Filial Piety in Chinese Thought and History

The phenomenon of filial piety is fundamental to our understanding of Chinese culture, and this excellent collection of essays explores its manifold role in Chinese thought and history. Often regarded as the key to preserving Chinese tradition and identity, its potentially vast impact on government and the development of Chinese culture makes it extremely relevant, and although invariably virtuous in its promotion of social cohesion, its ideas are often controversial.

A broad range of topics are discussed including not only Confucianism, with which filial piety is particularly associated, but also Buddhism and Daoism, making it essential reading for those studying Chinese culture, religion and philosophy. This is a multi-disciplinary effort that combines historical studies with philosophical analysis from an international team of respected contributors.

Alan K. L. Chan is Professor and **Sor-hoon Tan** is Assistant Professor at the Department of Philosophy, National University of Singapore.

Filial Piety in Chinese Thought and History

Edited by
Alan K. L. Chan and Sor-hoon Tan

RoutledgeCurzon
Taylor & Francis Group

LONDON AND NEW YORK

First published 2004 by RoutledgeCurzon
11 New Fetter Lane, London EC4P 4EE

Simultaneously published in the USA and Canada
by RoutledgeCurzon
29 West 35th Street, New York, NY 10001

RoutledgeCurzon is an imprint of the Taylor & Francis Group

© 2004 Alan K. L. Chan and Sor-hoon Tan for selection and editorial
material; individual contributors for their chapters

Typeset in Times by Graphicraft Limited, Hong Kong
Printed and bound in Great Britain by Antony Rowe Ltd, Chippenham, Wiltshire

British Library Cataloguing in Publication Data
A catalogue record for this book is available
from the British Library

Library of Congress Cataloging in Publication Data
A catalog record for this book has been requested

ISBN 0–415–33365–2

Contents

Contributors

Alan K. L. Chan is currently Vice-Dean, Faculty of Arts and Social Sciences, and Professor, Department of Philosophy, National University of Singapore. His works include *Two Visions of the Way, Mencius: Contexts and Interpretations* (ed.) and other studies on early Chinese philosophy and religion.

Sin Yee Chan is Assistant Professor at the University of Vermont. She has contributed essays to Kenneth Lieberthal, Shuen-fu Lin and Ernest Young (eds), *Constructing China*, and Cheng Chung-ying and Nicholas Bunnin (eds), *Contemporary Chinese Philosophy*.

Anne Cheng is University Professor of Chinese Philosophy at the Centre d'Etudes Chinoises at l'Institut National des Langues et Civilisation Orientales (INALCO), Paris. She is author of *Entretiens de Confucine, Etude sur le confucianisme Han: L'élaboration d'une tradition exégétique sur les classiques*, and *Histoire de la pensée chinoise*, and of chapters in M. Loewe (ed.), *Early Chinese Texts: A Bibliographical Guide* and J. A. Fogel et al. (eds), *Imagining the People: Chinese Intellectuals and the Concept of Citizenship, 1890–1920*.

Patricia Ebrey is Professor of History at the University of Washington, Seattle. Her works include *The Inner Quarters: Marriage and the Lives of Chinese Women in the Sung Period, The Cambridge Illustrated History of China, Confucianism and Family Rituals in Imperial China: A Social History of Writing about Rites*, and *The Aristocratic Families of Early Imperial China: A Case Study of the Po-ling Ts'ui Family*.

Ikeda Tomohisa is Professor at the University of Tokyo and specializes in early Chinese manuscripts. He has published widely on the Mawangdui silk manuscripts, including a major study of the *Wuxing pian*, and the Guodian bamboo manuscripts, including a book-length study of the Guodian *Laozi*.

Philip J. Ivanhoe is John Findlay Visiting Professor at Boston University. He is author of *Ethics in the Confucian Tradition: The Thought of Mencius* and *Wang Yang-ming* and *Confucian Moral Self-cultivation*, and of entries in *The International Encyclopedia of Philosophy* and *The Encyclopedia of Religion*. He has translated the *Laozi*, the *Mozi* (selected), and *Essays and Letters by Zhang Xuecheng*, and edited *Chinese Language, Thought, and Culture: Nivison and His Critics*, and other collections on Chinese Philosophy.

Keith N. Knapp is Associate Professor at The Citadel. He is author of entries in Yao Xinzhong (ed.), *Encyclopaedia of Confucianism*, and of two forth-coming books: *Accounts of Filial Offspring: The Confucian Ideology in Early Medieval China* and *Sanitizing Filial Piety: The Formation of the Twenty-four Filial Exemplars*.

Livia Kohn is Professor of Religion at Boston University. She is author of *God of the Dao: Lord Lao in History and Myth*, *Early Chinese Mysticism: Philosophy and Soteriology in the Taoist*, and *Taoist Mystical Philosophy: The Scripture of Western Ascension*. She has translated and edited several other works on Daoism.

Lee Cheuk Yin is Associate Professor at the Chinese Studies Department, National University of Singapore. He is author of *Collected Studies of Ming History* and co-author of *Emperor Chengzu of the Ming Dynasty: An Appraisal* and *Taoism: Outlines of a Chinese Religious Tradition*.

Yuet Keung Lo is Assistant Professor at the Chinese Studies Department, National University of Singapore. He has contributed to Kai-wing Chow *et al.*, *Imagining Boundaries: Changing Confucian Doctrines, Texts, and Hermeneutics*, and Kim-Chong Chong, Sor-hoon Tan and C. L. Ten (eds), *The Moral Circle and the Self: Chinese and Western Perspectives*. He is currently completing an annotated translation of an eighteenth-century anthology of Chinese Buddhist laywomen's biographies.

Mugitani Kunio is Professor of Chinese Thought at the Research Institute for the Humanities, Kyoto University. He has published extensively in early medieval religious Daoism (100–600 CE), including two major studies on the key Shangqing text, *Zhengao*.

A. T. Nuyen is Associate Professor at the Department of Philosophy, National University of Singapore. He is author of several articles on Chinese philosophy and continental philosophy in various international journals, and chapters in Knud Haakonssen and Udo Thiel (eds), *Kant and the Philosophical Theories of Human Nature in the 18th Century*, and Kim-Chong Chong, Sor-hoon Tan and C. L. Ten (eds), *The Moral Circle and the Self: Chinese and Western Perspectives*.

Lisa Raphals is Professor of Comparative Literature at the University of California, Riverside. Her works include *Sharing the Light: Representa-tions of Women and Virtue in Early China*, *Knowing Words: Wisdom and*

Cunning in the Classical Traditions of China and Greece, and contributions to C. Y. Li (ed.), *The Sage and the Second Sex*, B. W. Van Nordon (ed.), *Essays on the Analects of Confucius*, and *The International Encyclopedia of Philosophy.*

Sor-hoon Tan is Assistant Professor at the Department of Philosophy, National University of Singapore. She is author of *Confucian Democracy: A Deweyan Reconstruction*, entries in Yao Xinzhong (ed.), *Encyclopedia of Confucianism*, and essays in Alan Chan (ed.), *Mencius: Contexts and Interpretations* and Kim-Chong Chong, Sor-hoon Tan and C. L. Ten (eds), *The Moral Circle and the Self: Chinese and Western Perspectives.*

Acknowledgments

This present volume began at a workshop on "Conceptions of Filial Piety in Chinese Thought and History" organized by the Department of Philosophy and the Asia Research Institute, National University of Singapore (NUS), in 2002. With a research grant (no. R-106-000-006-112) provided by the NUS Faculty of Arts and Social Sciences, and additional funding from the Asia Research Institute and the Kwan Im Thong Hood Cho Temple, we were able to invite several scholars from Asia, North America and Europe to participate in the workshop. We would like to put on record our sincere gratitude to the sponsors for their generosity. We also thank our colleagues and students in the Department of Philosophy and the Asia Research Institute, whose support and assistance have made the workshop possible.

The Japanese version of Mugitani Kunio's chapter appeared in the Japanese publication *Society and Religion in Medieval China*. All the chapters in this volume were first presented at the workshop. We are grateful to the authors for being cooperative and patient in the editorial process. We have enjoyed working with them and have learned much from them. We are also grateful to Stephanie Rogers and Zoë Botterill at RoutledgeCurzon for their advice and assistance with the publication process.

Introduction

Alan K. L. Chan and Sor-hoon Tan

"Among the various forms of virtuous conduct, *xiao* 孝 comes first (*baixing xiao weixian* 百行孝為先)," declares a well known Chinese proverb. In the *Shuoyuan* 說苑, Confucius is quoted as saying, "Among human practices, none is greater than *xiao*."[1] *Xiao* is commonly rendered as "filial piety," although some contributors to this volume prefer "filiality." There is near unanimity among early Chinese thinkers about the importance of *xiao* in the Chinese ethos. Even though the legalist *Hanfeizi* condemns filial piety for undermining loyalty to the ruler, it took filial piety very seriously, devoting a whole chapter to arguing against it.[2] The concept of *xiao* in its mature formulation serves to define the ideal relationship between parent and child, which helps to secure the place of the family at the center of the Chinese ethical worldview. It would not be an exaggeration to say that the concern with *xiao* pervades all aspects of Chinese culture, both past and present.

Some scholars contend that the character *xiao* appears in the oracle bones; most agree that it occurs in Western Zhou (1045–771 BCE) sources, frequently as a verb in texts about the performance of sacrifices.[3] According to Donald Holzman, "The earliest appearance of the word for filial piety is on a bronze vessel that can be dated to the very last years of the Shang dynasty or the earliest years of the Zhou, that is, roughly around 1000 BCE. The etymology of the character is, for once, clear. It shows an old man being supported by a child."[4] Holzman remarks that "probably at the very earliest stages in their history, the Chinese gave filial piety an extremely exalted position – treated it as something one might almost call an absolute, a metaphysical entity."[5]

Keith Knapp observes that the earliest meaning of *xiao* seems to be connected with "providing food offerings to one's ancestors."[6] However, during the Western Zhou dynasty, it already "encompassed service to both living parents and ancestors."[7] And "while the general meaning of *xiao* as selfless devotion to the welfare of one's elders remained constant over time, the particulars of *xiao* – the concrete actions recognized as embodying it and to whom it was addressed – were often subject to change."[8] Knapp's comparison of the meaning of *xiao* in the Western Zhou and Spring and Autumn period sources with its meaning in Confucian philosophical texts of the early and late Warring States period argues that the Confucians fundamentally reinterpreted *xiao*. Confucians "de-emphasized the earliest meaning of *xiao*, feeding one's elders, and instead accentuated a derivative meaning of obeying one's parents, and by further extension, obeying one's lord."[9]

The Han dynasty, during which Confucianism was established as a state orthodoxy, is also characterized by official promotion of filial piety, systematically making unfilial conduct a punishable crime and rewarding acts of filial piety.[10] With few exceptions, Han emperors adopted *xiao* as part of their title. At least as early as the end of the Former Han dynasty (206 BCE to 8 CE), praise of filial piety enters more and more frequently into the dynastic histories and other historical works. Holzman's study describes "the peculiar passion [for filial piety] that took hold of the country at the beginning of the Later Han dynasty (25–220 CE)," and explains how "the excesses to which filial piety was carried at that time illustrate an aspect of Chinese psychology that, once understood, will help us appreciate much that usually remains incomprehensible in Chinese history." According to Holzman, the centrality of the homage children rendered to their parents and ancestor worship in Chinese culture, which create a strong tie binding succeeding generations one to another, explain both its enduring character and the difficulty of adapting it to the modern world.[11]

The transformation of filial piety into the keystone of Han morality appears full blown in the *Xiaojing* 孝經 (*Classic of Filial Piety*), which became established during the early Han period (206 BCE to 220 CE). According to Xun Shuang 荀爽 (128–190 CE), "the statutes of the Han dynasty require the entire empire to intone the *Xiaojing* by heart." *Zhao Qi* 趙岐 (*c.* 110–201 CE) in his commentary to the *Mencius* tells us that the Emperor Wen (179–157 BCE) appointed an Erudite (*boshi* 博士) to teach the *Xiaojing*.[12] This text was basic to classical Chinese education, and part of the school curriculum right up to the twentieth century. Although some Chinese intellectuals during the May Fourth movement condemned filial piety as "the source of all evil" – having the effect of turning "China into a big factory for the production of obedient subjects" – one of its key figures, Hu Shih, in a speech given in Taiwan in 1954, reversed that extreme iconoclastic attitude toward Chinese classics, and promoted the study of the *Xiaojing* specifically.[13]

Throughout Chinese history, stories of filial sons and daughters, represented not only in texts but also in pictorial and dramatic forms, occupied a cherished place in the popular imagination. In traditional China, the primacy of *xiao* translated into a political ideal that aspires to "govern all under heaven with the virtue of filial piety." Today, in the face of the forces of modernization and globalization, *xiao* has been singled out as a key to preserving Chinese tradition and identity, although it has also been argued that, as commonly conceived, filial piety is fraught with patriarchal and authoritarian prejudices and would thus require radical reformulation if it were to contribute to the development of Chinese culture. Whether filial piety is seen as the "essence" of culture or a burden of the past, it remains integral to the Chinese heart-mind and, given the impact of Chinese tradition on Korea and Japan, to the larger East Asian cultural environment.

While the significance of *xiao* is not in dispute, its meaning and practice in Chinese thought and history demand careful scrutiny.[14] Filial piety achieves intellectual prominence as a Confucian concept, but it also informs Daoism and Chinese Buddhism. While some attention has been given to *xiao* in Buddhism, few studies are available on the role of filial piety in religious Daoism.[15] Filial piety may be a shared ideal in China, but it is open to interpretation and has been made to support diverse and at times competing interests.[16] Earlier studies have already shown that it cannot be assumed that the concept was understood in the same way over the long course of Chinese history. Even within Confucianism, it is clear that the meaning of *xiao* can be interpreted in different ways, especially in relation to other key Confucian virtues. For example, does not "service to both living parents and ancestors" seem to presuppose a deeper filial love? If so, what is the relationship between *xiao* and *ren* (love, benevolence, or humanity), which is regarded by many commentators, traditional and modern, to be pivotal to the Confucian enterprise? Interpretations of *xiao* may also differ in view of the possible conflict between filial devotion and loyalty to the state. Indeed, can the tension between the two be resolved? In today's context, assuming that *xiao* is a necessary condition for the ethical life, can it be reconceived in ways that would meet the demands of modernity? At the practical level, the expression of *xiao* cannot but be influenced by changing sociopolitical circumstances. Perception of gender roles renders the development of the concept of filial piety more complex.

The fourteen chapters in this volume seek to interrogate the concept and practice of *xiao* from a variety of critical perspectives. They do not claim to be able to provide a comprehensive account of the many faces of filial piety or filiality, but together they make a significant advance in tackling the difficult questions that surround the concept and practice of *xiao* in Chinese thought and history. The first chapter deals with the meaning of the concept in early Confucian and Daoist texts. The next seven chapters explore the phenomenon of *xiao* in Chinese politics and religion in specific historical periods and are thus arranged conveniently in chronological order. The remaining studies cross into philosophical territory and the continued relevance of the concept as a virtue or practice. The multidisciplinary approach of the book is deliberate and reflects the authors' commitment to breaking disciplinary barriers in Asia research.

The recently excavated silk and bamboo texts from China provide us with more materials for understanding the role of filial piety in the early Chinese thought of various traditions, separately as well as in their interaction with one another. Ikeda Tomohisa examines the concept of *xiao* in the *Laozi* and the *Zhuangzi* in the light of the bamboo texts discovered in Guodian, Hubei province, in 1993. Although there is evidence that Daoist philosophy was critical of the Confucian understanding of *xiao* even then, Ikeda draws out

an ambivalence toward filial piety by comparing two concepts of *xiao* in
the pre-Qin to Han versions of the *Laozi* and the concept in the Guodian
Confucian texts, *Yucong* 語叢. He argues that early Daoist thought has
two contrasting evaluations of filial piety. One is negative, rejecting it as
an alienation of natural virtue, resulting from the world falling away from
a pristine nature and "non-acting (*wuwei* 無為)" – this usually takes the
form of criticizing Confucian conceptions of filial piety, and persists in the
conflict between Daoism and Confucianism.

There is a more positive attitude to filial piety, which Ikeda traces to a
passage (19) in the Guodian *Laozi* (A) affirming the value of filial piety as
part of human "natural endowment," part of what is so without any artificial striving on one's part. He suggests that the Daoists might be the first to
advocate filial piety as a value based on its being part of human nature, and
argues that the thinking on filial piety in the Guodian texts *yucong* reveals
Daoist influence on Confucianism of that period. But as Daoist thought
moved from emphasizing the negative to emphasizing the positive aspects of
filial piety, it also increasingly accepted the Confucian definition of the worldly
requirements of filial piety, even as it attempted to give filial piety a Daoist
reading by relating it to wider philosophical and religious issues.

That Confucianism has always adopted a positive attitude to filial piety
does not mean that its advocacy of filial piety is straightforward and
unproblematic. In upholding filial piety as a central virtue, Confucianism is
often caught in the tension between conflicting interests in society and competing prerogatives. Anne Cheng explores the tension between "private"
local interests and those of the newly established centralized state during the
Han period by examining the thorny issue of vengeance. While the ritual
requirement for a son to seek revenge for the murder of his father or ruler is
emphasized in canonical sources of the early imperial era, it is a crime under
the laws of the land to commit murder. The question of vengeance thus puts
into sharp relief the need to negotiate between the rites and the laws, the
two major regulators of sociopolitical order in Chinese history, when
scholars and officials attempted to establish filial piety as a fundamental
value in the emergent Confucian "orthodoxy" during the Han dynasty.

While the promotion of filial piety as a Confucian virtue in the Han
dynasty requires resolution of certain conflicting social and political prerogatives, Keith Knapp's study of *xiao* in the early medieval period after the
fall of Eastern Han shows how a change between the relative importance of
family and state could affect the meaning of filial piety as an ethical concept.
The role of filial piety as a central pillar of Han Confucian orthodoxy is
clearly evident not only in philosophical texts of the period, but also in the
numerous popular texts and pictorial depictions of "reverent care" (*gongyang*)
in early medieval China (third to sixth centuries), which Knapp examines.
These tales elevate the concept of *yang* 養, which the *Analects* criticizes as
inadequate fulfillment of the requirements of filial piety, to an exalted form
of care, *gongyang* 供養. By showcasing filial sons who suffered varying

degrees of deprivation to furnish their parents with food and clothing, the authors of these tales convey the message that sons should subordinate their welfare to that of their parents and further the family's interest rather than their own. Knapp shows that these tales view the simple act of feeding parents as a tangible means of expressing love, affirming filial obligation, and strengthening the hierarchical structure of the family. In a period when kin solidarity was an important ingredient in the maintenance of power and prestige, early medieval Confucians envisioned *gongyang* as a crucial means for cementing the bonds that held elite families together. The authors of tales about reverent care are more interested in service to the family than in service to the state, according to Knapp, which reflects the weakness of the central government and the dominance of "magnate" families at that time.

The importance of filial piety as a bond on which the strength of families depends is distinct from its place within Confucian ethics, so much so that when Confucianism fails to ensure filial piety, other means are found. According to Yuet Keung Lo, the "Scripture on Young Woman Yuye" (*Yuyenü jing*), which was putatively translated into Chinese around the third century when Buddhism was gaining followers while Confucianism declined, actually spoke to the household reality of clan-based families in the period under review, where a crisis of conflict seemed to be brewing between daughters-in-law and parents-in-law. Lo argues that the moral precepts in this scripture reinforce the Confucian sense of propriety for women and reflect a perceived need to reassert moral order at a time when the Confucian orthodoxy was losing its hold on the elite. The *Yuyenü Jing* was widely circulated during the third and fourth centuries and illustrates the mutual borrowing between Confucianism and Buddhism in Chinese society. The scripture's exclusive focus on the role of the daughter-in-law, whose conduct is portrayed as pivotal in ensuring harmony in the family, and the classification of women according to their social and family roles are unprecedented. Though modeled on Confucian ethics, in contrast to Confucian texts up to that period, which usually accorded women only the virtues of "reverence" and "obedience" and reserved the virtue of filial piety almost exclusively for men, the scripture praises women for "loyal and filial" service to their parents-in-law.

As the introduction of Buddhism into China produces some interesting changes in Chinese views of filial piety, the evolution of Daoism from the early thinking in texts such as the *Laozi* and the *Zhuangzi* to the religious Daoism of medieval China also brings about new ways of understanding and practicing filial piety in Chinese society. Livia Kohn provides a fascinating account of the complex role of *xiao* in early medieval Daoism. On the one hand, the Daoist doctrine of "inherited evil" – the belief that one must bear the consequences of the sins of one's ancestors – seems to view kinship bonds as a potential obstacle to religious attainment. On the other hand, incorporating the Buddhist doctrine of karma, medieval Daoism also portrays filial piety as a significant factor in obtaining good karma. The Daoist "synthesis" lies in extending the value of *xiao* to the cosmic realm. Although medieval Daoism advocates going beyond the family in the quest for transcendence and salvation, this is only possible if one's ancestors were at peace. Hence, various rituals were developed to expiate not only one's sins but also those of one's ancestors. Filial descendants hoped to transfer their forebears from the realm of the dead – called "Fengdu" in Daoist sources – to the paradise of immortality in the Daoist heavens. Indeed, as Kohn argues, the concept of *xiao* in medieval Daoism finds meaning in a larger soteriological project, which goes beyond one's own religious needs and those of one's family. As a religious Daoist concept, *xiao* is ultimately concerned with universal salvation.

Mugitani Kunio's discussion of the concept of the authentic parent to elucidate the role of filial piety in Daoism during the Six Dynasties period also shows that filial piety is not concerned merely with the biological parent–child relation. Mugitani further asserts that what the world considers filial, as pertaining to biological parents, actually obstructs religious attainment. Drawing from a large number of Daoist scriptures that have not been adequately studied in any language, Mugitani's study brings to light another important aspect of the religious Daoist conception of filial piety. As distinguished from biological parents, Daoist sources articulate the idea of "authentic parents," a pure form of "vital energies" (*qi* 氣) that arises from the Dao and crystallizes into a life-giving spiritual power (*shen* 神). In this context, biological parents are but vehicles, as it were, in the process of our coming to be. As such, biological parents are of lesser significance in the larger network of Daoist values. In the quest for transcendence and union with the Dao, the physical body and all "worldly" bonds must be transformed, although filial piety remains a necessary condition in the process of spiritual development.

While Ikeda brings out the complex interaction between Confucianism and Daoism in early Chinese thought, Kohn's and Mugitani's discussions of medieval Daoist religion attend to the interaction between Daoism and Buddhism. Kohn shows how medieval Daoism integrated Buddhist worldview and rituals into its religious practices and organization and highlights how Daoism learnt from Buddhism in incorporating filial piety. Mugitani locates the concept of the "authentic parent" against the background of the contests among Daoism, Buddhism and Confucianism during the Six Dynasties to Sui and Tang. Adding to Yuet Keung Lo's study of the *Yuyenü Jing*, Mugitani provides further examples of Chinese Buddhism's accommodation of filial piety during the critical years of its entry into Chinese society. Despite this "sinicization" of Buddhism evident in Buddhist scriptures that reconcile Buddhist teaching with filial piety, even promote filial piety, during the Six Dynasties to the Sui and Tang dynasties, Daoism sided with Confucianism in attacking Buddhism for being against filial piety.

The tension between state and family evident in Anne Cheng's study of vengeance in the Han dynasty continued to be a problem in later dynasties.

Patricia Ebrey examines a case where filial piety posed a serious political problem, when a reigning emperor had to contend with the wishes of his living father. This happened when the Emperor Huizong of the Song dynasty abdicated in favor of his son, Qinzong. Ebrey's analysis focuses on the relation between Huizong and Qinzong after the former's abdication in 1125 and shows how, for emperors with living parents, their sense of filial obligation could come into conflict with what their officials urged them to do for reasons of state. Ebrey looks at the rhetoric of filial piety – the arguments used and classical allusions evoked – by Qinzong's officials, who urged him to place more restrictions on Huizong, forcing the latter back to the capital, Kaifeng, and making him effectively a prisoner in his palace. The events narrated in the chapter are fascinating in their own right, but the larger picture is also important: with the value of filial piety deeply entrenched, delicate negotiations are needed to ensure that the requirements of both family and state are met.

The tension between the demands of family and those of the state on a person prompted many debates over the priority and relationship between the Confucian virtues of loyalty and filial piety. Despite various attempts to ground loyalty on filial piety, the latter continued to pose problems to the imperial state throughout China's history. Lee Cheuk Yin examines how the *Classic of Filial Piety* (*Xiaojing*) attempts to resolve the conflict between filial piety and loyalty so as to consolidate monarchical rule. In so doing, it politicizes the ethics of filial piety. Comparing the *Classic of Filial Piety* with the *True Accounts of Filial Devotion* (*Xiaoshun shishi*), compiled with commentaries by Emperor Chengzu (1360–1424) of the Ming dynasty, Lee argues that the politicization of *xiao* that began in the Han period reached its height in Emperor Chengzu's idea of "transferring filial piety to loyalty" (*yixiao weizhong*). The *True Accounts of Filial Devotion* contains 207 stories of exemplary filial conduct, all reinforcing the fundamental assertion that filial piety and loyalty both stem from the "principle of heaven."

Philosophically, the ethical answer to the tension between family commitments and loyalty to the ruler or state depends in part on the relationship between the virtue of *ren* and the virtue of *xiao* in Confucianism. Alan Chan traces the debate on this relationship, especially in terms of their relative priority. Translating passages from the *Later Han History* on the *ren–xiao* debate, he shows how, during the Han period, whether *xiao* "comes before" (*xian*) *ren* attracted intense discussion among Confucian scholars. As *ren* gradually takes on universal significance, it demands adjustment to the meaning of *xiao* as it appears in the Confucian classics. This poses a serious hermeneutical challenge and necessitates the deployment of certain terms of relations to clarify the *ren–xiao* relationship. In this context, the chapter examines such metaphors as "roots" (*ben*) and "branches" (*mo*), "before" (*xian*) and "after" (*hou*), and "inner" (*nei*) and "outer" (*wai*). By examining how the debate over *ren* and *xiao* proceeded via the various uses of these relational metaphors, Chan illustrates how filial piety gains meaning from its relationship with *ren*, and how its meaning changes with new configurations and balances between the two. These terms of relations play an important role not only in resolving the *ren–xiao* debate but also more generally in the development of Chinese philosophy.

The relationship between filial piety and *ren* is also interesting from the psychological perspective. Sin Yee Chan explores the moral psychology of the claim that filial piety is the basis of *ren*, evaluating it against the background of several psychological theories. She argues that filial piety and commiseration, as the basis of *ren*, are affective altruistic concerns. Whereas the latter is directed at any suffering individual, the former is directed at particular individuals of special significance to the moral agent. Combined with a learning process in which rituals play a key role, the connection between *xiao* and *ren* reveals the Confucian view of moral development. This is at odds with Lawrence Kohlberg's theory, which emphasizes reasoning in the form of universal principles. It is also incompatible with psychoanalytic theories that deny the genuineness of affective concerns. In contrast, Piaget's theory, which draws a parallel between affective development and cognitive development, provides psychological backing for the relation between *xiao* and *ren* presented in this argument. Sin Yee Chan suggests that despite its ability to illuminate moral development, there is a difficulty in understanding, and sometimes a reluctance to accept, the close relationship between the two concepts because most people conceive morality as pertaining to general benevolence and principles of justice, requiring transcendence of a narrow egoistic world and particularistic relationships.

Philip Ivanhoe considers the nature of *xiao* as a virtue from the perspective of contemporary moral philosophy, arguing for retention of part of the traditional Chinese thinking about filial piety and jettisoning of other parts. Taking the emotion of filial love as the basis of the virtue and elucidating the nature of that love by examining some important features of the parent–child relationship, he argues that traditional justifications of *xiao* as an expression of gratitude are unconvincing, although there are other compelling reasons for cultivating and valuing filial piety. With illustrations taken from both Western and Chinese literary classics, Ivanhoe shows that the true basis for the gratitude of filial piety lies not in the gift of life but in the care given for the receiver's own sake, and that one cannot really repay one's parents for such care. The most one can do is to cultivate a reciprocal feeling and live out an attitude of loving care, appreciation and reverence for one's parents. Filial piety cannot be reduced to a duty or to other virtues like friendship; it is a distinct and important virtue in its own right. The parent–child relationship is unequal and this inequality is what makes filial piety an appropriate paradigm for the ruler–subject relationship.

A. T. Nuyen addresses the contemporary criticism of filial piety as conservative and oppressive amidst renewed interest in "family values." Nuyen's analysis draws on Gadamer's hermeneutics and attempts to find a place for the concept of filial piety in contemporary ethical theory. He agrees with the view that if *xiao* entails absolute obedience to one's parents then it has no relevance for ethics in the twenty-first century, but proposes a fresh interpretation of the Confucian classics in which the concept of *xiao* takes the father figure as a symbol of tradition. On this reading, what is commonly taken to be absolute obedience to the father turns out to be respect for tradition. There is room for not following one's immediate father, even as one obeys the way of the fathers in a to-and-fro process of understanding the tradition. The criticism of *xiao* as oppressive thus seems misplaced.

Modern life prompts us not only to re-examine and even replace interpretations of filial piety as mostly about obeying one's father, but also to question an apparent gender bias in traditional literature on filial piety. Lo's study of the *Yuyenü Jing* touches on how, even during the Han dynasty, women were hardly ever described as filial, and women's virtues were understood mostly in terms of devotion to their husbands and parents in law. Lisa Raphals and Sor-hoon Tan, both of whom prefer the translation of "filiality," explore further the gender question from philosophical perspectives. Raphals focuses specifically on the gender divide in the articulation of *xiao*. Citing textual evidence from the Warring States period to the Ming dynasty, and drawing on theories of emotions that emphasize social construction ("nurture") in contrast with those that view emotions as biologically determined ("nature"), she shows how the emotion of filiality is gendered and functions differently in the lives of men and women. Whereas, for men, *xiao* is deemed to have been genetically defined through life, a woman's filial devotion is expected to shift to her husband's ancestral lineage at marriage. Historically, Raphals argues, the conception of women's virtues became increasingly circumscribed by their family roles and *xiao*, construed as loyalty to the family and the state, came to replace other virtues, especially intellectual virtues, that were once valued highly in the education of women.

Sor-hoon Tan examines the filial conduct of daughters-in-law depicted in texts from the Pre-Qin period to the Han dynasty to draw more general lessons about the nature of filiality. Although early Confucian texts rarely bestow the virtue of filiality on women, Tan argues that the figure of the filial daughter-in-law begins to gain prominence from the Han dynasty. Drawing from Ban Zhao's *Admonitions for Women* (*Nüjie*), Liu Xiang's *Biographies of Women* (*Lienü zhuan*), and the *Book of Rites* (*Liji*), Tan examines the extension of filiality to daughters-in-law within Confucian ethics between the Warring States and the end of Han dynasty. The filial requirements of a daughter-in-law and their importance in family harmony illuminate the connection between filial ethics and a more general relational ethics that provides food for thought even today. Confucian texts present the filiality of a daughter-in-law as an extension of both a daughter's and a son's *xiao*. By-passing the nature–nurture debate, Tan argues that the Confucian view of *xiao* reflects a normative endorsement of the feelings of attachment that develop in a nurturing relationship, which exists usually, but not always, between biological parents and child. *Xiao* is construed in ritual actions. Tan cautions against any "top-down" approach to revive outmoded rituals of *xiao*, although she is sensitive to the role rituals play in our daily lives and argues that this is the dimension we need to attend to if we wish filial piety to continue to be relevant in our ethical life.

The chapters in this volume display the variety and richness of the Chinese tradition in the understanding and practice of filial piety. The concept is important not only in Confucianism, but also in Daoism and Buddhism, and its evolution over time reveals how these adapt to changing circumstances, how they in turn modified the social and historical environment, and the interesting impact they have on one another within Chinese society. Both exalting filial piety as a supreme virtue and blaming it for everything that went wrong in Chinese society are over-simplistic attitudes to adopt toward filial piety. Historically filial piety has played important roles in shaping the character and the life of Chinese society and the Chinese people; it has also caused all kinds of problems at various levels and in various areas of Chinese life. Understanding how it functions as well as malfunctions in Chinese thought and history gives us a better grasp of the past that provides a better basis for understanding Chinese societies today, and shows us interesting possibilities for how filial piety might continue to play a role in modern life.

Notes

1 3.4/19/20, D. C. Lau and Chen Fong Ching (eds), *A Concordance to the Shuoyuan*, Hong Kong: Commercial Press, 1992.

2 "Loyalty and Filial Piety 忠孝," in Wang Xianshen, *Hanfeizi jijie* 韓非子集解, Beijing: Zhonghua shuju, 1998, pp. 465–69. Translated in W. K. Liao, *The Complete Works of Han Fei Tzu*, London: Probstain, 1959, Volume. 11, Book 20, Chapter 51.

3 Keith Knapp, "The *Ru* Reinterpretation of *Xiao*," *Early China*, 20, 1995, 195–222, pp. 197–8. Kang Xuewei (*Xianqin xiaodao yanjiu* 先秦孝道研究, Taipei: Wenjin, 1992, p. 9) maintains that the character in the sense of filial piety appears in the oracle bones. Hsiao Hsin-I ("A Preliminary Interpretation of the Origin of the Concept of *Hsiao* in the Shang Period," *Chinese Culture*, 19, no. 3, 1978, 5–19, pp. 9–11) and Li Yumin ("Yinzhou jinwen zhong de 'xiao' he Kong Qiu 'xiaodao' de fandong benzhi," *Kaogu Xuebao* 考古學報, 1974, p. 19) believe that *xiao* appears in the oracle bones only as part of a place name or personal name. Zhou Bokan ("Xiao zi guyi kao 孝字古義考," in *Zhongguo shi xinlun*, Taipei: Taiwan Book Co., 1985, pp. 64–76, p. 66), Fang-chih Huang Jacobs ("The Origin and Development of the Concept of Filial Piety in Ancient China," *Chinese Culture*, 14, no. 3, 1973, 25–32, p. 28), Xu Fuguan ("Zhongguo xiaodao sixiang de xingcheng yanbian ji qi zai lishi de zhu wenti 中國的孝道思想的形成演變及其在歷史的諸問題," in his *Zhongguo sixiangshi lunji* 中國思想史論集, Taizhong: Donghai Private University, 1959, p. 158), and Donald Hozman ("The Place of Filial Piety in Ancient China," *Journal of the American Oriental Society*, 118, no. 2, 1998, 185–99, p. 186) all deny that *xiao* appears in the oracle bones.

4 Holzman, "The Place of Filial Piety," p. 187.

5 Ibid., p. 185.

6 Knapp, "*Ru* Interpretation," p. 199.
7 Ibid., p. 196. See also Holzman, "The Place of Filial Piety," p. 188.
8 Knapp, "*Ru* Interpretation," p. 197.
9 Ibid.
10 Textual portrayal of unfilial conduct as a crime to be punished dates back to the "Announcement to the Prince of Kang 康誥" in the *Shangshu* 尚書. James Legge, *The Chinese Classics*, vol. 3, Hong Kong: Hong Kong University Press, 1961, p. 392.
11 Holzman, "The Place of Filial Piety," pp. 185, 199.
12 *Later Han History* (*Hou Hanshu*), Beijing: Zhonghua shuju, 1997, juan 62, p. 2051; Preface to the *Mencius* in the *Thirteen Classics*, Ruan Yuan (ed.), 8a. Both cited in Holzman, "The Place of Filial Piety," p. 191.
13 For condemnation of filial piety during the May Fourth movement, see "On Filiality" in Wu Yu, *Collected Essays* 吳虞文錄, Shanghai: Oriental Books, 1922, p. 15. Filial piety was also a target in the anti-Confucianism campaign in communist China. Hu Shih's speech is cited in Yan Xiehe, preface to the *Xiaojing baihua zhuyi* 孝經白話注譯, Taipei: Ruicheng shuju, 1980, p. 14.
14 The contemporary significance of *xiao* in East Asian culture was underscored in a conference in Korea on "Filial Piety and Future Society." The proceedings (Han'guk Chongsin Munhwa Yon'guwon, 1995), mainly in Korean but with several contributions in English, demonstrate a clear concern to locate in filial piety an anchor for social harmony and order. Similarly, attention is drawn to the continued relevance of filial piety in East Asian societies in several articles in Walter Slote and George de Vos (eds), *Confucianism and the Family*, Albany: State University of New York Press, 1998.
15 See Alan Cole, *Mothers and Sons in Chinese Buddhism*, Stanford, CA: Stanford University Press, 1998.
16 An excellent study in this regard is Norman A. Kutcher's *Mourning in Late Imperial China: Filial Piety and the State*, New York: Cambridge University Press, 1999, which provides a detailed analysis of the attempt during the early Qing dynasty by the newly victorious Manchu rulers to make use of traditional Confucian mourning rites to gain the support of the literati and to lend a measure of legitimacy to their conquest.

1 The evolution of the concept of filial piety (*xiao*) in the *Laozi*, the *Zhuangzi*, and the Guodian bamboo text *Yucong*

Ikeda Tomohisa

As is well known, the term "*xiao*" (filial piety) appears only twice in the current version of the *Laozi*. First, in Chapter 18, the *Laozi* states:

> When the Great Dao declines, there are benevolence and rightness. When knowledge and wisdom emerge, there are great achievements. When the six family relationships are not in harmony, there are filial piety [*xiao*] and compassion. When a country is in disorder, there are loyal ministers.[1]

Second, Chapter 19 of the current *Laozi* reads:

> Abandon sagacity and discard wisdom; then the people will benefit a hundredfold. Abandon benevolence and discard rightness; then the people will return to filial piety [*xiao*] and compassion. Abandon skill and discard profit; then there will be no thieves or robbers . . . Therefore let the people . . . manifest plainness, embrace simplicity, reduce selfishness, have few desires.

> 絕聖棄智, 民利百倍. 絕仁棄義, 民復孝慈. 絕巧棄利, 盜賊無有 . . . 故 . . . 見素抱樸, 少私寡欲.

In these instances, the *Laozi* seems to offer two contrasting assessments of *xiao*. Whereas in Chapter 18 it views *xiao* as negative or at best a secondary virtue, in Chapter 19 it gives a positive assessment or at least assigns a higher value to filial piety as compared with benevolence and rightness. This is one of the key problems that confront interpreters of the *Laozi*. Although many scholars have attempted to explain the apparent contradiction, it seems difficult to reach a coherent interpretation that would reconcile these two views of *xiao*. However, with the discovery of the Guodian bamboo texts, which include fragments of *Laozi*, the *Yucong* 語叢 (a collection of sayings associated with the Confucian school), and other Confucian writings, I believe we can now resolve this difficulty.[2] This is the focus of the present chapter. To situate the concept of *xiao* in the *Laozi* and the *Yucong* in proper context, I begin by examining a number of passages from the *Zhuangzi*, which serve to bring out the evolution of *xiao* in early Daoist philosophy.

Repudiation and affirmation of *xiao* in the *Zhuangzi*

The concept of *xiao* appears in Chapters 4 ("In the World of Men"), 12 ("Heaven and Earth"), 14 ("The Turning of Heaven"), 26 ("External Things"), 29 ("Robber Zhi"), and 31 ("The Old Fisherman") of the *Zhuangzi*.[3] On the surface, as in the *Laozi*, the *Zhuangzi* also seems to present a conflicting picture. Whereas some passages seem to repudiate *xiao*, others affirm it. In what follows I describe these two positions simply as the "negative" (N) and "positive" (P) views of *xiao*, respectively. The problem, again, is that two opposing and contradictory views of the concept appear to be featured in the same work.

Four instances of the negative view of *xiao* may be identified in the *Zhuangzi*. Chapter 12 of the *Zhuangzi* (N1) gives the following account:

> Chi-zhang Man-Ji said, "Everybody wants to see the world well ordered. If it had been so already, what point would there have been in calling in the man of the Yu clan? The man of the Yu clan was [like] medicine to a sore. But to wait until you go bald and then buy a wig, to wait until you get sick and then call for a doctor, to prepare the medicine like a true filial son [*xiaozi* 孝子] and present it to your loving father, wearing a grim and haggard look – this the true sage would be ashamed to do. In an age of Perfect Virtue the worthy are not honored, the talented are not employed. The rulers . . . and the people . . . do what is right and proper but they do not know that this is rightness. They love one another but they do not know that this is benevolence. They are faithful but they do not know that this is loyalty.[4]

A second example comes from Chapter 14 (N2):

> Tang . . . asked Zhuangzi about benevolence . . . Zhuangzi said, "Perfect benevolence knows no [familial] affection." [Tang] said, ". . . where affection is lacking, there will be no love, and if there is no love, there will be no filial piety [*xiao*]. Can you possibly say that perfect benevolence is unfilial?" Zhuangzi replied, "No, it is not so. Perfect benevolence is truly exalted! It can certainly not be fully described by *xiao*. And what you are talking about is not something that surpasses filial piety, but something that doesn't even come up to it . . . To be filial out of respect is easy; to be filial out of love is hard. To be filial out of love is easy; to forget parents is hard. To forget parents is easy; to make parents forget you is hard. To make parents forget you is easy; to forget the whole world is hard. To forget the whole world is easy; to make the

whole world forget you is hard. Virtue . . . rests in nonaction. Its bounty enriches ten thousand ages, and yet no one in the world knows this. Why all . . . this talk of benevolence and filial piety? Filial piety, brotherliness, benevolence, rightness, loyalty, trust, honor, integrity – for all of these you must drive yourself and make a slave of Virtue. They are not worth prizing.[5]

Third, according to *Zhuangzi* Chapter 26 (N3):

External things cannot be counted on . . . There is no ruler who does not want his ministers to be loyal. But loyal ministers are not always trusted . . . There is no parent who does not want his son to be filial [*xiao*]. But filial sons are not always loved. Hence, Xiao Ji grieved and Zeng Shen sorrowed [both were paragons of filial piety in early Chinese writings] . . . Delight and sorrow . . . trap man on either side so that he has no escape. Fearful and trembling, he can reach no completion. His mind is as though trussed and suspended between heaven and earth, bewildered and lost in delusion. Profit and loss rub against each other and light the countless fires that burn up the inner harmony of the mass of men . . . so that in time all is consumed and the Dao comes to an end.[6]

Fourth, in Chapter 29 (N4), the famous "Robber Zhi" states:

Robber Zhi [in a great rage] said, "This must be none other than that crafty hypocrite Kong Qiu [Confucius] from the state of Lu! Well, tell him this for me. You make up your stories, invent your phrases . . . you pour out your flood of words, your fallacious theories. You eat without ever plowing, clothe yourself without ever weaving. Wagging your lips, clacking your tongue, you invent any kind of 'right' and 'wrong' that suits you, leading astray the rulers of the world, keeping the scholars of the world from returning to the root, capriciously setting up ideals of 'filial piety' [*xiao*] and 'brotherliness', all the time hoping to worm your way into favor with the lords of the fiefs or the rich and eminent! Your crimes are huge, your offenses grave. You had better run home as fast as you can, because if you don't, I will take your liver and add it to this afternoon's menu!"[7]

At the opposite end of the interpretive spectrum, the following seem to provide a positive view of *xiao*. First, consider *Zhuangzi* Chapter 4 (P1):

Confucius said, "In the world there are two great decrees: one is fate and the other is rightness. That a son should love his parents is fate – you cannot erase this from his heart. That a subject should serve his ruler is rightness – there is no place he can go and be without his ruler, no place he can escape to between heaven and earth. These are called the great decrees. Therefore, to serve your parents and be content to follow them anywhere – this is the perfection of filial piety [*xiao*]. To serve your ruler and be content to do anything for him – this is the peak of loyalty. And to serve your own mind so that sadness or joy do not sway or move it; to understand what you can do nothing about and to be content with it as with fate – this is the perfection of virtue. As a subject and a son, you are bound to find things you cannot avoid."[8]

Second, Chapter 12 (P2) seems to reinforce the same message:

When a filial son [*xiaozi*] does not fawn on his parents, when a loyal minister does not flatter his lord, they are the finest of sons and ministers. He who agrees with everything his parents say and approves of everything they do is regarded by popular opinion as an unworthy son; he who agrees with everything his lord says and approves of everything his lord does is regarded by popular opinion as an unworthy minister. But in other cases men do not realize that the same principle should apply. If a man agrees with everything that popular opinion says and regards as good everything that popular opinion regards as good, he is not, as you might expect, called a sycophant and a flatterer. Are we to assume, then, that popular opinion commands more authority than one's parents, or is more to be honored than one's lord? Call a man a sycophant and he flushes with anger; call him a flatterer and he turns crimson with rage. Yet, all his life he will continue to be a sycophant . . . [and] a flatterer . . . See him spread out his robes, display his bright colors, put on a solemn face in hopes of currying favors with the age – and yet he does not recognize himself as a sycophant or a flatterer . . . This is the height of foolishness![9]

Third, in Chapter 29 (P3) we find "Robber Zhi" saying:

There is no one more highly esteemed by the world than the Yellow Emperor, and yet even the Yellow Emperor could not preserve his virtue intact, but fought on the field . . . until the blood flowed for a hundred *li*. Yao was a merciless father, Shun was an unfilial son [*buxiao* 不孝], Yu was half paralyzed, Tang banished his sovereign . . . King Wu attacked his sovereign . . . All these . . . men are held in high esteem by the world, and yet a close look shows that all of them for the sake of gain brought confusion to what is authentic within them, that they forcibly turned against their true form and inborn nature. For doing so, they deserve the greatest shame![10]

Finally, Chapter 31 (P4), "The Old Fisherman," has this to say:

The stranger said, "By 'authenticity' I mean purity and sincerity in their highest degree. He who lacks purity and sincerity cannot move others. Therefore he who forces himself to lament, though he may sound sad, will awaken no grief. He who forces himself to be angry, though he may sound fierce, will arouse no awe. And he who forces himself to be affectionate, though he may smile, will not create harmony. Genuine sadness need make no sound to awaken grief; genuine anger need not show itself to arouse awe; genuine affection need not smile to create harmony . . . What is genuine [in one's nature] may be applied to human relationships in the following ways. In the service of parents, it is love and filial piety [*xiao*]; in the service of the ruler, it is loyalty and integrity . . . In loyalty and integrity, service is the important thing . . . in the service of parents, their comfort is the important thing. In seeking to perform the finest kind of service, one does not always try to go about it in the same way. In assuring comfort in the serving of one's parents, one does not question the means to be employed . . . Rites are something created by the vulgar men of the world; authenticity is that which is received from Heaven. By nature it is the way it is and cannot be changed."[11]

The passages cited above account for all the occurrences of the concept of *xiao* in the *Zhuangzi*.

Consider, first of all, the passages that seem to give a positive assessment of *xiao*. At first glance, P1 (Chapter 4) seems to rank *xiao* highly. However, the text quite clearly considers those who "serve their own mind" as superior to or on a higher level than those "who serve their parents" and those "who serve their ruler." Thus, both the "perfection of filial piety" and the "peak of loyalty" are virtues that rank below the "perfection of virtue," or they may be particular virtues encompassed by "the perfection of virtue." The reason for suggesting the latter is that the *Zhuangzi* here defines virtue as "to understand what you can do nothing about and to be content with it as with fate" (知其不可奈何, 而安之若命), which means putting into practice filial piety and loyalty as a matter of fate and duty. From this perspective, this kind of *xiao* is something that one cannot but do. Although the *Zhuangzi* affirms filial piety here, it seems to be a passive or resigned recognition, a "low-level" affirmation.

The view of *xiao* in P2 (Chapter 12) seems to resemble that in P1. But its positive assessment of *xiao* is in fact even more flaccid. Indeed, it may even be classified as one of the examples of a negative view of *xiao*. This is because the assertion that "the finest of sons and ministers" are those who do not "fawn on their parents" and "flatter their lord," respectively, is but a judgment of the mundane world, of popular opinion. The *Zhuangzi* evidently does not hold in high regard the judgment of the "vulgar" or mundane world, but fundamentally questions it and considers it "the height of foolishness."

P3 (Chapter 29) offers a similar account of *xiao* to P2. Although it seems to affirm the value of *xiao*, the assertion that "Shun was unfilial" is made only to dispel the commonly held view that Shun was filial and was thus "held in high esteem by the world." In other words, the context makes it clear that the point of the *Zhuangzi* here is to challenge conventional standards and judgment. It offers a critique of a world driven by self-interest and is not concerned with promoting *xiao*. The chapter goes on to say that "those who are regarded by the world as worthy officers" and "those who are regarded by the world as loyal ministers," on closer inspection, can all be shown to be "not worth valuing." From this, it is clear that the *Zhuangzi* is consistent in its critique of the value discrimination of the mundane world. Thus, to the *Zhuangzi*, whether Shun was filial or unfilial is not the issue. From this perspective, one might as well classify this passage as an example of a negative view of *xiao*.

P4 (Chapter 31) focuses on the concept of "authenticity" or "genuineness" (*zhen* 真), which the text defines as "purity and sincerity in their highest degree." As an expression of what is authentic or genuine in one's nature in the realm of human relationships, filial piety should be affirmed. As we shall see, this passage provides an important clue to explaining the concept of filial piety in *Laozi* Chapter 19. At this point, it may be noted that "The Old Fisherman" (Chapter 31) is among the latest of the *Zhuangzi* chapters and has been dated by many scholars to the early Former Han dynasty (206 BCE to 8 CE). In addition, the concept of *zhen* (authenticity) appears to be an ancient Daoist concept. For example, Chapter 21 of the *Laozi* describes the Dao as "elusive," although "its essence is very real [*zhen*]."

In sum, the above analysis shows that there is only one instance (P4) in the *Zhuangzi* – a late addition of the early Former Han dynasty – in which *xiao* is unequivocally regarded as positive. Further, it is noteworthy that all the passages that may be seen to present a positive account of filial piety place *xiao* alongside loyalty (*zhong* 忠).[12] I come back to this point later. Other than P4, the "positive" accounts in fact provide only a weak affirmation of *xiao*, which may warrant reassigning them to the group of passages that repudiate *xiao*. Thus, one may conclude that the *Zhuangzi* holds a predominantly negative view of *xiao*. This seems to connect with the negative view of *xiao* in Chapter 18 of the *Laozi* cited above.

Why does the *Zhuangzi* assume such a negative view of *xiao*? Turning to the negative passages, we see that in Chapter 12 (N1) it is only when the "loving father" has fallen ill or hurt himself that the "filial son" appears on the scene to bring him medicine and tend to his needs. The sage, according to the *Zhuangzi*, would be "ashamed" of this kind of filial piety. The reason is that this kind of filial piety only arises after the ideal state of health of the father – that is, the ideal human condition, which the *Zhuangzi* describes as the "perfection of virtue" – has for certain reasons come to suffer harm. Filial piety, in this sense, is a "substitute" constructed to fill the resultant lack. Like "benevolence," "rightness," and other Confucian virtues, it represents a symptom of humanity's alienation from the Dao, from the ideal state of "perfect virtue," and thus testifies to the regressive development of human civilization.

According to Chapter 14 (N2), similar to the analysis we find in N1, "perfect benevolence" far surpasses the kind of "filial piety" and "affection" championed by the Confucians. The passage "to be filial out of respect" → "to be filial out of love" → "to forget parents" → "to make parents forget you" → "to forget the whole world" → "to make the whole world forget you" signals an ideal ethical and spiritual development. Compared with the ideal state of "perfect virtue" in which "self" and "world" merge into one, filial piety is but one of the least significant ethical concepts. Not only that, in their application, filial piety, together with other Confucian virtues such as "brotherliness, benevolence, righteousness, loyalty, [and] trust," have the effect of worsening the alienation from the ideal state of perfect virtue. In this sense, they are pernicious virtues.

N3 (Chapter 26) links filial piety with loyalty to show that *xiao* represents an "external thing" that cannot be depended on. The text here hints that human beings would end up being controlled by "external things" if we develop a close relationship with them. And this is precisely what we would need to avoid. Instead, one should hold fast to the absolute Dao that is always "dependable." Thus, the *Zhuangzi* concludes in this passage with the warning that "in time all is consumed and the Dao comes to an end." This agrees with the analysis of N1 and N2, which rejects *xiao* because it reflects and contributes to alienation from the Dao. The *Zhuangzi* here emphasizes that the mind, along with loyalty, filial piety, and other "external things," has itself become corrupted and "undependable." Consequently, anxiety and delusion pervade the mind, which exacerbates the state of alienation and regression from the absolute Dao.

Finally, in N4 (Chapter 29), the *Zhuangzi* criticizes pointedly that the Confucians advocate filial piety and brotherly respect merely to gain the favors of the rich and powerful. What should be noted is that filial conduct here is contrasted with the "root" (*ben* 本), which can only refer to the Daoist conception of the Dao. From this perspective, *xiao* is judged to be directly opposed to the absolute Dao, the source and root of the created order. As such, of course, it must be repudiated.

In view of the above, the critique of *xiao* in the *Zhuangzi* is based on its concern with alienation or regressive development of human civilization. As the origin and foundation of the world, the Dao and virtue signify an ideal state, which for whatever reasons began to suffer decline. As it continued to deteriorate, Confucian morality, with *xiao* at its core, came into being as a purported remedy. This testifies to the "fallen" state of the world, but more seriously Confucian morality is also seen to add to the decline of the pristine virtue of the Dao, because it creates an even greater sense of alienation. On this basis, the *Zhuangzi* thus considers *xiao* and other Confucian virtues to be false or pernicious virtues.

Repudiation of *xiao* in the various versions of the *Laozi*

Chapter 18 of the current version of the *Laozi*, cited above, asserts that filial piety arises only after family relations have been torn by disharmony. The Chinese text, divided into four sections, reads:

(1) 大道廢, 有仁義. (2) 智慧出, 有大偽. (3) 六親不和, 有孝慈. (4) 國家昏亂, 有忠臣.

The two Mawangdui *Laozi* manuscripts give a similar version.[13] Comparing the three versions, it is apparent that the transmission of Chapter 18 of the *Laozi* has been relatively stable. The reason underlying the text's rejection of *xiao* agrees with that of the *Zhuangzi* discussed above. Like the *Zhuangzi* passages, the *Laozi* here envisages an ideal state in which family relations are naturally in harmony and the country is in complete order. For reasons not explained in the text, this ideal state became corrupted; consequently, Confucian morality marked by benevolence, rightness, filial piety, and loyalty attempts to arrest the decline of the Dao, which only adds to the adverse "mutation" of pristine virtue. The point I would emphasize here is that the *Laozi* and the *Zhuangzi* give the same reason for their rejection of filial piety.

Section 2 is of particular interest because, as we shall see shortly, it is not found in the Guodian version of Chapter 18 of the *Laozi*. The phrase *dawei* 大偽 in section 2 merits special attention. It is often taken to mean "great hypocrisy," but in my view *wei* should be understood in the sense of "achievement," "effort," or "accomplishment." The first halves of sections 1, 3, and 4 – decline of the Dao, family discord, and political disorder – all point to a problem, a lamentable state of affairs. The first half of section 2, "emergence of knowledge," presumably should be performing the same semantic and literary function and thus should be understood as referring to a serious defect. In parallel, the second halves of sections 1, 3, and 4 – "benevolence and rightness," "filial piety and compassion," and "loyal ministers" – are all treasured highly by the world, though they now come under Laozi's criticism. Thus, *dawei* should also signify something valued by the mundane world.

In this context, "knowledge" reflects the Daoist view that clever schemes and cunning know-how characterize the state of a world that is already alienated from its source and original order. Such knowledge leads to *wei* 偽, man-made achievement and accomplishment, in the same sense as the word is used in the *Xunzi*. In other words, *wei* is likely used interchangeably with *wei* 為 (action), and the passage takes aim at Xunzi's advocacy of human effort and learning. In any event, the assertion "When knowledge and wisdom emerge, there are great achievements" suggests that the ideal state characterized by the absence of knowledge in the sense of cleverness and cunning has already been forgotten and that artificial effort and achievement have come to be cherished by the world.[14]

Chapter 18 appears in the recently discovered Guodian *Laozi* "C" text as follows:

(故)大道(廢), (焉(有)(仁)義. 六(親)不和, (焉)(有)孝(慈). 邦(家)(昏)(亂), (焉)(有)正臣.[15]

Neither the Guodian *Laozi* "A" text nor the "B" text contains this chapter. What is striking is that as compared with the Mawangdui manuscripts and the current (Wang Bi) version, section 2 is missing. It would appear that this section did not figure in early *Laozi* manuscripts like the Guodian bamboo text, and was inserted into the *Laozi* only when the Mawangdui texts were made, as the *Laozi* gradually evolved into its mature form. If I am right in suggesting that section 2 is particularly concerned with Xunzi's sense of Confucian practice, this would suggest that the *Laozi* "C" text discovered at Guodian may have come before Xunzi's thought became widely known and circulated.

Without the second section, indeed, *Laozi* 18 seems clearer. Benevolence, filial piety and loyalty arise only after the pristine Daoist order, natural family harmony, and political order have been corrupted. Moreover, the fact that section 2 is missing in the Guodian version may enable us to understand better the current *Laozi*. I have on several occasions suggested that the ideal Daoist order "for certain reasons" has fallen into disuse or has been damaged or corrupted. Although it is not articulated in the Guodian text, it is possible that the cause of the decline of the Dao, the disharmony in family relations, and political disorder is precisely the kind of arbitrary and artificial "knowledge" and the kind of "great achievements" that stem from it. Is there any evidence to support this?

Consider, for example, that in N1 (Chapter 12) the *Zhuangzi* seems to be suggesting that the reason for the loss of perfect virtue has to do with honoring the worthy and employing the talented. More precisely, when people "know" what they are doing to be in accord with "rightness" and when they "love one another" and "know" that to be benevolence, the knowledge of morality has come to motivate and inform human action, which signals the loss of natural order and harmony.

Similarly, N2 (Chapter 14) traces the loss of perfect virtue to the rise of filial piety, benevolence, and other Confucian virtues. Yet, at a deeper level, what led to the emergence of filial piety and other forms of artificial goodness in the first place was the direct opposite of "forgetting the world" and "making the world forget you." It is also opposed to the "non-action" (*wuwei* 無為) and "naturalness" (*ziran* 自然) of perfect virtue that brings about order without anyone "knowing" it. This seems to agree well with the emphasis in the Mawangdui and current versions of *Laozi* 18 that knowledge and artificial human action bring about the decline of the Dao.

In N3 (Chapter 26), we see the *Zhuangzi* calling attention to the problem of the mind having become an "external thing." This again seems to support the interpretation here that knowledge and human intervention is directly responsible for the eclipse of the Dao. In Chapter 29 (N4), scholars were led astray from their "root" by the Confucian ideals of filial piety and brotherliness. The Confucians "eat without ever plowing" and mouth "fallacious theories." This seems to suggest that the problem, according to the *Zhuangzi*, lies in the intellectualization and capricious theorizing characteristic especially of the Confucians, which serve only to corrupt the natural order of the Dao.[16]

Based on this analysis, it seems clear that the earliest versions of the *Laozi* and the *Zhuangzi* share the same basic idea that human innovation and knowledge has much to do with the decline of the natural Daoist ideal state. Filial piety, in this view, is the result of the loss of harmony and contributes to the further deterioration of the world. In contrast, the later Mawangdui versions added the idea that "when knowledge and wisdom emerge, there are great achievements" and placed it alongside the other three sections. In this way, all four sections now equally testify to the loss of genuine virtue, whereas the reason for the initial decline of the Dao has become blurred. This new development opens the possibility that filial piety may be interpreted as having a more positive value, as it may be taken to have arisen from a natural process of differentiation. Although the textual changes may appear small, a different interpretation of *xiao* may follow as a result.

Affirmation of *xiao* in the various versions of the *Laozi*

Now we turn to Chapter 19 of the *Laozi*, which as mentioned seems to provide a positive assessment of *xiao*. The *Laozi* says, "Abandon sagacity and discard wisdom; then the people will benefit a hundredfold. Abandon benevolence and discard rightness; then the people will return to filial piety and compassion." The two Mawangdui *Laozi* manuscripts carry essentially the same reading. The natural *xiao* of the people is evidently meant to contrast with the morality of benevolence and rightness. The reason for this opposition may have to do with the problem of desire, as the concluding line of Chapter 19 – "manifest plainness, embrace simplicity, reduce selfishness, have few desires" – seems to suggest, but it is not explained explicitly in the text.

Chapter 19 appears in the Guodian *Laozi* "A" text as follows:

(絕)(智)弃(辯), 民利百(倍). (絕)(巧)弃利, (盜)(賊)(無)(有). (絕)(偽)弃慮, 民(復)(孝)(慈). . . . (示)(素)保(樸), 少(私)(寡)欲.

Abandon knowledge and discard distinctions; then the people will benefit a hundredfold. Abandon skill and discard profit; then there will be no thieves or robbers. Abandon (artificial) effort and discard deliberations; then the people will return to filial piety and compassion . . . Manifest plainness, embrace simplicity, reduce selfishness, have few desires.

This differs significantly from the Mawangdui and current versions. In this discussion, I will concentrate on the phrase "(絕)(偽)弃慮, 民(復)(孝)(慈)." The Guodian text uses a variant for the word "*wei*" 偽, but following the editors of the Guodian texts, the identification should not pose any major difficulty.[17] However, the Guodian editors may have been too hasty in concluding that *wei* means "hypocrisy" or what is false.[18] This is because the words *wei* and *lei* 慮 here parallel "knowledge [*zhi* 智] and distinctions [*bian* 辯]" and "skill [*qiao* 巧] and profit [*li* 利]," which are all at least on the surface positive terms. Thus, *wei* 偽 should also be interpreted in a positive sense; otherwise the critical irony conveyed in this passage and so characteristic of the *Laozi* as a whole would have been lost. For this reason, *wei* should be read in the sense of conscious "effort," "achievement," or "accomplishment," as in the case of *Laozi* Chapter 18 discussed earlier.

Turning to the word read as *lei* 慮 here, the Guodian editors had at first suggested that the word comprises three components: "虎" on top, "且" in the middle, and "心" at the bottom. However, the middle component should be read not as "且" but as "田", since the common script "田" is often written as "目" in texts from the Chu region where the Guodian texts are found. Moreover, to read the character as *lei* would also yield better sense in the light of the passage as a whole. The Guodian editors here cite Professor Qiu Xigui's 裘錫圭 view that the character here should be read as *zha* 詐 (deception), i.e. in a negative sense.[19] However, as in the case of *wei*, the character *lei* should not be taken as a derogatory term here. Indeed, Qiu Xigui has since revised his earlier view that the character here is a variant of *zha* and now agrees that it should be read as *lei*.[20]

On the basis of the above analysis, the Guodian *Laozi* "A" text affirms the value of the "filial piety" of the people as something that is opposite to what comes out of artificial human effort and planning. The reason seems to be that whereas the former stems from the people naturally, the latter is typified by Confucian morality, which is the result of deliberate human intervention. Filial piety in the first sense is universal and inborn, intrinsic to the natural order and completely effortless or unlearned. This kind of filial piety does not reflect a product of alienation from the Dao or a remedy or substitute that is forced on the people. On the contrary, the Guodian *Laozi* considers this kind of filial piety to be a part of the pristine virtue of the Daoist world, a world in which the people are naturally filial and compassionate, and thieves and robbers are unheard of. This new line of thinking is continued in the Mawangdui and current versions of the *Laozi*, despite changes in the wording of the chapter. Even in the opening line of Chapter 19, the Mawangdui and current versions' "abandon sagacity and discard knowledge" reflects the same line of thought as the Guodian's "abandon knowledge and discard distinctions" and is similar also to the idea of "abandon [artificial] effort and discard deliberations."

Up to this point, we can see that all four versions of the *Laozi* Chapter 19 affirm filial piety. Chapter 18 of the *Laozi* in the two Mawangdui versions, with the added second section, also holds out the possibility that filial piety may be viewed as positive. They are thus not contradictory as commonly understood. The argument should become clearer if we compare these two chapters with Chapter 31 (P4) of the *Zhuangzi*. As mentioned, most scholars agree that the "Old Fisherman" chapter is one of the latest in the current *Zhuangzi*. In this chapter, it is clear that filial piety is paired with loyalty and integrity and affirmed as positive. They are affirmed because they are functions of what is "authentic" or genuine (*zhen*) in human relationships. What does "authenticity" mean? Towards the end of the passage, the *Zhuangzi* explains, "Rites are something created by the vulgar men of the world; authenticity is that which is received from Heaven. By nature it is the way it is and cannot be changed" (禮者，世俗之所為也。真者，所以受於天也，自然不可易也). The "authentic" or "genuine" is what human beings naturally receive from heaven; it is directly opposed to rituals and mundane or vulgar culture, which refer essentially to Confucian morality. Authentic filial piety thus rises from the virtue of Dao, an expression of the naturalness and nonaction. In terms of textual transmission and the development of Daoist philosophy, when the Guodian "A" version of Chapter 19 and the two Mawangdui versions of Chapter 18 were established, a new, positive account of *xiao* came into place. This view then finds sharper expression in the "Old Fisherman" chapter of the *Zhuangzi*, under the influence of the mature *Laozi*.

Older versions of *Laozi* Chapter 18 such as the Guodian "C" version share with other Daoist currents the view that the Confucian conception of *xiao* formed a part of the manmade rational system that came into being with the decline of the Dao, when family relations were no longer in harmony. As such, *xiao* must be rejected. In contrast, the "new" *Laozi* represented by Chapter 19 of the Guodian "A" version affirms filial piety as a genuine component of the order of nature. The Mawangdui versions of Chapter 18 represent a transition, a point at which section 2, missing from the Guodian "C" text, has become an integral part of the chapter. The "Old Fisherman" chapter of the *Zhuangzi* later brings this to fruition.

Thus, Daoist philosophy, based on the *Laozi* and the *Zhuangzi*, may be said to have gone through a decisive turn from rejecting *xiao* as artificial and false to affirming it as genuine and natural. This shift is not arbitrary but reflects changes in the meaning and practice of filial piety in ancient Chinese society, about which more will be noted later.

Xiao in the Guodian Chu bamboo texts, *Yucong*

Recently discovered among the Guodian bamboo texts, the *Yucong* 語叢 comprises four separate collections entitled simply *Yucong* I, II, III, and IV. They reflect Confucian influence. Many scholars have argued that the Guodian Confucian corpus, including the *Yucong* collection, belonged to the school of Zisi 子思, the grandson of Confucius, and Mencius. In my view, however, as the following analysis demonstrates, the *Yucong* does not belong to the "Zisi–Mencius" school. Let me consider several preliminary questions to put the discussion in context.

As Li Zehou has noted, although many of the Guodian texts are clearly Confucian in orientation and include a dialogue between Duke Mu of Lu 魯穆公 and Zisi, it remains unclear whether they belong to the so-called "Zisi–Mencius school." "On the contrary," Li proposes, "the bamboo texts clearly subscribe to the view that 'benevolence is internal and rightness is external' [仁內義外], which agrees with Gaozi's 告子 position and opposes that of Mencius. Thus, the conclusion that the bamboo texts belong to the 'Zisi–Mencius school' seems to have been made in haste and may not be accurate. On the contrary, the overall impression that I gain from reading these bamboo texts is that they may be closer to the *Liji* [Book of Rites] and the *Xunzi*."[21]

Ren Jiyu earlier argued that the so-called "school of Zisi and Mencius" never even existed.[22] In examining the date and authorship of the *Wuxing* 五行 text discovered at Mawangdui, I have also argued in detail that the so-called "Zisi–Mencius school" did not exist. The central philosophy of the *Wuxing* reflects not only the thought of Mencius but also that of Xunzi. In addition, there is evidence that the *Wuxing* was influenced by Daoist, Mohist, and Legalist thinking.[23] To regard the Guodian Confucian corpus as belonging to the "Zisi–Mencius school" thus seems overly restrictive and simplistic; it does not do full justice to the complexity and diversity of early Chinese thought.

Yucong I contains the following remark:

為孝，此非孝也. 為弟，此非弟也。不可為也，而不可不為也。為之，此非也。弗為，此非也。[24]

Literally, the passage may be translated:

To practice filial piety, this is not filial piety. To practice brotherliness, this is not brotherliness. This should not be done. Yet [filial piety and brotherliness] must not be left undone. To practice them would be wrong; not to practice them would be wrong.

It would be difficult to interpret this passage from the perspective of traditional Confucian doctrines. However, if we recognize that the Guodian Confucian texts were written under the influence of the Daoist philosophy of *wuwei* (nonaction) found especially in the *Laozi* and the *Zhuangzi*, the meaning of this passage can be understood readily. Translated with this in mind, the passage reads:

To practice filial piety, this is not [genuine] filial piety. To practice brotherliness, this is not [genuine] brotherliness. [This kind of filial piety and brotherliness] should not be practiced. Yet [genuine filial piety and brotherliness] cannot be left undone. To practice them [in the sense of performing rituals of filial piety and brotherliness] would be wrong; not to practice [genuine filial piety and brotherliness] would be wrong.

On the one hand, the "practice of filial piety" (*weixiao* 為孝) points to a repudiation of *xiao* as a deliberate and artificial ritual act. This agrees with the older Daoist view of *xiao* as a symptom of the alienation from the Dao. On the other hand, the text also says that filial piety "must not be left undone" or more precisely that "it is not permissible [*buke* 不可] not to practice [*xiao*]." This agrees with the "new" Daoist view in affirming the need to follow the kind of *xiao* that stems naturally from the depth of one's being. The negation of the former, both philosophically and as a literary device, adds to the force of the affirmation of genuine *xiao* that accords with *ziran*. Elsewhere in *Yucong* I, we also read, "[The relationship between] father and son reaches both the above and the below" (父子, 至上下也), which may be taken as pointing to the authentic *xiao* that characterizes the nature of the Daoist world.[25] Further, *Yucong* III states, "The *xiao* of the father and the love of the son is not [deliberate or artificial] action" (父孝子 (愛), 非(有)為也).[26] Perhaps the first clause should be emended to read "the love of the father and the *xiao* of the son"; in any event, the second clause clearly places the Daoist view of *xiao* in the fold of *wuwei*. This gives a new meaning to *xiao*, which contrasts sharply with the Confucian view of *xiao* as conscious and deliberate acts that require effort, patience, and self-denial. From the original negative view of *xiao* in certain sections of the *Laozi* and the *Zhuangzi* to the redefinition and affirmation of *xiao* in these classics and the *Yucong*, we see the transformation of a key concept and a major shift in intellectual orientation.

Conclusion: the two views of *xiao* in historical context

The two views of *xiao* in the *Laozi* and other texts should be understood in the larger context of the development of early Chinese sociopolitical and intellectual history. Much research remains to be done in this difficult field; by way of conclusion, I will briefly discuss two related issues, leaving aside the more technical historical details.

First, from the Daoist perspective, the Confucian view of *xiao* serves to justify and maintain the older "feudal" sociopolitical structure based on kinship-ties and lineage that was already in decline. This is the kind of *xiao* that needs to be repudiated. In contrast, the view of *xiao* as an expression of naturalness and nonaction that the Daoists themselves seek to affirm seems to be oriented towards supporting a different political structure – one that reflects a higher degree of centralization and political unity, with the country organized into commanderies and districts and with the father and village elders serving as heads at the local level.

The former view of *xiao* based on the ancient Chinese kinship-based political system is closely related to the development of Confucianism from Confucius to Mencius and Xunzi. Confucianism regards kinship and blood ties to be the foundation of moral and political order. It looks back to the Western Zhou as the "golden age" and attempts to defend or restore the early Zhou model of government characterized by benevolent rule and ritual efficacy. However, kinship obligations come easily into conflict with political allegiances, which conflict crystallizes in intellectual discourse as the tension between filial piety and loyalty (*zhong*). In this regard it is no accident that, with the exception of *Laozi* Chapter 18 and *Zhuangzi* Chapter 26 (N3), none of the passages that hold a negative view of *xiao* parallels *xiao* with *zhong*.

In comparison, the latter view of *xiao* assumes a different sociopolitical model that is based on the authority of the father figure. This is reflected in the *Xiaojing* (*Classic of Filial Piety*) and in the "Zhong Xiao" chapter of the *Hanfeizi*. Politically, this suggests a unified structure in which the ruler on top commands absolute obedience from the people below. Filial piety should serve this political edifice and does not conflict with loyalty. In principle, there is no inherent contradiction between *xiao* and *zhong*. This is because the relationship between father and son is seen to be the same as that between ruler and subject. In the passages that affirm *xiao* cited above, with the exception of *Laozi* Chapter 19, *zhong* and *xiao* are thus typically mentioned together.

The development of thought is never clear-cut; the exceptions I mentioned perhaps testify to the complexities of this development. Although the Daoists may object to the Confucian sense of filial piety, mutual influences are also to be expected. The Daoist view may have influenced the *Hanfeizi*, but that is a separate issue. What is clear is that the Daoists rejected the Confucian sense of *xiao* on the grounds that it is artificial and contrary to *ziran*. The same reasoning extends to other Confucian virtues; from the Daoist perspective, virtue can only be defined as what is authentic or genuine, which arises spontaneously from human nature, endowed by heaven and ultimately by the Dao. This sets up a direct confrontation with the Confucian emphasis on ritual propriety. During the Wei–Jin period (third to fifth centuries), this formed the basis of the debate between "orthodox teachings" (*mingjiao* 名教) and *ziran*. The evolution of the concept of *xiao* in the *Laozi*, the *Zhuangzi*, and the Guodian *Yucong* thus relates to the larger issue of the development of Chinese philosophy.

Notes

This chapter was translated by Alan K. L. Chan.

1 Translator's note: The author refers to the Wang Bi W 王弼 (226–249) version of the *Laozi* as contained in the "Daoist Canon" (*Daozang*). Translations from the

Laozi are based on Wing-tsit Chan, *The Way of Laozi*, Indianapolis: Bobbs-Merrill, 1963, and D. C. Lau, *Lao Tzu Tao Te Ching*, Harmondsworth: Penguin Books, 1963, with modification where necessary, especially in the light of the author's understanding of the text.

2 Translator's note: In 1993, some 800 inscribed bamboo slips were discovered in a tomb at Guodian 郭店, near Jingmen 荊門, Hubei province. The tomb, located near the old capital of the state of Chu 楚, a major political and cultural center in early China, is generally dated to about 300 BCE. The bamboo texts have been transcribed and published in *Guodian Chumu zhujian* 郭店楚墓竹簡, Beijing: Wenwu chubanshe, 1998. Three groups of bamboo slips, identified simply as "A," "B," and "C" and containing about 2,000 characters, correspond with 31 chapters of the current *Laozi*. On the Guodian find and especially the three groups of *Laozi* texts, in English, see especially William G. Boltz, "The Fourth-century BC Guodian Manuscripts from Chuu and the Composition of the *Laotzyy*," *Journal of the American Oriental Society*, 119, no. 4, 1999, 590–608; Sarah Allan and Crispin Williams (eds), *The Guodian Laozi*, Society for the Study of Early China and Berkeley: The Institute of East Asian Studies, University of California, 2000; and Robert G. Henricks (trans.), *Lao Tzu's Tao Te Ching: A Translation of the Startling New Documents Found at Guodian*, New York: Columbia University Press, 2000.

3 Scholars are generally of the opinion that the first seven chapters, the so-called "inner chapters" (*neipian* 內篇) of the current thirty-three chapter version of the *Zhuangzi* were written by Zhuangzi himself, whereas the remaining "outer chapters" (外篇) and "miscellaneous chapters" (雜篇) were put together by his disciples, successors and later writers. Consequently, the inner chapters are often thought to be the oldest and the most valuable in studying Zhuangzi's philosophy. In contrast, the outer chapters came later and are less valuable, and the miscellaneous chapters, the latest and the least valuable. I have argued elsewhere, however, that this is hardly the case. See Ikeda Tomohisa, *Zhuangzi "Dao" de zhexue ji qi yanbian* 莊子「道」的哲學及其演變, Taipei: Guoli bianyiguan, 2001, Chapter 2. Translator's note: Translations from the *Zhuangzi* are based on Burton Watson, *The Complete Works of Chuang Tzu*, New York: Columbia University Press, 1968, with modifications where appropriate.

4 Watson, *Complete Works of Chuang Tzu*, p. 138.

5 Ibid., pp. 155–6.

6 Ibid., pp. 294–5.

7 Ibid., pp. 324–5.

8 Ibid., pp. 59–60.

9 Ibid., pp. 138–9.

10 Ibid., pp. 328–9.

11 Ibid., pp. 349–50.

12 In comparison, among the "negative" passages only Chapter 26 (N3) mentions *xiao* together with "loyalty."

13 For the two Mawangdui silk manuscripts of the *Laozi*, which date to the second century BCE, see Robert Henricks (trans.), *Lao-tzu Te-tao ching: A New Translation Based on the Recently Discovered Ma-wang-tui Texts*, New York: Ballantine Books, 1989.

14 The criticism of the *Laozi* and the *Zhuangzi*, of course, is not limited to *xiao* but also extends to other key Confucian virtues such as benevolence, rightness, and ritual propriety. See especially *Laozi* Chapter 38 and *Zhuangzi* Chapter 9 ("Horses' Hoofs"). The latter depicts a world in which "perfect virtue" prevails. "Then along comes the sage, huffing and puffing after benevolence, reaching on tiptoe for rightness, and the world for the first time has doubts"; Watson, *The Complete Works of Chuang Tzu*, p. 105. See also *Huainanzi*, Chapters 2, "Shu zhen xun"

俶真訓, and 11, "Qi su xun" 齊俗訓; in *Huainan Honglie jijie* 淮南鴻烈集解, *Xinbian zhuzi jicheng* edition, Beijing: Zhonghua shuju, 1989, pp. 58–9 and 343. In both places, the *Huainanzi* emphasizes that benevolence and rightness arise only after the Dao and genuine virtue have been abandoned.

15 Translator's note: Chinese characters in brackets are modern equivalents accepted by the author. In this instance, they agree with the transcription given in *Guodian Chumu zhujian*, p. 121; see also *The Guodian Laozi*, p. 224, and Robert Henricks, *Lao Tzu's Tao Te Ching*, p. 114.

16 See n. 14 above; cf. Ikeda Tomohisa, *Zhuangzi*, Chapter 12.

17 *Guodian Chumu zhujian*, p. 111.

18 *Guodian Chumu zhujian*, p. 113, n. 3.

19 Ibid.

20 See my *Kakuten Sokan Rōshi kenkyū* 郭店楚簡老子研究, Tokyo: Tokyo University, 1999, pp. 53, 59, n. 5.

21 Li Zehou 李澤厚, "*Chu du Guodian zhujian yinxiang jiyao* 初讀郭店竹簡印象紀要," in *Li Zehou zhexue wencun* 李澤厚哲學文存, vol. 2, Anhui: Anhui Wenyi chubanshe, 1999. As is well known, the *Mencius* opposes Gaozi's view that "benevolence is internal and rightness is external" (e.g. *Mencius* 2A2, 6A4). The *Guodian* text entitled *Liude* 六德, however, supports this view; see *Guodian Chumu zhujian*, p. 188.

22 Ren Jiyu 任繼愈, *Zhongguo zhexue fazhanshi, xian Qin* 中國哲學發展史, 先秦, Beijing: Renmin chubanshe, 1983, 「孔孟之間的儒家傳承」、三「思孟學派考辨. This is based on the *Wuxing* 五行 text discovered at Mawangdui. I may add that in March 2000, at an international conference in Beijing on the *Yijing*, I asked Professor Ren whether the discovery of *Wuxing* among the Guodian bamboo texts would necessitate a change in his opinion about the "Zisi–Mencius school," to which he replied, "No need whatsoever."

23 See my *Maōtai hanbo hakusho Gogyōhen kenkyū* 馬王堆漢墓帛書五行篇研究, Tokyo: Kyūko shoin, 1993, Part 1, Chapter 2. See also my *Kakuten Sokan Gogyō no kenkyū* 郭店楚簡五行の研究, in *Kakuten Sokan no shisōshi teki kenkyū* 郭店楚簡の思想史的研究, Vol. 2, Tokyo: Tokyo University, 1999.

24 *Guodian Chumu zhujian*, *Yucong* I, p. 195.

25 Ibid., p. 196.

26 *Guodian Chumu zhujian*, *Yucong* III, p. 209.

2 Filial piety with a vengeance

The tension between rites and law in the Han

Anne Cheng

In an article entitled "Ritualisme et juridisme," Léon Vandermeersch describes the rites of ancient China as "mechanisms which rule social relationships *a priori*."[1] He then quotes the *Da Dai Liji* – "Rites condemn beforehand, penal law condemns afterwards" – and comes to the conclusion that "in China penal law has always been, with reason, treated as being essentially heterogeneous with the rites."[2] One is also reminded of the famous sentence in the *Liji*: "Rites do not reach down to commoners; punishments do not reach up to high officials."[3] The whole Chinese, especially Confucian, vision is dominated by the centrality of the principle of harmonization (*he* 和), of which the rites (*li* 禮) are expressions *par excellence*, while penal law (*xing* 刑), which strives to dissuade through its harshness and, at worst, inflicts correction *a posteriori*, appears as a simple makeshift. In view of the complex relationships that exist in Chinese tradition between particularistic rites and universalistic laws, the case of ritual murder carried out by vengeance is problematic and has, in fact, never ceased to give food for thought to experts both on classical sources and on legal texts.

Murder commanded by the duty of vengeance can only strike us as a paradox: while it proceeds from ritualism, it nonetheless strikes *a posteriori*, just as penal sanction would do. Moreover, instead of contributing to harmony as rites are supposed to do, vengeance is an act of violence that imperils social order. How, then, are we to resolve the contradiction inherent in an act that is supposed to restore social harmony, while jeopardizing it? This is a crucial question that is tentatively broached by canonical sources, especially the Gongyang commentary on the *Spring and Autumn Annals* (*Chunqiu Gongyang zhuan*), which is known to have played a central role in the formation of Han imperial ideology.[4]

Vengeance as a ritual act

In pre-imperial China, one of the major ritual prerogatives of Zhou aristocracy resided in the exclusivity of ancestor worship by virtue of the "lineage law" (*zongfa* 宗法), according to which every cadet branch of the royal lineage reproduced the royal rites in its own fief, and every cadet branch of the ducal lineages reproduced in its turn the rites of the ducal court within its own clan.

These perpetual struggles for the acknowledgment of lineage and consequently for ancestor worship account for the cases of vengeance in the Spring and Autumn period. But in the evolution, perceptible from the Warring States onward, toward a state system where central power exerted a growing control over the whole of the population, the "vertical" ramification of the lineage law tended to disappear to give place to a "horizontal" segmentation, with the clan as a basic unit. From then on, it was the clan, as a kin unit, that was the basis for the levy of troops and taxes, forced labor, and collective sanctions,[5] as well as for the moral obligation of vengeance between kinsmen as formulated by the ritual treatises and their commentaries. As Mark Lewis aptly summarizes, "The principle of collective liability for punishment on the basis of households was the legal expression of this new institutional order, just as the obligation to avenge immediate relatives was its moral expression in Confucian ritualist theory . . . In the state advocated by Shang Yang a man would judge and punish those people whom he would avenge in the world of the *Gongyang*."[6] The *Gongyang zhuan* indeed appears as the major canonical authority in which vengeance is presented as a moral obligation, in that it illustrates one of the fundamental human relationships.

The importance of requital (*bao* 報) as a basis for ritual relations is a well known fact.[7] It is in terms of reciprocity (*shu* 恕) that Confucius himself defined his central value of humaneness (*ren* 仁).[8] However, while he clearly condemned the spirit of vengeance, the ritual treatises of the late Warring States and early imperial era justify it on the basis of reciprocity. There is therefore a distinction to be made between the Confucian ethic and the specialization in rites characteristic of the *Ru* 儒, namely between the original teaching of Confucius, which placed filial piety at the basis of human quality, and the ritualistic spirit, which gears it toward the duty of vengeance.[9]

From the ritualistic perspective, however paradoxical it may seem compared to its declared ideal of harmony, vengeance is perceived as an eminently moral act: far from infringing upon social hierarchy, it is quite to the contrary its very warrant, in that it brings to life the personal bonds of reciprocity, which weave the social fabric. In the present case, reciprocity does not obey the law of retaliation, in that vengeance is not a settling of accounts between the victim and her or his avenging relative. One can therefore be quits as much through the received benefits (*bao en* 報恩) as through the offence undergone (*bao chou* 報仇).[10] Given that vengeance appears as the assertion of the reciprocity of obligatory bonds, it eventually turns the violent act, which it is in itself, into a ritualized act.

Vengeance in the ritual treatises

In the ritual treatises of the Han period, notably the *Liji*, the duty for a son to avenge the death of his father or mother is presented as absolute:

One should not bear the same Heaven as the murderer of one's father. One should never turn aside one's weapon if one encounters the murderer of a brother. One should not dwell in the same state with the murderer of a friend.

Zixia asked Confucius: "How should one live without having avenged a father or mother?" The Master replied: "Sleep on straw with your shield as pillow and do not take office. Do not share the same Heaven [with the murderer]. Even if you meet him in the market or court strike him without turning aside your weapon." "Might I ask how one should live without having avenged a brother?" "If you take office it should not be in the same state. If you are sent on a mission at the command of your prince, do not attack if you meet him on the way." "Might I ask how one should live if one has not avenged an uncle or cousin?" "Do not be the leader [in seeking revenge]. If the one in charge is capable then follow behind him with your weapon."[11]

Compiled in the early Han period, the Gongyang commentary on the *Chunqiu* delivers a strikingly similar lesson:

Chunqiu: In winter, the duke and a man from Qi hunted in Hao.

Gongyang: Why did the duke hunt with a man of low rank? [It was in fact] the marquis of Qi. If so, why is he referred to as "a man"? To conceal [the fact that the duke] hunted together with his enemy.

Sub-commentary by He Xiu: According to the rites, one does not bear the same Heaven as the murderer of one's father or mother. One does not dwell in the same state as the murderer of a brother. One does not share the same neighborhood with the murderer of a member of one's clan. One does not share the same marketplace or the same court with the murderer of a friend.[12]

The ritual treatises and the Gongyang commentary thus agree in saying that vengeance is a moral obligation, and that the degree of obligation is directly proportionate to the closeness of kin between the victim of the offence and his (or her) avenger, exactly on the model of the funeral and mourning rites, which, significantly enough, must be kept up until vengeance is actually drawn. In that respect, vengeance is closely associated with the mourning rites, for which it represents both a substitution and a condition, in that it too depends on the various degrees of kinship.

It is interesting to note that, in another major ritual treatise such as the *Zhouli* (which, because of its textual links to pre-Han Legalist strains in administrative theory and practice, is generally recognized as emphasizing the use of laws as a system of rewards and punishments to control wayward elements in society), the degree of obligation may also be measured by the physical distance beyond which one is not bound to go to seek vengeance:

the closer the murdered relative was in kin, the farther the avenger is supposed to go to seek vengeance.[13] Such a distance is translated by the *Zhouli* in terms of physical distance, which the "conciliator" (*tiaoren* 調人), a kind of arbiter or third party representative of higher authority, places between the avenger and the offender by sending the latter into exile. In this way, a system of "equivalences" is established according to hierarchical relationships and familial bonds:

> The one guilty of enmity toward a father is expelled beyond the seas; the one guilty of enmity toward an older or younger brother is expelled over a thousand *li* away; the one guilty of enmity toward uncles or cousins is not permitted to live in the same domain.
> The case of enmity toward a lord is viewed the same as that of a father; that toward a teacher or elder, as toward a brother; that toward a master or a friend as toward an uncle or cousin.[14]

The apology for vengeance in the Gongyang

If the Gongyang agrees with the ritual treatises to present an apology for vengeance, it is the only canonical source to go as far as to urge it over nine, or even a hundred, generations:

Chunqiu: The marquis of Ji greatly left his state.

Gongyang: What does "greatly left" mean? It means [his state] was destroyed. Who destroyed it? Qi destroyed it. Why does it not say "Qi destroyed it"? It is tabooed for the sake of Lord Xiang. The *Chunqiu* observes taboos for the worthy. What is worthy about Lord Xiang? He was avenging an offence. What offence? His distant ancestor Lord Ai was boiled at the Zhou court because the [then] lord of Ji had slandered him. In acting for this reason Lord Xiang's devotion to serving his ancestors was total. What does "total" mean? When Lord Xiang was about to seek vengeance upon Ji he divined, and the prognostication said, "You will lose half your army." "Even if I die for it, this would not be inauspicious."
How many generations is a "distant ancestor"? Nine generations. After nine generations should one still avenge an offence? Even after a hundred generations one still should.
Can the cadet lineage of a hereditary minister also do so? No. Why can a state? The [successive] lords of a state are a single body. The shame of the previous lords is the shame of the present lord. The shame of the present lord is the shame of the previous lords. How can the lords of a state be a single body? The lords of a state regard the state as their body, and the [status of] the feudal lords being hereditary, they are a single body.

The present state of Ji had committed no crime. Is this not simply [venting] anger? No. If of old there had been an enlightened Son of Heaven, then the lord of Ji would certainly have been executed and there would be no Ji. The fact that the lord of Ji was not executed and that until today Ji still exists means that there has been no enlightened Son of Heaven . . . If there had been an enlightened Son of Heaven, could Lord Xiang have acted in this manner? He could not. If he could not, then why did Lord Xiang do this? Whenever above there is no Son of Heaven and below there is no hegemon, it is allowed to act according to [one's own feelings] of affection or hatred.[15]

Such an exaltation of vengeance in the Gongyang is quite remarkable: the Gongyang usually considers the destruction of a state as the "worst of evils." But in the present case, it is credited to a "worthy man" because it proceeds from vengeance. Let us note, by the way, that the above said "worthy man" committed incest with his younger sister and eventually assassinated her husband so that their liaison could go on unhindered.

The Gongyang, then, urges a ritual regulation of vengeance, which, however, can only be carried out in the perennial framework of a state and not within the private framework of a clan: it is no longer a matter of the "lineage law," in which the clan was but a reduced-scale reproduction of a realm; from now on, the political and the familial domains are clearly distinguished. The case of Wu Zixu 伍子胥 (late sixth to early fifth centuries BCE), one of the most famous stories of vengeance in Chinese literature, perfectly illustrates, in its Gongyang version, the distinction drawn in the early Han between the affairs of the state and those of the clan. The story begins with the execution of Wu Zixu's father (together with his elder brother) by King Ping of Chu. Wu Zixu then leaves Chu to beg assistance from Wu. The king of Wu, Helü (ruled 513–494 BCE), offers to levy troops to help Wu Zixu to take vengeance on Chu, but is met by a refusal from Zixu, who claims it is a matter of personal vengeance, involving, what's more, a mere commoner:

> A feudal lord does not raise an army for the sake of a commoner. Furthermore, I have heard it said that "serving one's prince is like serving one's father." A subject will not avenge his father to the detriment of his prince.

After hearing these gallant words, Helü gives up on attacking Chu. Some time later, Chu exerts its tyranny on the small state of Cai, which turns to Wu for support. Only then does Zixu join the troops of Wu to inflict punishment on Chu (from state to state), while seizing the opportunity to wreak his personal vengeance. The Gongyang concludes this episode with the following moral:

It is rightly said: "Serving one's ruler is just like serving one's father." In what sense was it an opportunity [for Wu Zixu] to take vengeance? When the father does not receive a just execution the son ought to avenge him. If the father receives a just execution and the son avenges him, this is the way of "pushing against the blade" [i.e. the vengeance will simply attract vengeance in return]. It avenges the grievance but does not eliminate the harm.[16]

Whereas other sources provide a more or less detailed description of the vengeance of Wu Zixu, who is said to have flogged the grave of the Chu king, or alternatively to have unearthed his body before flogging it, the Gongyang version stands out quite prominently in that, while concentrating exclusively on the episode of vengeance, it refrains from making any mention of "emotional" gestures that would appear as expressions of strictly private feelings.[17] It all happens as if the Gongyang version wanted to erase the outrageous character of a vengeance which, carried out as it is out of filial piety, nevertheless culminates in the desecration of a royal grave. In the present case, Wu Zixu finds a chance to wreak vengeance only by transforming it into a *raison d'état*.

It is interesting to note that the "old text" (*guwen*) tradition, as represented, for instance, in the *Zuozhuan*, is to be distinguished from the "new text" (*jinwen*) position expressed in the Gongyang by absolutizing the ruler's will, which is none other than that of Heaven itself and against which no vengeance whatsoever could ever be directed:

Whenever a lord has killed a subject without reason, the Gongyang says the son is justified to seek vengeance. This is why Zixu's attack against Chu was lauded by the *Chunqiu*. But according to Mr Zuo [the presumed author of the *Zuozhuan*], the lord's decree is Heaven itself, so vengeance is not allowed.[18]

It must, however, be specified in this respect that the Gongyang takes care to stipulate that the duty of vengeance exists if, and only if, "above there is no Son of Heaven, and below there is no hegemon"; that is to say, if the supreme authority does not fulfill its function. When it does function, it is the role of the ruler to punish offenders.[19] One can here perceive the relationship between vengeance and penal sanction, which plays a crucial role in Han legal thought and most particularly in the Gongyang tradition.

Canonical authority and force of law

The Gongyang commentary constitutes a privileged reference, being, within the whole Confucian canonical literature, the most often quoted and implemented text in the ethico-legal field. In the Former Han, the Gongyang was used as a sort of hermeneutic grid to interpret the canonical text of the

Chunqiu, the annals of Lu in which Confucius was supposed to have passed his moral judgments (literally "praise and blame," *baobian* 褒貶) by means of a coded language. One of the interpretive modes defined by the Gongyang had a legal function, since the *Chunqiu* was read as a collection of precedents to be used to "collate decisions" and settle litigious legal cases. Dong Zhongshu, an expert on the *Chunqiu* in the Gongyang tradition at the Imperial Academy, is credited with a *Gongyang Dong Zhongshu zhiyu* (*Cases Settled by Dong Zhongshu on the Basis of the Gongyang*).[20] The few cases that have been preserved amply illustrate Dong's predilection for the particularism of the ritual frame of mind over the pure objectivity of the law by declaring innocent a father who has attempted to cover up for his son (by reference to the famous case of the stolen sheep in the *Analects*) or a wife who has killed her husband so as to avenge his mother, toward whom he had failed to pay his filial obligations.[21]

The Gongyang testifies to the strong tensions between the opposing centralistic and "feudal" aspirations at work in the early Han empire. While the former, of Legalist inspiration, gives primacy to the law, the latter endeavors to defend the traditional values and exalt the ancient ritual code.[22] In the ritual treatises of the early Han, the rites are presented as essential in the harmonization of the sociopolitical community and the prevention of disorder, while the laws play only a secondary role by intervening most of the time *a posteriori* to sanction an already committed crime. Rites and laws appear to be as complementary as the roots and the branches:

> [The ruler's moral] instruction is the root of governing, while legal judgments are the branches. They differ in their domains but are one in their implementation, and can therefore only follow on each other. This is why the superior man gives them such importance.[23]

But what is to be done in cases such as murder committed out of vengeance, where rites and law are in total contradiction? What makes vengeance a special case is that it is both a ritual and a violent, if not bloody, act, which means that it brings out both the ritual spirit (*li* 禮) and brutal force (*li* 力), which are as a rule antithetic in *Ru* ethics. Moreover, by presupposing the punishment of an armed force that substitutes itself for the sanction of the law, it raises the question of the priority to be given to either the state or the clan. At this point, the notion of "balancing the circumstances" (*quan* 權), central in the Gongyang tradition, intervenes to present a particular act not in its objective result (according to the Legalist view of the taxation of crimes), but as the manifestation of an intention, a subjective will.[24] Thus an analogous type of relationship holds between the great constant principles (*jing* 經, those edicted by Confucius in his choice of formulation in the *Chunqiu*) and the necessary adaptation to circumstances (*quan*) as between ethico-ritualistic prescriptions (*yi* 義) and legal judgments (*fa* 法). The difficulty that lies in conciliating the moral and ritual obligation of vengeance and the social constraints imposed by law was to remain one of the major dilemmas in legal theory and practice throughout the whole of Chinese imperial history.

Filial piety and loyalty to the ruler

In the Gongyang commentary, the duty of vengeance appears as the absolutizing of filial piety (*xiao* 孝), which is paralleled with the loyalty of the subject to his ruler (*zhong* 忠): "If, after the murder of their ruler, the subjects do not punish the murderer, they are not [true] subjects. If a son does not avenge [the death of his father], he is not a [true] son".[25] This analogy finds an echo in the *Bohutong* of the Later Han:

> A son is entitled to avenge his father because he has the same obligation toward him as a subject toward his ruler. The reason why a loyal subject or a filial son cannot tolerate [the murder of his ruler or father] is that his affection and obligation cannot be removed from him.[26]

Vengeance here appears as one of the major articulations between the two fundamental bonds of Confucian ritualism, which also happen to be the two central issues of the Han dynasty: the blood bond between father and son, doubled as it were by the political bond between ruler and subject. It was during the Han period that the *Ru* proceeded to assimilate filial piety, a central value in Confucian ethics, to the loyalty of the subject to the ruler and the state. One may here perceive the attempt made by the *Ru* to gain imperial patronage and to achieve political legitimation in the eyes of a centralizing power by integrating Legalist criticisms. Whatever the case, the theme of loyalty to the ruler and to the dynasty tends to stiffen somewhat, turning from a basically ethical and relativistic interpretation with Confucius and Mencius[27] into a cosmologico-religious and absolutist interpretation with the Han authors, notably Dong Zhongshu. Such interpretation aims at lumping together loyalty and filial piety, making the latter into an absolute duty, in that it is founded in nature and includes religious references to ancestor worship. Thus filial piety not only becomes the proper characteristic of Han emperors (who are posthumously styled *xiao*, "filial") and a decisive criterion in the process of recommendation of candidates to official functions, it furthermore finds itself integrated in the cosmological scheme of the Five Phases (*wuxing*) by way of its association with the central phase Earth and the color yellow.[28] In the cosmological scheme of Dong Zhongshu, loyalty to the ruler, just like a son's piety toward his father, is as "natural" as the submission of Earth to Heaven.

The idea of modeling and founding political loyalty on filial piety was amply illustrated in the *Xiaojing* (*Classic of Filial Piety*), "discovered" in the middle of the Former Han and immediately promoted to the status of a canonical work for which a chair was established at the Imperial Academy by Emperor Wen (ruled 179–157 BCE). Its only purpose was to construct not only a vague analogy, but a systematic identification between loyalty and filial devotion, which could then be used as a paradigm extensible to all sorts of relationships that no longer had anything to do with blood bonds: superior/inferior, master/disciple, patron/client, etc.

Ritual vengeance and legal punishment

We have seen that vengeance is considered by ritual sources as a moral act expressing reciprocity, which characterizes the fundamental relationships of Confucian society. But if one starts considering penal sanctions as being equally founded on reciprocity, one could be led to conclude, through a kind of syllogistic reasoning, that there is some equivalence between vengeance and punishment by law.[29] In particular, one cannot help seeing in vengeance over nine generations as urged by the Gongyang an echo of the utmost punishment envisaged by Han law; that is, capital execution with "extermination of the clan" (*mie zu* 滅族), some legal texts speaking more specifically of the "nine categories of kinship" (*jiu zu* 九族). The whole question is to elucidate what these nine categories might have corresponded to: if we are to believe the canonical authorities of the "new text" orthodoxy, they corresponded to persons belonging to three different clans: those respectively of the father, the mother and the wife. According to the "old text" tradition, they are meant to designate persons who bear the same clanic name, scaling from the great-great-grandfather down to the great-great-grandson (according to the famous exegete of the Later Han Zheng Xuan, the term *zu* is used to designate specifically the paternal clan).[30] In practice, it seems that "extermination of the clan" involved the execution of the offender together with his parents (and probably his paternal grandparents), his wife and children (and probably his grandchildren), and his brothers and sisters (in all likeliness including those who were married). However the case may have been, from these most complex listings emerge the kinship relations that are likely both to determine the penal punishment and to dictate the obligations of vengeance, namely those derived from the ritual rules of mourning.

Did Han law eventually succeed in substituting itself for the obligation of vengeance? The founder of the dynasty, Emperor Gaozu, inaugurated his reign in 206 BCE by decreeing that "anyone who kills a man will pay with his life."[31] But it is not clear from this general prohibition whether it considers as murder the act of vengeance, which, it seems, continued throughout the Han to be perceived as a duty as well as a, if not legal, at least legitimate sanction. The question of vengeance brings to light the ever present tension in the Han between the sense of "private" duty and imperial law, between state centralizing tendencies and local centrifugal ones. The way cases of vengeance were dealt with is revealing of a certain weakness of Han laws: even the officials of the imperial bureaucracy, who were supposed to enforce the emperor's decrees, were in practice rather lax, if not overtly tolerant, toward murderers by vengeance, probably under popular pressure, ever ready to pay homage to their heroism and selflessness. All the dynastic histories concerning the Han (*Shiji, Hanshu, Hou Hanshu*) testify to the frequent resort to "professional avengers," armed adventurers in the tradition of the "knights errant" (*youxia* 遊俠) of pre-imperial times, who put their competence in the service of the great, eventually organized into an authentic "mafia" operating in the shadow of the bureaucratic network.[32] As a rule, avengers, often quoted as examples of filial piety, yield a fairly positive image in Han historical sources.[33] Confronting imperial law, which prohibits murder for the sake of social order, centrifugal tendencies make reference to canonical sources such as the ritual treatises and the Gongyang commentary to present an apology for vengeance as a fundamental obligation akin to that of mourning.

Vengeance by the end of the Han

Starting from the restoration of the Han after the Wang Mang interregnum (9–23 CE), and while a refeudalizing process is at work, the emphasis is no longer placed on the centralizing of power, but on family interests. The type of analogy that had, in the early days of the dynasty, made it possible for loyalty to the ruler to achieve legitimation by finding a natural grounding in filial piety tends to be reversed in Later Han in the legitimation of filial piety placed at the very heart of Han institutional practices. As was shown by Michael Nylan, the Han state would end up stuck on the ambiguity that had been its very foundation by perpetuating confusion between force of law and morality through ritual conduct.[34] The dynasty was doomed to disappear, plagued by its own contradictions, notably the one between the will to centralize power by grounding it on the force of law and the will to promote a meritocracy whose criterion was a virtue of filial piety known and recognized by all, but ending up in a merely ostentatious performance in which the act of vengeance featured among the most spectacular feats.[35]

By the end of the first century, the "law on insults" (*qingwu fa* 輕侮法) permitted violent revenge to be taken for the sake of relatives who had in fact suffered little more than a serious offence to their personal dignity.[36] But as was pointed out by a councilor to Emperor He (ruled 88–106), such a law would fling the door open to chaos and it was in effect hastily abolished. The *Hou hanshu* tells about the interesting case of Su Buwei, whose biography is hardly more than the protracted story of his quest for vengeance for the death of his father.[37] After missing by a hair the chance to kill his father's murderer, a man called Li Gao (who only saved his life by happening to be in the toilet!), Su Buwei had to be content with assassinating Li's concubine and child, and unearthing Li's father's corpse in order to cut off the head and expose it in the market place. Only after carrying out such a grim task did Su Buwei allow himself to return home and perform the proper rites of mourning for his own father. At this point, Su's biography adds that only He Xiu (129–182), a Later Han eminent exegete on the Gongyang, provided canonical justification for such a bloody revenge by comparing it to that of Wu Zixu. Not only was Su Buwei unpunished for his avenging crimes, he was even allowed to take up service again in the administration of his commandery before he was caught up in his turn by Li Gao's avenger, who exterminated him along with sixty members of his family.

By the very end of the Han, at a time when imperial power had the greatest difficulty imposing its control on the great clans and local magnates who were involved in endless and ruthless vendettas, as is shown clearly by the Su Buwei saga, Xun Yue 荀悅 (148–209) attempted to formulate a compromise between vengeance as moral obligation and legal punishments:

> Answer to a question: "Taking vengeance was a right in ancient times."
> Someone said: "Should we leave the people free to take vengeance?"
> I said: "No."
> He said: "Then, what should we do about it?"
> I said: "There should be both freedom and restriction of action – there should be a chance [for people] to remain alive and for them to be killed. These should be systematized according to what is right and decided according to law; this is called establishing both right and the law."
> He asked: "What does this mean?"
> I said: "In accordance with the statute on taking vengeance in ancient times, those from whom vengeance for the death of a person's father is sought should be forced to evade [the hand of the avenger by moving] to a different province, one thousand *li* away; and for the death of a person's brother, to a different commandery five hundred *li* away; and for the death of a person's paternal uncle or cousin, to a different district one hundred *li* away. He who succeeds in taking vengeance upon those who do not avoid him in this way should be considered not guilty, whereas he who succeeds in taking vengeance upon those who try to avoid him in this way should be executed. Violating the royal prohibition against [killing] is a crime; taking vengeance is a right, but this right is forfeited by the crime. [Consequently, when vengeance is taken] those who follow the royal ordinance are considered obedient, while those who violate the royal ordinance are considered disobedient. [The determination of who is not guilty and] should stay alive and [who is guilty and] should be executed ought to be made according to whether one is considered obedient or disobedient. [The only exception to the above rule is that] those who go to or remain at their official missions will not be considered as not trying to avoid [vengeance]."[38]

Taking inspiration from the passage of the *Zhouli* quoted earlier, which called for a "voluntary avoidance of vengeance," meaning that the person sought out for vengeance had to leave his residence for a faraway place where he could never be found – the distance being inversely proportionate to the closeness of kin between the victim and the would-be avenger – Xun Yue attempts to define clearly and precisely the relationships between the moral obligation of vengeance and the pre-eminence of the law (what he calls the "royal ordinance").

One may conclude that the influence of the "legalized Confucianism" characteristic of the Gongyang, which leaves its mark on the beginnings of the first centralized empire in China, is still to be felt toward the end of the imperial era. Up to the latter part of the Qing dynasty, the tension remains between the respective domains of penal laws and of rites: in the minds of theoreticians of the law, the problem is to find a regulating principle between "human feelings," which are taken into account in the rites, and the constraints imposed by public order and state security.[39] But, contrary to the predominant conception in the early imperial period of the primacy of rites, to which laws are only supposed to bring their support, the polarity seems to be inversed by the end of the period. Thus, the sentence quoted at the start of this chapter – "Rites condemn beforehand, penal law condemns afterwards" – is replaced by this other adage: "Penal norms sketch an overall framework, the rites stick to human relations."[40]

Notes

1 Léon Vandermeersch, "Ritualisme et juridisme," in A. Blondeau and K. Schipper (eds), *Essais sur le rituel, Colloque du centenaire de la Section des Sciences religieuses de l'Ecole Pratique des Hautes Etudes*, vol. 2, Louvain and Paris: Peeters, 1990, reprinted in *Etudes sinologiques*, Paris: Presses Universitaires de France, 1994, pp. 209–20; see p. 211.

2 Vandermeersch, "Ritualisme et juridisme," p. 219; cf. *Da Dai Liji*, Chapter 46, *Licha*.

3 *Liji*, Chapter 1, *Quli*; cf. S. Couvreur, *Li Ki: ou mémoires sur les bienséances et les cérémonies, texte Chinois, avec une double traduction en Français et en Latin*, 1899, Paris: Cathasia, 1950 reprint, vol. 1, p. 53.

4 The Gongyang tradition, as it was elaborated during the Han period, from Dong Zhongshu to He Xiu, is the object of my *Etude sur le confucianisme Han. L'élaboration d'une tradition exégétique sur les Classiques*, Paris: Collège de France, Institut des Hautes Etudes Chinoises, 1985.

5 This is the so-called principle of "collective liability" (*lian zuo* 連坐) established by Qin law: the sanction for certain heavy crimes was not limited to the individual but extended to members of his family, neighbors, or, in the case of an official, to his immediate superiors or subordinates or to those who had recommended him to office.

6 Mark Edward Lewis, *Sanctioned Violence in Early China*, Albany: State University of New York Press, 1990, pp. 92–3.

7 See, for instance, L. S. Yang, "The Concept of 'Pao' as a Basis for Social Relations in China," in J. K. Fairbank (ed.), *Chinese Thought and Institutions*, Chicago: University of Chicago Press, 1957, pp. 291–309.

8 For example, *Lunyu* 4.15 and 5.11.

9 See B. E. Wallacker, "Han Confucianism and Confucius in Han," in D. T. Roy and T. H. Tsien (eds), *Ancient China: Studies in Early Civilization*, Hong Kong:

Chinese University Press, 1978, p. 227: "There was a difference between common respect for the past and the recognition of the values of Confucius as its repository and transmitter, on the one hand, and acceptance of the specific values of the *Ru*, on the other hand. The *Ru* were a partisan group who believed, we must assume, in such articles as the superiority of rites over law, kin relationships over those imposed by the state."

10 See, for instance, Chapter 6 *"Fu en"* of the *Shuoyuan* 說苑.

11 *Liji* Chapter 1, *Quli*, and Chapter 2, *Tangong*; cf. Couvreur, *Li Ki*, vol. 1, pp. 56 and 147–8.

12 *Chunqiu Gongyang zhuan* (with He Xiu's sub-commentary of Later Han), Duke Zhuang, fourth year, winter, in Ruan Yuan (ed.), *Chongkan Songban Shisan jing zhushu* edition, Kyoto: Chūbun shuppansha, 1974 reprint, p. 4832. T. Makino, *Chūgoku kazoku kenkyū* (Studies on family and lineage in China), Tokyo: Seikatsu sha, 1944, reprinted in *Makino Tatsumi chosaku shū*, 2 vols, Tokyo: Ochanomizu, 1980, vol. 2, pp. 4–15, presents the relevant occurrences and analyses their differences. See also T. Nishida, "Fukushū to keibatsu" (Vengeance and Punishment), in *Chūgoku keihō shi kenkyū* (*Studies on the History of Chinese Penal Law*), Tokyo: Iwanami shoten, 1974, pp. 95–120. In English, one may also read the rather summary article by Michael Dalby, "Revenge and the Law in Traditional China," *The American Journal of Legal History*, 25, no. 4, 1981, 267–307. For studies bearing more specifically on cases of vengeance in the Gongyang, see Li Xinlin, *Chunqiu Gongyangzhuan yaoyi*, Taipei: Wenjin chubanshe, 1989, Chapter 4, and T. Hihara, *Shunjū Kuyōden no kenkyū*, Tokyo: Sōbunsha, 1976, pp. 72–98.

13 T. Makino, *Chūgoku kazoku kenkyū*, p. 421, provides a synopsis of the "tarification" of distances of banishment based on ancient sources.

14 *Zhouli*, *"Diguan tiaoren,"* *Zhouli zhushu* edition, in Ruan Yuan (ed.), *Chongkan Songben shisanjing zhushu*, 1815, *juan* 14, pp. 10b–13a.

15 *Chunqiu Gongyang zhuan*, Duke Zhuang, fourth year, fourth month, pp. 4830b–31b.

16 *Chunqiu Gongyang zhuan*, Duke Ding, fourth year, winter, eleventh month, pp. 5074b–75a. On the expression "pushing against the blade," see the sub-commentary by He Xiu: "It is not correct that a son should avenge his father [in such circumstances] and the son should be punished in turn. This coming-and-going is what is called 'pushing against the blade'." See also Duke Xiang, twenty-ninth year, eighth month, where Jizi forgives Helü of Wu the murder of his elder brother with the following argument: "You have killed my elder brother. If I were to kill you in turn, then fathers and sons, elder and younger brothers would have to kill one another in a never-ending process."

17 The different versions of Wu Zixu's story, as found in *Zuozhuan*, *Lüshi Chunqiu*, *Huainanzi*, *Shiji*, etc., have been studied by David Johnson in several articles; see "Epic and History in Early China: The Matter of Wu Tzu-hsü," *Journal of Asian Studies*, 40, no. 2, 1981, and "The *Wu Tzu-hsu Pien-wen* and Its Sources," Parts I and II, *Harvard Journal of Asiatic Studies*, 40, 1980, 93–157 and 465–507. In contrast with the official characterization of the act of vengeance given in the Gongyang version, in the *bianwen* version described by David Johnson, Wu Zixu vows he will catch King Ping of Chu alive, rip out his heart and tear it to pieces, before exterminating his clan down to the ninth degree.

18 Xu Shen, *Wujing yiyi*, *Wujing yiyi shuzheng* edition, in Ruan Yuan (ed.), *Huang Qing jingjie*, 1825–1829, *juan* 1248, p. 44a. On this passage, see H. van Ess, *Politik und Gelehrsamkeit in der Zeit der Han – Die Alttext/Neutextkontroverse*, Wiesbaden: Harrassowitz, 1993, pp. 264ff.

19 Such an argument is to be found again in the Song in the writings of Wang Anshi; see *Wang Wengong wenji* 32, Shanghai: Shanghai renmin chubanshe, 1974, pp. 383–4.

20 According to the biography of Ying Shao, the author of the *Fengsu tongyi*, in *Hou hanshu, juan* 48, Beijing: Zhonghua shuju, 1982, p. 1612, the *Gongyang Dong Zhongshu zhiyu* originally included 232 cases, only a few of which have been preserved in various collections and compendia. For a study of the few extant cases, see Cheng Shude, *Jiu chao lü kao*, Beijing: Zhonghua shuju, 1963, pp. 163ff; and G. Arbuckle, "Former Han Legal Philosophy and the *Gongyangzhuan*," *British Columbia Asian Review*, 1, 1987, 1–25. See also O. Oba, "Kandai no kesshi hi," in *Kansai daigaku bungakubu ronshu*, 1975, 271–87.

21 *Lunyu* 13.18: "The Governor of She said to Confucius, 'In our village there is a man nicknamed "Straight Body." When his father stole a sheep, he gave evidence against him'. Confucius answered. 'In our village those who are straight are quite different. Fathers cover up for their sons, and sons cover up for their fathers. Straightness is to be found in such behaviour'"; as translated in D. C. Lau, *Confucius: The Analects*, Harmondsworth: Penguin Books, 1979.

22 On the "Confucianizing of the law" or the "legification of Confucianism," which is to be observed mainly in the "new text" (*jinwen*) ideology of Former Han, see T. T. Ch'ü, *Law and Society in Traditional China*, Paris: Mouton, 1961, p. 278, and my article "Le statut des lettrés sous les Han," in C. Le Blanc and A. Rocher (eds), *Tradition et innovation en Chine et au Japon, Regards sur l'histoire intellectuelle*, Montréal: Presses de l'Université de Montréal, 1996, pp. 69–92.

23 Su Yu, *Chunqiu fanlu yizheng*, Chapter 5, *Xinbian zhuzi jicheng* edition, Beijing: Zhonghua shuju, 1992, p. 94.

24 On this point, see S. A. Queen, *From Chronicle to Canon: The Hermeneutics of the Spring and Autumn, According to Tung Chung-shu*, Cambridge: Cambridge University Press, 1996, especially Chapter 6.

25 *Chunqiu Gongyang zhuan*, Duke Yin, eleventh year, pp. 4795b–6a. The idea that a man who has not been avenged is to be considered as being deprived of a son or of subjects is similarly attributed to Dong Zhongshu; see Su Yu, *Chunqiu fanlu yizheng*, Chapter 1.

26 Chen Li, *Bohutong shuzheng*, *Xinbian zhuzi jicheng* edition, Beijing: Zhonghua shuju, 1994, *juan* 5, *Zhufa*, p. 219.

27 See, for instance, *Lunyu* 3.19.

28 In the same vein, Dong Zhongshu provides loyalty to the ruler with a cosmic justification, grounded on a far more cosmological than philological "etymology": the graph *zhong* 忠 (loyalty) is supposed to designate a total devotion to one single objective, while the graph *huan* 患 (calamity) would denote the duplicity of a mind pursuing two different objectives; see Su Yu, *Chunqiu fanlu yizheng*, Chapter 51, pp. 346–7.

29 A. F. P. Hulsewé refutes such an equivalence, noting that a condemned person is said to be "requited" (*bao* 報) and adding about this particular term: "It shows that the crime was 'requited' by the punishment, the one as it were neutralizing the other. It is not a matter of avenging the deed on the perpetrator; rather it is the one act (the crime) which is counterbalanced by the other (the punishment)"; see Hulsewé, *Remnants of Han Law*, Leiden: Brill, 1955, p. 80.

30 See T. T. Ch'ü, *Han Social Structure*, Seattle: University of Washington Press, 1972, pp. 294–5, n. 198.

31 See A. F. P. Hulsewé, *Remnants of Han Law*, p. 333.

32 See, for instance, Chapter 124 of the *Shiji*, which is devoted to the *youxia*.

33 See the references given by Mark Lewis in *Sanctioned Violence in Early China*, p. 90 and notes 137ff.

34 In her article "Confucian Piety and Individualism in Han China," *Journal of the American Oriental Society*, 116, 1996, 1–27, Michael Nylan notes that the Han state had "a marked inability to disentangle private obligation from public duty."

35 M. Nylan, "Confucian Piety," n. 173, refers to the anecdote told in Chapter 4 of Ying Shao's *Fengsu tongyi* concerning a Zhou Dang, a student who keeps invoking the *Chunqiu* prescription to "seek vengeance" as a mere excuse to antagonize all his neighbors. According to Nylan, this kind of story gives an idea of the deterioration of the social fabric by Later Han.

36 See T. Makino, *Chūgoku kazoku kenkyū*, pp. 450–1.

37 See the biography of Su Buwei in *Hou hanshu, juan* 31, pp. 1107–9. For further information, see R. De Crespigny, *Emperor Huan and Emperor Ling*, Canberra: Faculty of Asian Studies, Australian National University, 1989, vol. 2, pp. 127–8, and H. van Ess, "The Old Text/New Text Controversy: Has the 20th Century Got It Wrong?," *T'oung Pao*, 80, 1994, 161–2. On He Xiu, see my *Etude sur le confucianisme Han* cited above in n. 4.

38 Xun Yue, *Shen jian, Zhuzi jicheng* edition, Hong Kong: Zhonghua shuju, 1978 reprint, p. 11; translation borrowed from C. Y. Ch'en, *Hsün Yüeh and the Mind of Late Han China*, Princeton, NJ: Princeton University Press, 1980, pp. 136–7.

39 See, for instance, J. Bourgon, "Shen Jiaben et le droit chinois à la fin des Qing," unpublished doctoral thesis, Paris, EHESS, 1994.

40 This was a common adage by the late Qing, taken up by Shen Jiaben (1840–1913), "Chongke Minglü xu (Preface to the reprint of the Ming code)," *Shen Jiyi wencun*, Chapter 6, p. 3b, in *Shen Jiyi xiansheng yishu, Jiabian, ce* 24; quoted by Bourgon, "Shen Jiaben," pp. 489 and 504.

3 Reverent caring

The parent–son relationship in early medieval tales of filial offspring

Keith N. Knapp

Ziyou 子游 asked about filial piety [*xiao* 孝]. The master said, "Today's filial piety is called being able to provide sustenance [*yang* 養]. As for dogs and horses, both are provided sustenance [*you yang* 有養]. But, if one does not show respect [*jing* 敬], wherein lies the difference?

(*Analects* 2.7)

As the above passage indicates, Warring States *Ru* 儒 ("Confucians") emphasized that *xiao* did not merely consist of *yang*, i.e. nurturing parents with food or physical care. This should be automatic and in no way is virtuous behavior. For them what counted were acts that either pleased or honored parents. Yet many early medieval (100–600) accounts of filial piety concern *yang*. In fact, close to half of these narratives are about offspring who diligently fulfill their parents' material needs and desires. With the exception of mourning, motifs about nurturing far outnumber any other theme in the filial piety stories. But if Warring States *Ru* were at pains to disassociate *xiao* from *yang*, why was caring for parents such an important theme in the early medieval narratives? How could the meaning of *xiao* seemingly revert to one of its earliest meanings; that is, "presenting food"?[1]

To understand this change one must remember that, due to the fall of the Eastern Han (25–220) and the disunion of China, the early medieval period was one that witnessed the decline of central authority and the increasing political importance of local elite families whose strength resided in their ability to form extended households that could control large amounts of land, men, and access to public office.[2] The authors of the early medieval tales largely defined *xiao* as *yang* because it was precisely this concrete and archaic aspect of filial piety that most benefited the solidarity of extended families, by simultaneously expressing love, creating obligation, and signaling hierarchy. Since food is the premier life-giving substance, no act communicated regard better than its bestowal; no act expressed apathy more than its denial. By stressing *yang* as *xiao*, early medieval authors also underlined that service to one's family took priority over service to the state. At the same time, though, early medieval authors modified the concept of *yang* by heralding the relatively new concept of *gongyang* 供養 (reverent caring), which differs from *yang* in that it is an act of nurturing that reveals the parents' superior status and the child's inferior status. *Gongyang* combines the concepts of *yang* and *jing*, thereby enabling one to display respect for one's parents through the manner in which one meets their physical needs.[3]

To establish these points, this chapter first shows how authors of filial piety tales before the Eastern Han attached little importance to the motif of nurturing parents. By examining the four levels of self-deprivations that early medieval filial children are portrayed as enduring to respectfully care for their parents, it then shows the overriding importance that later authors attached to the concept of *gongyang*. The purpose of the *gongyang* motifs was to demonstrate that a strict, vertical hierarchy should exist within the home, and that sons should utterly subordinate their interests to those of the extended family.

This chapter also pays heed to the identity of the recipients of *gongyang*. In recent years, scholars have increasingly examined the *Ru* conceptualization of the parent–child relationship. Since texts such as the *Analects* (*Lunyu* 論語), the *Book of Rites* (*Liji* 禮記), and the *Classic of Filial Piety* (*Xiaojing* 孝經) almost exclusively talk about the relationship between father and son (*fuzi* 父子) and only mention mothers in the compound *fumu* 父母 "father and mother," Alan Cole contends that *Ru* filial piety only concerns a son's responsibilities to his father and male ancestors.[4] Shimomi Takao 下見 隆雄, on the other hand, believes that it was the mother–son relationship that was of primary importance in early Confucianism. Since the Chinese family system entrusted the mother with rearing, protecting, educating, and punishing children, sons felt dependent upon and fearful of her. Consequently, Chinese sons were all "Mama's boys," which insured that they would forever do the bidding of the patrilineal family, which the mother represented.[5] I argue that the authors of the early medieval filial piety accounts went to neither extreme and valued both mother–son and father–son ties.[6]

The creation of "reverent caring"

Toward the end of the Warring States period (481–221 BCE), the term *gongyang*, which denotes the special feeding of elders, begins to appear in the literary sources. The fundamental meaning of *gong* 供 is "to provide" or "to supply," but it also has the extended meanings of "to offer respectfully" and "to present sacrifices." In the past, *gong* was also interchangeable with the character *gong* 恭, "to respect" or "to be reverent." *Yang*'s most basic meaning is "to feed" or "to provide sustenance," from which comes its extended meanings of "to raise," "to nurture," and "to cultivate." Thus, *gongyang* means something like "reverent caring " or "providing sustenance in a respectful fashion." That is, one presents food or material support as if one was offering it to a superior.[7] Undoubtedly, because the term stressed the deferential manner in which the gift was given, translators adopted it to describe Buddhist offerings that nourished either the mind or the body.[8]

The reader should note that, even though I translate *gongyang* as "reverent caring" to emphasize the broad scope of the actions it includes, given the tales' emphasis on the giving of food, in many cases the term could just as easily be translated as "reverent feeding."

The implicit, hierarchical aspect of *gongyang* becomes evident in statements that contrast caring for a child with caring for a parent. When trying to decide whether to support his mother or infant child, the filial exemplar Guo Ju 郭巨 said: "If we care for [*yang*] our son, I will be unable to engage in my occupation, which will hinder my effort to reverently care for [*gongyang*] our mother. We should kill the child and bury him."[9] Note that Guo merely "*yang*"s his child, but he "*gongyang*"s his parents. Furthermore, his decision makes it apparent that *gongyang* supersedes *yang* and is devoted to one's superiors. But what does reverent care entail? How did one use nurturing to indicate higher status?

One of the most common means of performing *gongyang* was offering delicacies to parents during the morning and evening audiences (*dingxing* 定省), which were daily ceremonies in which sons and daughters-in-law would wait upon their parents (like servants) and serve them food, especially tasty morsels. The commentator Zheng Xuan 鄭玄 (127–200) says that, by presenting parents with delicacies, sons and daughters–in-law are expressing their love and respect (*aijing* 愛敬).[10] Serving delicacies honored parents because such foodstuffs were costly and difficult to obtain. Statements by contemporaries attest to the fact that reverent care required wealth; thus an elderly Wang Chong 王充 (27–97) complained that, due to his family's poverty, he did not receive *gongyang*.[11] Hence, reverent care usually consisted of children honoring their parents by providing them with prestigious foodstuffs. Having determined the ordinary requirements of *gongyang*, let us now look at how tales from before the Eastern Han and early medieval filial piety stories treated the theme of nurturing.

A scarcity of reverent care

Before the Eastern Han, the compound *gongyang* appeared infrequently in extant texts and stories with nurturing motifs were few in number. The earliest text that contains the compound *gongyang* with the meaning of reverent care is the late third-century BCE *Hanfeizi* 韓非子. After that, the term appears, albeit infrequently, in a limited number of Western Han texts.[12] Filial tales with nurturing motifs before the Eastern Han are also rare, and popular early medieval reverent care motifs seldom appear, if at all, before the Eastern Han.

Even the few exemplary acts of caring that do exist in early narratives are often not the story's main focus. In the two cases in the *Zuozhuan* 左傳 where a filial son saves food for his parent, that act itself is only a minor motif. For instance, when Zhao Dun 趙遁 inquired why a starving man, Ling Zhe 靈輒, put aside half of the food Zhao gave him, Ling replied that, having been away for three years, he wanted to return home and give it to his mother. If the tale stopped here, it would resemble an early medieval filial piety tale; but the *Zuozhuan* goes on to say that years later, when Zhao was ambushed, one of his attackers came to his aid and saved him: this was no other than Ling who was repaying Zhao for his past kindness.[13] In short, the tale is not about filial piety *per se*, but instead about goodness requited. Similarly, in the *Zuozhuan*, Ying Kaoshu 穎考叔 uses setting aside food for his mother as a reminder to Duke Zhuang of his unfilial behavior – what is important here is not the nurturing motif itself but Ying's subtle remonstrance.[14] One might argue that these anecdotes' nurturing motifs are not emphasized because they are embedded in the *Zuozhuan*'s larger narratives; however, when Zhao Dun's story reappears in the *Shuoyuan* 說苑 (first-century BCE) it is again a story about kindness requited; indeed, the starving man's filial act was so unimportant that he is not even identified.[15]

Another characteristic of nurturing stories before the Eastern Han is that the filial exemplar's actions are not so excessive that others cannot replicate them. To illustrate the filial piety of King Wen 文王 and King Wu 武王 of the Zhou, the *Book of Rites* states that the former would check upon his father thrice daily, and if his father was not feeling well, it would affect King Wen's mood and countenance. Thus, his behavior was noteworthy for two reasons. First, he went to check on his father not twice a day as required by the rites, but thrice a day. Second, not only did he diligently perform all of the necessary rites, but he was also genuinely affected when his father was not well. Nevertheless, unlike later reverent care accounts, he does not personally serve meals to his father, and his concern for his father's welfare far outweighs in importance the presentation of food. As for King Wu, when his father (King Wen) became ill, for twelve days he nursed (*yang*) him continuously and would only eat when he did.[16] King Wu obviously suffers terribly on his ill father's behalf. Yet his self-deprivations are not so extreme that it would be impossible for others to emulate them, i.e. his actions are not superhuman.[17] In short, both kings Wen and Wu are filial exemplars whose actions are exceptional, but not extraordinary.

A Western Han (206 BCE to 8 CE) caring theme that does have a number of stories devoted to it is that of a son who, to nurture his elderly parents, either takes a humble office or declines a high one. The message of the former motif is that even though the Way no longer prevails or the ruler is immoral, a poor filial son takes any office, no matter how low, to ensure that his parents are amply provisioned.[18] This illustrates the frequently mentioned principle that "One whose family is poor and parents old is not selective in choosing office."[19] The message of the latter motif is that a filial son refuses high office because it interferes with taking care of his parents on two counts: first, it means one must live far from home, thereby making it impossible for him to personally serve his parents;[20] second, it might force him to place his lord's interests before his parents'. Thus, after refusing a ministerial position, Zengzi stated: "My parents are old. If one receives a salary from another person, he will be anxious about the affairs of that person. I cannot endure distancing myself from my parents to serve another."[21] Put another way, to ensure one's parents are well cared for, a gentleman should be willing to sacrifice his ambitions. As Xu Fuguan 徐復觀 has pointed out, this meant that parents were even more important than personal integrity.[22]

One last motif related to office holding and nurturing parents takes the form of a moral dilemma: a filial son must decide whether to serve his lord or care for (*yang*) his parent. The exemplar, in the end, resolves the dilemma by committing suicide to atone for being either unfilial or disloyal. For example, while supporting (*yang*) his mother, Bian Zhuangzi 卞莊子 thrice retreated in battle and suffered insult as a consequence. After completing the mourning rites for his mother, during a battle, he brought back three enemy heads to atone for his previously retreating trice. He then sacrificed himself fighting for his lord.[23] Tales like this one show that a gentleman would rather die than be either disloyal or unfilial.[24] Significantly, none of these narratives prioritizes either filial piety or loyalty: both are equally important and more precious than one's own life.[25]

In stories before the Eastern Han, female exemplars are also placed in filial dilemmas, but unlike male exemplars, their problems have little to do with the state, and everything to do with the family.[26] The overwhelming majority concerns women who confront a danger that threatens their relatives. A wife typically has to choose between being loyal to either her father or husband, or between her brother and husband. She usually commits suicide to avoid disloyalty to either one.[27] In other cases, a mother has to choose between saving her own child or a relative's child. Almost invariably, she saves the child that is not her own, whether it is her brother's child, master's child, or stepchild.[28]

The female protagonists of these tales explain their actions through the Legalist dichotomy of *gong* 公 and *si* 私. When the commander of the enemy's army asked the Righteous Aunt of Lu (*Luyigu* 魯義姑) why she would abandon her own beloved child to save her elder brother's, she replied that saving her own son is an act of private love (*siai* 私愛), whereas saving her brother's son is a communal duty (*gongyi* 公義). If she puts her private love ahead of her communal duty, her countrymen will ostracize her.[29] According to the *Hanfeizi*, *si* means self-absorption, while opposing self-absorption is called *gong*.[30] In other words, *si* consists of realizing personal concerns, whereas *gong* consists of manifesting shared ones. This story thereby implies that, even within a family, one could have a conflict between *si* and *gong* interests. Hence, I translate *gong* as "communal" rather than the more usual translation of "public." Since a woman relies on her children first for status within her husband's family and later for material support, by sacrificing her own child, she endangers her own welfare. Thus, by discarding her own son in favor of her brother's, the Righteous Aunt of Lu slighted her own self-interests to realize her natal family's communal interests. This sacrifice earns her countrymen's approval because she exhibits the commonly shared value of subordinating one's personal interests to those of the group. This illustrates what Norman Kutcher has called the Confucian "parallel conception of society." That is, since a person's obligations to his or her parents and lord (and by extension the larger community) are similar, if the person is loyal to one, he or she will also be loyal to the other.[31]

Multiple layers of self-sacrifice in early medieval tales

In stark contrast to narratives before the Eastern Han, in which nurturing is but a minor concern, early medieval accounts show that, while one's parents are alive, no aspect of *xiao* is more important. Like their predecessors, early medieval stories indicate that *gongyang* consists of furnishing parents with delicacies; however, underscoring its importance, the authors emphasize the deprivations that filial children inflict upon themselves to secure these luxuries. In fact, the authors of these tales depict filial exemplars as subjecting themselves to four levels of increasingly severe self-deprivation.

At the simplest level, filial exemplars temporarily deny themselves food. This might take the form of a filial son either refusing to eat if a parent has not yet taken food, or forgoing a delicacy, which he then presents to his parent. Such acts are often credited to filial sons when they are but young children. For example,

> Zhao Xun 趙循 [or Zhao Gou 趙狗] had a filial nature. When he was five or six, whenever he obtained something that was sweet or delicious, he never dared to eat it himself. He would always first take it and feed it to his father. When his father went out, Zhao would wait until he returned and only then ate. If his father did not return in time for a meal, leaning against the gate, he would cry and await him.[32]

Zhao's actions differ significantly from those of the *Zuozhuan*'s Ling Zhe and Ying Kaoshu. First, the sole purpose of this story is to call attention to Zhao's exemplary filial piety; it is not merely a device to explain the unfolding of a larger narrative. Second, unlike the *Zuozhuan* stories, the account portrays his behavior not as a one-time act but as habitual conduct. Third, whereas the former involved adults, Zhao was merely a boy of six. This tale's central message is: if a boy could perform reverent care in such a manner, how much more should adults.

Forgoing luxuries, especially delectable foods, that one's parents could not have was a popular motif in the early medieval tales. If parents could not enjoy them, there was no reason why someone of less importance, such as their son, should. Thus, when asked to explain why he would bother to exchange the rice he received as his salary for wheat and millet (less prestigious and cheaper grains), He Ziping 何子平 (417–477) said, "My parents live in the east, hence they are not always able to obtain rice. How could I allow myself alone to enjoy polished rice?"[33] This urge to furnish parents with superior foodstuffs was so strong that some filial exemplars found miraculous ways of sending delicacies home.[34] Other filial children strenuously avoided luxuries that they were not able to provide their dead parents while they were still alive. For example,

> Zeng Shen 曾参 once ate fresh fish. It was extremely delicious; however, he spat it out. Someone asked him why. He answered: "While my mother was alive, she did not know what fresh fish tasted like. I have now tasted its exquisiteness and spat it out, and for the rest of my life I will not eat it."[35]

In other words, the pleasures one could enjoy later in life should be dictated by the pleasures that one was able to provide his parents: a son could not treat himself better than he treated his parents.

The second level of self-deprivation is that of a filial son who undergoes severe physical hardship to reverently care for his parents. Securing delicacies for one's parents was so important that this motif often emphasizes that the child can only do so through physical torment. One account tells us, "Even though winter was at its height and the cold was at its worst, Wang Yan's 王延 (258–318) body was not completely covered by clothing, but the food of his parents was always extremely delicious."[36] Similarly, Huang Xiang 黄香 (56–106) "in winter had neither a quilt nor pants, but his father had extremely tasty foods."[37] In other words, even though these filial sons could feed their parents ordinary food, to provide them with special treats they sacrificed their most basic needs, such as keeping themselves warm.

The most common motif that illustrates this level of deprivation is that of a filial son searching for a food that is difficult, if not impossible, to obtain, usually because it is out of season. In each case, though, the filial offspring acquires the desired object because his willingness to endure intense suffering causes heaven to intervene on his behalf. The most famous tale of this kind is that of Wang Xiang 王祥 (185–269), who, in the dead of winter, to get the carp that his stepmother so desperately wanted, endeavored to break the ice of a pond with his bare hands.[38] Many tales suggest that filial sons even risked their lives to obtain their parent's desired food. For example, due to his mother's fondness for the water from a river's main current, Wei Tong 隗通 (*fl.* 6–2 BCE) always rowed out into the treacherous waters to get it for her.[39] In short, these accounts stress that reverent care is so important that any sacrifice is justifiable. Surely the *Book of Rites'* compilers did not intend that a son endanger his life to supply his parents with delicacies for their morning or evening meal.

The reason for going to such extremes is that reverent care required that a filial son should obtain whatever his parent desired. The tale of Liu Yin 劉殷 (*fl.* 300–318) makes this evident.

[His] great-grandmother, Woman Wang, in the depth of winter desired violets [*jin* 菫], but she did not say anything. As a result, for ten days she did not eat her fill. Yin thought her mood was strange and asked her why. Woman Wang told him. At that time Yin was nine years old. He thereupon grieved and cried in the marshes [after searching there in vain for violets]. He said, "My sins are extremely grave. While young I have already received the punishment of my parents' death. Now Woman Wang is in the hall of my home, but this month she has lacked a week's nourishment [*wu xunyue zhi yang* 無旬月之養]. Yin is a son, but he cannot obtain that which his parent wants. Emperor of Heaven and Lord of the Earth, I hope that you will show me pity." The sound of his crying voice did not stop for half a day. Thereupon, he suddenly heard something like the voice of a person say, "Stop, stop crying." Yin desisted and looked at the ground. Violets were growing there. He took more than a bushel of them and returned home. Even after eating the plants, their number did not diminish. Only when violets came into season did they decrease.[40]

Liu is inconsolable because he feels that he has neglected his primary duty as a son – he has failed to *yang* his grandmother. Nevertheless, she has been given sustenance each day, just not the food she desires. Thus he has failed to reverently care for her. For the creator of this story, then, a son who cannot obtain the parent's desired food is not a true son.

A similar motif is that of a filial child who undergoes hardships to nurse his parent back to health or to secure the medicine that will do so. As previously mentioned, King Wu was lauded for taking care of his father for an astonishing twelve days without sleeping. Yet, for early medieval authors, a near fortnight was not nearly astonishing enough. Thus, they credit exemplary sons with nursing their parents for years on end without sleeping.[41] To further emphasize the extraordinary nature of their acts, Heaven often rewards their efforts by providing them with the medicinal food that cures the parent's illness.[42] Obtaining whatever medicine the parent needs is just a variation of obtaining whatever food one's parent wants. Both motifs end with the presentation of something that is ingested; that is, a form of food. Another important aspect of this motif is that the filial son's feats cannot be replicated in reality: the tales' authors vest him with superhuman powers of endurance and supply a sympathetic Heaven.

The third level of self-deprivation is that of exemplary sons who engage in socially demeaning acts to reverently care for their parents. Even though the protagonists of the early medieval tales were primarily men from locally prominent, upper class families, the tales often portray them, on their parents' behalf, performing menial or disgusting tasks, which were usually done by servants or slaves.[43] Filial sons, thus, do distasteful, even appalling, things to restore or ensure their parent's health, such as sucking pus out of wounds, tasting vomit, or sampling feces.[44] Their willingness to do so was admirable precisely because they enthusiastically performed these acts that were normally considered repulsive.[45]

In other stories, despite servants or slaves being available, filial sons insist on doing all the menial tasks necessary for their parents' care. That is because, since only the son knows how much his parents have sacrificed on his behalf, only he can serve them with the sincerity and devotion that they deserve. Although a Tang (618–907) tale, an account of the monk Shi Daoan 釋道安 (d. 600) explicitly makes a point that is implicit in early medieval tales.

> When Daoan first came to Zhongxing temple, he brought along his mother. Every morning he would visit her. With his own hands he would boil rice for her and only after doing so would he go to lecture. Even though he had more than enough servants, he would never allow anyone to help. Even when it came to drawing water and chopping wood, he had to use his own hands. He told someone: "My mother was able to give me birth and feed me; if I don't do this myself how can this be called reverent care."[46]

Since a mother displays love for her child by performing a myriad of menial tasks on his behalf, the child who received that tender nurturing must repay it in kind. That is, he too must perform all the tasks necessary for nurturing his mother, no matter how trivial. Due to this kind of thinking, Jiang Ge 江革 (*fl.* 25–84) would not even let his wife or children prepare his mother's meals.[47] This notion resonates with Confucius' belief that, if he did not personally perform the sacrifice, it was as if it was not performed at all (*Analects*, 3.12).

Some exemplars did not stop at serving their parents food but insisted on personally growing it. Yang Zhen's 楊震 (d. 124) filiality vividly conveys this ideal:

> When young Yang was fatherless and poor, he lived alone with his mother. He borrowed land to plant crops to provide his mother with reverent care. Once his students helped him plant some indigo seeds. When he saw the sprouts, he pulled them out and planted them a little further back. His canton and hamlet praised him as filial.[48]

Obviously, Yang did not have to play the part of a farmer. Yet he insisted upon it so that his mother would dine on food produced by her own son. One tale, doubtless apocryphal, even presents an emperor, Han Wendi 漢文帝 (reigned 179–157 BCE), tilling the soil for his mother.[49] Of course, if even the emperor can grow his own parents' food, how much more so should an ordinary gentleman. In early medieval narratives, then, the act of tilling the soil to support one's parents had little to do with one's economic situation, but much to do with contemporary notions of filial piety.

One of the most common early medieval motifs is that of a filial son who *gongyang*s his parents by either "hiring out his physical labor for a wage" (*yongren* 傭賃) or "selling himself" (*zimai* 自賣). For example, Guo Ju and his wife both hired out their labor (*yongren*) to provide his mother with reverent care; Shi Yan 施延 (*fl.* 126–145) hired himself out as a soldier at a courier station and used his monthly salary to reverently care for his mother; Su Cangshu 宿倉舒 sold himself to provide his starving parents with nine *hu* (roughly 180 liters) of barley; Jiang Shi 姜詩 (*fl.* 60 CE) and his wife both hired themselves out to support their mother, and so on.[50] Strikingly, despite the existence of wage laborers and bondservants since at least the Warring States period, this motif of working as a hired laborer to support one's parents does not exist in any surviving anecdotes that predate the Eastern Han.[51] Likewise, early medieval authors often portray filial sons as performing other lower-class occupations, i.e. those that did not require an education, to furnish parents with *gongyang*.[52] Exemplary sons became hired laborers or indentured servants not because they needed to feed their parents, but because they wanted to provide them with delicacies. An early third-century version of the tale of Dong Yong 董永 relates that "He had to borrow money to reverently care for his father; he hired out his labor to provide his father with sweet and fatty meats."[53] In short, filial sons did not take on these mean occupations because their parents were starving, but because they wanted to feed them in style.

This motif of becoming wage-laborers and debt-bondsmen to reverently care for parents is significant on two counts. First, it indicates that, on his parents' behalf, a son should willingly assume the status of one of the most despised members of society. As in Rome, due to their servitude and dependence upon others, hired laborers were nearly at the bottom of society.[54] Men of somewhat comparable status, such as menials or artisans, were viewed as so lowly that early medieval governments prohibited them from attending schools, becoming officials, or even marrying commoners.[55] If circumstances forced members of the upper class to perform such labor, it was thought to be embarrassing.[56] In fact, being a wage-laborer was perceived as so base that the word *yong* 傭 was often used as an insult.[57] Becoming a wage-laborer or bondsman signaled not only poverty but social abasement as well. To guarantee that their parents were cared for in an exalted manner, filial exemplars thus willingly degraded themselves. But why would they be portrayed as happy to do so?

From other early medieval sources, we know that the *Ru* vision of an ideal family was one in which the rites were used to illuminate the superiority of senior family members and the inferiority of junior ones. In fact, relations between father and son should resemble that between a lord and his retainer, as this account of Fan Hong 樊宏 (d. 51) indicates:

> His father Chong 重 was warm-hearted and generous, but he also had rules and regulations. The three generations of his family held its wealth

in common. During the morning and evening audiences, his sons and grandsons would pay their respect to him, as if they were in court.[58]

Since family members work and reside together and are intimate with one another, there is always the danger that lines of authority within the family will become blurred. By following the rites, the formality of the court, which highlights distinctions between ranks, replaces some of the intimacy of the home. Thus, even though Fan Hong's father was generous and warm-hearted, the existence of rules and regulations within the household produced hierarchy-affirming formality. Accounts with the same theme are numerous.[59]

The motif of a filial son who acts the part of either a servant or a hired laborer stresses that he elevates the status of his parents by degrading his own. For Confucians, humbling oneself is an essential means by which one honors others; hence, the *Book of Rites* states that one should always humble oneself before others.[60] Confirming that this lesson was not lost on early medieval men, Liu Shao 劉邵 (*fl.* 250) in his *Renwu zhi* 人物志 points out:

> Human feelings always desire to be superior. So a man likes humility in others. Humility is the willingness to be below [*xia* 下] others. Being below others means yielding and giving to others. Therefore no matter whether a man is wise or foolish, if you meet him with humility, he will have a pleased appearance.[61]

Although Liu was speaking in general terms, the benefits of humility doubt-lessly held true within the family as well. Exemplary sons who acted like servants or wage laborers humbled themselves by acting as if they were socially inferior to their parents. And what could express inferiority better than engaging in the tasks of the lower class?[62]

An exemplary son also endeavored to humble himself and exalt his par-ents through the kind of food he ate and offered them. In China, food has long been used as a status indicator because particular foods were associ-ated with certain social classes. During the early medieval period, meat, wine, and rice (except in the south where rice was common) were luxury foods that the rich usually enjoyed, while vegetables, millet, wheat, beans, and water were the daily fare of the poor.[63] Significantly, the food that a filial son offered to his parents was upper-class fare, whereas the food that he, his wife, and children ate was that of poor commoners.[64] Tales in which an upper-class man eats at the home of a poor exemplary son reveal how filial children could use food to affirm hierarchy.

> Mao Rong 茅容 [second century] was over forty and tilled the soil. Once, together with other men of his ilk, he avoided a rainstorm by sitting under a tree. The majority of men squatted, but Mao alone sat in a dignified manner. Guo Tai 郭泰 [128–169] observed this and thought it was extraordinary. He began conversing with Mao who thereupon invited Guo to spend the night at his home. Since the sun had already set,

he slaughtered a chicken for food. Guo thought that this was to be his meal. But before long Mao presented [*gong*] it to his mother. He provided himself and his guest with the same meal of vegetables. Guo stood up and bowed to him saying, "You are more worthy than I am."[65]

A similar story about the exemplar Yue Yi 樂頤 (late fifth century) of the Southern Qi, which is consciously modeled after that of Mao Rong, makes this point even more bluntly.[66] Both of these anecdotes show that, in the homes of the truly filial, the status of parents is so high that even high-ranking guests merit lesser treatment.

Tales that spoke of dire supernatural consequences for those who did not provide reverent care also underscore the importance of familial hierarchy. For example, after being sick for many years, Zhu Xu's 朱緒 (fifth century) mother suddenly desired to eat wild rice stew. Zhu tasted it first, liked it, and then gobbled it up. His mother angrily retorted, "If Heaven is conscious may you choke to death." When Zhu heard this, his heart became heavy and blood immediately began to run out of his body. By the next day he was dead.[67] Not only did Zhu fail to give his mother what she desired, he also denied her that which might have cured her. He thereby contravened not only *gongyang*, but also *yang*, i.e. doing the minimum necessary to keep one's parents alive. Although not numerous, such tales make it evident that the spirit world detests sons and daughters-in-law who violate the dictates of reverent care.[68]

The second important point about the motif of filial sons becoming hired laborers is that it reveals a remarkable shift. In filial piety tales from before the Eastern Han, when a son was in dire financial circumstances, he would compromise his integrity and take whatever governmental office he could obtain to reverently care for his parents. Early medieval exemplars, on the other hand, resort to doing manual labor for others or selling themselves. In short, for their parents' sake, filial sons were willing to suffer not only personal hardship, but also public humiliation in an era that put a premium on the distinctions that separated gentlemen (*shi* 士) from commoners (*shu* 庶).

The final and highest level of self-deprivation was sacrificing one's wife and/or children for the sake of one's parents. Tales that illustrate this theme usually take the form of a moral dilemma in which a filial son must choose between two unpalatable options. Yet the choices involved and the solutions resorted to in early medieval stories are far different from those found in tales featuring male protagonists that circulated before the Eastern Han. Rather than having to choose between one's father or lord, in early medieval stories a son must choose between saving either his parent or child, or his brother's child or his own. Strikingly, these dilemmas more closely resemble those of women in tales from before the Eastern Han, insofar as they concern choices about the family rather than choosing between the family or state. The best known early medieval filial dilemma is that of Guo Ju, who when faced with choosing to provide for his elderly mother or his young son, decides to bury his son alive so that he can continue to reverently care for his mother.[69] Since he must be alive to do so, he forgoes suicide and, like the female exemplars of earlier stories, endeavors to kill his son. Even the rationale Guo gives for burying his son alive – "We can have another son, but we will never have another mother" – resembles that which led a concubine in the *Zuozhuan* to tell her father of her husband's plot to kill him.[70] In other tales, again like female exemplars, early medieval filial sons end up attempting to kill their own children to save those of their siblings.[71] In short, early medieval authors were putting male protagonists in story lines that in the past were solely associated with women.

The ideology that underlies early medieval filial dilemmas is also that of fulfilling "communal interests" at the expense of "private interests." By sacrificing his own wife and children, an exemplary son is abandoning that which is often most dear to him, i.e. his own conjugal family. Underlining their emotional importance to the son, classical *Ru* works often say, "filial piety decreases with the appearance of a wife and children."[72] In fact, early medieval men viewed one's wife and children as an extension of one's self.[73] By sacrificing them, a man thereby surrenders that which he shares with no one for his parents whom he shares with his brothers. That is, he casts aside his private interests for the agnatic family's communal interests. Moreover, he sacrifices his future well-being to repay his parent's past kindness. An inscription accompanying an illustration of the Guo Ju story on a fifth-century coffin affirms that this is indeed what contemporaries perceived him as doing. It reads, "One who cannot cast aside their selfish interests [*si*] cannot be given this [pot of gold]."[74] In other words, the inscription's creator interpreted Guo's sacrifice as done to realize communal interests. The prominence that this story had in early medieval art underscores how compelling this message was for its early medieval audience.[75]

The supremacy of society over state

The feminization of early medieval filial dilemmas suggests that the question of which comes first, the family or the state, was no longer that important. Unlike their male predecessors, early medieval filial sons who are caught in moral dilemmas display no concern for the state at all. Instead, like the female exemplars, their concerns are related to the family. Almost none of the early medieval accounts shows a filial son struggling to fulfill the requirements of both filial piety and loyalty.[76] This lack of concern for the government is best exemplified in the tale of Zhang Ti 張悌 (sixth century), who became a bandit to provide his mother with reverent care.[77] Oftentimes, the state is only present in the tales insofar as it rewards the filial child's conduct; that is, its significance only lies in its sanctioning of familial virtues. Loyalty's absence in these accounts seems to confirm Tang Changru's 唐長孺 argument that, during this period, it was far less esteemed than filial piety.[78]

The early medieval stories lack concern for the state because they reflect the interests of the local elite. Lu Yaodong 逯耀東 has noted that early medieval historians paid little attention to court politics and instead mostly wrote about affairs that concerned local elite families, of which they were members.[79] But what were the interests of such families? As the power and reach of the central government declined in the Eastern Han and local elite families took on more governmental functions and social importance than ever before, maintaining order and generating solidarity within these large, extended families became an urgent problem for patriarchs. One way of instilling order within a large family was to impose a rigid hierarchy within it, based on the *Ru* vision of an ideal household; that is, one in which parents came before children, brothers came before wives, and sons gladly did their seniors' bidding. Hence, early medieval filial dilemmas advocate sublimating one's self-interests to keep the extended family together. It is precisely this concern for maintaining family unity that led the creators of these stories to put their male protagonists into what used to be female dilemmas. Thus, just as women in the past were urged to discard their children – that is, their personal interests – for those of the extended family, men were now being urged to do the same.

During this era, the most important trait that an official could have was to be unselfish. In fact, an official's loyalty was merely a function of his selflessness, as Ren Yan 任延 (d. 69) makes clear: "I've heard it said that a loyal retainer has no self-interests [*busi* 不私] and that a retainer with private interests is not loyal. Enacting the upright and upholding communal interests [*gong*] is the moral code of retainers."[80] The filial dilemma stories promote this same idea. A truly filial son is one who cleaves to his family's communal interests at the expense of his own private ones. That is to say, within the family he is totally selfless and is concerned only with the extended family's welfare. Early medieval authors assume that, before holding office, if a man strives to fulfill his extended family's *gong* interests, he will surely continue to be selfless when in office. A filial son's incorruptibility in office is thus an extension of his selflessness at home. This assumption probably explains why famous exemplary sons were showered with offers of public office and the common early medieval saying: "Loyal retainers must be sought in the families of filial sons" (求忠臣必於孝子之門). Since both families and the community at large prized selflessness, this type of conduct provided sons with a means of gaining fame.[81]

Requiting the care-debt

A lingering question is: why does a filial son have to sacrifice so much to reverently care for his parents? The answer is that he must repay the immense debt he owes them for feeding and raising him when he was a child. Hence, when his parents become infirm and helpless with age, he must carry out his end of the reciprocal bargain.[82] Due to the Chinese Buddhist emphasis on the mother–son relationship, Alan Cole has felicitously called this obligation a "milk-debt." That is, a son must forever repay with filial piety the toil, blood, and pain that his mother has expended in raising him.[83] Since *Ru* writings emphasize that one has to repay both parents for their roles in raising oneself, I will call this obligation the "care-debt." In early China, besides expressing love or care, the presentation of food, or by extension material support, creates obligation. If one feeds a man, he is obligated to repay your kindness.[84] This sense of obligation was so strong that it could be used as a means to control others.[85] In the same way, a child is obligated to repay his parents for the food and care they provided him as a helpless child. The following poem from the *Shijing* 詩經 (*Classic of Poetry*) emphasizes the debt that a child owes both his parents.

> Without a father, on whom can one rely? Without a mother, on whom can one depend? Abroad one harbors grief, at home one has nobody to go to. Oh father, you begat me, oh mother, you fed me [*ju* 鞠], [both of] you comforted and reared [*xu* 畜] me, you looked after me, constantly attended to me, abroad and at home you carried me in your bosom; I wish to requite your goodness, but Heaven goes to excess![86]

Note that a number of the words used in this poem, such as *ju* and *xu*, are synonyms of *yang*. Thus, it explicitly relates that the author wants to repay his parents for the *yang* that he received as a child, by caring for them in their old age. That *yang* is the basis of the parent–child relationship can also be seen in the *Ru* rationale for mourning parents for three years. One owes them three years of suffering, deprivations, and unremitting attention because for the first three years of a child's life his parents breast-fed and intensively cared for him.[87] It is probably not a coincidence that in medieval China a child was usually thought to suckle for three years.[88]

Requiting the care-debt is precisely the rationale that underlies the early medieval tales' emphasis on reverent care. This message comes across most clearly in lore about filial crows.

> Crows are compassionate birds. They are born in the deep woods. From outside of their high nests, holding food in their beaks, the parents place it into their chicks' mouths. Without waiting for the chicks to cry, the parents on their own accord present them with food. When the parents' wings fatigue and they can no longer fly, their children's wings are already fully developed. Flying to and fro, the children bring food and return regurgitation [*fanbu* 反哺] for their mother. Since birds are like this, how much more should humans! Crows bring food in their beaks to feed their young, and children bring food in their beaks to feed their mother. These birds are all *xiao*.[89]

Crows are filial because they present food to their elderly parents, just as their parents fed them when they were young; that is, they "feed in return" (*fanbu*).[90] This association of filiality with crows was so well known that the first-century work *Shuowen jiezi* 說文解字 simply defines crows as "filial birds."[91] In fact, by the Eastern Han, crows and the idea of *fanbu* became emblems of filial piety.[92]

The tale that best embodies this principle of "feeding in return" is that of the Xing Qu 邢渠, whose behavior literally approximated that of the crow. Xing's father was old and could not chew food because he had no teeth; thus, Xing always masticated (*bu*) food for him. After he did this for a while, his father became healthy and miraculously grew a new set of choppers.[93] In other words, Xing regurgitated food for his father, as a crow would for its mother. The key word in this passage is *bu* 哺, whose basic meaning is "to masticate" or "regurgitate," and whose extended meaning is "to feed."[94] In pre-modern China, parents often masticated solid food for children.[95] A filial piety story suggests this was a common practice well beyond infancy.[96] Hence, just as his father supplied him with food and perhaps even chewed it for him when he was a helpless infant, Xing was now doing the same. Put another way, now that his father resembled a helpless infant in that he was toothless, Xing was "feeding in return" (*fanbu*), which means he was reversing roles and parenting his parent. Underscoring the importance of this concept, the image of Xing Qu feeding his father was the most commonly illustrated filial piety story in the Eastern Han – at the Wu Liang shrine, there are more depictions of this filial piety tale than of any other.[97] Obviously, the idea of *fanbu* that was embodied in the image of a son parenting his parent touched the hearts of contemporaries, and thereby became a popular motif in funerary art.

One of the most popular tales, the filial grandson Yuan Gu 原谷, suggests what might happen to those who refuse to reverse roles. One day, Yuan Gu's father and mother decided that his grandfather was too old to be useful, so they decided to get rid of him. Yuan followed his father, who used a litter to carry the grandfather to the mountains. After his father abandoned the old man, Yuan grabbed the litter and brought it home. When his father asked him why, he replied, "Perhaps later you too will become old and will not be able to work again. Merely in order to do the right thing, I have retrieved it." Terrified and ashamed, his father realized the error of his ways, retrieved the old man, and served him in a filial manner.[98] Whereas the story of the filial bird praised crows because they willingly reverse roles, the tale of Yuan Gu makes the same point, but from the angle of self-interest. Yuan's virtuous act consists of saving his grandfather by reminding his father of the reciprocity that underlies *yang*. That is to say, one parents elderly, infantile parents not only because of the care-debt one owes them, but also because, in doing so, one hopes that in turn one's children will parent oneself. The frequency with which this story appears in early medieval art belies the importance of the role reversal motif. In the early medieval period, with the exception of Ding Lan 丁蘭, no filial tale was as commonly portrayed as the Yuan Gu story, and its image appears in places as far apart as Sichuan and North Korea.[99]

Mothers and fathers

Alan Cole has skillfully shown that indigenous Chinese Buddhist sutras, while hardly ever mentioning the care-giving role of the father, put increasing stress on the unlimited debt that a son owes his mother, due to her endless travails in raising him and the vast amount of milk he took from her through breast-feeding.[100] From the filial piety stories on role reversal, however, we can see that *Ru* believed that the care-debt was owed to both parents. The role-reversal stories do not single out requiting the debt owed to one's mother, as the examples of Xing Qu and Yuan Gu have already demonstrated. Moreover, although the care-debt one owed one's parents was great, it was not unlimited and could be repaid by providing parents with the same care and love they gave one as a child.

The importance of fathers also becomes apparent upon looking at the modification of the Shun legend, which early medieval authors refitted with motifs that stressed *xiao* as reverent care. In the earliest versions of the story, Shun's stay at Mount Li was merely a method by which the sage emperor Yao tested his worthiness to rule; Shun's filiality thereby consisted of his continued love for his parents, despite their many attempts on his life.[101] However, early medieval versions stress how Shun endeavored to materially support his estranged and physically distant parents.[102] It is precisely Shun's effort to nurture him that stirs his father's heart. According to one version of the tale, Shun's father dreamt that a phoenix carried rice in its mouth to feed him, and he then realized it must be his son. Later, upon finding coins among the rice his wife had brought back from the market, he knew that Shun must have put them there; thereupon he repented his sins.[103] By having a bird bring food to him, this version underscores that Shun is performing "feeding in return." It is precisely this act of *fanbu* that makes his father appreciate how much his son loves him and how reprehensible his own behavior has been.

Note too that this story squarely focuses on the father–son relationship. It is only due to his stepmother's lies that Shun's father turns against him. It is Shun's father who realizes that his son must be his benefactor, who searches for him, and who joyfully embraces him in the market. Shun miraculously cures his father's ailment. Shun's stepmother, on the other hand, cannot connect with her stepson. Despite his love for her, she consistently attempts to kill him. Even after repeated demonstrations of his benevolence, she fails to recognize that Shun is providing for her. In short, this is a tale that celebrates the father–son relationship, which should normally be an emotionally rewarding one, if it were not for the machinations of evil women.

Underscoring the significance of this modified version of the Shun tale is the fact of its great prominence in the Northern and Southern dynasties. Out of the twelve artifacts from this period adorned with scenes of filial piety tales, it appears on six. Even more impressively, on the Guyuan lacquered coffin which has multi-scene depictions of six filial piety stories, the

Shun tale merited eight scenes, far more than any other. Thus, if the mother–son relationship was truly predominant in early medieval China, someone forgot to tell the artisans who created this coffin and other artifacts that feature filial tales about fathers and sons.

Yet, despite the importance of the Shun story, even a casual glance at tales with reverent care motifs reveals that many concern the mother–child bond. More likely than not, an exemplary son's actions would be devoted to his mother. When looked at statistically, out of eighty-two tales with reverent care motifs, fifty-two of the recipients were mothers, or 63 per cent. Fathers or fatherly figures, on the other hand, were recipients in twenty-one of the tales, or 25 per cent of the total. Tales in which both parents received reverent care account for about 12 per cent.[104] Obviously, for these accounts' compilers the mother–child bond was of tremendous importance. Since affection is often expressed in Chinese culture through the presentation of a favorite food, perhaps even more telling is the fact that tales with the motif of a filial son who desperately seeks after his parent's favorite food entirely feature mothers as the recipients of reverent care.[105] A filial son seemingly caters only to his mother's whims, not his father's.

Nevertheless, fathers are not entirely neglected. By combining anecdotes in which fathers are the recipients of reverent care with those in which both parents are, we discover that fathers receive *gongyang* in 37 per cent of the tales. The numbers become even more impressive when we look at images of the stories, particularly from the Eastern Han. Due to the popularity of stories of Dong Yong and Xing Qu, 50 per cent (twenty-three out of forty-six) of the represented reverent care stories from this era feature fathers.[106] Pictorial representations from the Northern and Southern Dynasties have fathers as the recipients in 33 per cent of the images and mothers in 38 per cent. The difference between the written accounts of filial children and the pictorial representations is that the percentage of stories showing reverent care given to both parents is much greater in the latter: 29 per cent of the images have both parents as recipients. Taken together, this means that fathers receive reverent care, whether alone or together with their wives, in 62 per cent of the images. Obviously, both artisans and their patrons valued providing reverent care for both parents.

Why then are mothers rather than fathers more often the recipients of reverent care in the written accounts? The predominance of mothers could be due to demographic factors. Mothers might have been the main recipients because husbands were much older than their wives and tended to die well before them. Based on her examination of epitaphs from the Six Dynasties period, Jen-der Lee has noted that, although some upper-class women married younger men, on average their spouses were seven years their senior. Moreover, they spent an average of 18.6 years in widowhood.[107] Although Lee's sample is far too small to be conclusive, it does suggest that numerous upper-class males would grow up in households in which their father had died early and that were headed by their mother. Thus, mothers loom so large in the filial piety accounts perhaps because they tended to outlive their older husbands.

Conclusion

Early medieval filial piety stories with reverent care motifs are important for four reasons. First, they elevate the humble concept of *yang* to an exalted form of nurturing, *gongyang*, which calls attention to a parent's superior status within the household. Early medieval authors emphasized *gongyang*'s importance by showing filial sons who gladly endured various types of deprivations to furnish their parents with luxurious food and clothing.

Second, the authors emphasized reverent care because it conveyed a message that heads of local elite families wanted to communicate to their descendents: that adult sons should subordinate their own wishes to those of their parents. Moreover, no matter what their actual social status was, within the family they should recognize their inferior status, and strive to further the family's collective interests rather than their own personal ones. The incentive for sons was that if they were able to do this, not only would harmony prevail within the extended family, they would also attract the interest of the outside community by showing themselves to be selfless men.

Third, reverent care motifs indicate that the narratives' compilers were more interested in service to the family than that to the state. Exemplary sons in the tales neither worry about fulfilling the demands of loyalty nor see government service as a means to provide reverent care. Instead, they worry about the solidarity of their families and find ways within local society to honor their parents. Hence, in many ways, these tales reflect the weakness of government during the early medieval period and the importance of extended families.

Fourth, the authors of the early medieval stories privileged neither the relationship between mother and son nor that between father and son. Both were important. Obviously, the former was viewed as the more intimate one; nevertheless, illustrations of these tales make it evident that their audience also attached much importance to the father–son tie.

Notes

1 See K. Knapp, "The *Ru* Reinterpretation of *Xiao*," *Early China*, 20, 1995, 199–222, pp. 197–204.
2 For studies that document this transformation, see D. Grafflin, "Social Order in the Early Southern Dynasties," PhD dissertation, Harvard University, 1980, Chapter 1; R. de Crespigny, "The Three Kingdoms and Western Jin: A History of China in the Third Century," *East Asian History*, 1, 1991, 1–36, and *East Asian History*, 2, 1991, 143–65; and C. Holcombe, *In the Shadow of the Han*, Honolulu: University of Hawaii Press, 1994, Chapter 2.
3 Concerning the hierarchical implications of the word *jing*, see K. Knapp, "The *Ru* Reinterpretation of *Xiao*," p. 206, n. 40.

4 A. Cole, *Mothers and Sons in Chinese Buddhism*, Stanford, CA: Stanford University Press, 1998, pp. 14–31.

5 T. Shimomi 下見隆雄, *Kō to bosei no mekanizumu*, Tokyo: Kenbun shuppan, 1997, pp. 95–129, 169–84, and his *Jukyō shakai to bosei*, Tokyo: Kenbun shuppan, 1994, pp. 253–71.

6 Although daughters and daughters-in-law were also required to provide reverent care, they usually had to do even more to be viewed as filial; consequently, this chapter only examines the relationship between parents and sons. With regard to the special filial piety required of women, see the chapters in this volume written by Sor-hoon Tan and Yuet Keung Lo.

7 Gu Yewang's 顧野王 (519–594) *Yu pian* 玉篇 provides one gloss of *yang* as "to prepare delicacies to respectfully feed [*gongyang*] superiors [*zunzhe* 尊者]." See *Yuanben Yupian canjuan* 元本玉篇殘卷, Beijing: Zhonghua shuju, 1985, pp. 84 and 286.

8 For a Buddhist definition of *gongyang*, see W. E. Soothill and L. Hodous, *A Dictionary of Chinese Buddhist Terms*, London: Kegan Paul, Trench, Turbiner & Co., 1934, p. 249.

9 Li Fang 李昉 (925–996) *et al.*, *Taiping yulan* 太平御覽, Taipei: Taiwan Commercial Press, 1986, *juan* 811, p. 8b. The *Hanfeizi* 韓非子 also clearly makes this distinction: "If as an infant, his parents feed [*yang*] him meagerly, he will grow up bearing a grudge against them. When the son fully matures and becomes an adult, his reverent care [*gongyang*] of his parents will be skimpy. His parents will be angry and scold him." See Wang Xiansheng 王先慎, *Hanfeizi jijie* 韓非子集解, *Zhuzi jicheng* edition, Shanghai: Shanghai shudian, 1985, *juan* 11, p. 204.

10 Ruan Yuan 阮元, *Liji zhushu* 禮記注疏, *Shisanjing zhushu* edition, Taipei: Yiwen yinshuguan, 1983, *juan* 27, p. 5b.

11 D. C. Lau *et al.* (comp.), *Lunheng zhuzi suoyin* 論衡逐字索引, Hong Kong: Commercial Press, 1996, 85.372. See also *Hanfeizi jijie*, *juan* 49, p. 339.

12 The *Hanfeizi* employs this compound three times. Among Western Han texts, it appears in the *Liji* once, the *Xinxu* 新序 once, *Zhanguo ce* 戰國策 once, *Huainanzi* 淮南子 twice, *Shiji* 史記 trice, and the *Lienü zhuan* 列女傳 once.

13 D. C. Lau *et al.*, *Zuozhuan zhuzi suoyin* 左傳逐字索引, Hong Kong: Commercial Press, 1995, B7.2.3 (Duke Xuan, 2).

14 After vowing to not see his mother again until reaching the afterworld, Duke Zhuang asked Ying Kaoshu why he did not eat the meat broth that the duke had just bestowed upon him. Ying replied that he wanted to take it to his mother with whom he shared all his food. This made Duke Zhuang realize his mistake in vowing not to see his mother until they met in the afterlife. The narrator of the story thus praises Ying Kaoshu for transforming Duke Zhuang's behavior. See D. C. Lau *et al.*, *Zuozhuan*, B1.1.4 (Duke Yin, 1).

15 D. C. Lau *et al.*, *Shuoyuan zhuzi suoyin* 說苑逐字索引, Hong Kong: Commercial Press, 1992, 6.18.

16 D. C. Lau *et al.*, *Liji zhuzi suoyin* 禮記逐字索引, Hong Kong: Commercial Press, 1992, 8.1; J. Legge (trans.) *Li Chi*, 2 vols, New Hyde Park: University Books, 1967, vol. 1, pp. 343–4.

17 One Western Han exception to this would be Yuan Ang's 袁盎 account of Emperor Wen's 漢文帝 (reigned 179–157) filiality. There, Yuan asserts that when Emperor Wen's mother was sick for three years, his eyelids never closed, he never changed clothes, and would always first taste his mother's medicine. Thus, his filiality surpassed that of even Zengzi. See K. Takigawa 瀧川龜太郎, *Shiki kaichū kōshō* 史記會注考證, Taipei: Hongshi chubanshe, 1986 reprint, *juan* 101, p. 2738; and Ban Gu 班固 (32–92), *Hanshu* 漢書, Taipei: Hongye shuju, 1978 reprint, *juan* 49, p. 2269. Unless otherwise stated, all references to the dynastic histories are from the *Zhonghua shuju* edition.

18 This of course ran counter to early *Ru* attitudes toward office holding, according to which one should not hold office unless the Way prevailed or one could serve a worthy ruler. See R. Eno, *The Confucian Creation of Heaven*, Albany: State University of New York Press, 1990, pp. 43–52. This change indicates the overwhelming importance of *xiao* in the Han.

19 This phrase appears in many Han *Ru* works. See D. C. Lau *et al.*, *Hanshi waizhuan zhuzi suoyin* 韓詩外傳逐字索引, Hong Kong: Commercial Press, 1992, 1.1, 1.17, 7.7; *Shuoyuan*, 3.5; D. C. Lau *et al.*, *Xinxu Zhuzi Suoyin* 新序逐字索引, Hong Kong: Commercial Press, 1992, 5.30; D. C. Lau *et al.*, *Lienü zhuan zhuzi suoyin* 列女傳逐字索引, Hong Kong: Commercial Press, 1994, 2.6; Fan Ye 範曄 (398–445), *Hou hanshu* 後漢書, Taipei: Hongye shuju, 1977 reprint, *juan* 39, p. 1294, *juan* 81, p. 2678; and *Kongzi jiayu* 孔子家語, Taipei: Shijie shuju, 1983, *juan* 2, p. 17.

20 An example of this is Zilu 子路 who said he would gladly exchange his present exalted position and its lavish benefits for when he ate plain food and carried heavy burdens on behalf of his parents. In other words, the rewards of high office are not comparable to the satisfaction obtained in nurturing one's living parents. See *Shuoyuan* 3.5 and *Kongzi jiayu*, *juan* 2, p. 17.

21 *Kongzi jiayu*, *juan* 9, p. 88.

22 Xu Fuguan 徐復觀, *Lianghan sixiangshi* 兩漢思想史, Taipei: Xuesheng shuju, 1979, vol. 3, pp. 39–42.

23 See *Xinxu*, 8.14, *Hanshi waizhuan*, 10.13, and *Hanfeizi jijie*, *juan* 19, p. 345. For other stories with this motif, see that of Zhuang Zhishan 莊之善 (*Hanshi waizhuan*, 1.21, *Xinxu*, 8.9) and Shen Ming 申鳴 (*Hanshi waizhuan*, 10.24, *Shuoyuan*, 4.14).

24 As Kristina Lindell notes, this type of story illustrates the *Ru* tenet that a sage would rather choose death than act immorally. See her "Stories of Suicide in Ancient China," *Acta Orientalia*, 35, 1973, p. 180.

25 The tale of Shen Sheng 申生 is an exception to this pattern of virtuous suicide. Contriving to establish her own son as crown prince, Shen's stepmother, the Lady Liji 驪姬, convinced his father that Shen tried to poison him. When someone told Shen that he should either flee to another kingdom or explain the situation to his father, he refused to do either. His rationale was, "Without Lady Ji, my father cannot rest in comfort, cannot eat his food with satisfaction. If I try to excuse myself, the blame will fall on Lady Li. My father is an old man – I could never be happy with such a course of action." See *Zuozhuan*, B5.4.6 (Duke Xi, 4); the translation is from B. Watson, *The Tso Chuan*, New York: Columbia University Press, 1989, pp. 23–4. In sum, Shen sacrificed himself not to save his father's life, but merely to save him from embarrassment and to insure his comfort. In a way, by trying to make sure his father was happy and comfortable, he died in an effort to reverently nurture his father. This is perhaps why this tale was one of the few Warring States narratives that early medieval authors incorporated into their collections of filial piety stories.

26 For an exception, see *Lienü zhuan*, 5.3.

27 Ibid., 5.7, 5.14, and 5.15.

28 Ibid., 5.6, 5.8, and 5.12.

29 Ibid., 5.6.

30 *Hanfeizi jijie*, *juan* 49, p. 345.

31 See A. Kutcher, *Mourning in Late Imperial China: Filial Piety and the State*, Cambridge: Cambridge University Press, 1999, pp. 2–3.

32 See *Taiping yulan*, *juan* 414, p. 2a and Xu Jian 徐堅 (659–729), *Chuxue ji* 初學記, 3 vols, Beijing: Zhonghua shuju, 1962, *juan* 17, p. 421. A similar tale is told of Yin Yun 殷惲 when he was seven years old. See *Chuxue ji*, *juan* 17, p. 421, and *Taiping yulan*, *juan* 414, p. 1b.

33 Shen Yue 沈約 (441–513), *Songshu* 宋書, Taipei: Dingwen shuju, 1980 reprint, *juan* 91, pp. 2257–8; *Taiping yulan, juan* 413, p. 8a; and Ouyang Xun 歐陽詢 (557–641), *Yiwen leiju* 藝文類聚, 2 vols, Shanghai: Shanghai guji chubanshe, 1999, *juan* 20, p. 371.

34 While fulfilling corvée labor obligations in one prefecture, Du Xiao 杜孝 filled a bamboo tube with fish and sent it down the river to his wife in another prefecture, so that she could present the fish to his mother (*Chuxue ji, juan* 17, p. 422, *Taiping yulan, juan* 411, p. 5b, and *Yiwen leiju, juan* 96, p. 1673).

35 *Taiping yulan, juan* 862, p. 2b. For a similar anecdote see *Taiping yulan*, 413.7b–8a, and *Songshu, juan* 93, p. 2295.

36 *Taiping yulan, juan* 412, p. 5b, and *Jinshu* 晉書, Taipei: Dingwen shuju, 1980, *juan* 88, p. 2290.

37 *Taiping yulan, juan* 412, pp. 4a–b; *Chuxue ji, juan* 17, p. 420; and Yang Yong 楊勇, *Tao Yuanming ji jiaojian* 陶淵明集校箋, Taipei: Zhengwen shuju, 1987, *juan* 8, p. 320.

38 Unlike its later versions, none of this tale's early ones have Wang Xiang laying or sleeping on the ice. In each case, he is trying to physically break the ice open. See *Taiping yulan, juan* 26, p. 9b, *Chuxue ji, juan* 3, p. 60, Yang Yong, *Shishuo xinyu jiaojian* 世說新語校箋, Taipei: Taiwan jidai shuju, 1975, *juan* 1, p. 14, *Yiwen leiju, juan* 9, pp. 179–80, and Fang Xuanling 房玄齡 (576–648) *et al.*, *Jinshu* 晉書, *juan* 33, p. 989. According to yet another version, while waiting on the shore to spot carp, day after day Wang braved a severe winter wind. See Yu Shinan 虞世南 (558–638), *Beitang shuchao* 北堂書鈔, Tianjin: Tianjin guji chubanshe, 1988, *juan* 158, pp. 4a–b.

39 *Taiping yulan, juan* 389, p. 5b and *juan* 411, p. 6a. The *Huayang guozhi* 華陽國 志 and *Shuijing zhu* 水經注 say that his name is Wei Xiang 隗相 and his style is Shutong 叔通. See Liu Lin 劉林, *Huayang guozhi jiaozhu* 華陽國志校注, Chengdu: Bashu shushe, 1984, *juan* 10b, p. 780, and Zheng Dekun 鄭德坤, *Shuijing zhu gushi* 水經注故事, Taipei: Yiwen yinshuguan, 1974, p. 178.

40 *Jinshu, juan* 88, p. 2288.

41 See the accounts of Han Wendi (*Yiwen leiju, juan* 20, p. 370), Fan Liao 樊僚 (*Taiping yulan, juan* 412, p. 4b), Cai Yong 蔡邕 (*Taiping yulan, juan* 414, p. 2b), Bao Ang 鮑昂 (*Taiping yulan, juan* 414, p. 2b), and Li Mi 李密 (*Jinshu, juan* 88, p. 2274).

42 See the accounts of Xiahou Xin 夏侯訢 (*Taiping yulan, juan* 411, p. 7a), Miao Fei 繆斐 (*Taiping yulan*, 411.7b), Liu Lingzhe 劉靈哲 (*Taiping yulan, juan* 411, p. 3b), and Xiao Ruiming 蕭叡明 (ibid.).

43 For some of the tasks that early medieval servants and slaves performed, see C. M. Wilbur, *Slavery in China during the Former Han Dynasty*, New York: Klaus Reprint Co., 1968, pp. 178–84, pp. 382–92, and Wang Yi-t'ung, "Slaves and Other Comparable Social Groups during the Northern Dynasties (386–618)," *Harvard Journal of Asiatic Studies*, 16, 1953, 293–364, especially pp. 331–44.

44 The earliest filial piety story with this motif only appears in the Western Han. According to the *Shiji*, despite his own advanced age, Shi Jian 石建, a high official, returned home every five days from his post to wash his father's undergarments and chamber pot. See *Shiji, juan* 103, pp. 5–6, and *Hanshu, juan* 46, p. 2195.

45 These acts illustrate the Confucian principle that "in serving one's parents what is difficult is controlling one's countenance" (*Analects* 2.8). On the repulsiveness of sucking pus from sores and the difficulty of looking pleased while doing so, see the story of Emperor Wen and Deng Tong 鄧通 (*Taiping yulan, juan* 742, p. 5a).

46 Daoxuan 道玄, *Xu gaoseng zhuan* 續高僧傳, Shanghai: Shanghai guji chubanshe, 1991, vol. 24, p. 307b; cited in Cao Shibang 曹仕邦, "Sengshi suozai Zhongguo

sengtu dui fumu shizun xingxiao de yi xie shilie 僧史所載中國僧徒對父母師尊行孝的一些實例," in Xu Fuguan xiansheng jinian lunwenji bianji weiyuanhui (ed.), *Wenshi yanjiu lunji* 文史研究論集, Taipei: Xuesheng shuju, 1986, pp. 195–6.

47 Yuan Hong 袁宏 (328–376), *Hou Hanji* 後漢記, Taipei: shangwu yinshuguan, 1975, p. 135. For a similar account, see that of Ji Shao 稽紹 in *Taiping yulan*, *juan* 412, p. 5a.

48 *Hou hanshu*, *juan* 54, p. 1760. For a similar story about Wang Pou 王裒, see *Jinshu*, *juan* 88, p. 2278, and Chen Shou 陳壽 (233–297), *Sanguozhi* 三國志, Taipei: Dingwen shuju, 1983, *juan* 11, p. 348.

49 See Wang Sanqing 王三慶, *Dunhuang leishu* 敦煌類書, 2 vols, Gaoxiong: Liwen gongsi, 1993, vol. 1, p. 214. The *Hanshu* conversation, upon which this account is based, says nothing about the emperor working the land to provide the empress dowager with food. See *Hanshu*, *juan* 49, p. 2268.

50 *Taiping yulan*, *juan* 411, pp. 1a–b, *juan* 413, pp. 7a–b, and *juan* 414, p. 2b. For other examples of filial children working as hired laborers to support their parents, see Xing Qu (*Taiping yulan*, *juan* 411, p. 6a and *Yōmei bunko Xiaozi zhuan* 陽明文庫孝子傳 [ms. n.d.], *juan* 1, p. 4b); Ji Mai 紀邁 (*Taiping yulan*, *juan* 411, pp. 7b–8a); Shendu Xun 申屠勳 (*Taiping yulan*, *juan* 413, p. 7a); Li Du 李篤 (*Taiping yulan*, *juan* 414, pp. 1a–b); Xuan Yan 旋延 (*Taiping yulan*, *juan* 414, p. 2b); and Zhan Qin 展勤 (*Yiwen leiju*, *juan* 97, p. 1683).

51 For the appearance of wage-laborers in China, see Watanabe Shinichirō 渡邊信一郎 *Chūgoku kodai shakai ron* 中國古代社會論, Tokyo: Aogi shoten, 1986, p. 22; for the appearance of slaves and bondsmen, see E. G. Pulleyblank, "The Origins and Nature of Chattel Slavery in China," *Journal of the Economic and Social History of the Orient*, 1, 1957–8, 185–220.

52 Thus, Zhang Kai 張楷 sold medicine (*Hou hanshu*, *juan* 36, p. 1243), Cheng Jian 程堅 polished mirrors (*Taiping yulan*, *juan* 411, p. 1b), Shentu Fan 申屠番 was a lacquer artisan (*Hou hanshu*, *juan* 53, p. 1751), and Guo Yuanping 郭元平 became a carpenter and tomb-builder (*Songshu*, *juan* 91, p. 2244).

53 See Zhao Youwen 趙幼文, *Cao Zhi ji jiaozhu* 曹植集校注, Beijing: Renmin wenxue chubanshe, 1984, pp. 326–9, and *Songshu*, *juan* 22, p. 627. For similar statements about Jiang Ge, see *Tao Yuanming Ji*, *juan* 8, p. 321, and *Hou hanshu*, *juan* 39, p. 1302.

54 For the low social status of hired laborers in Roman society, see M. I. Finley, *The Ancient Economy*, Berkeley: University of California Press, 1985, pp. 41–2, 65–7.

55 See S. Pearce, "Status, Labor, and Law: Special Service Households under the Northern Dynasties," *Harvard Journal of Asiatic Studies*, 51, no. 1, 1991, pp. 115–16 and 123–9, and Wang Yi-t'ung, "Slaves and Other Comparable Social Groups," p. 326.

56 For instance, when his father died, Wu You 吳祐 refused to accept funerary presents and instead shepherded pigs in a marsh. One of his father's former subordinates told him, "Your father was a minister with a salary of 2,000 piculs of rice, yet you engage in such base pursuits. Even though you are shameless, what is your former lord [i.e. his father] supposed to do?" (*Hou hanshu*, *juan* 64, p. 2099) Even though Wu's biography includes this incident to show his incorruptibility, his elder's comments reveal how this behavior was commonly envisaged.

57 Yan Zhitui 顏之推 (531–91) says that in the north after a man who has remarried dies, "sons slander their [step-] mothers by calling them 'concubines'; younger brothers dismiss their elder [half-] brothers as 'hired laborers' [*yong*]." See Wang Liqi 王利器, *Yanshi Jiaxun jijie* 顏氏家訓集解, Taipei: Mingwen shuju, 1984, *juan* 4, p. 47, which is cited in Watanabe, *Chūgoku kodai shakai ron*, p. 168.

58 *Hou hanshu*, *juan* 32, p. 1119.

59 See the accounts of Zhou Xie 周燮 (*Hou hanshu, juan* 53, p. 1742), Zhou Liang 周良 (*Hou hanshu, juan* 53, p. 1743), Hua Xin 華欣 (*Shishuo xinyu, juan* 1, p. 10), and Cai Kuo 蔡廓 (*Songshu, juan* 57, p. 1573).

60 *Liji*, 1.7 and 33.10.

61 *Renwu zhi, Sibubeiyao* edition, Taipei: Zhonghua shuju, 1983, *juan* 2, p. 12a; this translation has been modified from that of J. K. Shryock, *The Study of Human Abilities: The Ren Wu Chih of Liu Shao*, New York: Kraus Reprint Corporation, 1966, p. 137.

62 In the *Lienü zhuan*, Jing Jiang 敬姜 criticizes her son Wenbo 文伯 because he allows his friends to wait upon him as if he was their father or elder brother. She tells him this is not appropriate behavior for someone who is young and whose position is low. He thereupon corrects his behavior by only associating with men who are older and more worthy than himself. When with them, he opens his lapels, rolls up his sleeves, and personally serves them food. When his mother sees this she admiringly states, "You have become an adult" (*Lienü zhuan*, 1.10). Stories that show filial sons becoming slaves or hired laborers are making the same point, but in a more exaggerated way.

63 See Qu Xuanying 瞿宣穎, *Zhongguo shehui shiliao congchao* 中國社會史料叢鈔, 2 vols, Shanghai: Shanghai shudian, 1985, vol. 1, pp. 127–8, 134–5; Yu Yingshi, "Han China," in K. C. Chang (ed.), *Food in Chinese Culture*, New Haven, CT: Yale University Press, 1977, pp. 74–6; and David R. Knechtges, "Gradually entering the Realm of Delight: Food and Drink in Early Medieval China," *Journal of the American Oriental Society*, 117, no. 2, 1997, p. 230; and K. C. Chang, "Introduction," *Food in Chinese Culture*, pp. 15–17.

64 For instance, while in office, Kong Fen 孔奮 would only give his mother the choicest of foods, yet his wife and children merely ate vegetables (*Tao Yuanming Ji, juan* 8, p. 320, and D. C. Lau *et al.*, *Dongguan hanji zhuzi suoyin* 東觀漢記逐字索引, Hong Kong: Commercial Press, 1994, 15.11); Li Du 李篤 was a copyist at night so that he could buy his mother meat and millet seed, but his wife and children merely ate vegetables (*Taiping yulan, juan* 414, pp. 1a–b); and Xue Bao used rice to offer sacrifices to his dead parents, but he merely ate taro (Wang Xianqian 王先謙, *Hou hanshu jijie* 後漢書集解, Beijing: Zhonghua shuju, 1984, *juan* 39, p. 2a).

65 *Yiwen leiju, juan* 20, p. 370 and the *Taiping yulan, juan* 414, pp. 1b–2a. That one would expect the prestige food to go to the honored guest can be seen in a story about Tao Kan's 陶侃 (259–334) mother, Woman Zhan 湛氏. An important visitor unexpectedly stayed at their home in mid-winter. She ripped apart her bedding and gave the hay stuffing to her guest's horse to eat, and secretly cut her hair and sold it to her neighbors, so that she could present delicacies to their venerable visitor. See *Jinshu, juan* 96, p. 2512. Woman Zhan is admirable precisely because of the extreme sacrifices she makes to do the right thing: lavishly entertain an important guest.

66 When Yue Yi served dried fish and salted vegetables to his guest, a high official, the latter flatly stated "I cannot eat this," at which point, Yue's mother came out with the several kinds of delicacies that she was normally served. Upon seeing this the guest said, "You surpass Mao Rong and I am not equal to Guo Tai" (Xiao Zixian 蕭子顯 [489–537], *Nanqishu* 南齊書, Taipei: Dingwen shuju, 1980 reprint, *juan* 55, p. 964).

67 Li Yanshou 李延壽 (612–678), *Nanshi* 南史, Taipei: Dingwen shuju, 1980 reprint, *juan* 73, p. 1815. This story appears in the biography of the filial son Xiao Ruiming who, upon hearing of Zhu's unfiliality, was so emotionally overwrought that he could not eat for several days. After first planning to personally mutilate Zhu's corpse, Xiao changes his mind when he considered that doing so would only serve to pollute his knife.

68 A story about Xiang Sheng's 向生 wife, which perhaps dates to the Tang, shows a daughter-in-law who undermined reverent care in even a worse way. See Wang Chongmin 王重民 *et al.*, *Dunhuang bianwen* 敦煌變文, Taipei: Shijie shuju, 1980, vol. 2, p. 909.

69 *Yiwen leiji*, *juan* 83, p. 1424. A story that strikingly resembles this one, but lacks the child being saved through divine intervention, is that of Guo Shidao 郭世道. See *Taiping yulan*, *juan* 413, p. 8a; and *Songshu*, *juan* 91, p. 2243. A tale involving a similar choice is that of Zhao Zi 趙咨. See *Yiwen leiju*, *juan* 20, p. 370, and *Hou hanshu*, *juan* 39, p. 1313.

70 For this phrase see *Dunhuang bianwen*, vol. 2, pp. 886, 905. As for the *Zuozhuan* story, when a concubine found out that her husband planned to assassinate her father, she asked her mother what to do. Her mother replied, "All men are potential husbands, but you have only one father. How could there be any comparison?" See *Zuozhuan*, B2.15.2 (Duke Huan, 15). The translation is from B. Watson, *The Tso Chuan*, p. 12.

71 For example, while fleeing rebels, despite his mother's objections, Liu Ping 劉平 abandoned his own son to save his dead brother's daughter. When the child persisted in following them, Liu Ping tied him to a tree (*Hou hanshu*, *juan* 39, pp. 1295–6).

72 See *Mengzi*, 5A1; *Hanshi waizhuan*, 8.23; *Shuoyuan*, 10.9.

73 For example, when in office, He Ziping devoted his entire salary to his mother and would spend none of it on his own wife and children. When someone asked him about this, He replied, "It is merely that I hope that my salary will principally be put to use in supporting my parent, and not put into use on my own behalf" (*Songshu*, *juan* 91, p. 2258). In other words, if he used his salary to benefit his wife and children, he would be using it to benefit himself.

74 Han Kongle 韓孔樂 and Luo Feng 羅豐, "Guyuan Bei Wei mu qiguan de faxian 固原北魏墓漆棺的發現," *Meishu yanjiu* 美術研究, 2, 1984, 5–6.

75 This story appears more frequently on remaining artifacts from the Northern and Southern Dynasties (317–589) than any other. Out of the twelve Northern and Southern Dynasties artifacts that are adorned with filial piety narratives, the Guo Ju story appears on eight – two-thirds. Since one would expect that artisans usually decorated tombs with images of the most popular stories, the frequency of its depiction is a good measure of the welcome it received.

76 The only exception to this is in the *Hou hanshu* biography of Liu Ping (*juan* 39, p. 1296), which describes how as an official he loyally served the governor of his commandery Sun Meng 孫萌. Characteristically for the early medieval period, the lord he showed loyalty to was not the ruler, but his immediate superior.

77 Zhang Ti's family was poor and had nothing with which to reverently care for his mother. He told his rich neighbor about the situation, but he lent him nothing. Zhang Ti could not overcome his anger, so he joined with four of his friends and became a bandit. Of the clothes and goods he obtained this way, he did not retain a coin for himself (*Nanshi*, *juan* 74, p. 1836).

78 See "Zhongxiao xianhou lun 忠孝先後論," in Tang Changru, *Wei-Jin Nanbeichao shilun shiyi* 魏晉南北朝史論拾遺, Beijing: Zhonghua shuju, 1983, pp. 238–53. Another piece of evidence that confirms Tang's supposition is the timing of the appearance of the dynastic histories' special chapters dedicated to filial sons and loyal retainers. The first chapter dedicated to filial sons in a dynastic history appears in the third century, whereas the first dedicated to loyal officials (*Zhongyi zhuan* 忠義傳) only appears in the *Jinshu*, which was completed in 644. Tellingly, even though "Biographies of the Filial and Righteous" usually took pride of place among collective biographies in histories written during the Six Dynasties period, in dynastic histories compiled during the Tang, the former always come after the "Biographies of the Loyal and Righteous."

79 Lu Yaodong, "Wei-Jin biezhuan de shidai xingge 魏晉別傳的時代性格," in Guoji Hanxue huiyi lunwenji weiyuanhui (ed.), *Zhongyang yanjiuyuan guoji Hanxue huiyi lunwenji* 中央研究院國際漢學會議論文集, Taipei: Zhongyang yanjiuyuan, 1981, p. 643.

80 *Hou hanshu, juan* 76, pp. 2462–3.

81 On the connection between selflessness and fame, see *Jinshu, juan* 75, pp. 1968–9.

82 For a discussion of reciprocity as the basis of Chinese social relationships in general and the parent–child relationship in particular, see L. S. Yang, "The Concept of *Pao* as a Basis for Social Relations in China," in J. K. Fairbank (ed.), *Chinese Thought and Institutions*, Chicago: University of Chicago Press, 1957, p. 302.

83 See A. Cole, *Mothers and Sons*, pp. 73, 81–7.

84 For an example of a story that illustrates this, see that of Guan Zhong 管仲 in *Hanfeizi jijie, juan* 12, p. 230.

85 By accepting the food of another man, one's life is no longer one's own. Since that man has enabled one to live, one must repay that kindness by providing him with service, even if it means sacrificing one's own life. See *Lienü zhuan*, 2.14, for comments that make this connection between food and control explicit.

86 Mao, no. 202. I have slightly modified Karlgren's translation. See his *Book of Odes*, Stockholm: The Museum of Far Eastern Antiquities, 1974, pp. 152–3.

87 *Analects*, 17.21, and *Liji*, 39.8. A Tang story about an elder brother who reared (*ruyang* 乳養) his two infant sisters throws light on this belief. When the brother died, his sisters were grief-stricken and decided to mourn him for three years. They justified their behavior by saying, "Although the three-year rites do not exist for brothers, we relied upon him to be fed and raised (*juyang* 鞠養), how is it possible to treat him like an ordinary person?" See *Taiping yulan, juan* 422, pp. 4a–b.

88 Indigenous Chinese Buddhist sutras state that infants drink their mother's blood for three years. For instance, the *Fumu enzhong nanbao jing* 父母恩重難報經, supposedly translated by Kumarajiva, states, "For three years you drank your mother's white blood" (*Dunhuang bianwen*, vol. 2, pp. 675, 677). Jen-der Lee notes that early medieval Chinese believed that breast-feeding should last for at least two years. See her "Wet Nurses in Early Imperial China," *Nannü*, 2, no. 1, 2000, 17–18. With regard to later Chinese beliefs that a child suckled for three years, see C. Furth, "From Birth to Birth: The Growing Body in Chinese Medicine," in A. B. Kinney (ed.), *Chinese Views of Childhood*, Honolulu: University of Hawaii Press, 1995, p. 178, and P. Y. Wu, "Childhood Remembered: Parents and Children in China, 800 to 1700," in A. B. Kinney (ed.), *Chinese Views of Childhood*, p. 137.

89 *Yomei bunko xiaozi zhuan, juan* 2, p. 25b.

90 As Cheng Gongsui 成公綏 (230–273) stated, "Crows have long been taken as an auspicious sign because they 'feed in return' [*fanbu*] and recognize [the principle of] *yang*" (*Yiwen leiju, juan* 92, p. 1593).

91 Xu Shen 許慎 (*c.* 58–147), *Shuowen jiezi zhu* 說文解字注, Shanghai: Shanghai guji chubanshe, 1981, *juan* 4, p. 56a. The Confucian *chenwei* "apocryphal texts" are replete with explanations of why crows are deemed filial. See *Taiping yulan, juan* 920, p. 1b, and *Yiwen leiju, juan* 92, p. 1591.

92 See Guo Moruo 郭沫若, "'Wu huanbu mu' shike de buchong kaoshi 烏還哺母石刻的補充考釋," *Wenwu*, 4, 1965, 2–4, and the song about the Sage-emperor Shun in Cai Yong's 蔡邕 (133–192) *Qincao* 琴操, Shanghai: Commercial Press, 1937, *juan* 2, p. 15.

93 *Taiping yulan, juan* 411, p. 6a, and *Yomei bunko xiaozi zhuan, juan* 1, p. 4b.

94 Xu Shen, *Shuowen, juan* 2, p. 15b.

95 Charlotte Furth has noted that Sun Simo 孫思邈 (581–682) thought parents should give their infants pre-chewed food as soon as they were two months old and that the standard term for infant feeding was *rubu* 乳哺, "to suckle and masticate," which referred to both liquid and solid nourishment. See C. Furth, "From Birth to Birth," p. 188, n. 53. For information on when medieval doctors thought that infants should begin eating pre-chewed solid food and what types of solid foods they should eat, see Hsiung Ping-chen 熊秉真, "To Nurse the Young: Breastfeeding and Infant Feeding in Late Imperial China," *Journal of Family History*, 20, no. 3, 1995, 217–39, and her *Youyou: Chuantong Zhongguo de qiangbao zhi dao* 幼幼: 傳統中國的襁褓之道, Taipei: Lianjing, 1995, pp. 118–22.

96 When the seven-year-old Cheng Zeng mournfully grieved for his departed mother, "his grandmother pitied him, and masticated [*jue* 嚼] meat for him to eat. When he discovered it was flavorful he spat it out." See *Taiping yulan*, *juan* 413, p. 7a, and *Yiwen leiju*, *juan* 20, p. 371.

97 See Kuroda Akira 黑田彰, *Kōshiden no kenkyū* 孝子傳の研究, Kyoto: Shibunkaku shupan, 2001, p. 214.

98 *Taiping yulan*, *juan* 519, p. 3a. Stories about the abandonment of elderly were common throughout Asia and Yuan Gu's tale was known in both medieval Korea and Japan. For information on stories of the abandonment of the elderly, see Takahashi Morikō 高橋盛孝, "Kirō setsuwa kō 棄老說話考," *Kokugo Kokubun* 國語國文, 7, no. 9, 1938, 90–8. Interestingly, the story of Yuan Gu is now circulated in South Korea as an oral tale. See R. L. Janelli, and D. Y. Janelli, *Ancestor Worship and Korean Society*, Stanford, CA: Stanford University Press, 1982, p. 52.

99 See Kuroda Akira, *Kōshiden no kenkyū*, p. 214.

100 A. Cole, *Mothers and Sons*, passim.

101 See *Mencius*, 5A1 and 5A2; *Lienü zhuan*, 1.1; *Xinxu*, 1.1; *Shiji*, 1.44–50; Ruan Yuan, *Shangshu zhushu* 尚書注疏, *Shisanjing zhushu* edition, Taipei: Yiwen yinshuguan, 1983, *juan* 2, pp. 24a–b; *Lunheng*, 85.366.

102 How he did so depends on the version of the story. According to an encyclopedia fragment from Dunhuang, he did this by refusing payment for the rice he sold them at the market (*Dunhuang bianwen*, vol. 2, p. 901). In another version, he buys firewood from his stepmother for twenty times its ordinary price (Ningxia bowuguan 寧夏博物館, *Guyuan Bei Wei mu qiguanhua* 固原北魏墓漆棺畫, Yinchuan: Ningxia renmin chubanshe, 1988, p. 11).

103 Dao Shi 道世 (d. 683), *Fayuan zhulin* 法苑珠林, Shanghai: Shanghai guji chubanshe, 1991, *juan* 49, p. 361.

104 This tally comes from examining each story from Mao Panlin's 茆泮林 *Gu xiaozi zhuan* 古孝子傳, Shanghai: Shangwu yinshuguan, 1936, Tao Yuanming's *xiaozhuan* 孝傳 and the *Yomei bunko Xiaozi zhuan*. In cases where the recipients are grandfathers or male masters, I count them as a father.

105 For examples, see the tales of Wang Xiang, Jiang Shi, Wei Tong, and Liu Yin.

106 Inscriptions at the Wu Liang shrine and on the Dawenkou pictorial stones identify the "wooden parent" whom Ding Lan is reverently caring for as his father rather than his mother. If all the Eastern Han Ding Lan representations were taken to be his father, then images with fathers as recipients would rise to 58 per cent.

107 J. D. Lee, "The Life of Women in the Six Dynasties," *Journal of Women and Gender Studies*, 4, 1993, pp. 62–5.

4 Filial devotion for women

A Buddhist testimony from third-century China

Yuet Keung Lo

Most studies on filial devotion (*xiao*) tend to focus either on the virtue as transgender moral excellence or on the relationship between the male child and his parents. This peculiar focus, of course, can be justified since the majority of our textual records on the subject portray filial devotion in transgender terms or illustrate the virtue in praxis, usually involving a male child either as a paragon or a travesty of it. It appears that only a male child can be called filial or unfilial. The female child seems to belong to a different moral category altogether. Indeed, the *Xiaojing* 孝經 (Classic of Filial Devotion) has virtually nothing specific to say about female children as bearers of the highly acclaimed virtue.[1] Similarly, Liu Xiang's 劉向 (77–6 BCE) *Lienü zhuan* 列女傳 (Biographies of Women), a monumental work that would sanction womanly behavior in China for ages to come, classified various types of women according to their virtues or the lack thereof, and the category of filial devotion was curiously missing. Where were the girls and women when praises for filial devotion were administered? Historical evidence seems to compel us to conceptualize *xiao* in a broader matrix of cultural and political underpinnings.

This chapter addresses the issue of filial devotion exemplified in the persons of female practitioners from the second to fourth centuries. Specifically, it argues that as far as young girls of nubile age were concerned, the virtue most esteemed and expected of them then was devotion to their husbands and their parents-in-law; their filial status was grounded on their pious devotion to the needs of their parents-in-law and their abilities to maintain and contribute to the harmony, stability and continuation of their newfound families. While indigenous texts from the period in question seem to offer no explicit, coherent didactic exposition on the role of filial daughters-in-law, a Buddhist scripture entitled *Yuyenü jing* 玉耶女經 (Scripture on Young Woman Yuye), which was putatively translated into Chinese around the third century, presents a unified and sustained *vade mecum* on womanly conduct, with unequivocal emphasis on the propriety of daughters-in-law in aristocratic families. In this scripture such propriety was identified as "loyal and filial" (*zhongxiao* 忠孝). Given the specific aristocratic setting of the story in the scripture, this chapter proposes that the scripture actually spoke to the household reality of clan-based families in the period under review, where a crisis of conflict seems to be brewing between daughters-in-law and parents-in-law. The moral prescriptions in the scripture echoed and reinforced Confucian propriety for women, which might have been popularized among the elite families in the short tract on womanly conduct titled *Nüjie* 女誡 (Admonitions for Women) by Ban Zhao 班昭 (*c.* 49 to *c.* 120), even as Confucian ritualism and moralism had begun to lose their grip on members of lesser aristocratic families in the second century when the Han empire was approaching its eventual debacle. Authentic or not, the scripture, then, appears to be a clarion call to reassert moral order in the clan-based families, which took upon themselves the mandate to reinvigorate and perpetuate the Confucian ritual order and, ultimately, to legitimize their own political, social, and moral standing.

The extratextual condition

From the arrival in 168 CE of An Shigao 安世高, the earliest known translator of Buddhist scriptures in China, until the end of the Western Jin period (265–316), China had borne unwilling witness to the collapse of the Han empire in 220, then an interregnum plagued with incessant warfare among three competing kingdoms, and a short-lived reunified empire under the Jin for about 50 years. During this time, the Chinese social structure was maintained and dominated by powerful clan-based families, which had arisen as a social and political power since at least the first century BCE.

The rise of clan-based families was, in part, precipitated by the adoption of Confucianism as the state orthodoxy during the Han dynasty. The Five Confucian Classics became the official curriculum for the civil service examinations. Success in the examinations guaranteed the candidate a passport into officialdom. "It is better to leave your son a copy of a Confucian classic than a trunk of gold 遺子黃金滿籯不如一經" – this was the advice offered by a popular aphorism circulated in eastern China during the last two centuries preceding the Common Era.[2] This, of course, surprised nobody. In addition to the annual civil service examination based on the Confucian classics, the Han government also recruited, on a regular basis, young people of filial devotion and moral integrity (*xiaolian* 孝廉). Once the successful scholar became a government official, his earnings and privileges helped to raise the status of his family. As his wealth grew over time, the scholar-official began to share it with members of his extended family and clan. We learn that numerous scholar-officials were extremely frugal themselves, yet they distributed their wealth among the so-called nine relations (*jiuzu* 九族) of their families as well as members in their villages and clans.[3] This twin policy of civil service recruitment worked to promote a Confucian ethos and contributed to the rise of powerful clan-based family networks throughout the empire.

By the end of the Western Han dynasty (206 BCE to 8 CE), scholar-official families had become the ruling elites, intellectual vanguards, and moral leaders in society. Taking advantage of their political privileges, scholar-officials managed to increase their land holdings at the expense of the common people. To protect their vested interests, scholar-officials as an interest group would and could torpedo reform proposals designed to curtail their expanding power. In the end, their power and influence grew so pervasive and overwhelming that the usurpation of the Western Han empire by Wang Mang 王莽 (reigned 9–23) would not have been possible without the support of the scholar-official families. Their moral and military support also proved to be indispensable to the subsequent founding of the Eastern Han dynasty (25–220).[4]

Clan-based scholar-official families continued to grow during the Eastern Han and into the fourth century. Many of the powerful scholar-official families such as the Wangs 王 of Langye 琅邪 (modern-day Shandong Province) and the Zhengs 鄭 of Xingyang 滎陽 (modern-day Henan Province), which were to dominate the sociopolitical arena later, began to flourish. Politically, both the Han and Jin dynasties emphasized rule by virtue, particularly the virtue of *xiao*. As Emperor Zhang 章 of Han (reigned 76–88) proclaimed, "Filial devotion is the culmination of all virtues and the beginning of the myriad forms of goodness 夫孝, 百行之冠, 眾善之始也."[5] All Han and Jin emperors were given a posthumous title bearing the character *xiao*, "filial," which affirms the emperor's moral legitimacy to the throne and his legacy to his descendants.[6] The same title was frequently conferred on the descendants of the imperial family when they were enfeoffed.[7] Indeed, the practice of naming after the virtue of filial devotion became so widespread that male children of any social background were often named *xiao* in the Han and Jin periods.[8] In the social and ethical spheres, then, filial virtues were promoted religiously in lockstep with government sanction.

During the Han and Jin periods, the *Xiaojing*, a short text that came to be a popular primer, epitomized the ultimate importance of filial devotion as a personal, familial, as well as political, virtue. Filial devotion was heralded as the "basis of virtue and the inspiration of transformative teachings"; the perennial principle of Heaven; the standard of the earth; and the norm of conduct for the people."[9] For personal cultivation, filial devotion provided a basis; and for politico-moral transformation, it became a strategy for recruitment to government office and for political edification. As Patricia Ebrey has observed, "filial piety came to be considered a political virtue, tied to loyalty to the emperor."[10] Family ethics and political success joined in a convenient symbiosis of *realpolitik*. Filial devotion was recognized as a universal virtue, which serves to "regulate the family, govern the state, and perfect the world."[11] At the behavioral level, filial devotion was concretized, mediated, and performed with rituals. To sustain the power and status of their families, scholar-officials saw the strategic importance of maintaining and enforcing a class-confirming system of rituals among their kin. Thus family rituals and role-based behavioral propriety took on paramount importance in a class-conscious aristocracy and permeated the everyday life of landed scholar-official families. It became imperative for scholar-official family members to study the elaborate systems of rites as well as the social etiquette that prescribed proper behavior for all occasions imaginable.

Ritual thus became the proper basis for family life. It should be noted that high-ranking official positions and substantial salaries were never the sole qualification that defined what it was to be a scholar-official family. In fact, the majority of the great families in the Eastern Jin (317–420) had slipped into poverty.[12] Instead, it was moral acclaim and ritual identity that distinguished a scholar-official family and its members. According to Chen Yinque 陳寅恪, during the Wei–Jin period, although there was a distinction between a great clan and a small clan, as long as a man was reputed for his talents and abilities, he would be qualified as a "person of renown" (*mingshi* 名士), regardless of his actual family background. Most importantly, if a woman was known for her knowledge and observance of ritual propriety, she could even be married into a great clan.[13] A young woman of good breeding distinguished herself from an underbred one primarily on account of her rite-consciousness and her ritualized character.

Perhaps the example of Wang Zhan 王湛 (249–295) suffices to illustrate this point. Wang came from a prestigious aristocratic family. When he was still young, he went against the ritual convention of parental matchmaking and sought on his own the hand of the daughter of Hao Pu 郝普, who was the Prefect of Luoyang. As it turned out, the bride was not only beautiful but also virtuous, and she eventually became the maternal model of the Wang family. When he was asked how he could tell his wife was such a model woman, Wang said, "I once saw her at the well drawing water. In every movement and gesture she never departed from her normal manner, and never once did she cast an improper glance. It was by this that I knew."[14]

In this context, marriage in the third and fourth centuries had also become a means of social mobility and a strategy for forming political alliances.[15] Consider the case of Li Luoxiu 李絡秀, reportedly an extraordinarily beautiful and talented lady from Ru'nan 汝南. When she agreed to be a concubine of Zhou Jun 周浚, then General Pacifying the East, her father and brothers would not give their consent. But she prevailed on them, saying, "Since our household is 'ruined and in trouble,' why grudge a lone daughter? If we contract a marriage with a noble family, hereafter we might be greatly benefited." After she was married to the Zhou family, she told her sons, "The only reason I compromised my integrity to become a concubine in your family was to provide for my own household. If you don't treat the members of my family as you would your own kin, I for my part don't care to live out my remaining years."[16] It is revealing to examine how Li was chosen by the general. We are told that once, when Zhou Jun was out hunting, a violent rainstorm broke out just as he was passing by the home of the Li family. As it turned out, none of the men were at home. Luoxiu, upon hearing that there was a noble person outside, with the help of a female slave slaughtered pigs and goats and prepared food and drink for dozens of men. Everything was carried out to perfection, and Zhou did not hear anyone. When he peeked surreptitiously, all he saw was a lone girl, who was unusually beautiful. That was Luoxiu. And he took the opportunity to seek her for a concubine.[17] The case of Li Luoxiu suggests that desirable women might not belong to any fixed class or rank. Their grace, beauty, charm, and virtue could serve them in place of noble birth and lineage. These traits then became their claim to nobility. Daughters from humble families could join the ranks of great ladies from aristocratic families on account of their talent and ritual training. For daughters from prominent families, good breeding could be the lifeline to their continued membership in the higher reaches of the sociopolitical echelon.

When the Xie 謝 family tried to seek the hand of the youngest daughter of Zhuge Hui 諸葛恢 (d. 345), they were rejected. At that time, the Zhuges were one of a few powerful families, whereas the Xies were not. After Zhuge Hui died, the Zhuge family declined; nonetheless the Xie proposed again, and this time they were successful. When Wang Xizhi 王羲之 (321–379) got wind of the wedding, he went over to the Xie family to take a look at the bride. And he found that "she still had the good breeding bequeathed by her father . . . her manners were correct and fastidious, her appearance and dress shining and neat."[18] Wang was known for his carefree personality and indifference to conventional behavioral norms, yet he was enticed to see for himself the grace and charm of a well bred daughter from a once prestigious family. Clearly, daughters needed to be groomed for their marketability and the prosperity of their family, especially when it was already in decline. Good breeding might remain the only redeemable asset available for a struggling family.[19]

Ritual training and family harmony

Women from aristocratic families in early medieval China obviously received their ritual training from their families. Common texts of elementary learning from the Han period such as the *Analects* and the *Xiaojing* provide little specific instruction on womanly virtues, and as far as filial devotion is concerned, women seem to be totally deprived of that honor. Even in the *Lienü zhuan* where concrete models of womanly virtues are presented, filial daughters (*xiaonü* 孝女) are curiously missing. Instead, the classics on rituals played a crucial role in defining the role of women and in guiding social behavior. For instance, the *Da Dai Liji* 大戴禮記 (Elder Dai's Record of Rites) defines the female sex as "to follow (女者, 如也) . . . ; that is, to follow the teachings of men and thus fulfill the rationales in their teachings (言如男子之教, 而長其義理者也). For this reason, a woman is called a *furen* (婦人), or someone who is subservient to others (服於人)."[20] Clearly, obedience and subservience are pivotal in the Confucian conception of women. More specifically, a woman is someone who "obeys (服也), and that means to subdue herself and obey in accordance with the rites (以禮屈服也)"; she "submits herself to family affairs and to serving others" (服於家事, 事人者也).[21] Women, at least those from an aristocratic background in early medieval China, were, then, expected to be ritualistic performers of obedience.

It is clear that the conception of women in Confucian canonical writings centers on the notion of service (*shi* 事), rendered in accordance with prescribed rituals. This view is also evident in the *Xiaojing*, which classifies filial devotion by social ranks from the Son of Heaven to the common people. Women were not given a specific place in this system; instead, they seem to share the kind of filial devotion practiced by the common people (*shuren zhi xiao* 庶人之孝). The Classic explains the way of being filial for the common people as follows. They observe the laws of nature and use the resources of the earth to the best advantage. They take good care of themselves and practice frugality in order to support their parents, or literally "feeding one's parents" (*yang fumu* 養父母).[22] If women also come under this category, their filial devotion would be defined chiefly in terms of their ability, and perhaps willingness, to provide for their parents. Given such mundane and routine duties required of the female child, it is not surprising that the term *xiaonü* (filial daughter) is such a rare commodity in didactic literature for women.[23]

For most women, their services would be directed to their husbands and parents-in-law. If they performed, they would be praised as "submissive" (*fu* 服), "obedient" (*shun* 順), or "respectful" (*jing* 敬), and honored as exemplary "wives" or "daughters-in-law." Indeed, the *Mencius*, citing the authority of a time-hallowed ritual tradition, explicitly characterizes "obedience" as the "proper" (*zheng* 正) virtue of wives and daughters-in-law.[24] In a word, if women were "submissive" and "obedient," they could be deemed bona fide "women."

Filial devotion as a gendered virtue

With regard to womanly conduct, the "Neize" 內則 ("Rules for the Inner Quarters") chapter of the *Liji* 禮記 (*Book of Rites*) provides further details. It spells out the rules and etiquette for girls and women of all ages and the minutiae of everyday behavior in the inner quarters in service of their parents and parents-in-law. Two points concerning the relationship between daughter-in-law and parents-in-law are of particular interest. First, although the text focuses primarily on the obligations of sons and daughters-in-law, it also contains specific rules of propriety for parents when they interact with their sons and daughters-in-law. In other words, moral obligation and ritual respect are meant to be mutual. For instance, parents-in-law are advised to be fair and impartial to their daughters-in-law and not to play favorites. When their daughters-in-law are less than respectful, they should not resent them; instead, they should try to be patient and educate them.[25]

Second, although the son and his wife are equally obligated to serve the parents/parents-in-law, the text reserves the term *xiao* for the son and describes the model daughter-in-law only as respectful (*jing*).[26] Thus it seems that the moral labels *xiao* and *jing* are gender-specific and tend to privilege the male over the female in the moral hierarchy.[27] The case of Jiang Shi 姜詩 and his wife from the early first century can best illustrate this gender division of virtue.

According to the *Hou hanshu*, both Jiang and his wife treated his mother very well. Jiang's conduct was characterized as "extremely filial 至孝," while his wife was "obedient and particularly devoted 奉順尤篤."[28] Jiang's mother was fond of eating hashed fish, with company, so husband and wife often worked together to prepare such a meal and invited an old lady in their neighborhood to eat with her. It is not clear how the virtuous couple differed in their support of the same elderly woman; if anything, it would appear that Jiang's wife was sacrificing more of herself in serving her mother-in-law,[29] although only Jiang Shi was praised as "filial." Interestingly, when a horde of raiding robbers came to loot Jiang's village, as soon as they found out that Jiang lived there, not only did they restrain themselves from looting, but they also offered rice and meat to Jiang as a gesture of respect. They said, "We will for sure alarm the spirits if we are going to disturb a man of profound filial devotion 驚大孝必觸鬼神."[30] Why is it that despite their equal dedication to supporting the same woman, only the son was honored with the virtue of filial devotion, by both the apparently morally conscious robbers and later historians? In fact, people later built a shrine in Jiang's village to worship him for his extraordinary filial devotion;[31] his wife was not given any recognition at all.

According to the *Da Dai Liji*, the daughter-in-law should be productive in the inner quarters; she should not go beyond 100 *li* to attend a funeral; she should not be dictatorial but always consult others before she takes action; she should always speak with evidence; and when she travels at night, she should always carry a candle with her. If she can do all these, she is considered "trustworthy" (*xin* 信)," and trustworthiness is the template for womanly virtues (所以正婦德也).[32] It is noteworthy that *xin* literally means "true" or "authentic" and this meaning seems to be implied in the *Da Dai Liji*: *xin* defines not only a woman's integrity but also her "authenticity"; that is, who she is. The "Jiaotesheng" chapter of the *Liji* elaborates the meaning of "trustworthiness" further. It says, "Trustworthiness finds expression in serving others; it is the virtue of the daughter-in-law 信, 事人也; 信, 婦德也."[33] Evidently, in Confucian canonical teachings, men and women are defined in different moral terms and their conduct is evaluated differently. In the end, the identity of girls and women is circumscribed within the inner quarters, yet they fall short of being filial. They can only aspire to be respectful daughters and trustworthy daughters-in-law. It is little wonder, then, that while filial devotion was rigorously promoted in early medieval China, and at least eight different collections of biographies of filial sons from the period survived in the seventh century, there was not even one single anthology for filial daughters.[34]

According to the "Rules for the Inner Quarters," children start learning numbers and directions at the age of six. Presumably this includes both boys and girls. At age seven, however, boys and girls are seated separately and they do not eat together anymore. At age ten, children begin to leave their home to learn how to read and write, and they stay with their teachers. It appears that girls will not continue with their formal studies and are typically married off when they turn fifteen.[35] It is not clear how much learning girls will have received before marriage. Once they are married, they will stay in the home of their parents-in-law and will be under their authority. In other words, the education of the daughter-in-law lies largely in the hands of her parents-in-law. We have seen that, according to the "Rules for the Inner Quarters," parents-in-law do have the moral obligation to educate their daughters-in-law. Such a home-based learning environment helps to foster family cohesiveness, which no doubt would be desirable to clan-based families.[36] However, the young daughter-in-law will be under the guidance of her parents-in-law and taught to serve the interests of her new family only; often, she is basically left to fend for herself, alone.[37]

If we imagine for a moment the situation of a young teenage girl who is married, through parental arrangement, to a husband whom she most likely has never met before, and who will have to negotiate with an entirely new family that might be far away from her home town, the prospect certainly looks grim and scary. How can a young daughter-in-law prepare herself to face her future? The *Nüjie* by Ban Zhao fills an important gap in this regard, especially given the lack of instruction of any kind for young girls in the *Xiaojing* and the conservative nature of the "Rules for the Inner Quarters."[38]

Traditionally, the *Nüjie* has been viewed in a conservative light; in fact, it has been criticized for being instrumental in imposing a physically constricting and spiritually denigrating ideology for women in traditional China.[39] That the text was written by a woman almost stigmatizes it as a betrayal of the female sex. A recent study, however, has cast doubt on this view and argued convincingly that the text was in fact a handbook of survival skills from a loving grandmother for her young granddaughters who were going to marry into alien families.[40] Instead of asking young girls to be submissive by virtue of their inherently inferior nature, Ban Zhao actually advised them to seek personal survival in an often hostile environment by resorting to a strategy of dissimulation. Viewed in this light, whereas the didactic "Rules for the Inner Quarters" is written from the perspective of the parents and parents-in-law and highlights how they should be served and obeyed, the *Nüjie* is strategic by design and composed for the survival and benefit of the defenseless daughter-in-law.

Once the young daughter-in-law assumes her new role, she must learn to cope with her unfamiliar situation on a day-to-day basis – the postnuptial education she will receive from her in-laws is not entirely different from what may be considered "on-the-job" training. The teenage daughter-in-law will now be under the watchful eyes of her parents-in-law and must take an active interest in the instructions she receives from them, which are no longer a mere litany of otiose etiquettes and rites but bear directly on her personal well-being and the reputation of her family in the complex world of postnuptial politics.

The most fundamental principle of personal survival is to play the role of the inferior and weak (*beiruo* 卑弱), so Ban Zhao advised her granddaughters. The sole duty of the wife is service to her husband, according to the *Nüjie*, and failure to fulfill such duty would lead to the collapse of moral order.[41] Strategically, she has to win the favor of her parents-in-law; she has to earn their love by yielding (*qucong* 曲從) to their wishes.[42] As demonstrated below, the spirit of Ban Zhao's advice is virtually identical to the Buddhist wisdom authorized by the *Yuyenü jing* in its various translations.

The *Nüjie* was not intended for public consumption and was not made known to a wide audience probably until Fan Ye (398–445) recorded it in the biography of Ban Zhao in the *Hou hanshu*. Meanwhile, a climate of family conflict seems to have prevailed in early medieval Chinese society. Specifically, as the following account of the divorce of Deng Yuanyi 鄧元義 in the second century illustrates, the conflict between daughters-in-law and parents-in-law began to flare up across social strata. Deng's wife "served her mother-in-law very prudently 事姑甚謹," but the latter simply loathed her and went as far as to lock her daughter-in-law up in an empty room and curtail her daily provisions. As a result, the young wife became emaciated, yet she never uttered a word of complaint. In the end, her father-in-law found out what had happened from his grandson. With tears in his eyes, he lamented, "How could one imagine a mother-in-law to have done something so terrible!" And he sent the young wife back to her parents. Later, she remarried a certain Ying Huazhong 應華仲, who was recruited to government office. One day, as Ying was going to court with his wife, Deng was among the onlookers by the roadside watching the procession. As he saw his former wife, Deng told the people around him that "she was my former wife. Although she did not actually do anything wrong, my mother treated her very badly. In fact, I have always loved her very much."[43] Deng's confession indicates that the divorce was not voluntary. His personal tragedy was by no means singular; on the contrary, it must have been a fair reflection of a larger social reality. Although Deng came from a high-ranking scholar-official family, there is evidence that the conflict between the daughter-in-law and the parent-in-law was widespread.

The famous popular ballad "Southeast the Peacock Flies 孔雀東南飛," which probably dates to the late second or early third century, captures the tragic drama of such a conflict in an ordinary family.[44] In the song, a junior official named Jiao Zhongqing 焦仲卿 is caught in a dilemma: he loved his wife Liu Lanzhi 劉蘭芝 dearly, but his mother disliked her, apparently because of her homeliness. Liu Lanzhi was married at seventeen and appears to have followed every instruction for the daughter-in-law as dictated in the "Rules for the Inner Quarters." She would start working at cockcrow and not retire until late at night. Neither did she violate any propriety or commit any offense. But her mother-in-law never quit nitpicking and complained that her daughter-in-law failed to observe propriety (*wu lijie* 無禮節) and behaved as she wished (*zi zhuanyou* 自專由).[45] The conflict could not be resolved and the couple was forced to divorce. Liu was determined not to marry again. When her mother forced her, she took her own life, and upon discovering it her husband also hanged himself. The ballad was composed by one of their contemporaries, who wanted to publicize it as a warning to merciless mothers-in-law. While the song extols the loftiness of romantic love, it belies the daughter-in-law and parent-in-law conflict, which was evidently quite common toward the end of the Han dynasty.

The late second-century story of the exemplary daughter-in-law Zhang Lixiu 張禮修 also attests to this problem, albeit ending on an optimistic note. Zhang Lixiu married Zhao Song 趙嵩, whose mother was a mean and ruthless woman, and she treated Zhang horribly. However, Zhang never showed any resentment, and even when her own parents tried to intercede on her behalf, she would only blame everything on herself without implicating her mother-in-law. Her exemplary conduct eventually moved her mother-in-law, who became kind and affectionate to her. Enthused, those who knew her story said, "Why shouldn't all daughters-in-law behave in the way Zhao's wife did? She moved her nasty mother-in-law to change her behavior. She can really be considered the teacher of daughters-in-law."[46]

It is revealing that the people chose to extol Zhang's extraordinary virtues rather than denounce her mother-in-law's unethical behavior. Evidently, the onus of moral responsibility was on the daughter-in-law. Zhang followed the Confucian prescriptions for the daughter-in-law to a fault and therefore earned the accolade of being the "teacher of daughters-in-law" (*fushi* 婦師). The fact that she was given that honor is itself a reflection of the cultural collective unconscious that took the moral asymmetry between the daughter-in-law and mother-in-law for granted. Hence, there was a necessity to profile the exemplary daughter-in-law for all to emulate. It was under such peculiar historical circumstances that Zhang Hua 張華 (232–300) informed his readers that he knew of a special kind of black magic that would make women filial and obedient (*xiaoshun* 孝順) daughters and daughters-in-law.[47] It would seem that Zhang Hua was actually expressing a kind of collective wishful thinking of his time. Daughters-in-law were just too unruly; it would be like a dream come true if only some magical potion could cure their unruly behavior once and for all.

Buddhist testimony

Such a magical potion remained elusive. Nevertheless, to arrest this growing social malady, some help did come from the spiritual authority of

Buddhism. The evidence can be found in the *Yueyenü jing*, a short scripture of about 2,000 characters. The scripture survives in five different versions under different titles. They are:

1   *Foshuo Yuyenü jing* 佛說玉耶女經 (Scripture on Young Woman Yuye as Spoken by the Buddha), translator unknown[48]
2   *Yuyenü jing*, translator unknown[49]
3   *Yuye jing* (Scripture on Yuye), which is also known as *Zhangzhezi yi Fo shuo zifu wujing jing* 長者子詣佛說子婦無敬經 (Scripture on an Elder's Son who Complained to the Buddha of His Daughter-in-law's Irreverence), translated by Dharmaranya 曇無蘭 during the Eastern Jin dynasty[50]
4   *Foshuo Asuda jing* [*Aśuddha-sūtra*] 佛說阿遫達經 (Scripture on [Elder] Aśuddha as Spoken by the Buddha), translated by Gunabhadra 求那跋陀羅 (394–468).[51]
5   The Yuye story appears in the *Ekottarāgama* (*Zengyi ahan jing* 增一阿含經), even though the protagonist is now called Sujātā 善生 instead.[52]

According to Dao'an 道安 (314–385), in his highly reliable Buddhist catalogue *Zongli zhongjing mulu* 綜理眾經目錄 the first two versions date to the Western Jin dynasty.[53] The authenticity of the scripture is unquestionable because it was apparently excerpted from one of the earliest Pāli Nikyās, the *Ekottarāgama* (*Zengyi ahan jing* 增一阿含經), which was translated into Chinese by Sanghadeva 僧伽提婆, who came to China in the second half of the fourth century and in 397 arrived in Jiankang 建康 (modern-day Nanjing), the capital of Eastern Jin. Given that the story in the five versions of the scripture is essentially the same, we will base our discussion of the scripture on the *Yueyenü jing* because it puts forth the message for the daughter-in-law most forcefully and coherently,[54] and it comes from the late third and early fourth centuries, the period under our discussion.

The *Yueyenü jing* explicitly states that its purpose is to admonish unruly daughters-in-law. Yuye, the protagonist of the story, is a defiant young woman who has recently married into a wealthy aristocrat's family named Anāthapindika. To the outrage and frustration of her parents-in-law, she shows no respect to them and disobeys her husband. As they complain, she simply "does not observe womanly propriety" (*buyi fuli* 不以婦禮). In the end they become so chagrined that they go to seek the help of the Buddha. The dialogue between the Buddha and Yuye constitutes the core of the scripture. Yuye is given a thorough and detailed lecture on the evil nature of being a woman. At the end of the lecture, the Buddha reminds Yuye of the Ten Precepts and the Three Obeisances (*trisarana*) in Buddhism as well as the favorable and unfavorable retribution for well behaved and ill behaved daughters-in-law.[55]

The scripture defines women solely by what they do and characterizes their various behaviors by assigning a role-based label to them. Thus, *meifu*

妹婦, the women who act like a sister, are those who, among other things, "serve (*shi* 事) their husbands with uttermost respect and sincerity."[56] Similarly, *zhishifu* 知識婦, women who act like a good friend, are those who "are respectful, obedient, and devoted in serving [*shi*] their husband,"[57] and *bifu* 婢婦, women who act like a maid, are those who "aspire to womanly conduct. . . . They serve [*shi*] their husbands in the way they serve [*shi*] their parents-in-law."[58] As we will see, the maid-like women's behavior toward their husbands and parents-in-law is extolled as "loyal and filial." Such role-based definitions of women are clearly in keeping with the service-oriented conception of women in the Confucian tradition as stipulated in the *Xiaojing*.[59] In fact, the virtues expected of the consummate daughter-in-law in the *Yuyenü jing* reinforce those mandated in Han Confucian doctrine, especially those articulated in the "Rules for the Inner Quarters."

Women, the scripture insists, do not have an identity of their own. Their identity and self-worth are defined by others: parents who give birth to them; husbands whom they have to care for; parents-in-law whom they have to serve. Traditionally, the Confucian doctrine of "three followings" (*sancong* 三從) stipulates that a woman should follow her father while at home, her husband after she marries, and her son after her husband dies. Notably, the *Yueyenü jing* modifies this triangular dependency by replacing the son with the parent-in-law. This is precisely the reason why the scripture was selected for translation, to offer a Buddhist solution to the pressing problem of conflicts between daughter-in-law and parent-in-law.

In the story, the young Yuye undergoes a rigorous regimen of socialization in the Anāthapindika household, a process that is earnestly enforced as soon as she joins her newfound family. The absence of Yuye's husband in the story suggests that the task of socialization falls entirely on the shoulders of his parents. The role of the parent-in-law looms large. The fact that Yuye is all by herself in the story also suggests that she has no other source of moral authority to resist, if she wants to, the socialization she is compelled to go through. Her parents must have given their tacit approval even if it were their obligation to share the burden of the task. In fact, Chinese parents in general urged their daughters to obey the authority in their newfound families, so at least the *Lienü zhuan* would advise.[60]

Given the constant interaction between the daughter-in-law and parent-in-law in a virtually round-the-clock process of instruction and admonition, friction and resentment can easily arise. In the scripture the solution to this family conflict is given in the form of a catalogue of daughters-in-law with a variety of twists in character. Yuye is presented with an array of models for the good daughter-in-law (*shanfu* 善婦) and evil daughter-in-law (*efu* 惡婦), each with a detailed description. The seven models of a daughter-in-law are: women who act like a mother (*mufu* 母婦); women who act like a sister (*meifu* 妹婦); women who act like a friend (*zhishifu* 知識婦); women who act like a daughter-in-law (*fufu* 婦婦); women who act like a maid (*bifu* 婢婦); women who act like an enemy (*yuanjiafu* 怨家婦); and women who act like a murderer (*duomingfu* 奪命婦).[61] Of these models, two seem to stand out:

fufu and *bifu*. The former is significant because the *Yueyenü jing* is about how a daughter-in-law is supposed to conduct herself, and the latter because it is what the protagonist decides to emulate.

Let us first examine what these two models are. *Fufu* refers to women who "nourish and support their parents-in-law with uttermost devotion and effort, and they never complain. They cultivate womanly propriety without lapse or negligence. They never propose anything improper, nor do they conduct themselves unceremoniously. And they always act in favor of harmony. Such are women who act like a daughter-in-law."[62] As a proposed model to address Yuye's defiant and improper conduct, *fufu* seems to be right on the mark, but why is it not the choice for Yuye?

The reason for Yuye to choose otherwise is the option of *bifu*. As the Buddha explains, women who act like a maid are those

> whose hearts are always fearful and those who never dare to be over-weening. They are loyal and filial, fulfilling every moral obligation [*zhongxiao jinjie* 忠孝盡節]. They do not use foul language, nor do they indulge themselves in wanton behavior. They guard themselves with propriety in the way a subject serves his king. When they are in their husbands' favor, they do not become arrogant. If they were flogged, they would accept the punishment with respect. And when subject to scolding and abuse, they remain silent. Pain or pleasure, their bodies will enjoy it all the same. Their affection for their husbands is undivided. They aspire to womanly conduct, and are never particular about their clothing and food. They serve their husbands in the way they serve their parents-in-law.[63]

The description of *bifu* is the longest and most detailed of the seven models presented in the scripture. Moreover, unlike that of *fufu*, it includes obligations to both the husband and parents-in-law, which provide more specific moral guidance for the exemplary daughter-in-law. In this sense, the description of *bifu* is probably tailored to address the specific transgressions of Yuye mentioned earlier in the scripture. But the language used in the description is noteworthy. It is the first time that a daughter-in-law's behavior was considered "loyal and filial." Previously, *zhong* and *xiao* were gender-specific terms of moral qualities and social honor reserved for males under normal circumstances in the Chinese moral universe. Yuye's choice was thus most significant – it seems that women were finally admitted into the preserve of *xiao*, even though the object to which the virtue was applied had now switched from their parents to their parents-in-law.

It should be clear that the *Yuyenü jing* is essentially a catechism for womanly conduct that aims particularly at the role of the daughter-in-law. Doctrinally, there is nothing profound or reactionary about the scripture's view on women and on the moral obligations of the daughter-in-law. Yet documents describing symbolic actions are hardly innocent, transparent texts; they were written or translated by authors or translators with various intentions and strategies. Viewed in its historical context, the *Yuyenü jing* reflects a serious concern with the role of women, especially as daughters-in-law, in maintaining domestic and social harmony.

Early classical texts such as the *Yijing* 易經 (Book of Changes) and the *Liji* consistently emphasize the importance of familial relationships, but invariably the focus is on the parent–child relationship and the husband–wife relationship. In contrast, the relationship between the daughter-in-law and the parent-in-law is hardly mentioned in Confucian canonical writings. The appearance of the *Yuyenü jing* at this juncture of Chinese history was no coincidence. In fact, between the third and fifth centuries a large number of short Buddhist scriptures on women appeared.[64] Many of them were excerpts from longer scriptures, whereas others appear to be free-standing scriptures of particular themes and lessons. The *Yuyenü jing* itself, as mentioned, was part of the *Ekottarāgama* and was made a self-contained scripture. These thematic scriptures arguably were created for particular historical exigencies. Once the need that demanded their presence was gone, they would lose their relevance, which may partly explain the subsequent loss of many of these scriptures. The sudden flood of instructional literature is indicative of the preoccupation with the issue of womanly behavior in early medieval China. The *Yuyenü jing* fulfills a social need in its historical milieu. It addresses the thorny problem of conflicts between daughters-in-law and parents-in-law in aristocratic families and at the same time, offers concrete, practical instructions for the grooming of young girls of nubile age from elite families in anticipation of marrying an honorable husband from a family of social prestige and political influence.

Conclusion

It seems self-evident that the relationship between daughters-in-law and parents-in-law is perennial, and no doubt attempts to deal with this family problem are as old as the problem itself. Yet in the case of Chinese history we are no longer able to know what these attempts might have been and how successful they were in their times due to the lack of historical evidence. What seems unique about third-century China is that considerable attention was given in a variety of textual sources to the conflict between daughters-in-law and parents-in-law. This singular phenomenon suggests that the perennial family conflict demanded an urgent redress. To a certain extent, the cornucopia of pre-third-century Confucian canonical texts that attempted to prescribe the behavior of young girls before and after marriage obliquely belied the anxiety over this family conflict and articulated some possible solutions. The third century witnessed an increasing openness and acceptance of Buddhism in China, which indicates, to some extent, inadequacy in the indigenous Chinese tradition to cope with its inherited problems. Meanwhile, the embrace of the foreign doctrine made it possible for many aristocratic families in this time to confront the conflict between daughters-in-law and parents-in-law with new spiritual resources. The appeal to Buddhist authority in the third century was in all likelihood a new social and ideological strategy to address this perennial family problem.

The fact that the *Yuyenü jing* was translated five times within a short span of roughly two hundred years is unprecedented in Chinese Buddhist history. In addition to addressing a real concern in aristocratic families, the scripture also fed the official propaganda of filial devotion that needed nourishment in a time of precarious stability and order in the mid-third century. The Buddhist elements in the scripture, such as the Ten Precepts and retribution, are like window dressing that points up the central message of how to be the consummate daughter-in-law. The meaning of the scripture cannot be understood apart from the historical circumstances and cultural milieu that inform it.

The daughter-in-law occupies a pivotal position in the *Yuyenü jing* because she is perceived as a problem. The Buddhist solution revolves around role obligations and role performance – an approach that resonates perfectly with Confucian ethical principles. A consummate daughter-in-law can now earn the honor of being "loyal and filial," which has previously been reserved for the male sex. The Buddha's endorsement as reflected in the scripture seems to suggest that the Buddhist monastic order condoned, if not supported, secular marriage practices and other family-related matters. No conflict between secular conventions and religious sanctions is evident.

As we have seen, the *Xiaojing* elevates *xiao* to a universal virtue. As such, it transcends gender differentiation. In the real world of familial relations, however, conceptions of *xiao* are always gender-based. In the moral universe of the *Xiaojing*, the daughter-in-law is a new entity, calling for new conceptual assimilation and appropriation. The Classic could no longer contain her because of her gender. We thus have an inherent contradiction here. The Buddhist advocacy of female filiality in the *Yuyenü jing*, then, poses a challenge to the male tradition of filial devotion. Filial devotion for women now takes on a new cultural meaning in the person of the daughter-in-law.

Despite its touted intrinsic moral value, filial devotion is highly pragmatic. As the *Yuyenü jing* demonstrates, it is, in fact, far more important for a particular conception of filial devotion to work than for it to be logically sound. As soon as a particular conception of filial devotion ceased to be adequate, it would be modified even if that might contradict its earlier presuppositions. This did not seem to bother people at that time because, while filial devotion as a normative value was sacrosanct, the conception of it as a virtue in praxis was provisional. The *Yuyenü jing* signals a reconceptualization of *xiao* among the aristocratic clan-based families in the third and fourth centuries. To both the Confucian-minded scholar-officials and the Buddhist-minded sympathizers, the conflict between the daughter-in-law and the parent-in-law must be dealt with. Defiant and unruly daughters-in-law needed to be brought under control. Instead of being browbeaten into submission, daughters-in-law were now put on a moral pedestal if only they could practice the new ethic of familial harmony.

In this concerted effort, the Confucian-minded aristocratic elites and their Buddhist allies attempted to build an imagined community of ritual propriety centering on the universal virtue of filial devotion. Perhaps for the first time, filial devotion as a manmade moral label had truly transcended gender boundaries. As noted earlier, Zhang Hua announced that he knew of a special magic that would transform women into filial and obedient (*xiaoshun*) daughters and daughters-in-law. The attribution of *xiaoshun* by a non-Buddhist scholar to girls and women right at this historical juncture should not be a mere coincidence. The problem must have been deeply and widely felt. In the end, women were assimilated into the moral sphere of filial devotion and, willing or not, became its guardians and co-perpetuators of the reconceptualized virtue that could now be consummated across gender boundaries. Further research will have to be undertaken to determine if the thoughtful attention accorded the daughter-in-law in third-century China had anything to do with the changes in or perhaps formation of Chinese patriarchy.

Notes

1 Parts of the *Xiaojing* as we have it today were already in circulation in pre-Qin times, but the text itself was probably not finalized until the early Han dynasty. See W. Boltz, "*Hsiao Ching*," in M. Loewe (ed.), *Early Chinese Texts: A Bibliographical Guide*, Berkeley: Society for the Study of Early China and the Institute of East Asian Studies, University of California, 1993, pp. 141–53.
2 See Ban Gu 班固 (32–92), *Hanshu* 漢書, Beijing: Zhonghua shuju, 1983, *juan* 73, p. 3107.
3 There are two different interpretations of *jiuzu* in Han times. It can either refer to all family members from nine generations, four anterior to and four posterior to the individual in question. Or it can refer to four kinds of relatives from one's paternal family, three from one's maternal family, and two from the family of one's wife. See also Anne Cheng's discussion in this volume.
4 My analysis of clan-based families in the Han period follows that of Yu Yingshi 余英時. See his "The Relationship between the Establishment of the Political Authority of the Eastern Han and Powerful Clan-based Families 東漢政權之建立與士族大姓之關係," in Yu Yingshi, *The Intellectual Class in China: The Early Period* 中國知識階層史論: 古代篇, Taipei: Lianjing chuban shiye gongsi, 1980, pp. 109–203.
5 See the "Biography of Jiang Ge," in *Hou hanshu* 後漢書, *juan* 39, p. 1303.
6 The only exception is Gaozu 高祖 Emperor (reigned 206–196 BCE) of Han, who was the founding emperor of the Han dynasty.
7 See the "Biography of Liu Ban" in *Hou hanshu*, *juan* 39, p. 1303.
8 For instance, see *Hou hanshu*, *juan* 39, pp. 1298, 1301.
9 *Xiaojing zhushu* 孝經注疏, in Ruan Yuan 阮元 (1764–1849) (ed.), *Shisanjing zhushu* 十三經注疏, 8 vols, Taipei: Yiwen yinshuguan, 1976, Chapter 7, *juan* 8, p. 28b.
10 P. Ebrey, "Women, Marriage, and the Family," in P. S. Ropp (ed.), *Heritage of China: Contemporary Perspectives on Chinese Civilization*, Berkeley: University of California Press, 1990, p. 203.
11 The importance of the *Xiaojing* can hardly be overestimated. Nearly sixty commentaries and studies on the *Xiaojing* from the early medieval period survived in the seventh century. These include a version of the Classic prepared by Emperor

Mu 穆 of Jin (reigned 345–361), who personally lectured on the Classic at court at least twice, and a Tobanese translation from Emperor Xiaowen 孝文 of Northern Wei 北魏 (reigned 471–499). See the *Suishu, juan* 4, pp. 923–4. Emperor Xiaowu 孝武 of Jin also had lectured on the Classic to his officials at court; one such occasion took place on the ninth day of the ninth month in 375. See the *Shishuo xinyu* 世說新語, *juan* 3, p. 90, in R. B. Mather (trans.) *A New Account of Tales of the World*, Minneapolis: University of Minnesota Press, 1976, p. 71.

12 He Qimin 何啟民, "A Study of the Economic Situation of the Aristocratic Families in the Southern Dynasties 南朝門第經濟之研究," in his *Essays on Aristocratic Families in Medieval China* 中古門第論集, Taipei: Xuesheng shuju, 1978, pp. 139–87; see especially pp. 146, 166–83.

13 Chen Yinque, *Political History of the Tang Dynasty: A Draft* 唐代政治史述論稿, in *Collected Works of Chen Yinque*, 5 vols, Taipei: Liren shuju, 1982, vol. 3, p. 71.

14 *Shishuo xinyu, juan* 19, p. 15; as translated in R. B. Mather, *New Account*, p. 349; cf. *Shishuo xinyu, juan* 19, p. 16. Wang has a biography in the *Jinshu (juan* 75, pp. 1959–60), but his wife is not mentioned.

15 The imperial practice of selecting brides from the families of high-ranking officials may have percolated down to the lower social strata. In 273, Emperor Wu 武 of Jin proclaimed that children from the families of ministerial officials were not allowed to marry until the imperial talent selection was over. Many of the young girls thus selected would become concubines in the palace. Although the Emperor did attempt to curb hypergamy a year later, which testifies to the prevalence of the practice, he did not impose restriction outside the palace. *Jinshu, juan* 3, p. 63.

16 *Shishuo xinyu, juan* 19, p. 18; in R. B. Mather, *New Account*, p. 350. Li earned a spot in the "Biographies of Women" in the *Jinshu*, which reports the same story; see *Jinshu, juan* 96, pp. 2514–15. The fact that this episode was included in the official Jin history and that stories of this kind were widely circulated suggests that marriage as a means to forming an alliance with powerful families was common in early medieval China. Two other examples probably from the third century can be found in Chang Qu 常璩, *Huayang guozhi* 華陽國志. After Wang He 王和 in the Shu 蜀 region (modern-day Sichuan) became widowed, her elder brother tried to persuade her into marrying a prominent family for security. Yang Ji 陽姬 married an illustrious family, and as a result her two brothers obtained government posts and her own family was catapulted into prominence. See the biographical accounts of Wang He and Yang Ji in *Huayang guozhi jiaozhu*, Chengdu: Bashu chubanshe, 1984, *juan* 10b, pp. 769 and 785.

17 *Shishuo xinyu, juan* 19, p. 18; R. B. Mather, *New Account*, p. 350.

18 *Shishuo xinyu, juan* 5, p. 25; in R. B. Mather, *New Account*, p. 164. See also Zhuge Hui's explanation here of the marriages of his daughters to different families, which illustrates clearly the importance of forming a network of social alliances through marriage in early medieval China.

19 In the Song dynasty (960–1279), it was customary in high society for the wife's family to provide a lavish dowry, which often included land. See P. Ebrey, "Women, Marriage, and the Family," pp. 207–10; and her *The Inner Quarters: Marriage and the Lives of Chinese Women in the Sung Period*, Berkeley: University of California Press, 1993, especially, pp. 99–113. During the Jin period, although women relied mainly on their good breeding marked by ritual training to marry into aristocratic families, parents also had to prepare a dowry for their daughters, which could prove to be a financial burden for a family with many daughters. Thus in the year 275, Emperor Wu of Jin, in recognition of the fact that many generals and soldiers due for marriage had yet to find a wife, decreed

that families with five daughters were exempted from taxes, so that daughters could be married out. See *Jinshu, juan* 3, p. 64.

20 *Da Dai Liji*, Chapter 80, in Wang Pinzhen 王聘珍, *Da Dai Liji jiegu* 大戴禮記解詁, Beijing: Zhonghua shuju, 1983, p. 254. The "Jiaotesheng" 交特牲 chapter of the *Liji* also states that "a woman is someone who follows others [*furen, congren zhe ye* 婦人, 從人者也]"; see *Liji zhushu* 禮記注疏, in Ruan Yuan (ed.), *Shisanjing zhushu*, Chapter 11, *juan* 5, p. 506b.

21 Ban Gu, *Bohutong* 白虎通; cited in Wang Pinzhen's commentary on Chapter 80 of the *Da Dai Liji*, p. 254.

22 *Xiaojing zhushu*, Chapter 6, *juan* 8, p. 27a.

23 In the chapter on "Biographies of Women" in the *Hou hanshu*, we find one fourteen-year-old girl and a young mother described as *xiaonü* 孝女. In both cases, their filial devotion was directed to their father. See *Hou hanshu, juan* 84, pp. 2794, 2799. The epithet was probably accorded to them during the fifth century when the *Hou hanshu* was compiled. For a more detailed discussion of this issue, see Yuet Keung Lo 勞悅強, "The Invisible Woman in the *Classic of Filial Devotion* 孝經中的隱形女性," Occasional Papers in Chinese Studies, No. 151, October 2002, Department of Chinese Studies, The National University of Singapore.

24 *Mencius*, 3B2. The "Jiaren" 家人 (family members) hexagram in the *Yijing* 易經 (*Book of Changes*) also states that "it is beneficial to have a woman that is proper." The Judgment on this hexagram explains, "The woman has her proper role on the inside while the man has his on the outside. That the man and the woman fulfill their proper roles is the greatest principle of Heaven and earth. When the father acts like a father . . . the husband like a husband, the wife like a wife, then the way of the family is proper." *Zhouyi zhengyi* 周易正義, in Ruan Yuan (ed.), *Shisanjing zhushu, juan* 1, pp. 89c–d.

25 *Liji zhushu*, Chapter 12, *juan* 5, p. 521a.

26 *Liji zhushu*, Chapter 12, *juan* 5, pp. 520d–1a. "Respectfulness" is also identified as one of the virtues of the daughter-in-law in the *Mencius*, 3B2.

27 Based on extant sources, only a handful of women enjoyed the privilege of being recognized as a filial daughter-in-law (*xiaofu* 孝婦) before the Jin dynasty. For instance, in Liu Xiang's *Lienü zhuan*, only one woman is identified as *xiaofu*, a title given to her by Emperor Wen 文 (reigned 179–157 BCE) of Han, which suggests that women were not routinely recognized and praised as filial daughters-in-law. See the "Biography of Chen the Widowed Filial Daughter-in-law," in Liang Duan 梁端 (1800–1825), *Lienü zhuan jiaozhu* 列女傳校注, *juan* 4, pp. 9a–10a. *Xiaofu* is not a category in the *Lienü zhuan*; Chen is actually classified under the category of women who are "chaste and obedient" (*zhenshun* 貞順). See also the discussion by Sor-hoon Tan and Lisa Raphals in this volume.

28 See the biography of Jiang Shi's wife in the *Hou hanshu, juan* 84, p. 2783.

29 Jiang's mother was fond of drinking the water from a river that was six to seven *li* away from their home. Jiang's wife often went upstream to draw water for her. Once, when she was out getting the water, she ran into a windstorm and therefore could not come back in time. As a result, her mother-in-law suffered from thirst, and for this reason, Jiang kicked her out of their house.

30 *Hou hanshu, juan* 84, p. 2783. Jiang was recruited by the government on the basis of his filial devotion; *Hou hanshu, juan* 84, p. 2784.

31 According to the biography of Jiang Shi's wife, sweet water once sprang from underground somewhere near the couple's house. Almost a thousand years later, Ouyang Xiu 歐陽修 (1007–1072) reported that the spot where the water had allegedly sprung came to be called Spring of Jiang Shi. Once again, Jiang's wife was not given any credit. See Wang Xianqian 王先謙 (1842–1917), *Hou hanshu jijie*, Changsha: Shangwu yinshuguan, 1940, *juan* 84, pp. 3067–8.

32 *Da Dai Liji jiegu*, Chapter 80, pp. 254–5.

33 *Liji zhushu*, Chapter 11, *juan* 5, p. 506a.

34 On these anthologies, see *Suishu, juan* 4, p. 976. See also Keith N. Knapp's article in this volume.

35 On the age of marriage in the Han, see Yang Shuda 楊樹達, *A Study of Rituals Concerning Marriage and Death in Han China* 漢代婚喪禮俗考, 1933, Taipei: Huashi chubanshe, 1976 reprint, pp. 24–9. During the Jin, beginning in 273, Emperor Wu decreed that if parents did not marry their daughters who had reached seventeen, designated officials would do so on their behalf. *Jinshu, juan* 4, p. 63.

36 As Ebrey has observed, "Where men marry in their teens they usually stay in their parents' home, and their wives are under the authority of their mothers. Such arrangements make it easier for the senior generation to set the tone in child-rearing practices, religious and economic activities, and so on, which adds to social conservatism. Large extended families are easier to achieve when generations are short and new members (mostly brides) socialized at young ages." P. Ebrey, "Women, Marriage, and the Family," p. 198.

37 In some cases, even the grandmother-in-law was involved in the process of socialization. A loving mother could send some of her own maids along with her daughter when she marries. For both these points, see the biographical account of Wen Jijiang 文季姜 in *Huayang guozhi, juan* 10c, p. 825.

38 Ban Zhao herself cited a text called *Nüxian* 女憲 (*Regulations for Women*) twice in her *Admonitions for Women*. Apparently, it was some sort of practical guidebook on everyday conduct for women, but the text was lost.

39 For a study of Ban Zhao that includes a full translation of the *Nüjie*, see N. L. Swann, *Pan Chao: Foremost Woman Scholar of China*, New York: Russell and Russell, 1932. The study is somewhat dated but remains the only monograph available on Ban Zhao.

40 Y. S. Chen, "The Historical Template of Pan Chao's *Nü-chieh*," *T'oung Pao*, 82, 1996, 230–57.

41 *Nüjie*, Chapters 2 and 3, in *Hou hanshu, juan* 84, pp. 2788, 2789.

42 *Nüjie*, Chapter 6, in *Hou hanshu, juan* 84, p. 2790.

43 *Ru'nan ji* 汝南記, cited in the annotation to the biography of Ying Feng in *Hou hanshu, juan* 48, p. 1607.

44 A brief preface of unknown date states that the ballad was based on an actual event that took place during the Jian'an 建安 era (196–220). See Lu Qinli 逯欽立, *Complete Poems from the Pre-Qin through the Han-Wei and Nanbeichao Periods* 先秦漢魏晉南北朝詩, 3 vols, Beijing: Zhonghua shuju, 1983, vol. 1, pp. 283–6. For an English translation, see B. Watson (trans.) *The Columbia Book of Chinese Poetry: From Early Times to the Thirteenth Century*, New York: Columbia University Press, 1984, pp. 82–92. There is another ballad from about the same time that also deals with a separated couple. In this poem, the former wife runs into her divorced husband while coming back from picking plants in the mountains and earnestly asks him about his new wife. From her husband's honest and gentle reply, we can sense the lasting affection between the divorced couple and that they were not separated voluntarily. Theirs is most probably another case of forced divorce demanded by the unfortunate woman's former parents-in-law. For the poem, see Lu Qinli, *Complete Poems*, vol. 1, p. 334. For an English translation, see B. Watson, *Columbia Book of Chinese Poetry*, pp. 102–3.

45 Lu Qinli, *Complete Poems*, vol. 1, p. 283.

46 *Huayang guozhi, juan* 10c, p. 814.

47 Zhang Hua, *An Account of a Miscellany of Things* 博物志, Beijing: Zhonghua shuju, 1980, p. 141. Zhang was a key official whose advice was critical to the unification of China under the Jin; his opinions were widely respected in his time.

When the Jin came to power, Zhang was entrusted with the task of writing the history of the Jin and crafting the various political and ritual institutions for the new dynasty. Zhang appears to be a filial son; when his mother died, he observed the mourning in excess of the proper rites at the expense of his health. And when his cooperation was sought in a coup d'état soon after the Jin dynasty had been established, he declined on the grounds that the conspiracy would show itself to the world as an unfilial act (以不孝示天下). See Zhang's biography in the *Jinshu*, *juan* 36, pp. 1068–77.

48 *Taishō Tripitaka* (abbreviated to T.) 142(2). 863c16–864c4 (work no. 142, vol. 2, p. 863c, line 16 to p. 864c, line 4). According to the scripture itself, this version is also called *Yuye jing*. See T.142(2).864b29–c1.

49 This version is appended to the end of the first version in the *Taishō Tripitaka*; see T.142(2).864c8–865c14.

50 T.143(2).865c20–867a16. The alternative title is given in Tong Wei 童瑋, *Index to Twenty-two Kinds of Buddhist Canon* 二十二種大藏經通檢, Beijing: Zhonghua shuju, 1997, p. 668.

51 T.141(2).863a22–c10. Aśuddha was the father-in-law of Yuye in the scripture.

52 See T.125(2).820c5–821a23, story 9 in *juan* 49.

53 Sengyou 僧祐 (445–518), *Collection of Notes on the Tripitaka* 出三藏記集, *juan* 3, T.2145(55).17c11

54 For a detailed discussion of the five versions of the scripture, see Yuet Keung Lo, "Recovering a Buddhist Voice on Daughters-in-law: The *Yuyenü jing*," forthcoming.

55 The Ten Precepts and Three Obeisances are: "Seek refuge in the Buddha; seek refuge in the Dharma; and seek refuge in the monastic order. Do not kill. Do not steal. Do not engage in lewd indulgence. Do not lie. Do not drink liquor. Do not be foul-mouthed. Do not use lewd language. Do not be jealous. Do not be hateful and angry. Have faith that good conduct will be rewarded by good karma. These are the ten precepts; they are what female lay followers practice."

56 T.143(2).865a23–4.

57 T.143(2).865a28.

58 T.143(2).865b7–8.

59 Interestingly, material provision is also one of the key elements in the definition of motherly women (*mufu*), women who "love their husbands as a mother loves her son. Day in and day out, they nurture [*yang* 養] their husbands and care for them, never failing to serve them in a timely fashion." See T.143(2).865a21–2. In the scripture's definition of women who act like an enemy (*yuanjiafu*), failure to nourish and raise their children is one of their typical behaviors. See T.143(2).865b11.

60 For instance, see the biography of Meng Ji 孟姬 in Liu Xiang's *Lienü zhuan*, 4.3b. Mencius also appeals to the authority of ritual prescriptions that when a woman is ready to marry, her mother would admonish her on her departure that "she be respectful and cautious, and should not go against the wishes of her husband" (必敬必戒, 無違夫子). See *Mencius* 3B2.

61 T.142(2).865a17–20.

62 T.142(2).865a21–b2.

63 T.142(2).865b3–8.

64 The titles of these scriptures scatter in *juan* 2, 3, 4, and 5 of Sengyou's *Chu sanzang ji ji*. See T.2145(55).5b–40c.

5 Immortal parents and universal kin

Family values in medieval Daoism

Livia Kohn

The Daoist religion in medieval China developed in three major phases or stages. First, in the second and third centuries CE, there were the communal movements of Great Peace and Celestial Masters, whose followers lived together in family and village units, paid taxes to the religious leadership, and worked together in preparation of the millennial new age soon to arise. Following this, in the fourth and fifth centuries, new revelations from various Daoist heavens were received by aristocratic seekers, in both north and south China, and new schools grew, including Highest Clarity, Numinous Treasure, and the new Celestial Masters. Numinous Treasure in particular integrated large portions of the Buddhist worldview and ritual into the Daoist system, enhancing its growth into a fully organized religion. The third phase, finally, developed in the sixth and seventh centuries with the integration of the various Daoist schools into one system under the umbrella of the Three Caverns. More Buddhist doctrine and organization were integrated, and Daoism developed a full-fledged monastic institution together with more sophisticated doctrines and elaborate religious practices.

The concept of filial piety (*xiao*) in the context of these developments tends to focus on the relationship between the present generation and its ancestors and descendants. Ancestors were commonly seen as potential obstacles to the religious attainment of Daoists, mainly because their sins were visited upon their descendants and thus obstructed the latter's salvation. This notion was first formulated in the Later Han dynasty, in the context of the Great Peace movement, as the doctrine of "inherited evil." It meant that all misdeeds and negativity of the ancestors did not die with them but, unless expiated in some way or another, remained to haunt the descendants for generations.

This family consciousness of the early movements is also evident in their collections of rules, where living with the family and observing propriety toward one's relatives are emphasized as important virtues – as they are in the later rules of Complete Perfection. In addition, as Daoism developed further, the doctrine of karma and retribution was added to its family values, and filial piety became a key factor in the creation of good karma.

This is expressed both in medieval collections of rules and in the main Daoist scripture on filial piety, a text of the Tang dynasty.

In the various medieval schools of Daoism, on the other hand, otherworldly realization became more important than family relationships in this life, and practitioners were encouraged to not limit themselves to their own families but behave properly to everyone and spread universal virtue and salvation. However, this was possible only when one's ancestors were at peace – more specifically one's ancestors of seven generations who, as long as they lingered in a shadowy underworld or languished in the hells, would not allow the practitioner to attain full cosmic freedom. As a result, various rituals developed that focused on expiating one's own and the ancestors' sins, culminating in the transfer of one's forebears from the realm of the dead in Fengdu 酆都 to the registry of immortality in the Southern Palace (Nangong 南宮).

With the emergence of the monastic institution, moreover, a close connection was established between the good karma of becoming a monk or nun and previous behavior – both of oneself in former lives and of one's ancestors up to seven generations. Further, support of religious institutions in this life would lead to great benefits for generations to come, making donations to monasteries an act of responsible family planning. Beyond this, however, filial care expressed through the monastic connection was geared toward the transformation of the cosmos at large, to the universal salvation of the world, making family values in medieval Daoism part of a cosmic rather than personal endeavor.

Inherited evil

> If at this time [when the sinner dies], the reckoning is not complete and further disasters are needed, they will be visited upon the person's descendants, sons and grandsons. Should that not be sufficient either, they extend to his retainers and servants. The latter, of course, have no idea where they went wrong and only know that they are suffering from a reduced life expectancy.[1]

This is the gist of the doctrine of inherited evil (*chengfu* 承負), the key to understanding fate in medieval Daoism. It goes back to the ancient thinking of mutual reciprocity and the retribution of deeds caused by the ancestors. They, as early as the Shang dynasty (1766–1025 BCE?), were held responsible for good and bad fortune. Ancestors acted benevolently if they were treated well and given the right kinds of sacrifices, but caused disasters if neglected or offended.[2] Poor harvests, natural catastrophes, and other misfortunes were seen as caused by the "curse of an ancestor," and much political and religious energy was expanded to either pacify the ancestors or divine their will with the help of the so-called oracle bones.[3]

Under the Zhou (1025–256 BCE), the system of reciprocity on the social plane continued supernaturally with the notion that the dead could persecute or haunt the living for misbehavior and evil deeds, on occasion people even killing themselves so that they could become obnoxious specters and haunt their enemies in revenge.[4] Overlying this concept, a new level of reciprocity was developed with the idea of the "mandate of heaven/sky" (*tianming* 天命), which added a moral dimension to the ritual world of the Shang by indicating the right of a certain upright person or family to rule the country. In the Han dynasty (206 BCE to 220 CE), the notion of personal retribution of deeds was expanded to include good and bad fortune experienced in this life. It is documented in several anecdotes about military leaders who ordered massacres of enemy soldiers and found themselves in disgrace or dire straits later on, as well as in reports on immorality seekers who "practiced a variety of charitable acts – the feeding of orphans, the repair of roads and bridges, and so forth – in the quest for eternal life."[5] At the same time, collective punishments became the legal norm, holding entire families responsible for the misdeeds of one.

In medieval Daoism, the various notions of ancestral wrath, personal retribution, and collective punishments were joined in the doctrine of inherited evil. Indicating an especially close relationship between ancestors and descendants, it stated that the actions of the ancestors (*cheng*) were put as a load (*fu*) on the backs of their descendants.[6] As Ge Hong's 葛洪 *Baopuzi* 抱樸子 (Book of the Master Who Embraces Simplicity) warns:

> Whenever you interfere with or steal another's goods, the gods may take into account [the life expectancy] of your wife, children, and other members of your household in order to compensate for it, causing them to die, even if not immediately.[7]

In greater detail the notion was formulated in the *Taiping jing* 太平經 (Scripture of Great Peace, DZ 1101), dated in its first inception to the second and its reconstituted edition to the sixth century.[8] Here "inherited evil" meant that "when someone strives to be good but evil results, this is because he receives and transmits the mistakes men have formerly made."[9] The kind of evil that was inherited could be created physically in bad deeds or mentally in a hostile or resentful attitude. Its existence took some pressure off the present generation in that reasons for failure could be found among earlier family members, but at the same time heightened the responsibility of the individual for his many generations of descendants.[10]

Chengfu also extended to other social units beyond the family, such as the groups of five families that had joint responsibility according to the legal codes, and in the case of an emperor involving the fortune of the entire country.[11] Daoist practice, purifications, exorcisms, the establishment of an open and harmonious community, as well as individual meditations, were all geared toward the alleviation and eventual termination of this situation, in the hope of creating a purer world of Great Peace.[12]

The same notion is explained in considerable detail in the *Chisongzi zhongjie jing*, which consists of a dialogue between the two venerable immortals Huangdi 黃帝 (Yellow Emperor) and Chisongzi (Master Redpine). They raise various issues regarding fate and life, such as why people are different in their fortunes, why there are miscarriages and the deaths of infants, how one can improve one's lot, and how one can dissolve the sins already accumulated.[13] On inherited evil, the text says:

> The Yellow Emperor asked: "On occasion there are those dying while still in the womb or those who only live to a see a few years. They have not yet done anything in the world, so what prohibition or taboo would they have violated?"
>
> Master Redpine explained: "Things like these happen because the sins of the ancestors and forebears are bequeathed upon the descendants, causing them calamities. Since antiquity, heroes and wise men have established corresponding teachings, which have been documented in the books of the immortals. They all admonish people to do good and know the very incipience of evil, so that even from high antiquity on they can give nothing but good fortune to their numerous generations of descendants."[14]

Prosperous families, therefore, have to thank their long line of morally good ancestors for their good fortune, whereas slaves and outcasts are inheriting their forebears' bad inclinations. Moral rectitude or turpitude thus continues over generations, offering both consolation for bad situations and a good hope for the future. There is always opportunity for improvement, and if the entire world improves, Great Peace is reached.

The text is even more specific in defining the benefits and disasters caused by the good or bad deeds of one's forebears, stating that with increased deeds, fortunes increase also. For example, "200 good deeds will allow a person to be famous for many generations and cause his descendents to receive official employment," while "400 good deeds cause his sons and grandsons to be rich and noble for four generations, receiving outstanding official employment." Nine hundred good deeds will make his family bring forth sages, and for 1,000 good deeds his family will bring forth Immortals (4b). Similarly, bad deeds accumulate over generations.

> Three hundred evil deeds, and his family for generations will bring forth humble and lowly people. Four hundred evil deeds, and his sons and grandsons for generations will be poor and lowly, destitute and beggars . . . Seven hundred evil deeds, and his sons and grandsons will be the five kinds of rebels, unfilial and criminal people. Eight hundred evil deeds, and his family will bring forth rebellious ministers and unfilial sons who cause destruction and beheadings to the entire clan.
>
> (5a–5b)

It is interesting to note that filial piety and the lack of it are understood as themselves the result of irresponsible and unfilial behavior of people several generations back, thus creating a circular relationship between the misfortune and misbehavior of people in one generation and those earlier and later.

Families in this life

The early movements not only saw family relationships on the ancestral plane, but also placed a strong value on intergenerational integrity in this life. One of the earliest surviving codes of the Celestial Masters, for example, is the *Laojun shuo yibai bashi jie* 老君說一百八十戒 (*180 Precepts Revealed by Lord Lao*).[15] It does not address issues of filial piety *per se*, but emphasizes that followers should respect the harmony of others, never "causing a rift in other people's families," spying on their privacy, ignoring their taboos, or wrongly venerating their ancestors (nos 41, 99, 113, 159). Moreover, they should not "form a party or clique on the basis of their own families" (no. 61), but instead should burn incense and pray "for the good of the myriad families and the establishment of Great Peace on earth" (no. 152).

Along similar lines, the *Nüqing guilü* 女青鬼律 (*Nüqing's Statutes against Demons*, DZ 790), another fourth-century text of the Celestial Masters, says that lack of filial piety, resulting from bad family relations, will cause the subtraction of 180 days from one's life expectancy (1b–2a). Irresolute behavior and disrespect toward one's own and others' families, moreover, will bring the loss of 3,000 days and bad fortune for one's descendants for seven generations (2a). It also says:

> Do not live in a separate dwelling from your father or son or otherwise allow your family to scatter. Such violation will cause the subtraction of 22 days.

> Do not go against the orders of your parents and wander about in the four directions. Do not establish yourself as a man of perfect energy and claim you had harmonized it all by yourself. Such violation will cause the subtraction of 320 days.
>
> (2b–3a)

The notion that bad moral behavior has a direct impact on one's life expectancy stems from the belief that the celestial administration monitors people's deeds and adds or subtracts days of life accordingly. The first passage to describe this explicitly is found in the *Baopuzi* in connection with a description of the activities of the Three Corpses or Deathbringers (*sanshi* 三尸), supernatural parasites that monitor human behavior from within. It says:

> On every *gengshen* 庚申 day [of the sixty-day cycle], they [the Three Corpses] ascend to heaven and file a report on our misdeeds with the Ruler of Fates [*Siming* 司命]. Similarly during the last night of the

month, the Stove God makes a journey to heaven and reports on our behavior. For the more important misdeeds, three hundred days are deducted from our lives. For lesser sins, they take off three days.[16]

Again, filial piety is seen not only as a virtue in present relationships but as a behavior with cosmic consequences for one's own life and that of others.

Rules that honor and preserve family harmony are also found in the *Guanshen dajie* 觀身大戒 (*The Great Precepts of Self-Observation*, DZ 1364), a text of the fifth or sixth century that outlines a total of 300 integrated Daoist precepts and guidelines for advanced practice. Its first section on community rules emphasizes that Daoists should not live separate from their families (no. 121) or form a party on their basis (no. 119). They must not encourage others to leave home (no. 91), plot against their elders or parents (no. 176), or generally behave in an unfilial manner (no. 177). The very same precepts appear also in the *Zhongji jie* 中極戒 (*Precepts of Middle Ultimate*), the advanced rules of the later school of Complete Perfection, which generally placed a greater emphasis on filial piety, making it the first of their elementary ten precepts: "Do not be disloyal or unfilial, without benevolence or good faith. Always exhaust your allegiance to your lord and family, be sincere in your relation to the myriad beings."[17]

While this strong emphasis on filial piety as a religious rule dates from the Song and beyond, there is a clear sense that good relationships with one's family members are necessary for the advancement and salvation of religious followers. Most typically, lack of filial piety is understood as producing karma that will cause Daoists to suffer hell, bad rebirth, loneliness, and the inability to attain immortality. The clearest formulation of this view is found in the *Shier shangpin quanjie* 十二上品全誡 (*Twelve Highest Precepts with Explanation*, DZ 182), a text associated with the Numinous Treasure School. It says:

The Eleventh Precept: Do Not Fail in Filial Piety.

The Heavenly Worthy said: Among the students of the Dao, anyone who has received the precepts of the perfected must not lack in filial piety, be disobedient in his heart, or go against the wishes of his or her parents. Never fail to give them your proper respect and love, never turn your back upon your ancestors and kin. Never fail to think of them with loving care and gratitude, nor fail to develop proper feelings of shame.

People who fail in filial piety may expect six kinds of retribution:

1 They will be punished by the laws of the state.
2 They will be excluded from the community of sentient beings.
3 They will fall into hell and suffer from the ten kinds of torture.

4 They will be born as owls and the like, living in constant battle with their kin.
5 They will, even if born on the human plane, be burdened by past karma which ensures that they will suffer ever more vexations in personal relationships.
6 They will roam about hither and thither all alone, and the thunder of heaven will descend upon them and kill them.

Lack of filial piety is a great evil no perfected commits!

May all bad filial karma be dissolved completely!

(9a–b)

The retribution for lack of filial piety in the form of both earthly and heavenly justice and through punishment in the hells and by bad rebirth is further expanded in the *Taishang Laojun shuo bao fumu enzhong jing* 太上老君說報父母恩重經 (*Scripture on Repaying Parents' Kindness, Revealed by the Highest Lord Lao*, DZ 662).[18] This Daoist text, which dates from the Tang dynasty, is modeled on the Buddhist *Foshuo fumu en nanbao jing* 佛說父母恩難報經 (*Sutra on the Difficulty in Repaying Parents' Kindness, Spoken by the Buddha*), allegedly translated by An Shigao 安世高 of the Han dynasty but probably a later work.[19]

It begins with Lord Lao holding court in the heavens in the presence of 50,000 sages. Then the perfected Haikong Zhizang 海空智藏 rises and asks about repaying the kindness of one's parents.[20] Lord Lao appreciates the question and proceeds to give an extended sermon, which focuses on the hardships that parents, especially mothers, undergo in carrying and raising their children. He concludes by offering the assembled sages a vision of hell, where unfilial children are punished, and of heaven, where filial offspring enjoy the pleasures of the celestial halls. Neglecting one's parents, moreover, is described as being on the same level as slandering the Three Treasures and insulting Daoist recluses (5b), placing the personal practice into a larger cosmic context. The final section of the text, moreover, provides an autobiography of Lord Lao and his experience with his mothers in several incarnations, plus a description of the main monthly and annual rites to be held in honor of one's parents. The text echoes Buddhist arguments from the same period and claims that it was a foremost filial act to repay one's mother and save her from suffering in hell, preferably by either becoming a monk oneself or giving donations in support of the monastic institution.[21]

While medieval Daoists placed a certain emphasis on the need to honor one's parents in this life – and with the help of religious institutions and rituals – the more dominant tendency was to see parental care in the larger context of religious attainment and karmic retribution. If a person could not even feel compassion for the people who gave up so much to raise him, how could he ever develop the universal ethics necessary for the higher realization of the Dao?

Seven generations

A similar thinking in terms of karmic connection and the creation of a more universal mind is also at the forefront of the discussion of the Daoists' relationship to their ancestors. Most commonly these are described as one's ancestors of seven generations, a number adopted from Buddhism. The expression "parents of seven generations" occurs first in the *Yulanpen jing* 盂蘭盆經.[22] However, it refers not to ancestors but to the parents who raised the person for the past seven lives. The notion was therefore linked more with the doctrine of transmigration than with ancestral worship, but in Daoism it came to be strictly associated with the latter and led to particular concern with one's patrilineal ancestors of seven generations.[23]

The bad deeds and potential wrath of one's ancestors can be neutralized in several ways.[24] The best is to observe the basic precepts of the religion, which forbid – like their Buddhist counterpart – killing, stealing, lying, sexual misconduct, and intoxication, as well as the harboring of jealousy, hatred, ill will, and envy toward others. This basic moral attitude and behavior will give karmic relief to both self and ancestors. As the *Zuigen pin* 罪根品 (*The Root of Sin*, DZ 457), an early collection of Numinous Treasure rules, says:

> Anyone who upholds the precepts firmly will have his merit inscribed in the ten heavens. His good fortune will extend to his ancestors of seven generations, who will duly be taken out of the long night of the nine underworlds and ascend to the Southern Palace of the heavens. Oneself, one will enter the realm of light and, with good karma uninterrupted, attain spirit immortality.
>
> (1.6b)

The belief here was that the dead would be subject to the otherworldly administration of the Six Palaces of Fengdu. As the *Tianguan santu jing* 天關三圖經 (*Threefold Illustrated Scripture of Going beyond the Heavenly Pass*, DZ 1366), a manual of Highest Clarity visualizations and chants, describes it:

> Mount Fengdu is located in the north, in the position of the celestial stem *gui* 癸. Therefore the northeast is known as the Gate of Demons [*gui* 鬼], the root of the energy of death. The mountain is 2,600 miles high and 30,000 miles in circumference. Its grotto heaven begins right beneath the mountain; it measures 15,000 miles in circumference . . .
>
> Its Six Palaces are governed by the Northern Emperor. They are the Six Heavens of the demons and the ghosts of the dead. Here the institution that governs people's death is located. In all cases, a death summons is issued at these Six Palaces on Mount Fengdu.[25]

The Six Palaces are hell-type places, where the dead are not only administered but also punished. They have picturesque names, such as the Palace of Infamy and Death, of the Destruction of Faith, and of the Seven Ancestral Misdeeds, and show an early influence of Buddhist hells. Their officers are immortals of a low rank who work their way up to the higher realms in centuries of dedicated service. Even they, although no longer undergoing active punishment, still suffer from judgment and have to perform extended duties. In contrast to the ordinary dead and their officers, ancestors that have become immortals registered in the Southern Palace are happy and at ease.

As the *Shangpin dajie* 上品大誡 (*Great Precepts of the Highest Ranks*, DZ 177), another early scripture of Numinous Treasure, describes it:

> Anyone in the ten directions who observes the precepts will forever encounter splendid and prosperous families to be born in. He or she will be healthy and strong in body and mind. The gods of the earth will serve as his guards, and the officers of the Three Worlds will receive him formally. The souls and spirits of such a person's ancestors up to seven generations will ascend to the Southern Palace, where they will be clothed and feasted at heavenly banquets. They will all attain an early rebirth, where they inevitably return to the human plane and come to life in royal families. For ever and ever, in every generation, their karma will be linked with the Dao itself.[26]

The observance of the precepts thus offered a good initial way toward clearing one's own karmic burden and that inherited from one's ancestors. In addition, however, formalities of expiation were considered essential, notably a rite known as the "Purgation of Mud and Ashes" (*tutan zhai* 塗炭齋). This was essentially an elaborate ceremonial punishment, believed to "acquire the remission of sins, not only for the penitents but also for hundreds of thousands of their ancestors, parents, uncles, and brothers – living and dead. Its merit derived from 'suffering restraint', mortifying the flesh and fettering the body."[27] The ritual anticipated the tortures of hell and thus could ward off calamities threatening to strike in this life and the next; it closely imitated the trials undergone by criminals condemned by the courts of the world.

Participants would appear wearing sackcloth and with their faces smeared with soot. They would chant prayers of sin and repentance, then, guided by the officiant, undergo a ritual punishment. Gradually the rhythm of the chanting would increase, the tension of the punishment would rise, until the crowd, all excited, lost control in ecstasy and began to roll wildly in the mud. The master of ceremonies then calmed them down again, to move on toward the next crescendo.[28] A typical petition runs as follows:

We, this family _____,
Performing the Pure Rite for the Great Pardon,
Light lamps to display brightness,
And illuminate the heavens.
For three days and three nights,
Through all six [double-hour] periods,
We carry out repentance for our Pardon.
May our millions of forebears and ancestors,
All our fathers, mothers, uncles, brothers,
Whether dead already or to die in future,
Down to ourselves, participating here,
May we all
Be free from all the evil
For kalpas still to come!
For millions of generations,
We have committed sins and accumulated burdens.
Reverently we now trust in the method of this purgation:
May our family be complete and ordered!
May we be bathed and cleansed to purity![29]

Transfer registration

Another way to ensure the karmic purity and happiness of one's ancestors was to ritually transfer their registration from the realm of the dead in Fengdu to the registry of immortality in the Southern Palace. One form involved the practice of visualization and ecstatic excursions, during which the adept prayed for the transfer not only of his own registers from death to life but also of those of his ancestors. This is documented in the *Tianguan santu jing*, where adepts invoke the gods,

Oh, Yin Essence of Northern Womb!
Spirit Soul and Spirit of the Celestial Jade!
Oh, Nine Lords of Highest Jade!
Merge and transform ten thousand times into one single spirit!
Erase all my yang sins from the registers of Great Yin!
Transfer all my yin energy into the Realm of Great Yang!
Let me traverse the seven stars to cut off death!
Let me open up the six harmonies at the Heavenly Pass!
Let me free my ancestors for seven generations from the three bad
   rebirths!
Let us all come back to life in the Southern Palace![30]

Another form involves particular rituals at the time of burial. They are specified in the *Mingzhen ke* 明真科 (*Rules for the Illustrious Perfected*, DZ 1411), which says:

Take the five tablets of the "Perfect Text in Cinnabar Writing" and set up five tables in the courtyard to face the five directions. On each of them place one tablet of the text. Then take five pounds of pure gold [iron, in the case of commoners] and from one each cast a dragon, so you have five dragons altogether, which you place next to the tablets of the text. In addition, take [silk] painted in five colors as a pledge to the Five Emperors.[31]

For an emperor or a noble, one bolt of silk is used, with lesser amounts for people of descending ranks, just as aristocrats have their dragons made from gold while commoners use iron. The rite ensures that the deceased is covered in an appropriate garment during his wait for transformation, while the dragons, cast and pointed in the five directions, carry the message of his impending transfer in registration to all the relevant officers of the otherworld.[32] As the *Wulian jing* 五錬經 (*Scripture of Fivefold Purification*, DZ 369) says, "Through proper purification the souls of one's ancestors up to nine generations can leave their abode of perpetual night and enter the heavens of radiant light."[33]

Yet another common way of helping one's ancestors to an existence of permanent bliss is casting statues of Daoist gods, most commonly Lord Lao or the Heavenly Worthy, with inscriptions that implore the deity to grant entry into the heavenly halls to the donor's ancestors up to seven generations.[34] A nicely preserved object of this kind is the Sovereign Lord Lao of Yao Boduo 姚伯多, a statue dated to 496 that is today housed in the Yao District Museum.[35] Showing a rather sketchy image of the god in front, it has inscriptions on all its sides, focusing on the good fortune of the emperor and the state, the family's present generation, and their Yao ancestors. In relation to the latter, the text says:

We pray that
All the members of Daoist Yao Boduo's family –
His three forebears and five ancestors,
His fathers and mothers of seven generations,
All his relatives, long deceased or dead lately –
If currently in the three bad rebirths,
May speedily be rescued and liberated!
May they forever be separated from
The suffering of the dark hell prisons,
And ascend to the Southern Palace,
The true home of the immortals!
Should they, again, be reborn as humans,
May they have lords and kings for their fathers![36]

This passage also documents vividly the parallel belief in permanent otherworldly resting places of the ancestors and the possibility of them taking rebirth, containing good wishes, as it were, for all eventualities of a person's post-mortem destiny. Ideally, of course, all one's ancestors should be transferred to heaven, thus being entirely removed from the mutuality-based relationship between the dead and the living, needing no more feeding and causing no more havoc among their descendants. The transfer of one's ancestors to the heavenly halls of pure light thus simultaneously means the complete exoneration of the descendants from all kinds of inherited evil, assuring those presently living of a highly prosperous and fortunate life and increasing their own chances of a successful ascent to the heavens.[37] The transfer of ancestors to immortals is therefore not an entirely altruistic practice but has immediate consequences for the devotee's life, just as the various rituals of healing by easing ancestral suffering in the hells serve primarily the living, reinforcing yet again in a roundabout way the mutuality and filial piety dominant in mainstream Chinese religion.[38]

The monastic connection

With the establishment of an integrated Daoist organization in the sixth and seventh centuries, the karmic impact of filial piety was formulated in greater detail and the role of Daoists and their institutions as focal points of karmic activity increased. For example, the *Qianzhen ke* 千真科 (*Rules for the Thousand Perfected*, DZ 1410) says:

> Recluses should at all times have a loyal and upright demeanor – whether coming or going, moving or staying, you must strive to set all things and people right.
> First, set yourself right.
> Second, set your disciples right.
> Third, set both the excellent and the lowly right.
> Fourth, set the distant followers of the divine law right.
> Fifth, set the obstinate ordinary people right.
> Doing the first, you serve as a model for others.
> Doing the second, you help imbuing all with righteousness.
> Doing the third, you make both big and small to be obedient.
> Doing the fourth, you will help spread the righteousness of the divine law.
> Doing the fifth, you will widely increase wisdom and purity.
> Only one who can act like this truly deserves to be called a Daoist.
> If you don't even manage to do the first, you will be hated by others and your disciples will have no respect for you. They will come to think badly of their teachers and elders, and in the monastery there will be no proper rules and prohibitions. Big and small, noble and humble will be mixed together, there will be neither filial piety nor righteousness. The distant crowd of followers, too, will hate each other, ignorantly increasing their fields of sin. They will be quite unable to establish the

awe-inspiring kindness of the great Dao and there will be all sorts of evil and crime.[39]

Here Daoists are no longer concerned only with the attainment of immortality for themselves and the purification of their ancestors, but have become responsible for the transformation of the world at large into a better place and a realm of goodness and morality. If they do not set themselves right, they cause disrespect for themselves and by extension lack of filial piety and propriety among the wider populace. The responsibility for the moral salvation of the entire world is thus placed on their shoulders.

This enormous burden is justified in the *Yinyuan jing* 因緣經 (*Scripture of Karmic Retribution*, DZ 336) of the Sui dynasty, which is also cited at length in the *Fengdao kejie*.[40] It attributes great responsibility to monks and nuns because of their particular karmic standing:

> Whoever, over seven lives [in the seventh generation], rejoices in the Dao, honors the precepts and follows the divine law, gives freely in charity and aids the poor, prays for the living and helps save the dead, always acts with compassion and presents offerings to the Three Treasures without being slack or lazy, will be born in the body of an ordained monk or nun.[41]

Only those who have been involved with the Dao over many lifetimes or generations can therefore be monks or nuns of the religion. They should have the corresponding karmic strength and moral mettle to serve as ideal models. Accordingly, only people with a strong Daoist background are considered candidates for successful ordination. The *Fengdao kejie* specifies a total of twenty-five kinds of people who "can be caused to become ordained monks or nuns." The first five are:

1   Those whose families have worshiped the Dao for generations and who believe and delight in the divine law of the scriptures
2   Those who themselves over several lives have worshiped the Dao and who believe and delight in the divine law of the scriptures
3   Those who in this life actively worship the Dao and who believe and delight in the divine law of the scriptures
4   Those whose families have been pure and good for generations and have believed and worshiped the perfection of the right path
5   Those who themselves over several lives have been pure and good.[42]

The merits accumulated in this life are thus similar to those gained over several previous lives and match those created by one's family. The Daoist monk or nun is seen as the carrier of cosmic power by virtue of his or her good karmic deeds, which are enhanced by those of former lives and those created by the family. The individual thus never stands alone but is part of a larger unit, be it the continuity over lifetimes or the connectedness with a family. Only when the person is morally strong within this expanded context can he or she be a true moral catalyst and guide the world toward greater harmony and the practice of perfect filial piety.

Filial benefits for generations to come, moreover, are also closely linked with support for Daoist institutions and recluses. Venerating the Three Treasures will create filial sons over many generations, while copying the scriptures will cause one's descendants to be wise and sagely. Similarly, donating facilities for meditation and retreats brings nobility upon one's descendants, while providing incense and fragrant oils will cause one to have handsome sons and grandsons. Assisting others in becoming Daoist masters will cause one's descendants to attain rebirth in the Middle Kingdom, and practicing Daoist rites will cause them to flourish and to have ancestors who are well satisfied and bring good fortune.[43]

All these various activities are not ultimately geared toward creating a better fortune for individual families, although the enticement is certainly there. The final vision of Daoists, in setting up recluses as moral models and propagating the practice of a morality that integrates good deeds for religious institutions with success of future generations, is the cosmic transformation or universal salvation of the world at large. Ultimately, filial piety as a virtue directed toward one's own family must be superseded by the awareness of the karmic interconnectedness of all – family must be everybody's family, children must be everybody's children. The *Guanshen dajie* describes this:

> May I regard the parents of others like my own.
> May I regard the children of others like my own.
> May I regard the self of others more importantly than my own.
> May I regard the wounds and pains of others more importantly than my own.
> May I regard the shame and evil of others more importantly than my own.[44]

The text then summarizes the goal of this new vision by saying "May my fate and karma be cut off at its roots," propagating a state where all karmic connections and family relations have been dissolved into the greater and higher state of universal salvation.

Conclusion

Filial piety and care for the family were important values in medieval Daoism, as is evident from the various rules and scriptures dedicated to them. However, looking at the overall appearance of these values in the religion, it becomes clear that they are not values in and of themselves. Unlike in Confucian works, the hardships of the parents are emphasized little, and there are no stories about Daoists giving up major benefits or comforts to serve their parents. Instead, it appears that filiality and family care were seen as part of a larger goal, that of the cosmic transformation of all, of guiding the world toward the state of Great Peace. Ultimately, one's own family was less important than the family of all beings, and one's own ancestors were relevant mainly because they could become obstacles to one's attainment of immortality. Care for the parents in this life or for the family in future generations was important because it increased the good karma needed for Daoist achievements, just as the transfer of ancestors to the registry of immortality was essential because their status as "dead" would impede progress.

Family values in medieval Daoism were thus part of the larger picture of cosmic values, and the care offered to one's parents and kin was just one aspect of the veneration one should offer one's true divine parents, as well as of the care one had to develop for all beings and the universe at large. This understanding of filial piety and family values in Daoism matches the evidence also in Buddhism. Here monks were encouraged to leave the family and become recluses away from society, yet many sutras extolled the necessity and benefits of filial piety, and monks frequently made donations to monasteries and organized rituals for the sake of their parents.[45] Filial piety was not, as earlier scholars claimed, unimportant in India and rose to prominence only in Chinese Buddhism; nor was it a special feature of the latter.[46] It was always an essential virtue but not, as in Chinese mainstream or Confucian society, a virtue in and of itself or geared mainly toward the orderly functioning of social life. Instead, it was a virtue that taught caring first on a personal level, and was then expanded to involve care and compassion for all beings: beginning with the family, religious practitioners learned to develop empathy for all and grow into cosmic rather than personal or social beings.

This understanding is further borne out by the actual deeds of Daoists in medieval China. We do not have much information on the relationship Daoists had with their families, but we know that important leaders remained celibate, that women defied their families and social convention to enter Daoist convents, and that religious seekers gave themselves over to the gods even to the point of death in this life.[47]

The latter is especially poignant and also unusually well documented. It involves the life of Zhou Ziliang 周子良, a friend and disciple of the Highest Clarity patriarch Tao Hongjing 陶弘景 (456–536), and is described extensively in the latter's *Zhoushi mingtong ji* 周氏冥通記 (*Record of Mr Zhou's Communications with the Otherworld*, DZ 302). According to this, Zhou first met Tao in Yongjia in 509, when he was twelve years old, became Tao's disciple, and returned with him to the Highest Clarity headquarters on Mount Mao near Nanjing in 512, taking his aunt and his mother along. There he led a life of seclusion, silence, and meditation, beginning soon to have direct contact with various gods in dreams and actively pursued visions.[48] In the summer of 515, the gods presented him with a celestial job offer, informing him that:

at present there is a vacancy in our chancery, and we should like you to fill it. The title and functions will be specified later, and there is no need for overmuch discussion now. You will be summoned in the tenth month of next year, and so should make all necessary preparations.[49]

After being thus ordered to ascend and fill a post in the celestial hierarchy, Zhou continued to receive detailed instructions from the gods, including specifications on: where and how to build his hut; what to eat and how to prepare his food to assure the complete destruction of all body demons; how to perform breathing and gymnastic exercises to gain maximum purity in body and mind; and how to undertake the concoction of the elixir that would eventually transport him upward.[50] In the appointed month (10/516), Zhou readied himself for ascension by sweeping his hut and cleaning his utensils. On his last day, the twenty-seventh,

> he bathed in scented hot water and put on clean clothes. He played chess with [his friend] Wenxing and read books. From time to time he looked at the shadow on the sundial. A little after noon, he got up and said, "The time has come." He then tightened his belt, burned incense, and went to his teacher's scripture room. He did all the rituals addressing himself to the gods in the texts, then went directly back to his hut.[51]

There he lay down and downed the elixir, discovered shortly afterward by his mother and aunt, who were horrified to see him depart and cried: "What have you done, what have you done?"[52] Silencing them with a few words and a wave of his hand, Zhou gave up his earthly connection and passed on to his desired realm of the immortals, fulfilling a fate and realizing a virtue far beyond this world.

Notes

1 *Chisongzi zhongjie jing* 赤松子中戒經 (Essential Precepts of Master Redpine, DZ 185), p. 2a. This is a work of the fourth century. Texts in the Daoist Canon (*Daozang* 道藏, abbreviated DZ) are given according to K. Schipper, *Concordance du Tao Tsang: Titres des ouvrages*, Paris: Publications de l'Ecole Francaise d'Extrême-Orient 1975; page references are cited in the text. See also Livia Kohn, "Counting Good Deeds and Days of Life: The Quantification of Fate in Medieval China," *Asiatische Studien/Etudes Asiatiques*, 52, 1998, p. 842.
2 C. Brokaw, *The Ledgers of Merit and Demerit: Social Change and Moral Order in Late Imperial China*, Princeton, NJ: Princeton University Press, 1991, p. 28.
3 P. U. Unschuld, *Medicine in China: A History of Ideas*, Berkeley: University of California Press, 1985, p. 19.
4 H. Yamazaki 山崎宏, "Rikuchō Zui-Tō jidai no hōō shinkō" 六朝隋唐時代の報應信仰, *Shirin* 史林, 40, no. 6, 1957, p. 456; Y. H. Lin, "The Weight of Mt T'ai: Patterns of Suicide in Traditional Chinese History and Culture," PhD dissertation, University of Wisconsin, Madison, 1990, p. 73.
5 C. Y. Hsü, "The Concept of Predetermination and Fate in the Han," *Early China*, 1, 1975, p. 52; C. Brokaw, *Ledgers of Merit and Demerit*, p. 30.

6 B. Hendrischke, "The Concept of Inherited Evil in the *Taiping Jing*," *East Asian History*, 2, 1991, p. 8; see also Y. Kamitsuka 神塚淑子, "Taiheikyō no shōfu to taihei no riron ni tsuite 太平經の承負と太平の理論について," *Nagoya daigaku kyōyōbu kiyō*, 32, 1988, 41–75; Chen Jing 陳敬, "Taiping jing zhong de chengfu baoying sixiang" 太平經中的承負報應思想, *Zongjiao xue yanjiu* 宗教學研究, 1986, 35–9.

7 *Baopuzi*, DZ 1185, 6.7b; J. R. Ware, *Alchemy, Medicine and Religion in the China of* AD *320*, Cambridge, MA: MIT Press 1966, p. 117. The *Baopuzi* was compiled about 320 CE. Ware's study contains a complete translation of the "Inner Chapters"; for details on the life of the author, see N. Sivin, "On the 'Pao-p'u-tzu nei-p'ien' and the Life of Ko Hung," *Isis*, 40, 1969, 388–91; for more on Ge Hong and a translation of the "Outer Chapters," see J. Sailey, *The Master Who Embraces Simplicity: A Study of the Philosophy of Ko Hung (* AD *283–343)*, San Francisco: Chinese Materials Center, 1978.

8 Wang Ming 王明, *Taiping jing hejiao* 太平經合校, Beijing: Zhonghua, 1960. The textual history and composition of the *Taiping jing* is a knotty scholarly problem that has been written about variously. See especially B. Kandel, *Taiping jing: The Origin and Transmission of the "Scripture on General Welfare" – The History of an Unofficial Text*, Hamburg: Gesellschaft für Natur-und Völkerkunde Ostasiens, 1979; and J. O. Petersen, "The Early Traditions Relating to the Han-dynasty Transmission of the *Taiping jing*," *Acta Orientalia*, 50, 1989, 133–71; and *Acta Orientalia*, 51, 165–216. On its contents, see M. Kaltenmark, "The Ideology of the T'ai-p'ing-ching," in H. Welch and A. Seidel (eds), *Facets of Taoism*, New Haven, CT: Yale University Press, 1979, pp. 19–52.

9 B. Hendrischke, "Concept of Inherited Evil," p. 10.

10 Ibid., p. 11. The "extension of errors" or bad fortune to one's descendants is called *yanwu* and as such mentioned variously in early Daoist literature. See E. Zürcher, "Buddhist Influence on Early Taoism," *T'oung-pao*, 66, 1980, p. 137, n. 98; K. Akizuki 秋月觀英, "Rikuchō dōkyō ni okeru ōhōsetsu no hatten 六朝道教における報應說の發展," *Hirosaki daigaku jinbun shakai* 弘前大學人文社會, 33, 1964, p. 36.

11 B. Hendrischke, "Concept of Inherited Evil," pp. 16–17.

12 Ibid., pp. 18–19.

13 L. Kohn, "Counting Good Deeds and Days of Life," p. 837.

14 *Chisongzi zhongjie jing*, pp. 1b–2a; L. Kohn, "Counting Good Deeds and Days of Life," p. 844.

15 The text does not survive as a separate scripture in the Daoist canon. It is found in *Yunji qiqian* 雲笈七籤 (DZ 1032), 39.1a–14b; *Laojun jinglü* 老君經律 (DZ 786), 2a–12b; *Yaoxiu keyi jielü chao* 要修科儀戒律鈔 (DZ 463), 5.14a–19a. It is also extant in two Dunhuang manuscripts, pp. 4731 and 4562. For a discussion of its history and relevance, see H.-H. Schmidt, "Die hundertachtzig Vorschriften von Lao-chün," in G. Naundorf, K. H. Pohl, and H.-H. Schmidt (eds), *Religion und Philosophie in Ostasien: Festschrift für Hans Steininger*, Würzburg: Königshausen and Neumann, 1985, pp. 151–9; M. Kobayashi, "The Celestial Masters under the Eastern Jin and Liu–Song Dynasties," *Taoist Resources*, 3, no. 2, 1992, 17–45; B. Penny, "Buddhism and Daoism in *The 180 Precepts Spoken by Lord Lao*," *Taoist Resources*, 6, no. 2, 1996, 1–16. On the preface, see S. Maeda 前田繁樹, "Rōkun setsu ippyaku hachiju kaijō no seiritsu ni tsuite 老君說一百八十戒序の成立について," *Tōyō no shisō to shūkyō* 東洋の思想と宗教, 2, 1985, 81–94. A complete English translation is found in B. Hendrischke and B. Penny, "*The 180 Precepts Spoken by Lord Lao*: A Translation and Textual Study," *Taoist Resources*, 6, no. 2, 1996, 17–29.

16 *Baopuzi, juan* 6, pp. 5a–b; J. R. Ware, *Alchemy, Medicine, and Religion*, pp. 115–16; see also L. Kohn, "Kōshin: A Taoist Cult in Japan. Part II: Historical Development," *Japanese Religions* 20, no. 1, 1995, 34–55.

17 *Chuzhen jie* 初真戒, DZ 180. Similarly the *Yuqing jing* 玉清經 (*Scripture of Jade Clarity*, DZ 1312, 1.33a–b) and the *Daofa huiyuan* 道法會元 (*A Corpus of Daoist Ritual*, DZ 1220, 54.5a–b) place filial piety first among their precepts. See H. Hackmann, *Die dreihundert Mönchsgebote des chinesischen Taoismus*, Amsterdam: Koninklijke Akademie van Wetenshapen, 1931.

18 A shorter version of the same text and "Revealed by the Highest Lord of Dark Heaven" is found in DZ 663. Another very similar scripture is found in Chapter 7 of the *Taishang cibei daochang xiaozai jiuyou chan* 太上慈悲道場消災九幽懺 (*Repentences of the Highest Lord to Dissolve the Disasters of Ninefold Darkness and Celebrate Compassion*, DZ 543). For a comparison between these various Daoist and the Buddhist version of the text, see Xie Mingling 謝明玲, "Butsu setsu fubo enshō kyō to Taijō rōkun setsu hō fubo enshō kyō to so no kankei ni tsuite 佛說父母恩重經と太上老君說報父母恩重經とその關係について," *Tōyō daigaku kenkyū seiyin kiyō* 東洋大學研究生院紀要, 21, 1984, 219–32.

19 For the sutra, see *Taishō Tripitaka* (abbreviated T.) 684, 16.778–9. K. Ch'en, *The Chinese Transformation of Buddhism*, Princeton, NJ: Princeton University Press, 1973, pp. 37–40.

20 Haikong Zhizang is the main protagonist of a Tang philosophical Daoist text, the *Haikong zhizang jing* (Scripture of Haikong Zhizang, DZ 9), which is discussed in M. Sunayama 沙山稔, *Zui Tō dōkyō shisōshi kenkyū* 隋唐道教思想史研究, Tokyo: Hirakawa, 1990; S. Kamata 鎌田茂雄, *Chūgoku bukkyō shisoshi no kenkyū* 中國佛教思想史の研究, Tokyo: Shunjūsha, 1969, pp. 83–96.

21 For details on the mother–son relationship in Buddhism and arguments exploiting it to the benefit of the monastic and priestly institution, see A. Cole, *Mothers and Sons in Chinese Buddhism*, Stanford, CA: Stanford University Press, 1998.

22 *Ullambana Sūtra*; T. 686, 16.779–80; see S. F. Teiser, *The Ghost Festival in Medieval Chinese Religion*, Princeton, NJ: Princeton University Press, 1988.

23 Y. Kamitsuka "Lao-tzu in Six Dynasties Sculpture," in L. Kohn and M. LaFargue (eds), *Lao-tzu and the Tao-te-ching*, Albany: State University of New York Press, 1998, p. 78.

24 See P. Nickerson, "Taoism, Death, and Bureaucracy in Early Medieval China," PhD dissertation, University of California, Berkeley, 1996.

25 DZ 1366, 10b–11b; L. Kohn, *The Taoist Experience: An Anthology*, Albany: State University of New York Press, 1993, p. 265; see also C. Mollier, "La méthode de l'empereur du nord du mont Fengdu: une tradition exorciste du taoïsme médiévale," *T'oung-pao*, 83, 1997, 329–85.

26 DZ 177, 5b. The same is also emphasized in the *Taiji zhenren shuo ershisi menjie jing* 太極真人說二十四門戒經 (*Scripture of Twenty-four Precepts for Disciples Revealed by the Perfected of Great Ultimate*, DZ 183), 7a.

27 C. Benn, "Daoist Ordination and Zhai Rituals," in L. Kohn (ed.), *Daoism Handbook*, Leiden: E. Brill, 2000, p. 311.

28 H. Maspero, *Taoism and Chinese Religion*, trans. F. Kierman, Amherst: University of Massachusetts Press, 1981, p. 381.

29 *Wushang biyao* 無上秘要 (*Secret Essentials of the Most High*, DZ 1138), 50.1b–2a; L. Kohn, *The Taoist Experience*, pp. 109–10.

30 2b–3a; Kohn, *The Taoist Experience*, p. 260.

31 DZ 1411, 25b; L. Kohn, "Kōshin," p. 74.

32 Dragons were commonly accepted as messengers and frequently cast and thrown into streams in Tang ritual. See E. Chavannes, "Le jet des dragons," *Memoires concernant l'Asie Orientale*, 1919, 55–214.

33 L. Kohn, "Kōshin," p. 74, n. 4; see also S. Bokenkamp, "Death and Ascent in Ling-pao Taoism" *Taoist Resources*, 1, no. 2, 1989, 1–20.

34 S. Matsubara, *Chûgoku bukkyô chôkokushi kenkyû*, Tokyo: Yoshikawa kobunkan, plate 307b.

35 Y. Kamitsuka, "Nanbokuchō jidai no dōkyō zōzō 南北朝時代の道教造像," in M. Tonami 礪波護 (ed.), *Chūgoku chūsei no bunbutsu* 中國中世の文物, Kyoto: Kyoto University, Jimbun kagaku kenkyūjo, 1993, p. 251; see also S. Bokenkamp, "The Yao Boduo Stele as Evidence for the 'Dao-Buddhism' of the Early Lingbao Scriptures," *Cahiers d'Extrême-Asie*, 9, 1997, pp. 55–68.

36 Y. Kamitsuka, "Nanbokuchō," p. 258; and her "Lao-tzu in Six Dynasties Sculpture," pp. 75–6.

37 Some people whose ascent is assured will already be registered above and show this in specific signs on earth. As the *Housheng daojun lieji* 後聖道君列記 (*Annals of the Latter-day Sage, Lord of the Dao*; DZ 442) says, for example, "people [coming to life] with a jade name in the Golden Towers have sunshine in their eyes. They show pure teeth and white blood. Benevolent and compassionate in character, they love immortality. Bright and versatile, they are of high excellence" (9b).

38 See M. Strickmann, "Therapeutische Rituale und das Problem des Bösen im frühen Taoismus," in G. Naundorf, K. H. Pohl, and H. H. Schmidt (eds), *Religion und Philosophie in Ostasien*, pp. 185–200.

39 DZ 1410, 26a. That Daoists should be models for everyone is also emphasized in *Fengdao kejie* 奉道科戒 (*Rules and Precepts for Worshiping the Dao*, DZ 1125, 1.11b), a manual of monastic Daoism of the early seventh century; see L. Kohn, "The Date and Compilation of the *Fengdao kejie*: The First Handbook of Monastic Daoism," *East Asian History*, 13, 1997, 91–118; F. C. Reiter, *The Aspirations and Standards of Taoist Priests in the Early T'ang Period*, Wiesbaden: Harrassowitz, 1998.

40 On *Yinyuan jing*, see L. Kohn, "Steal Holy Food and Come Back as a Viper: Conceptions of Karma and Rebirth in Medieval Daoism," *Early Medieval China*, 4, 1998, 1–48.

41 *Yinyuan jing* DZ 336, 2.1b; *Fengdao kejie*, DZ 1125, 1.9a.

42 *Fengdao kejie*, section 7, 2.7b–8a.

43 *Shangpin dajie* 上品大誡, DZ 177, 8b–9a.

44 DZ 1364, 14b.

45 K. Ch'en, *The Chinese Transformation of Buddhism*, pp. 18–25; G. Schopen, "Filial Piety and the Monk in the Practice of Indian Buddhism: A Question of 'Sinicization' Viewed from the Other Side," in G. Schopen (ed.), *Bones, Stones, and Buddhist Monks*, Honolulu: University of Hawaii Press, 1997, pp. 56–71.

46 Y. H. Jan, "The Role of Filial Piety in Buddhism: A Reappraisal," in C. W. H. Fu and S. A. Wawrytko (eds), *Buddhist Ethics and Modern Society: An International Symposium*, New York: Greenwood Press, 1991, pp. 27–40.

47 Kou Qianzhi 寇謙之, Lu Xiujing 陸修靜, and Tao Hongjing all lived solitary and unmarried lives. For their biographies and several stories about women seekers, see the *Daoxue zhuan* 道學傳 (*Biographies of Students of Dao*) as discussed and translated in S. P. Bumbacher, *The Fragments of the Daoxue zhuan*, Frankfurt: Peter Lang, 2000.

48 W. C. Doub, "A Taoist Adept's Quest for Immortality: A Preliminary Study of the *Chou-shih Ming-t'ung chi* by T'ao Hung-ching," PhD dissertation, University of Washington, Seattle, 1971, pp. 43, 47.

49 M. Strickmann, "On the Alchemy of T'ao Hung-ching," in H. Welch and A. Seidel (eds), *Facets of Taoism*, New Haven, CT: Yale University Press, 1979, p. 161, n. 114.

50 W. C. Doub, "A Taoist Adept's Quest," pp. 49, 58, 68.

51 *Mingtong ji*, DZ 302, 1.3a; W. C. Doub, "A Taoist Adept's Quest," pp. 153–4.

52 M. Strickmann, "On the Alchemy of T'ao Hung-ching," p. 160, n. 113.

6 Filial piety and "authentic parents" in religious Daoism

Mugitani Kunio

The concept of *xiao* (filial piety) in Chinese culture has a long history. The concern with procreation and ancestor worship reaches deep into the ancient Chinese past. The family emerges as the organizing principle of society, and the resultant ethics of filial piety, especially in its Confucian form, becomes a defining feature of Chinese identity. While the Confucian ethical worldview permeates every level of Chinese life and culture, critical challenges do arise occasionally. The first major challenge occurred with the introduction of Buddhism into China. During the period of the Six Dynasties (third to sixth centuries), the Buddhist call to join the *sangha* and to lead a celibate life became a serious point of contention. Another critical current surfaced in religious Daoism, which from the third century attempted to formulate a doctrinal response to the dominant Confucian *xiao* worldview. In this chapter, I focus on this development in early medieval religious Daoist history.[1]

Birth and cosmogony in religious Daoism

What is the early Chinese understanding of the process of human birth? The *Guanzi* 管子 explains that birth arises from "the union of the essence and vital energy between a man and a woman" (男女精氣合).[2] The *Zhouyi* (*Book of Changes*) offers a similar account: "Heaven and earth mesh together, and the myriad things develop and reach perfect maturity; male and female blend their essences together, and the myriad creatures are formed and come to life."[3] This may be regarded as the common view of the generative process in early Chinese writings.

The union of male and female is understood to have been a process of the union of the yin and yang vital energies (*qi* 氣). What is the origin of this process? In Daoist understanding, of course, it is the Dao that generates all life. The *Laozi* has this to say: "The Dao gave birth to the One. The One gave birth to the two. The two gave birth to the three. The three gave birth to the myriad creatures. The myriad creatures carry the yin and embrace yang, and through the blending of *qi* they attain harmony" (Chapter 42). Although the interpretation of the "One" varies, there is little doubt that the

Dao is the source of all beings. During the Han period (206 BCE to 220 CE), based on the views of Dong Zhongshu 董仲舒 (*c.*179–104 BCE) and other Confucian scholars, the dominant interpretation makes use of the concept of "Origin" (*yuan* 元) or "Original *qi*" (*yuanqi*) to explain the concept of "One." Thus, the second-century CE scholar Wang Fu 王符 proposes in his *Qianfu lun* 潛夫論 (Comments of a Recluse) that the Dao is the source and root of all beings, whereas *qi* is the "function" of the Dao.[4] Similarly, Zhang Heng 張衡 (78–139), the great mathematician and astronomer, subscribes to the formula Dao → Original *qi* → myriad creatures in accounting for the generation of beings.[5] This also guides the commentaries to the *Laozi*. For example, the Heshang gong 河上公 commentary understands the *Laozi* to be saying in Chapter 1 that "The 'nameless' refers to the Dao. It is formless and therefore cannot be named . . . [The Dao] emits the vital energies and brings about the transformation [of nature] . . . and forms the root and beginning of heaven and earth."[6] On *Laozi* Chapter 21, Heshang gong also comments, "This states that the Dao endows [all beings with *qi*]. The myriad creatures come into being as they receive their vital energies from the Dao." This provides the basic theoretical framework for further elaboration in religious Daoist doctrines.

The fourth-century religious Daoist classic, the *Zhengao* 真誥 (*Declarations of the Perfected*), a foundational scripture of the *Shangqing* 上清 (Supreme Purity) sect, gives the following account: "The Dao from its original, undifferentiated state produces the original energy. When the original energy is formed, the Great Ultimate [*taiji* 太極] arises. The Great Ultimate is the father and mother of heaven and earth."[7] This clearly indicates that the Dao first produces the original *qi*-energy, which makes life possible, and that the "Great Ultimate," a concept found in the *Zhouyi* and central to Confucian philosophy, comes after the original *qi*-energy. Indeed, during the Six Dynasties period religious Daoist writings often offer a more elaborate theory of the fivefold transformation (*wuyun* 五運) of the Dao, providing a fuller account of the transformation of the original *qi*-energy to the genesis of beings.[8] At the same time, the religious Daoist sacred geography and pantheon headed by Yuanshi tianwang 元始天王 (Heavenly King of the Original Beginning) were being systematized. This is a complex development; but of primary theoretic or doctrinal interest is that the Dao, gods (*shen* 神), and *qi* are seen to form a triune whole. In this context, the concept of the "*qi* of the Dao" (*Daoqi* 道氣) comes to be widely used, which plays an important part in the subsequent development of Daoist teachings.[9]

Commenting on Chapter 42 of the *Laozi* cited above, the well known late-Tang Daoist master Du Guangting 杜光庭 (850–933) writes:

As to the genesis of the myriad creatures, it is the *qi* of the Dao that gives birth to them, and the yin and yang energies that nurture and allow them to grow . . . As to the birth of human beings, it is the Dao with its original *qi* that forms their essence and spirit; heaven with its *qi* of grand yang that enables them to move and to breathe; and the earth with its *qi* of pure yin that endows them with form and substance.[10]

In the same work, Du Guangting explains that the Dao endows human beings with "essence" (*jing* 精), "spirit" (*shen* 神), and *qi*.

> At the start of life, the Dao endows [a human being] with *qi*; heaven endows him with spirit, and earth, his essence. These three blend together to give [the person] his form. Human beings should [therefore] cherish his essence, nourish his *qi*, and preserve his spirit. [If they are able to do so] they will then live long. If [even] one of the three becomes dispersed or exhausted, then it would lead to imbalance and disorder and brings about disease . . . and death.[11]

This may be regarded as a typical account of cosmogony and human birth that stems from the religious Daoist traditions of the Six Dynasties. The "*qi* of the Dao" accounts for the genesis of all beings. For human beings, mirroring the structure of the macrocosm, the "essence," "spirit," and *qi* form an integral whole. Should harm come to one, then the whole person will suffer. The point to note is that all three are understood to be forms of *qi*, which constitute different aspects of the human being.

Providing a more detailed account of the process of human birth, a *Shangqing* (Supreme Purity) scripture states:

> *Qi*-energies bind into essence; essence transforms into spirit; spirit [completes the process and] changes into an individual being. Thus, the human being is an image of heaven and earth; the *qi*-energies operate naturally and spontaneously [according to their own principles]. The *qi*-energies of nature are all essences of the nine heavens. They . . . inform the embryo and nurture it. For nine months, the *qi*-energies fill out the embryo . . . which is born in the tenth month. In the first month, [conception takes place when] *qi* is received; during the second month, the soul [*ling* 靈] is endowed; during the third month, transformation evolves; during the fourth month, the essence solidifies; during the fifth month, the head and body take shape; during the sixth month, the human form is complete; during the seventh month, the spirits take their position [within the body]; during the eighth month, the nine apertures are illuminated. During the ninth month, the *qi*-energies of the nine heavens fill the entire body . . . and in the tenth month, the Lord of Life registers the person, who is then born.[12]

The process of human birth thus goes through a series of *qi*-transformations and is not completed until the person is duly recorded in the registry of life. Indeed, other Daoist scriptures testify that a host of deities are involved in this process, besides the "Lord of Life" (*siming* 司命). Birth is a significant event; it is not surprising that it is treated with awe and seriousness in religious Daoism. What is striking is that birth is characterized as a *religious* event – there is no mention of the involvement of human parents.

Authentic parents

The human biological parents seem to play little role in the process of birth, according to religious Daoist teachings, and function primarily as the arena in which the gods perform their creative acts. The *Shangqing* scripture referred to above also speaks of the "original father of the nine heavens" (*jiutian yuanfu* 九天元父) and the "mysterious mother of the nine heavens" (*jiutian xuanmu* 九天玄母).[13] They are the object of prayer and petition, especially for a safe delivery. But the divine father and mother play a larger role, as another Daoist scripture, the *Dongzhen taitan yinshu* 洞真太丹隱書 (*Secret Writings on the Great Elixir*, a Dongzhen scripture), explains:

> The original father and the mysterious mother are the ancestor of all life. The original father takes charge of the *qi*-energies . . . the mysterious mother takes charge of the essence, which transforms into the human embryo. The essence and the *qi* complete each other and the yin and the yang produce each other . . . After nine transformations . . . the human body is made complete. The body joins with the spirit. If the spirit departs, death would result; if the spirit is secure, life ensues.[14]

The original father (*yuanfu*) and the mysterious mother (*xuanmu*) – the word *xuan*, "mysterious" or "dark," also carries the connotation of sublimity and transcendence – are thus the divine source of all beings. Another *Dongzhen* scripture, the *Jiuzhen zhongjing* 九真中經 (*Central Scripture of the Nine Perfected*), similarly instructs:

> Human life begins with the ripening of the essence and the accumulation of *qi*, which are embodied in the embryo and thicken into blood . . . The five spirits decree a person's form and substance . . . The five viscera are mysteriously formed, each under the command of one of the five spirits. The human parents only know that they bring forth a new life, but they do not realize that it is the intervention of the divine lord and the five spirits [that makes life possible].[15]

In this account, the human parents play an insignificant role, although they assume that they are responsible for the birth of a new life. From conception to the eventual delivery of the newborn child, divine agents are at work every step of the way. One more example from another Daoist scripture should suffice to make the point. The *Dongxuan zhutian neiyin jing* 洞玄諸天內音經 (*Dongxuan Scripture of the Inner Sounds of All Heavens*) states:

Individual life arises from emptiness and that which is of itself so; because of [karmic] causes and conditions, one becomes attached to a womb and comes into being through a series of transformations. The fact that I was conceived by my parents does not mean that they are the origin of my life. They are not the authentic parents. One's father and mother are precious and occupy an exalted place. Because of the [karmic] causes and conditions that I bring, I am bound to my birth parents. To their kindness of carrying and nurturing me, I am indebted and must repay with ritual propriety. For this reason, I address them as father and mother. But the fact remains that though I receive a form, the body is not my [true] form. It is but like a house in which I temporarily dwell . . . Thus, those who obtain the Dao are no longer bound by their form . . . With a body, all manners of evil arise; without a body, one enters into the realm of naturalness and accords with the Dao in all one does. Then the body becomes one with the spirit. When this happens, one attains the authentic body and returns to the [divine] parents who bring life, and realizes the Dao.[16]

This passage evidently reflects Buddhist influence, but for our purposes the important point is that the human birth parents are to be distinguished from the "authentic parents," the true divine father and mother who create life. What is the relationship between these two sets of parents? The quotation above does not disparage the biological parents but recognizes the debt that a child owes to them. Nevertheless, their place remains firmly in the mundane world of conventional values governed by ritual propriety and their contribution counts little in the higher truth of the Dao. To realize spiritual enlightenment and Daoist immortality, a person must rely on the divine authentic parents, which entails the negation of one's worldly self in cultivating a spiritual body. This implies that in the pursuit of the Dao, one must also leave behind one's biological birth parents.

The idea of "authentic parents" figures commonly in Daoist scriptures from the late Six Dynasties to the early Tang in the seventh century. At times, it is understood more overtly in terms of the Buddhist analysis of mind as the source of all illusory phenomena. For example, the widely influential *Benji jing* 本際經 recognizes that life is constituted by *qi*-energies, but it explains further that all phenomena "are originally [contained in] one single thought" (*shi chu yi nian* 是初一念). In this context, the scripture goes on to say that the *qi*-energies "arise from emptiness and nonbeing . . . Thus it is said that [human life] is produced by the authentic parents. Through a series of changes and developments, the physical body is formed. Attached to the father and mother of the phenomenal world, the embryo is nurtured and born, complete with all the sensory apparatus."[17]

Biological parents are but an instrument of the divine. They offer an earthly abode for the transformation of life. The unseen hand of the divine is responsible for creation and should be recognized as our "authentic parents." There are two points to note here. First, as the eleventh-century encyclopedic Daoist collection *Yunji qiqian* 雲笈七籤 reports, at birth, each human being is endowed with an inner "spiritual light" (*lingzhao* 靈照), which renders possible the "return" to one's authentic parents, also described here as "original authenticity" (*benzhen* 本真), and the realization of Daoist immortality.[18] One's earthly existence poses serious obstacles to complete spiritual realization, but one's inner spiritual light is never extinguished and may be rekindled through Daoist rituals and practices. Second, although the biological parents are but an instrument, they are necessary. The reason seems to be that the *qi* of Dao is formless and nameless; it requires the mediation of being to bring about individuated physical forms. Thus, the divine authentic parents of all beings have to make use of biological parents in the process of earthly creation. However, this mediation comes with a price. Because biological parents are a part of the phenomenal world, they also contribute to the karmic causes and conditions that render the newborn child a creature of desire and illusion. The inner spiritual light becomes dim, and the inborn "original nature" (*benxing* 本性), also called the "Dao-nature" (*daoxing* 道性) in some sources, endowed by our authentic parents becomes corrupted. Human beings thus find themselves enslaved by desire and caught in the endless cycle of life, death, and rebirth. In this sense, the biological parents represent a hindrance to Daoist spiritual self-realization, although children must repay their parents for their kindness in bringing them up. This obviously raises questions about the Confucian conception of *xiao*.

The debate on filial piety

The debate on filial piety in early medieval China first arose between Confucianism and Buddhism. It would be useful to consider briefly the Buddhist–Confucian debate before we return to filial piety in religious Daoism. Probably the earliest extant record of this debate is that found in the Buddhist apologetic work, the *Mouzi lihuo lun* 牟子理惑論 (*Mouzi on the Settling of Doubts*), which discusses the meaning of *xiao* in two places.[19] First, the *Mouzi* addresses the criticism that by shaving one's head to join the *sangha*, Buddhist monks are being unfilial, since according to the *Xiaojing* (*Classic of Filial Piety*), the "beginning of filial piety" lies in taking care of one's body, every part of which is a gift from one's parents. In response, the *Mouzi* gives the example of a man from the state of Qi – a stronghold of Confucianism in early China – whose father fell into the water while crossing a river by boat. The son rescued him and had to apply considerable force, turning him upside down to draw the water out from his mouth. Thus, he was able to revive his father. If the son had "folded his hands" in accordance with the "normal" ritual norms and refrained from doing "violence" to his father, as the *Mouzi* drives home the point, his father would have died. This is why Confucius himself emphasized the importance of weighing the circumstances and making judgments that are timely and appropriate (*Analects* 9.30). The *Mouzi* goes on to cite other examples to bring out the point that to achieve "great virtue" one should not adhere rigidly to small ritual details. Now, as the text concludes, the monks gave up their wealth and left their family, and turned away from the world of desire, and this may be regarded as the "height of self-giving" – in what sense does it contravene the teachings of Confucius or deviate from the ideal of filial piety?

Second, the *Mouzi* has to confront the charge that by joining the *sangha* and leading a celibate life, Buddhist monks were committing the greatest sin against filial piety: namely, to leave no heir. The *Mouzi*, employing the language of philosophical Daoism, replies that family ties and worldly possessions are but the "excess" baggage of one's earthly existence; in contrast, purity and "non-action" (*wuwei* 無為) would lead one to the Dao. Ancient recluses such as Xu You 許由, Bo Yi 伯夷, and Shu Qi 叔齊, who renounced the world for a higher cause, were all recognized even by Confucius. Thus, the *Mouzi* concludes, Buddhist monks were in no way unfilial in joining the *sangha* and devoting their lives to cultivating the Way and virtue.

Criticisms of this kind appear frequently in polemic works against Buddhism. For example, Sun Chuo's 孫綽 fourth-century work the *Yu Dao lun* 喻道論 (*Explaining the Dao*) similarly contrasts the Confucian emphasis on *xiao* with the perceived Buddhist call for renunciation.[20] The Buddhist responses also generally follow the precedents established by the *Mouzi*. Two additional arguments may be mentioned. First, in spreading the Buddhist gospel and serving as a model for the world, the monks were also doing their families proud, which is an important element of filial piety recognized, for example, in the *Xiaojing*. Second, Buddhist scriptures themselves such as the *Fumu en nanbao jing* 父母恩難報經 and the *Yulan pen jing* 盂蘭盆經 actively promote filial piety. On the whole, Buddhist teachings of this period do not criticize *xiao* ethics but instead try to reconcile Buddhist teachings with it. This is generally well known and forms a part of the larger "sinicization" of Buddhism.

In this debate, religious Daoism generally sided with Confucianism against Buddhism, marshalling similar arguments. For example, the early Tang Daoist master Fu Yi 傅奕 in his *Gaoshi zhuan* 高識傳 (*Biographies of Enlightened Masters*) provides a couple of examples of Daoist critique of Buddhism centering on *xiao*.[21] The first example emphasizes that having no heir is the greatest of sins and attacks Buddhism as a "demonic religion" (*guijiao* 鬼教). The second charges that Buddhism advocates leaving behind one's parents and holding in contempt the authority of the king. In addition, Buddhist rituals are expensive and put a strain on limited state resources.

A more direct Daoist critique of Buddhism is recorded in Fa Lin's 法琳 *Bianzheng lun* 辯正論. According to this account, the Daoists argue that "Lord Lao", i.e. the divine Laozi, establishes a model, which centers on filial piety and loyalty, in order to save the world from evil. In contrast, "Buddhism teaches the people to abandon duty and their parents" and is opposed to both benevolence and filial piety. In response, reflecting a higher level of maturity in the development of Buddhism in China, Fa Lin explains that in the ceaseless samsaric cycle of life, death, and rebirth, the possibility that all sentient beings may become one's parents or enemies must be recognized. This is the reason why Buddhism teaches impartiality and seeks enlightenment and transcendence from all worldly attachments. At the same time, Fa Lin emphasizes that Buddhism, in fact, affirms filial piety. At the lowest level, filial piety is a matter of physical service, and at a higher level, filial piety involves mental labor; but at the highest level, filial piety is a soteriological enterprise. In embracing the Buddhist *dharma* and joining the *sangha*, the individual seeks enlightenment so as to bring salvation to his parents and all sentient beings. In contrast, Fa Lin charges, those who sought Daoist immortality by going into the mountains in search of perfected beings or to pursue spiritual purification through esoteric practices were concerned only with their own welfare. In this sense, it is the Daoists and not the Buddhists who are selfish and unfilial.[22]

Affirming worldly filial piety

In the process of localization, Buddhism cannot but address and affirm the pervasive Chinese concern with filial piety. To provide scriptural support, uniquely Chinese Buddhist scriptures such as the *Fumu enzhong jing* 父母恩重經 (*Scripture on the Great Parental Kindness*) came to be produced, highlighting the Buddhist view of filial piety. During the Tang period, this facilitated the discourse on "harmonizing" the three traditions of Confucianism, Buddhism, and Daoism.

As an indigenous tradition, religious Daoism perhaps did not face the same level of critical scrutiny. Nevertheless, the religious Daoist recluse who pursues spiritual cultivation and immortality offers a ready target for Confucian criticism. Traces of this debate can be found, for example, in Ge Hong's 葛洪 (*c.* 283–363) *Baopuzi* 抱樸子 (*Master Who Embraces Simplicity*). On the charge that the followers of the Way of immortality "turn their back to traditions and abandon the world" (*beisu qishi* 背俗棄世), the *Baopuzi* relates, "I have heard that keeping one's body without harm is what is meant by fulfilling filial piety. Does not the attainment of the way of the immortals, which enables one to enjoy everlasting life . . . far surpass this?" Furthermore, if one succeeded in attaining the Dao, his ancestors would be immensely proud of his achievement. In the realm of the immortals, nothing would be lacking. Among those who attained the Dao, none could compare with Laozi, whose descendants included notable figures. Thus, as the *Baopuzi* concludes, there is no cause for worry that those who pursue the Dao of immortality today would lack descendants or that ancestor worship would come to an end.[23]

Following the appearance of the Buddhist *Fumu enzhong jing*, similar Daoist scriptures arrived on the scene. Among them are the *Taishang zhenyi bao fumu enzhong jing* 太上真一報父母恩重經, which takes the form of a sermon by the "Heavenly Lord" (*tianzun* 天尊) emphasizing the need to repay the kindness of one's "authentic parents," and the *Taishang Laojun shuo bao fumu en zhong jing* 太上老君說報父母恩重經, which is clearly modeled on the Buddhist *Fushuo fumu enzhong jing* 佛說父母恩重經.[24] A typical Daoist scripture of this genre is the *Yuanshi Dongzhen cishan xiaozi baoen chengdao jing* 元始洞真慈善孝子報恩成道經, which explains that the scripture aims at "explaining to enlightened kings the need to govern the world with filial piety, and to filial sons [the need] to repay the kindness of their parents."[25] Although as compared with Buddhism there was perhaps no acute need for religious Daoism to defend itself against charges of "unfiliality," it nevertheless saw fit to highlight its contribution to establishing an ideal world order bound by filial virtues.

During the Six Dynasties, filial piety became a key element in religious Daoist doctrines. Although immortality remains the goal, few could attain it; for the majority, death poses a serious concern. In this context, filial piety becomes a condition for a blessed afterlife. For example, the *Zhengao* reveals that "those who are utterly filial and loyal would be appointed officials of the underworld when they die. After a hundred and forty years, they would then be able to receive instruction from an immortal on the great Dao."[26] From this, they would progress and became officials in the divine hierarchy, and further promotion can be expected once every 140 years. "A filial son can move the spirits and gods," the text also suggests, who would command birds and animals to guard his tomb. In comparison, "those who possess the virtue of a sage," though they would also be appointed officials to the lord of the underworld when they die, would require 1,000 years before they would be promoted, and a further 1,400 years before they could gain a place in the Daoist heavens. As the great Daoist master Tao Hongjing 陶弘景 (456–536) astutely observes, this would mean that "in terms of the span of time [required for promotion in the afterworld], those who possess the virtue of a sage do not match those who are loyal and filial."[27] The *Zhengao* also mentions that although generally practitioners of the Dao in their pursuit of immortality should avoid coming into contact with corpses, which would "harm their spirit and corrupt their *qi*-energies," they should nonetheless out of love attend the funeral for their parents, teachers, and masters. Indeed, the text instructs, they should mourn for them deeply, without regard for the harm that this outpouring of emotions would bring to themselves.[28]

Another important feature in many of the Daoist scriptures of the Six Dynasties period concerns the salvation of one's parents and ancestors. This is significant because religious Daoism, with its emphasis on immortality, is often perceived to be chiefly concerned with individual salvation. At most, it is able to bring benefit to a small group of people closely related to the adept. With the introduction of Buddhism and the increasing appeal of Mahayana universal salvation, religious Daoism responded by breaking out of its narrow individual focus. This can be seen in the development of the *Shangqing* (Supreme Purity) sect with its center in Maoshan 茅山 and especially in the teachings of the *Lingbao* 靈寶 (Numinous Treasure) scriptures, which incorporate a great deal of Buddhist influence. Here, the earlier Daoist emphasis on the pursuit of individual immortality is complemented by concerns with the afterlife, including rebirth, appointment to the ranks of divine officials, and salvation for one's ancestors. On this basis, rituals for the well-being of ancestors became an important part of religious Daoist practice. This not only suited perfectly the traditional Chinese concern for ancestor worship but also influenced the development of Buddhist rituals.[29]

Conclusion

As an indigenous tradition, religious Daoism drew from the different currents of beliefs in early China. These include the veneration of the "lord of heaven" (*tiandi* 天帝), astral worship, various forms of esoteric, "magical" arts, and other religious beliefs. Religious Daoism also reflects the interests of both state worship centered on the emperor and clan-based ancestor worship. During the Six Dynasties, religious Daoist doctrines began to take shape, in which the concept of filial piety plays a decisive role. The influence of Buddhism cannot be denied, although Daoism has its own contributions to make. The emphasis on loyalty and filial piety as a condition for appointment and promotion in the afterworld and the concern with salvation for one's ancestors that we find in the *Zhengao*, the representative scripture of the *Shangqing* sect, is a good example in this regard. Buddhism had to confront a more intense attack on its perceived denial of filial piety. What appears at first sight to be a call for renunciation and direct repudiation of traditional family ethics turns out in the end, as Buddhist apologetic works demonstrate, to contain a doctrine of "genuine" filial piety. When it is recognized that all sentient beings are creatures of desire subject to innumerable rebirths, the possibility that any being can become one's parents should be apparent. Moreover, with scriptures that are devoted to the virtue of filial piety, Chinese Buddhism shows that it seeks not confrontation but a way to coexist with native beliefs and traditions.

As religious Daoism developed during the Six Dynasties, the concept of *qi* assumed a central doctrinal position, bringing to light the fundamental unity of the Dao, divine beings, and *qi*. The concept of *qi* explains the sense in which all beings can be said to be creatures of the Dao. It also makes clear that the human body constitutes the abode of divine spirits. Unseen divine forces are at work in the birth of human beings; they are thus our "true" parents. One's biological parents are but the field in which divine creativity takes place. This need not entail a critique of filial piety. Instead, what this means is that religious Daoism subordinates conventional filial piety to a higher religious *xiao* devoted to the "authentic parents." This challenges the Confucian formulation of filial piety. Perhaps this also reflects an attempt to respond to Buddhism on the meaning of "true" filial piety. In any event, the concept of "authentic parents" constitutes an important aspect of religious Daoist doctrinal history, especially in terms of its relationship with Buddhism.

Notes

This chapter has been translated by Alan K. L. Chan.

1 Translator's note: A fuller version of this chapter in Japanese has been published as "Shin fubo kō" 真父母考, in Mugitani Kunio 麥谷邦夫 (ed.), *Chūgoku chūsei shakai to shūkyō* 中國中世社會と宗教, Kyoto: Dōkisha, 2002, pp. 19–38. Bibliographical references have been added in the notes; they do not refer necessarily to the same editions that the author has used.

2 *Guanzi* 39 "Shuidi" 水地, in Li Mian 李勉, *Guanzi jinzhu jinyi* 管子今注今譯, Taipei: Taiwan Shangwu, 1990, p. 676.

3 *Zhouyi*, *Xici xia* 繫辭下, as translated in Richard J. Lynn, *The Classic of Changes: A New Translation of the I Ching as Interpreted by Wang Bi*, New York: Columbia University Press, 1994, p. 85; for the Chinese text, see *Zhouyi jinzhu jinyi* 周易今注今譯, Taipei: Taiwan Shangwu, 1988, p. 428.

4 Wang Fu, *Qianfu lun*, 32 "Benxun" 本訓, in Peng Duo 彭鐸, *Qianfu lun jian jiaozheng* 潛夫論箋校正, Beijing: Zhonghua shuju, 1985, p. 367.

5 Zhang Heng, *Lingxian* 靈憲, as cited in *Hou Hanshu* 後漢書 (*History of the Later Han Dynasty*), "Tianwen zhi" 天文志 ("Treatise on Astronomy"), Beijing: Zhonghua shuju, 1982, p. 3215, n. 4.

6 Translator's note: Heshang gong (Old Master by the River) is portrayed in traditional Chinese sources as a teacher to the Han Emperor Wen (reigned 179–157 BCE). Scholars remain divided on the date of the Heshang gong commentary. Whereas most modern Chinese scholars would accept it as a Han product, probably Later Han, some Japanese scholars, including Professor Mugitani, would trace it to the Six Dynasties period. For the text of the Heshang gong commentary, see the modern critical edition by Zheng Chenghai 鄭成海, *Laozi Heshanggong zhu jiaoli* 老子河上公注斠理, Taipei: Zhonghua, 1971.

7 Translator's note: The *Zhengao* is said to be based on direct divine revelations given to Yang Xi 楊羲 (330–386). For an introduction to the *Shangqing* sect of religious Daoism, see Isabelle Robinet, *Taoism: Growth of a Religion*, Phyllis Brooks (trans.), Stanford, CA: Stanford University Press, 1997, Chapter 5. The *Zhengao* now exists in a twenty-book (*juan* 卷) version, in the *Daozang* 道藏 (Daoist Canon), Shanghai: Shanghai shudian, 1996, vol. 20, pp. 491–610. This passage is found at the start of *juan* 5, p. 516.

8 For example, the *Dongshen jing* 洞神經 describes the fivefold transformation of the Dao as follows: *taiyi* 太易 (primordial change) → *taichu* 太初 (primordial beginning, when the original *qi* begins to stir) → *taishi* 太始 (grand initiation) → *taisu* 太素 (grand purity) → *taiji* 太極; as cited in the Tang dynasty collection, *Daojiao yishu* 道教義樞 (Pivotal Teachings of Religious Daoism), *juan* 7, in *Daozang*, vol. 24, p. 828.

9 On this development, see Mugitani Kunio, "Dō to ki to kami: dōkyō kyōri ni okeru imi o megutte" 道と氣と神 – 道教教理における意義をめぐつて, in *Jinmin gakuhō* 人民學報, 65, 1989.

10 Du Guangting, *Daode zhenjing guang shengyi* 道德真經廣聖義, *juan* 33, in *Daozang*, vol. 14, p. 479.

11 Ibid., *juan* 46, p. 549, commentary on *Laozi* Chapter 72.

12 *Dongzhen jiudan shanghua taijing zhongji jing* 洞真九丹上化胎精中記經, as cited in the sixth-century Daoist work, *Wushang biyao* 無上秘要, *juan* 5, in *Daozang*, vol. 25, p. 12. This scripture appears under a slightly different title – *Shangqing jiudan shanghua taijing zhongji jing* – in *Daozang*, vol. 34, p. 82. See also *Jiutian shengshen zhang jing* 九天生神章經, in *Yunji qiqian* 雲笈七籤, *juan* 16, *Daozang*, vol. 22, p. 123.

13 *Shangqing jiudan shanghua taijing zhongji jing*, in *Daozang*, vol. 34, p. 82.

14 As cited in *Wushang biyao*, *juan* 5, *Daozang*, vol. 25, p. 13.

15 Ibid.

16 Ibid.

17 *Benji jing*, *juan* 4.

18 *Yunji qiqian*, *juan* 3, citing the *Sanbao zajing chuhua xu* 三寶雜經出化序, in *Daozang*, vol. 22, p. 15.

19 The *Mouzi lihuo lun* is preserved in the Buddhist collection, *Hongming ji* 弘明集, *juan* 1, in *Taishō shinshū Daizōkyō*, Tokyo, 1960, vol. 52, pp. 1–7; the discussion on *xiao* is found on pp. 2–3. Cf. Yoshikawa Tadao 吉川忠夫, "Kō to bukkyō" 孝と佛教, in *Chūgoku chūsei shakai to shūkyō*, pp. 1–18.

20 Sun Chuo's *Yu Dao lun* is also collected in the *Hongming ji*, *juan* 3; for a detailed study of *xiao* in Buddhism, see Michihata Ryōshū 道端良秀, *Chūgoku bukkyō to jukyō rinri* 中國佛教と儒教倫理, Kyoto: Heirakuji, 1968, and "Bukkyō to jitsusen rinri" 佛教と實踐倫理, in his *Tōdai bukkyō shi* 唐代佛教史, Tokyo: Hōzōkan, 1958. Translator's note: See also Livia Kohn's chapter in this volume; and Alan Cole, *Mothers and Sons in Chinese Buddhism*, Stanford, CA: Stanford University Press, 1998, for the scriptures mentioned below.

21 Fu Yi's views are discussed and criticized in the *Guang Hongming ji* 廣弘明集, *juan* 7, in *Taishō shinshū Daizōkyō*, vol. 52, p. 133. A similar debate is found in the *Neide lun* 內德論 (*On Inner Virtue*) by the Tang scholar Li Shizheng 李師政, in *Guang Hongming ji*, *juan* 14, p. 187.

22 Fa Lin, *Bianzheng lun*, *juan* 6, in *Taishō shinshū Daizōkyō*, vol. 52, pp. 529, 532–3.

23 Ge Hong, *Baopuzi*, 3 "Dui su" 對俗, in Wang Ming 王明, *Baopuzi neipian jiaoshi* 抱樸子內篇校釋, Beijing: Zhonghua, 1980, pp. 45–6.

24 The *Taishang zhenyi bao fumu enzhong jing* is found in the *Daozang*, vol. 2, pp. 30–1. For the *Taishang Laojun shuo bao fumu en zhong jing*, see *Daozang*, vol. 11, pp. 470–3.

25 *Daozang*, vol. 2, p. 33.

26 *Zhengao*, *juan* 16, in *Daozang*, vol. 20, p. 586.

27 Ibid.

28 *Zhengao*, *juan* 10, in *Daozang*, vol. 20, p. 553.

29 On this point, see Mugitani Kunio, "Shoki dōkyō ni okeru kyūsai shisō" 初期道教における救濟思想, *Tōyō bunka* 東洋文化, 57, 1977.

7 Imperial filial piety as a political problem

Patricia Ebrey

We are accustomed to thinking of filial piety as one of the elements of Chinese culture that held China together as a society. It made conforming to the requirements of the patrilineal family and the cult of the ancestors seem natural and right. In its more extended meanings, it provided ideological support for social and political inequalities of many sorts, motivating respect for the authority of village elders, landlords, officials, and the emperor. In the now somewhat dated language of sociology, filial piety was functional, not dysfunctional. It worked.

In this chapter, I will try to unsettle this comfortable understanding of the relationship between filial piety and Chinese society by showing that filial piety did not fit so perfectly with imperial rule. Confucian moral teachings required that emperors be paragons of filial piety, but to the scholar-officials with whom emperors governed an emperor who made decisions on the basis of his understanding of his filial obligations could be a threat to the state. To officials, imperial filial piety could be a dangerous thing.

No one writing from within the Confucian tradition ever disputed the principle that emperors must embrace filial piety. Emperors were supposed to be moral exemplars, and filial piety was viewed as a fundamental moral virtue. The ethical demands placed on rulers date back at least to the formulation of the "Mandate of Heaven": if rulers do not act virtuously, Heaven will send warnings in the form of untoward events or anomalous phenomena, and if they do not reform Heaven could even take the mandate away from them, another way of saying they would lose their thrones. On the list of the virtues rulers could not slight, filial piety occupied a prominent place. The *Classic of Filial Piety* opens with a discussion of the virtues of the former kings and asserts that "the filial piety of the Son of Heaven consists in serving his parents with complete love and respect so that his moral influence reaches the common people and he becomes a model for the distant regions in all directions."

An essential component of the ancient idea of filial piety was cult service to deceased ancestors, and throughout imperial Chinese history this element in imperial filial piety remained central and largely unproblematic. No one seriously questioned that among the most important rituals emperors had to perform were those involving their forebears. Over the centuries the literature on how imperial burials and ancestral sacrifices should be performed grew enormously.[1]

But service to parents did not end with material provision of their needs after death. In the *Analects*, Confucius says, "When your father is alive observe his intentions. When he is deceased, model yourself on the memory of his behavior. If in three years after his death you have not deviated from your father's ways, then you may be considered a filial child" (1.11). For emperors – and perhaps for most adult Chinese with adequate financial means – providing funerals, burials, and continuing offerings was not the difficult part. Much more challenging was dealing with living parents and adhering to deceased parents' ways. Already in the *Analects* the particular challenge this posed for rulers received acknowledgment: "Zengzi said, 'I have heard from the Master this about the filial piety of Meng Zhuangzi: Other dimensions of it can be attained by others, but his not changing his father's ministers or his father's government is difficult to match'" (19.18).

The imperial family was, of course, not a typical family. Princes did not get to spend much time with emperor-fathers, who were very busy men, with dozens of officials and consorts demanding their attention. Once a prince was appointed heir apparent, a group of officials largely took over his training. They did their best to inculcate in him Confucian teachings on filial piety and undoubtedly made sure that he observed basic proprieties such as daily calls on his parents, but they spent much more time with him than his father did, and did not necessarily strive to build up a warm relationship between father and son, satisfied with one that was formally correct. The crown prince had more time to spend with his mother, but given competition for favor among the emperor's consorts, he could well have acquired from her ambivalent feelings about his father. Added to this, the huge stakes involved in succession complicated family dynamics. In the imperial family, one heir succeeds to everything; once succession is settled, his brothers become expendable. Those with connections to the successful prince gain access to the vast resources of the throne; those connected to other sons become as marginal as the surplus sons themselves. Put another way, the power and status of a great many other people, ranging from court officials to consorts and eunuchs, depended on which son succeeded, giving them plenty of motivation to try to position themselves to be on the winning side. An emperor had to be wary of those surrounding any of his sons and is likely to have wanted his own spies keeping an eye on his sons, hardly the best foundation for warm, affectionate relationships.

Normally, once a prince became emperor, he no longer had a living father. His actions might reflect psychologically complex feelings toward his deceased father, but he had considerable freedom to act on his own. Many emperors, of course, had living mothers (birth mothers or legal mothers) to whom they were expected to show their filial devotion. The requirement that emperors treat their mothers with filial piety underlay the power of empress dowagers. Any student of Chinese history knows the difficulty young emperors had in dislodging empress-dowager regents who did not want to turn over power when young emperors came of age. Occasionally mothers could exploit the imperatives of filial piety even when their sons were grown. In the Tang, if it were not for the fact that Ruizong and Zhongzong had to observe the proprieties of filial piety, it would not have been as easy for Empress Wu to establish and maintain her dominance.

Occasionally emperors' filial obligations were made more complex by adoption. In both Song and Ming times officials and emperors came into conflict over an emperor's treatment of his natural father after he was made heir of the previous emperor. As Carney Fisher has shown so well, conflicting understandings of both the core of filial obligations and the essential nature of the imperial institution led to major crises in the reign of Yingzong in the Song and Shizong in the Ming. Officials felt called on to take stands, creating very public crises.[2]

Here I will look at yet another anomalous situation: emperors with living ex-emperor fathers. In some of these cases, the new emperor had coerced the abdication of his father, not the most filial of acts. But even when the abdication was unequivocally voluntary, the potential for conflict was great because the emperor's sense of filial obligations to his living father might conflict with what he or his officials took to be his obligations to the dynasty. There were more emperors with abdicated fathers than one might expect. During the Tang dynasty alone, four emperors started their reigns with their father/predecessor still alive. Gaozu abdicated to Taizong in 626 but lived until 635. Ruizong abdicated in 712 to Xuanzong but lived until 716. Xuanzong abdicated in 756 after he learned that Suzong had been enthroned, but lived until 762. In 805, after only a few months on the throne, Shunzong was forced by eunuchs to abdicate in favor of his son, Xianzong, who, however, did not have to reign with a living father for long, since Shunzong died in 806.

Abdication had some sanction in the Confucian classics, since Yao had abdicated in favor of Shun. The two were not related, so when Shun began his reign he owed deference to two men, his father Gu Sou and Yao. How this impinged on his ethical obligations was discussed by Mencius in two passages. In *Mencius* 5A4 an interlocutor posed the question of whether a ruler can treat his predecessor and/or his father as a subject. When Mencius insisted that Shun would not have treated them as subjects, the interlocutor cited a line from the *Odes* to the effect that everyone in the realm is the king's subject. Mencius argued first against taking a single line of an ode out of context, then offered this principle, "There is nothing a filial son can do greater than bringing honor to his parents, and there is no better way to honor one's parents than supporting them with the entire realm. To be the father of the Son of Heaven is the height of honor. To be supported by the entire realm is the ultimate of support."[3]

The other passage, *Mencius* 7A35, implied that Shun would have placed his filial obligations to his father above his political ones if ever required to make a choice. When someone asked what an officer of Shun's would do if Shun's father killed someone, Mencius replied that the officer would have to arrest him, because the officer had to follow the rules he was charged with enforcing. Shun himself, however, would abandon the kingdom (considering it of no more value than a worn out sandal) and hide out with his father somewhere along the seacoast, living happily with him. In other words, officials had an obligation to treat the king's father as just another subject, but the king himself had to treat him as a father, even at the cost of his throne.[4]

In imperial times, the actual relationship between emperors and retired emperors/fathers was undoubtedly shaped by many factors, including their personalities, the political factions dominant at court, who had urged the abdication, and a host of other matters. As a step toward a more nuanced understanding of the complexities of these situations, I now look closely at one case from the Song dynasty: the relationship between Huizong and Qinzong during the year that followed Huizong's abdication late in 1125.

Huizong and Qinzong

Huizong was born in 1082, during the reign of his father Shenzong, but he was not the eldest son, nor was his mother the empress, so he never had the pressure placed on him that was commonly placed on the heir apparent. Moreover, he never got to know his father or birth mother, as Shenzong died prematurely (age thirty-eight *sui*) in 1085, and his birth mother soon thereafter (his legal mother the empress Xiang 向 lived many more years). Shenzong's oldest son, Huizong's brother Zhezong, then ten *sui*, was enthroned, but real power was held by their grandmother (Shenzong's mother), Grand Empress Dowager Gao 高. She immediately reversed most of the political policies that had meant so much to Shenzong – the New Policies initiated by Wang Anshi 王安石 – and ousted and banished most of those who had served Shenzong. Huizong's upbringing seems to have been largely in the hands of wet nurses, eunuchs, and a series of tutors. He had a brother three months older than him and three more from eleven months to three years younger than him. This set of princes moved out of the palace to their own residences in 1098 when they were in their teens.

Once Empress Gao died in 1093 and Zhezong began ruling on his own, he reversed Empress Gao's policies and revived those of his father. A new round of ousting and banishing officials ensued. In 1100 Zhezong died at an even younger age than Shenzong, only twenty-five *sui*. He had no male heir and Empress Dowager Xiang selected Huizong over his slightly older brother to succeed. Huizong was then nineteen *sui*. Three months later his wife, Empress Wang, gave birth to his first son, Qinzong. Empress Wang lived until Qinzong was nine *sui*. Huizong would go on to have many more sons (thirty-four by the time he abdicated). Some of them, especially the third son Kai 楷, shared more of Huizong's interests in literature and art than Qinzong did. Still Qinzong's standing as the likely heir was never questioned and he was formally appointed heir apparent when he was sixteen *sui*. By the time he was nineteen, he had enough confidence in his standing that he was one of the few willing to voice objections to Huizong's pro-Daoist policies.

In his capacity as emperor, Huizong frequently evoked the memory of his father. Perhaps Zhezong had influenced him in this regard. Zhezong had been old enough to have known Shenzong and resented the way his grandmother destroyed his legacy. Whether Huizong also resented Gao is a matter for speculation, but whatever his motivations, after less than two years on the throne, Huizong sided unambiguously with the reformers and clamped down on political dissent. For nearly a quarter of a century, the substantial number of officials who detested the New Policies could do little but seethe.

As an emperor, Huizong worked to make his court a center of culture. He built up collections of ancient bronzes and jades, paintings and calligraphies. He had court scholars put together compendiums of court rituals, Daoist texts, medical manuals, and the like. He established the most comprehensive school system ever attempted in China and used it to recruit officials. He set up a court school for painters and calligraphers and undertook numerous building projects, constructing new palaces, temples, and office buildings. He developed a distinctive calligraphic style and let his calligraphy be widely seen by having it engraved on stone in every prefecture. He even was an avid painter and would give officials paintings he had made.[5]

Abdication

Early in Huizong's reign the Song army had some success on the northwest border, against the Qiang. This campaign was treated as a notable accomplishment since the Northern Song had not been able to gain the upper hand over its northern neighbors the Khitan Liao and Tangut Xia; military defeats had been dealt with by negotiated settlements involving hefty annual payments to the victors. A second opportunity to regain territory presented itself after 1117, when the upstart Jurchen Jin were gaining on their former overlords, the Liao. In 1120 Song entered into an alliance with the Jin in order to regain the Sixteen Prefectures – territories that Tang had held and that Song had long considered properly Chinese in the region of modern Beijing and Datong. To simplify a complex story, Jin proved a much less desirable neighbor than Liao and in late 1125 invaded north China on the pretext that Song had violated an agreement on the return of subjects.

With the Jurchen rapidly approaching Kaifeng from two directions, the court entered crisis mode. An official drafted an edict for Huizong in which he took all of the blame for the crisis on himself, saying that it was because he had excluded critics from his government that everything was going wrong.

Some officials began discussing among themselves the possibility that Huizong should abdicate, perhaps thinking the Jurchen would interpret the gesture as an apology and withdraw, perhaps thinking Huizong would not make an effective leader during war, or that they could manage a new young emperor more effectively. Li Gang 李綱, whose own account of these events survives, called on a court official he knew named Wu Min 吳敏 to discuss abdication. Li argued that the Jin would withdraw when they heard news of the abdication. When Wu Min asked if appointing Qinzong as regent would be enough, Li Gang cited the example of Xuanzong and Suzong in the Tang: Suzong's legitimacy had always been compromised by the fact that with his father out of the capital he had taken the throne without Xuanzong first abdicating. Huizong should not put Qinzong in that position, Li Gang argued, but instead transfer full authority to him before leaving. Wu Min then sought a private audience with Huizong, during which he tried to convince him that the dynasty would have a better chance if he abdicated. He urged him to make a decision within three days.

The next day Huizong agreed to abdicate and Wu Min, the grand councilor Li Bangyan 李邦彥, and Huizong began planning such details as where he should live (the Daoist temple built at the site of his princely mansion) and what title should be used for him (Lord of the Dao 道君). Huizong decided he had to claim illness as an excuse for abdicating, so when his officials were assembled, he faked a stroke. Pretending to be unable to talk or use his right hand, he used his left hand to write out the order that Qinzong be enthroned. Qinzong resisted very strongly, probably not wanting to take over in the middle of a crisis. Both Huizong and Qinzong used the language of filial piety:

> [The heir apparent, Qinzong] wouldn't accept the mandate. Tong Guan 童貫 and Li Bangyan placed the imperial robes on him, but the heir apparent rose and pushed them off, not daring to accept them. The emperor [Huizong] with his left hand wrote, "If you do not accept, you are unfilial."
>
> The heir apparent said, "If I accept, then I am unfilial."
>
> The emperor wrote to summon the empress. When she arrived, she told the heir apparent, "The emperor is old. He and I wish to entrust our lives to you." He still insistently declined. The emperor then ordered the eunuchs to carry the heir to Blessed Tranquility Hall and put him on the throne. The heir was definitely unwilling to walk, so the eunuchs used force to carry him.[6]

Soon after Qinzong was installed as the ninth emperor of the Song dynasty (12/24, 1125), Huizong prepared to leave for the southeast, presumably both for his personal safety and to give Qinzong the space to rule on his own.[7] He left at night ten days later, on 1/4, 1126, heading first to the southern capital at Yingtian, then Yangzhou, then Zhenjiang.

Contact between Qinzong and his father over the next several months is well documented because after the fall of the Northern Song many scholars devoted themselves to collecting accounts of all the events surrounding the fall. We thus have much more to go on than Tang historians do to disentangle the ways the two principals and those around them used the rhetoric of filial piety and the emotions intrinsic to the father–son relationship to negotiate the new situation. In the narrative below, I focus on instances that bear on these questions: Did the concepts of filial piety guide their actions, or were they mere window dressing? Did officials evoke filial piety when they wanted to convince Qinzong to adopt a course of action because they thought he truly was struggling to do the filial thing, or because they thought he needed a reason for his actions that could be publicly proclaimed? Did Qinzong fail to take actions he believed were in the interest of the state or himself because he believed they violate filial piety? How flexible was Huizong's understanding of the filial piety expected of Qinzong?

Qinzong and the retired emperor, lord of the Dao

Once Qinzong took the throne, those who had been excluded from Huizong's court expected to get their turn, as they had when Shenzong died. During the first few weeks, Qinzong continued to work with high officials who had served Huizong, especially the ones who had urged abdication, but from the start Qinzong received many memorials from those who wanted a total change of administrations. Just days after his accession, the National Academy student Chen Dong 陳東 called for the execution of Huizong's leading officials, including those no longer in office, such as the eighty-plus Cai Jing 蔡京, not active since 1120. Chen labeled them the "Six Traitors," a label that stuck (the list included Cai Jing, Wang Fu 王黼, Tong Guan, Liang Shicheng 梁師成, Li Yan 李彥, and Zhu Mian 朱勔). At this point, however, Qinzong's first concern was defending Kaifeng, then negotiating with the Jurchen to get them to leave, and finally raising the enormous sums of gold and silver that the Jurchen demanded.

On 1/28, well before the Jurchens left, Chen Dong submitted another inflammatory memorial, reiterating his demand that the "six traitors" be executed but going on to make a new accusation that Cai Jing's son Cai You 蔡攸, along with Tong Guan and Zhu Mian, had kidnapped Huizong and taken him south against his will. Chen wanted them brought back to be punished. In his view it was particularly dangerous to let the mobile palace get to the southeast, since Cai Jing's faction was strong in that area. Chen feared that Huizong's entourage might try to set up a separate government in the thousand counties of the south. He insisted that Qinzong should write out an edict in his own hand and send it to Huizong "inviting" him to return to the capital. Chen argued against those who said the Jurchen threat was the main problem of the moment, asserting that the "inner troubles" of evil officials were more serious than the outer ones of barbarian enemies.

Chen brought filial piety into his argument by noting that the physical separation between Qinzong and his father made it difficult for Qinzong to serve Huizong in the way a filial son should and by claiming that bringing Huizong back would manifest his filial piety.[8]

Chen Dong was not the only one worried about possible separatist plots on the part of Huizong's entourage. On 2/14, Chen Gongfu 陳公輔 submitted a memorial urging Qinzong to dismiss those officials who had served under Huizong, including the ones who had urged him to abdicate like Wu Min and Li Bangyan. He explicitly brought up the passage in the *Analects* that presents the ability to maintain a father's government as the height of filial piety, but argued against it:

> In my view, when Your Majesty was accumulating virtue in the Eastern Palace [i.e. heir apparent], you were modest and conscientious, withdrawing from responsibility on the grounds of lack of ability, all of which was appropriate to your role as son. Today you are in charge of the entire realm and manage the myriad states, which is your responsibility in your role as ruler. You should lead with the firmness of the Qian hexagram and persevere with the clarity of the Li hexagram. You should promote what is advantageous and get rid of what is harmful, in order to continue the unlimited blessings of your ancestors on the one hand and comfort the hopes of all living beings on the other. You should not get stuck on proposals to hold fast to the principle that "not changing the ministers or the government of his father is difficult to attain."[9]

Chen Gongfu then went on to argue that Huizong himself at the end had come to recognize that those around him were evil, and in his final edict had taken on the blame himself. Thus Qinzong, by getting rid of the ministers who had served Huizong, would be doing what Huizong would have done. Qinzong undoubtedly could see through this – emperors for centuries had routinely taken on the blame when anything went wrong, from comets to solar eclipses, droughts to uprisings, but their officials did not normally act as though they really meant everything they said. Moreover, Huizong had himself selected the officials to accompany him on his trip south more than a week after he had issued the edict of repentance. Still, by arguing that Huizong had come to his senses at the end, Chen Gongfu was giving Qinzong a way to claim that demoting, banishing, and executing Huizong's officials was a filial act.

A few days later, on 2/18, Tang Zhong 唐重 offered Qinzong another way to interpret forcing Huizong's return as a filial act. His argument was that Huizong was facing all sorts of dangers on his travels, which, since Qinzong is so filial, causes him anxieties. Alluding to Mencius 5A4, Tang implored, "Now that the peace agreement has been reached and the royal house is free from worries, it is right that you 'use the resources of the realm to take care of him'."[10]

As a result of urgings like these, on 3/1 Qinzong sent the official Song Huan with a letter to ask Huizong to return.[11] Qinzong's court, however, was not in full agreement on how much force to use to get Huizong back and on how real the rumors were that he or those around him were setting up an alternative government far from Kaifeng. The best evidence we have of the sorts of discussions that were taking place among officials in the capital is a long memorial that the mid-rank official Wang Zao 汪藻 sent to the grand councilors. Since he was not addressing Qinzong, he could use franker language in discussing what many clearly felt was the threat of the "mobile palace." Evidently these officials had been debating how the imperatives of filial piety applied to Qinzong's case, because Wang began by presenting his interpretation:

> I once noticed that Confucius explained the filial piety of the common person in this way: "He is cautious in his person and frugal in his expenditures in order to support his father and mother." From the common person on up, the higher his rank, the greater his virtue, up to the Son of Heaven, of which it is said, "His love and respect are complete in his service to his parents; and his virtuous teachings are a model for the land within the four seas."[12] Surely the patrimony of Son of Heaven is all under Heaven, but what does he see when he observes whether all under Heaven is peaceful or not? When the realm is peaceful, his parents will certainly be too. When the ancients talked of filial piety, they cited examples like those of Shun. Someone asked Mencius "When Shun was Son of Heaven and Gao Yao was officer, if [Shun's father] Gu Sou killed someone, what would he do? Mencius said, "He would arrest him." "Would Shun then not prevent it?" Mencius said, "How could Shun stop it? [The officer] had received [his charge]." The phrase "he had received" means that he had received the most public-minded way in the realm in order to bring order to the people. If we set this aside, we have no means to attain order."[13]

Note here that Wang Zao conveniently left out the next part of this passage in which Mencius says that Shun would consider possessing the empire no more essential than a worn out sandal and would abandon it in order to protect his father. Instead Wang argued that the welfare of the entire society could not be sacrificed for what is essentially a private relationship. He also advocated thinking very carefully about the phrase from Mencius, "supporting him with the whole realm," which he clearly did not want to be taken literally.

Wang himself was no fan of Huizong and thought Qinzong had no obligation to consult him. If, he argued, when the barbarians had first invaded, Huizong out of shame and fear had worked with Qinzong "to wipe away the humiliation to the dynasty, and soothe the hearts of the army and people," then it would be appropriate for Qinzong to invite Huizong back into the palace and consult with him morning and evening to "relieve his concerns about danger, doubt, disturbance, and worry." However, since Huizong had left when the siege was imminent without even giving a return date, Qinzong had no obligation to discuss policies with him. And Wang was even angrier at the entourage who had accompanied Huizong. "When the royal carriage left, officials in a state of fear let the state collapse and fled south. These criminals, saying they were part of the escort, without waiting to ask the court for permission, even high-ranking officers and close followers who had received generous rewards from the state, kept sneaking out, so that there were hardly any left by the ruler's side to protect the state."[14] That these men had gone unpunished, Wang claimed, weakened the credibility of Qinzong's court. Moreover, the mobile court issued its own orders, redirecting relief armies and causing confusion in command. Besides, the mobile court was expensive, using up 6,000 strings of cash a day, and some of the scoundrels associated with it were proposing that palaces be built and parks be purchased, all very costly.

Wang recommended sending a current grand councilor to invite Huizong back, but also proposed dealing directly with the military and civilian personnel attached to the mobile court. He proposed offering rewards to those who cooperated and threatening death to those who did not. By getting the mobile court back, "the sincerity of the father–son tie will have an effect." If this did not work, an even tougher approach was warranted: "If scoundrels still dare to obstruct things, then identify the worst among the officials of the mobile palace, from the commissioner on down, and replace them. Once those treacherous conspirators are gone, and the retired emperor hears upright words every day, he will not tarry any longer."[15]

Wang did not discount the possibility that everything would be fine once Qinzong and Huizong were reconciled, but wanted to convince Qinzong that he had to remember his other responsibilities and make sure that only one court was issuing orders:

> Once the mobile palace has returned and the two emperors are recon-
> ciled, even if the retired emperor suddenly pays no more attention to the
> myriad affairs, still we must keep in mind that there are many principles
> and obligations in the realm. Major matters should be carried out only
> after petitioning. That way, there will be unity of purpose above and
> unity of command below. The *qian* and *kun* forces will be restored and
> the dynasty will last forever. How could the filial piety of the emperor
> be greater than this?[16]

Two days after Wang wrote this memorial, Qinzong sent another letter to Huizong, again asking him to return. This document has the formality of a letter between two rulers, but includes many references to the Daoist ideas Qinzong knew interested Huizong. It also evoked the phrase from Mencius, "supporting with the entire realm." Qinzong appointed Zhao Ye 趙野 as the

Commissioner for Welcoming Back in charge of delivering it and had one of Qinzong's brothers accompany him, perhaps to remind Huizong that this was a family matter.[17]

Empress Zheng 鄭, Huizong's empress, had not gone as far south as Huizong had, and she agreed to return to Kaifeng before Huizong did. On 3/11 an official reported that the current rumor was that Qinzong wanted to open the main palace gate and invite the empress dowager to return and rule jointly with him, which he warned against on the grounds that power in the hands of consorts invariably was dangerous and that Qinzong was not a minor in need of guidance.[18] On 3/12, Qinzong's officials advised him not to let Empress Zheng into the palace. In this case, the officials avoided using the term *xiao*, arguing instead that the duty of a woman with a living husband is to be at his side, and as Huizong would not live in the palace, she should not either.[19]

As the capital recovered from the siege, tension between the two courts abated a little. On 3/15 Huizong sent a letter to Qinzong, reporting that the recent visit of Qinzong's envoy Song Huan had helped to clarify matters and smooth relations.[20] To try to reduce the paranoia of so many of the officials at Qinzong's court, Chen Gongfu submitted a memorial expressing his doubts about the rumors of separatist traitors seizing control of Huizong.[21] He first told Qinzong that Huizong's imminent return was "a response to the sincerity of Your Majesty's filial piety, a blessing for the realm." Then he argued that there were no grounds for comparing Qinzong's relationship to Huizong to the Tang case of Suzong and Xuanzong, an analogy others must have been evoking:

> Consider that the retired emperor ruled for a long time. Last year in the winter the northern barbarians invaded, and because he was tired of the cares of governing, he wanted to abdicate. Your Majesty is by nature extremely filial; deeply affected you wept and refused. Only after repeated parental instructions did you take the great seal. This has some similarity to the time in the Tang when Ruizong, because of an astral phenomenon and in response to Heaven's warnings, [abdicated to] the heir apparent, who entered in fear and trembling. But how could it compare to Suzong setting himself on the throne at Xingfu while Minghuang [Xuanzong] was traveling in Shu? In your case there should be feelings of joy between father and son; even a thousand or ten thousand years from now, no one will doubt [your motivations].[22]

Chen went on to try to convince Qinzong not to worry that Huizong would be angry at him for demoting and executing so many of his top officials. "These acts were all done with the dynasty in mind and were in accord with popular opinion, and were a way to follow through on the retired emperor's edict." Chen also reiterated the by then familiar argument that Huizong had in his last edict called for rooting out entrenched evils and that Qinzong had thus through his actions been honoring his father's intentions. Moreover, Chen argued, Huizong is a kind person and the father–son relationship a natural one: "Is the retired emperor closer to you or closer to his officials? In my opinion, no one is closer to him than Your Majesty." Chen worried, though, that Qinzong had not selected an adequately diplomatic official to carry his message to Huizong, and wanted someone else sent. "Should by any chance the retired emperor harbor the slightest suspicion, [the envoy] could immediately in an appropriate way earnestly and fully describe your Majesty's true filial sincerity and item by item explain that there is no difference between his edict of last year and the intentions behind your recent actions."[23]

> Chen urged a grand show when Huizong returned to the capital: The ritual of welcoming him should be done on a grand scale. Your Majesty should take the imperial carriage and go in person to welcome him at the suburbs. The empresses, consorts, princesses, and imperial relatives, down to the ministers, officials, scholars, commoners, and elders, should all come to meet him, so that he sees the contrast between the hurry of his past departure and the honor of his present return, and how this was possible only because Your Majesty bore the heavy burden entrusted to you, bringing some peace to the difficulties caused by the invasion, stability to the capital, getting administration restored, and making the people glad. When the retired emperor's heart has been soothed by such actions, he will appreciate that this is a time when "being the emperor's father is the height of honor" [allusion to *Mencius* 5A4].[24]

Should these courtesies not be enough to win over Huizong, once Huizong was back, Qinzong could control who talked to Huizong. "You should select from among your officials scholars of probity known for their virtuous behavior, scholarship, filial piety, and integrity to act as advisors to the retired emperor. They should attend him every day, joining him when he is at leisure, leading his sagely mind toward metaphysical truths so that he frees himself from the burden of worldly affairs."[25]

Another official who worried about the danger in aggravating the friction between the two courts was Li Gang. At an audience with Qinzong, Li Gang objected to plans to send Nie Shan 聶山 with soldiers to arrest key officials in Huizong's entourage such as Tong Guan, Cai You, and Gao Qiu 高俅. He used the example of Suzong and Xuanzong to make his case:

> In the past, when Suzong wished to excavate Li Linfu's tomb, Li Bi remonstrated, asking how Minghuang would take it. Suzong put his arm around Bi's neck and cried, "I hadn't thought that far." If [Nie] Shan's mission in fact succeeds, it will frighten the Lord of the Dao [Huizong], which would trouble Your Majesty. If the mission fails and it is discovered by these men, what if they took the Lord of the Dao

prisoner in the southeast and demanded the circuit of Jiannan? How would Your Majesty deal with it?[26]

The comparison with Li Linfu was apt because Tang contemporaries had been as quick to blame the An Lushan rebellion on former powerful chief minister Li Linfu as his own contemporaries were to blame the Jurchen invasion on Cai Jing and Tong Guan. When Qinzong asked what alternative he had, Li Gang proposed calling off the mission to arrest the leading members of Huizong's inner circle and instead gradually demoting and transferring them to get them away from Huizong.

Qinzong then sent Li Gang to call on both Empress Zheng and Huizong, perhaps seeing in Li Gang the sort of diplomatic person Chen Gongfu had recommended that he send as an emissary. Li called first on the Empress. He did his best to make the new decision not to let her into the palace seem less hostile than it really was. Once he entered the empress's boat, he tried to soften the new order that she live outside the palace, by telling her that given Qinzong's "sagely filial piety" (*shengxiao* 聖孝), nothing would be able to come between the two, no matter where she lived. When the empress did in fact return to Kaifeng on 3/19, the imperial guard was ready to prevent her from entering the palace. She, however, made no effort to enter.[27]

When Li Gang arrived at Huizong's place, according to his own record, "I fully reported on the emperor's sagely filial piety and affection, of his intention 'to use the empire to take care of him'," alluding to Mencius. Huizong's tears streamed down, and he acknowledged that Qinzong was filial. The two men then talked about everything that had happened since Huizong left the capital, with Li Gang trying to convince Huizong that Qinzong had made reasonable decisions, and Huizong similarly explaining why he had taken several steps that had raised suspicions about his intentions. For instance, Huizong said he had cut off the transmission of documents between the mobile palace and Qinzong's court because during the siege he thought that if messages were intercepted, the Jurchen would learn his location. In response to thirty-odd questions posed by Huizong, Li Gang explained such measures as the new honors granted to Sima Guang. The most persuasive part of Li Gang's message directly addressed the issue of filial piety. He told Huizong:

> The emperor is benevolent, filial, and cautious; his only concern is that he would not do as you would want him to. Every time he receives an inquiry from you, he becomes so anxious and frightened that meals cannot be served. Let me compare it to an ordinary family where the esteemed father has left and entrusted the family business to a son. Then fierce bandits rob and plunder and the son must make the decisions about what should be done. While awaiting the father's return, the son cannot but worry. The esteemed father ought to praise and comfort the son for coming up with a plan to preserve the fields and

gardens, and not make a fuss over the details. Now, when the current emperor was first on the throne, Your Majesty took a trip, which was just when the enemy invaded. To save the dynasty, he had no choice but to make minor changes in the government. Today the dynasty is no longer endangered and the four directions are calm. If Your Majesty now returns, in my view it would be a great comfort to His Majesty. There is no need to ask about the minor details.[28]

Li Gang was here trying to persuade Huizong that if he returned, he would be treated like a father who had returned from a business trip, and be put back at the center of things, certainly something no one at Qinzong's court intended. Whether Li Gang saw himself as deceiving Huizong toward a higher end, or saw himself as saving Huizong's face in a way Huizong would know was a polite fiction, is not clear from Li Gang's account.

Two days later, before Li Gang returned to Kaifeng, he had another meeting with Huizong, on which occasion Huizong offered written evidence that his intentions had always been to do the best for the dynasty. He produced a prayer that he said he had written the night before his abdication and gave it to Li Gang to show to the officials. It read in part:

I was formerly lord over the land within the four seas and looked after the myriad people, but my virtue was thin, and in managing things did not make the right choices. Fighting has broken out and no one is safe. Because I worry about the ancestral temples, the temples of the soil and grain, and all the people, I have already transferred the seals to my heir in order to conform to Heaven's desires above and to stop the armies below so that, as hoped for, near return and far become obedient, the world becomes peaceful, the dynasty has unlimited blessings, and those inside and outside enjoying the pleasures of peace.

If in this way the bandit-soldiers put down their weapons, after there is general peace, I will with all my heart observe the Dao and happily live in reclusion. May Heaven be my witness, I am not acting recklessly. Once the decision is made, even if there are crises, it will be a great sin to get involved with my old responsibilities. If in this prayer, something is not entirely appropriate, let the disaster that descends reach only my person, preserving the foundation of the dynasty and protecting the welfare of living beings. Let the five weapons be permanently set aside, the ten thousand countries all be at peace, I hope for true kindness and special attention.[29]

Huizong also asked Li Gang to explain to Qinzong why his journey had been so slow, and gave Li a personal note that read, "You have assisted the emperor in defending the dynasty. Anyone able to bring peace between a father and son so that all suspicion is resolved deserves to have his name passed down in the histories for ten thousand generations."[30]

Li Gang continued to play a conciliatory role after his return to Kaifeng. For instance, on 3/27 he argued with Geng Nanzhong 耿南仲 when the latter proposed dismissing all of Huizong's eunuch servants.[31] He was not entirely successful in this effort, however; when Huizong was finally welcomed back to Kaifeng, on 4/3, ten of the eunuchs with him were prevented from entering.[32] On 3/30 an official submitted a memorial impeaching Song Huan, above all on the grounds of connections to Wang Fu and Cai You, but explicitly charging that he had tried to drive a wedge between Qinzong and his father by telling Qinzong of Huizong's anger and reporting to the literati what Huizong had said.[33]

After his return to Kaifeng on 4/14, Huizong lived at the palace/Daoist temple, Dragon Virtue Palace 龍德宮, built several years earlier at the site of his princely mansion near the northwest corner of the city. Over the next several weeks, Qinzong, on the urging of his officials, gradually tightened control over Huizong and those with him. Officials were assigned to the palace and required to make daily reports on Huizong's activities. At one point they were given orders to question everyone who visited Huizong and confiscate any gifts he made to them.[34] Qinzong's visits to Huizong were rare, and Huizong was apparently invited to the palace only once, on 5/13.[35] Qinzong could not avoid visiting Huizong on his birthday in the tenth month, but the occasion did not go well. Shortly before, Huizong had said that the Jurchen were sure to return, and proposed that he go to Luoyang to organize an army there, but Wu Min had convinced Qinzong to reject this idea. At the birthday party, someone stepped on Qinzong's toes, and Qinzong refused the glass of wine Huizong offered him. Moreover, after this meeting, Qinzong had placards posted outside the Dragon Virtue Palace offering rewards to anyone who turned in people passing rumors about the two palaces. From this point on, we are told, there was no real communication between the two palaces.[36]

To finish the story, late in 1126 the Jurchen returned and set siege to the capital again. When the outer walls fell after a month, Huizong and Empress Zheng moved into the palace. One of the first demands the Jurchen made when negotiations were opened was that Qinzong turn over his father as a hostage. Qinzong refused on the grounds of filial piety, but he did send a younger brother and uncle, and also offered to go himself. Once under Jurchen control, Qinzong was put in the difficult position of having to deceive Huizong to get him to leave the relative safety of the palace. Neither Huizong nor Qinzong ever regained their freedom. Both were transported north, in separate parties as far as Yanjing, then together as they were transferred progressively further north, in 1130 reaching the remote town of Wuguo. The Jurchen treated both Huizong and Qinzong as former emperors, and Huizong, as the senior, seems to have regained his authority over the imperial family, a great many of whom were also transferred north. Both Huizong and Qinzong died in captivity, Huizong eight years later, Qinzong thirty-four.

As a postscript, I could add that Gaozong (1127–1162), Huizong's other son to succeed to the throne, had an even harder time reconciling his obligations to preserve the dynasty and to serve his parents, both of whom had been taken into captivity by the Jurchen. Many people wondered why he did not pursue ransoming his parents until after Huizong's death, and why he ransomed only his mother and not his brother Qinzong. On the other side were those who thought he was too conciliatory toward the Jurchens, suspecting him of putting his desire to get his mother back above getting the entire north back. Perhaps to soothe his conscience, in his late years after his mother had been returned, he was extremely devoted in his attentions to her. And once she died, he abdicated himself, though in his case his heir, Xiaozong, treated him with extreme deference.

Implications and reflections

Reading between the lines in these memorials and accounts of political decision-making, it seems evident that most of the officials at Qinzong's court saw Qinzong's qualms about the imperatives of filial piety as a problem of emperor management. They adopted the rhetoric of filial piety because Qinzong or other officials expressed their reservations in that language, but the logic underlying their proposed courses of action was a political one, not an ethical one. It was based above all on their distrust, verging sometimes on hatred, of those who surrounded Huizong and, one suspects, in some cases of Huizong himself. In their hands, the rhetoric of filial piety was extraordinarily malleable; Qinzong's officials were able to justify almost any action they saw as in the interest of the dynasty as an expression of filial piety, anything short of having Huizong killed. For Qinzong, however, the situation was not so simple. Like any child, he could not look on his father in an entirely dispassionate way, nor could he easily free himself from desire for his approval and fear of his disapproval. Qinzong had to deal with the psychology of father–son relations, the ethical rhetoric of filial piety, and the political requirements of a court in crisis.

Officials, even those generally viewed as strong advocates of a Confucian vision of government, such as Li Gang, found it was easy to elevate the more abstract side of filial piety – responsibility to ancestors and thus to the dynasty – above the more concrete side of filial piety – deference to the wishes and established ways of one's parents. Their commitment to Confucian teachings meant that they could not downgrade filial piety, but they were free to interpret it in very broad terms. Both because of the crisis of the invasion and because of the intense factional strife that had marred court politics for two generations, Qinzong's officials wanted his administration to be a genuinely new one, not one encumbered by the *Analects'* injunction against making changes in one father's administration, or Mencius' elevation of duty to father over duty to subjects. A change in emperors, to these officials, should mean an opportunity to change policies and personnel, not a period when change is forbidden.

Why were they so determined to force Huizong back to Kaifeng? One might have thought that moving some members of the imperial family out of the capital would increase the chances of the dynasty surviving – it was after all because Gaozong was out of the capital that he survived to rally Song forces after the fall of Kaifeng. To those around Qinzong, however, unity of command took absolute priority and the ambiguities created when Huizong was not under their full control were too great a cost. They could not instantly replace all the officials who had entered office under Huizong, but they did not want these men to doubt who was actually in charge.

The dire situation in the capital during the siege gave Qinzong little choice but to appoint to leading posts men untainted by association with Huizong's court. Once when Qinzong dismissed Li Gang, students at the National Academy staged a huge protest. But even if Qinzong accepted popular opinion concerning whom he should appoint as ministers, he was less comfortable than they were with overturning everything his father had done. He needed a great deal of reassurance, presumably to assuage pangs of guilt, as he demoted or executed his father's former officials and dismantled his projects. He does not seem to have been nearly as eager as his chief officials to force Huizong back to Kaifeng. From Li Gang's testimony I suspect that he dreaded having to face Huizong (though once he discovered that he could force Huizong to do as he wanted, Qinzong lost some of his trepidation about dealing with his father).

On the whole, Qinzong and Huizong did better when they could use intermediaries. Calm, well spoken intermediaries could offer comforting assurances of good intentions and avoid the danger of volatile personal confrontations. It was when Qinzong refused to take the cup of wine that Huizong collapsed in tears and communication between the two courts reached its lowest point. The two got along better when they had men like Song Huan and Li Gang carrying messages between them.

Some of the features of the relationship between Qinzong and Huizong were special to the circumstances under which Huizong gave up power. The factional style of politics, in which opponents are labeled traitors, had marred political life since the beginning of Shenzong's reign. The threat to the dynasty was not imagined, but real, calling for extreme measures. Both were men in their prime, Qinzong in his mid-twenties (older than Huizong when he took the throne), but Huizong only in his mid-forties himself.

Still, some of the elements of their relationship are best explained by reference to larger institutional and cultural structures rather than their particular circumstances. Qinzong received an education comparable to that of other princes who were prime candidates for the throne. The tutors appointed to educate him may have believed that new emperors should be encouraged to rethink the policies and personnel of their fathers, but still would have worked hard to inculcate in him the classical teachings on filial piety. After all, they had to train him for two roles and they could not predict when he would pass from one to the other. The dutiful deference to his father's wishes that an heir had to display to retain his position, perhaps decades into adulthood, was not always good preparation for guilt-free reversal of his father's policies after succession. Tutors who stressed only a prince's obligations to Heaven, the dynasty, and his subjects might well find that he was passed over for the succession, hardly a goal they would aim at. Qinzong, like other Chinese princes, had to be reared to be a prince as well as to be a ruler on his own.

Let me end with an issue for us to ponder. In Chinese fiction and drama, little has been made of the friction inherent in imperial father–son relations. One could easily imagine a Greek or Shakespearean tragedy that focused on the relations between Huizong, Qinzong, and Gaozong. Each had reasons to resent the others and blame the others for his plight. Qinzong's advisors always blamed Huizong's policies for the disaster. But if Qinzong had not forced Huizong to return to the capital, Huizong could probably have lived out his life in the south. Huizong and Qinzong both had reasons to wonder why Gaozong did not ransom them. The Chinese did write historical fiction about the court in this period, most successfully the *Xuanhe yishi* 宣和遺事.[37] This story draws heavily on historical sources, but none of the father–son tensions found in the historical sources I have quoted here are played up in the novel. The culturally painful topic of alien conquest is dealt with metaphorically in the novel, but not the more universal issues of father–son tensions. Qinzong and Huizong are shown as crying together during captivity, but not blaming each other. Do we learn anything interesting about the place of filial piety in Chinese culture from the relative silence of literature on the strains filial piety could create?

Notes

1 On this literature, see H. J. Wechsler, *Offerings of Jade and Silk: Ritual and Symbol in the Legitimation of the T'ang Dynasty*, New Haven, CT: Yale University Press, 1985; J. L.Watson and E. S. Rawski (eds), *Death Ritual in Late Imperial and Modern China*, Berkeley: University of California Press, 1988; P. Ebrey, "Portrait Sculptures in Imperial Ancestral Rites in Song China," *T'oung Pao*, 83, 1997, 42–92; J. P. McDermott (ed.), *State and Court Ritual in China*, Cambridge: Cambridge University Press, 1999.
2 C. T. Fisher, "The Ritual Dispute of Sung Ying-tsung," *Papers on Far Eastern History*, 36, 1987, 109–38; *The Chosen One: Succession and Adoption in the Court of Ming Shizong*, Boston: Allen and Unwin, 1990.
3 *Mengzi zhushu*, *Shisan jing zhushu* edition, 9A, pp. 9a–12a; cf. J. Legge (trans), *The Chinese Classics*, Hong Kong: Hong Kong University Press, 1961 (reprint of Oxford, 1865–1895 edition), vol. 2, pp. 350–4.
4 *Mengzi zhushu* 13B.6b–7b; cf. J. Legge, *Chinese Classics*, vol. 2, pp. 469–70.
5 I am currently working on a book on this topic and have given papers on several aspects of it, only one of which has appeared in print so far: "Taoism and Art at the Court of Song Huizong," in S. Little (ed.), *Taoism and the Arts of China*, Berkeley: University of California Press, 2000, pp. 94–111.

6 Yang Zhongliang 楊仲良, *Tongjian changbian jishi benmo* 通鑑長編紀事本末, Guangya shuju, 1893, *juan* 146, p. 9a.

7 Dates (12/24, etc.) give month and day in the Chinese lunar calendar.

8 Xu Mengxin 徐夢莘, *Sanchao beimeng huibian* 三朝北盟會編, Taipei: Dahua shuju reprint of punctuated edition, *jia* 315–20.

9 Ibid., *jia* 367.

10 Ibid., *jia* 398.

11 Huang Yizhou 黃以周, *Xu zizhi tongjian changbian shibu* 續資治通鑒長編史部, Shanghai: Shanghai Guji Chubanshe, 1986, *juan* 54, p. 6b.

12 Both from the *Classic of Filial Piety*.

13 Xu Mengxin, *Sanchao, jia* 425.

14 Ibid., *jia* 426.

15 Ibid., *jia* 427.

16 Ibid., *jia* 427.

17 *Jingkang yaolu* 靖康要錄 (anon.), *Congshu jicheng* edition, *juan* 3, pp. 62–3.

18 Ibid., *juan* 3, pp. 63–5.

19 Ibid., *juan* 3, pp. 65–6.

20 Xu Mengxin, *Sanchao, jia* 430–1; *Jingkang yaolu, juan* 4, p. 67.

21 *Jingkang yaolu, juan* 4, pp. 69–70; Xu Mengxin, *Sanchao, jia* 431–2; Huang Yizhou, *Xu zizhi tongjian, juan* 54, p. 8a.

22 *Jingkang yaolu, juan* 4, p. 69.

23 Ibid.

24 Ibid., *juan* 4, pp. 69–70.

25 Ibid., *juan* 4, p. 70.

26 Li Gang, *Jingkang chuanxin lu* 靖康傳信錄, *Congshu jicheng* edition, *juan* 2, p. 16. On this source and its author, see J. W. Haeger, "Sung Government at Midstream: Translation of and Commentary on the *Ching-k'ang ch'uan-hsin lu*," PhD dissertation, University of California, Berkeley, 1971, and "1126–27: Political Crisis and the Integrity of Culture," in J. W. Haeger (ed.), *Crisis and Prosperity in Sung China*, Tuscon: University of Arizona Press, 1975.

27 Li Gang, *Jingkang chuanxin lu, juan* 2, p. 17.

28 Ibid., *juan* 2, p. 18.

29 Yue Ke 岳珂 (1183–?), *Tingshi* 庭史, Beijing: Zhonghua shuju, 1983, *juan* 8, p. 93. Later Huizong gave a copy of this prayer to Li Gang when he visited him in 1126/3. The *Jingkang yaolu, juan* 4, pp. 74–5, records it after describing that visit, but does not mention when the prayer was first written.

30 Li Gang, *Jingkang chuanxin lu, juan* 2, p. 18. Li later showed this document to Qinzong, who added his own thanks to it and returned it to Li. Li not only treasured it but also had copies of it printed. Li Gang, *Liangxi ji* 梁溪集, *Siku quanshu* edition, *juan* 161, pp. 1a–2b.

31 Xu Mengxin, *Sanchao, jia* 440–1.

32 *Jingkang yaolu, juan* 4, p. 89. See also Xu Mengxin, *Sanchao, jia* 445.

33 *Jingkang yaolu, juan* 4, p. 85.

34 *Jingkang yaolu, juan* 4, p. 93; Xu Mengxin, *Sanchao, jia* 445.

35 Xu Mengxin, *Sanchao, jia* 470.

36 Ibid., *jia* 564.

37 For a translation see W. O. Hennessey, *Proclaiming Harmony*, Ann Arbor: Center for Chinese Studies, University of Michigan, 1981. On the historical sources used by the author, see his "Classical Sources and Vernacular Resources in *Xuanhe Yishi*: The Presence of Priority and the Priority of Presence," *Chinese Literature: Essays, Articles, and Reviews*, 6, 1984, pp. 33–52.

8 Emperor Chengzu and imperial filial piety of the Ming dynasty

From the *Classic of Filial Piety* to the *Biographical Accounts of Filial Piety*

Lee Cheuk Yin

Filial piety in pre-Qin Confucian thought

Historically, the concept of "filial piety" was already well developed as early as the Zhou dynasty.[1] During the chaotic and turbulent Spring and Autumn Periods, the Confucian school advocated "rectification of names," proper human relationships, and that rulers relieve the people's agony. For them, the idea of filial piety enjoyed a primary position of importance.

The word *xiao* (孝, filial piety) appeared seventeen times in the *Analects* and twenty-seven times in the *Mencius*. To Confucius, it was the starting point of fulfilling an ideal moral character. There are four passages in Book II of the *Analects* in which Confucius explained the meaning of filial piety to his disciples:

> When your parents are alive, comply with the rites in serving them; when they die, comply with the rites in burying them; comply with the rites in sacrificing to them.[2]
>
> (2.5)

> Give your father and mother no other cause for anxiety than illness.
>
> (2.6)

> Nowadays for a man to be filial means no more than that he is able to provide his parents with food. Even dogs and horses are, in some ways, provided with food. If a man shows no reverence, where is the difference?
>
> (2.7)

> What is difficult to manage is the expression on one's face. As for the young taking on the burden when there is work to be done or letting the old enjoy the wine and food when these are available, that hardly deserves to be called filial.
>
> (2.8)

From the above definitions given by Confucius, it can be said that he viewed filial piety as not just providing material needs and ritual burial. That is, the practice of filial piety should not be thought of as merely fulfilling a formality, but should be carried out as a natural and spontaneous product of filial affection. It should be a desire of the innermost heart and practiced with respect and sincerity.

In discussing filial piety, Mencius embraced the views of Confucius and further elaborated the concept. He even approached the concept from another angle by explaining the conditions for being "unfilial." He said: "There are three ways of being unfilial, and to have no posterity is the greatest of them" (4A26). The three unfilial behaviors, according to the annotations by Han scholar Zhao Qi 趙岐, are: deceiving your parents with flatteries and leading them to ignore righteousness; not entering public service and making a career when parents are old and living in poverty; not marrying and having no posterity to carry on the ancestral sacrifice.[3] In other words, filial piety encompasses not only direct filial duty toward one's parents – that is, respect and support for one's parents during their life and sacrifice to them after their death – but also indirect filial duty toward one's clan to carry on the family line so that ancestors will continue to be worshiped by the future generations. Mencius also mentioned five conditions by which a son would be considered unfilial by society:

> There are five things, which are said, in the common practice of the age to be unfilial. The first is laziness in the use of one's limbs, without attending to the nourishment of his parents. The second is gambling and chess playing and being fond of wine without attending to the nourishment of his parents. The third is being fond of goods and money, and selfishly being attached to one's wife without attending to the nourishment of one's parents. The fourth is to follow the desires of one's ears and eyes, so as to bring one's parents into disgrace. The fifth is being fond of bravery, fighting and quarrelling so as to endanger his parents.
>
> (4B30)

Although it seems that a son is bound by many conditions in order to be filial, filial piety never implies blind obedience to one's parents. One may and ought to reason with one's parents when their orders conflict with righteousness, such as orders to commit crimes or tell lies. In such circumstances blind obedience is considered to be deleterious to parents and run counter to the true spirit of filial piety. Both Confucius and Mencius said that when the son sees his parents' faults, he is under an obligation to expostulate them gently and humbly. When they do not indicate an inclination to follow his advice, he should show an increased degree of reverence, but should not abandon his purpose. Moreover, according to Mencius, even if the admonition arouses the parents' anger, this is not regarded as unfilial.

Thus, it can be seen that any claim of lack of filial piety ought to be measured by the attitude and behavior on both sides.

Pre-Qin Confucian scholars considered filial piety toward one's parents to be the most important ethic in human relationships, more important than one's loyalty to the country. As a matter of fact, the relationship between father and son is natural and unalterable. No matter how bad one's father is deemed to be, the relationship cannot be changed. On the other hand, the relationship between ruler and minister is acquired, one can choose whether or not to serve the monarch, the relationship can be cast off and is changeable.[4] Loyalty (*zhong*) as a moral ethic that maintains ruler–minister relationships is a professional obligation rather than an innate duty; this obligation is relative, reciprocal, and not absolute. Unlike filial piety, which is "the root of benevolence,"[5] loyalty is neither the most basic ethic nor a necessary condition of attaining benevolence.

Comparing filial piety with loyalty, the former has a broader coverage, inclusive of the latter, but not vice versa. Therefore, it is said that a filial son will certainly be a loyal minister, whereas a loyal minister is not necessarily a filial son.[6] Pre-Qin Confucians believe that if one can fulfill the requirements of filial piety, by extension of the virtue he will also fulfill the requirements of loyalty. However, although the virtue of filial piety is bound up with the virtue of loyalty, there are situations in which they will contradict each other. When a choice has to be made between filial piety and loyalty, pre-Qin Confucians gave priority to filial piety. In Book 13 of the *Analects* we find the following conversation:

> The Duke of She said to Confucius, "In my hometown, there is a straight and upright man. When his father stole a sheep, he gave evidence against him." Confucius said, "The straight and upright men in my hometown are of a different type. Fathers conceal the misconduct of their sons, and sons of their fathers. Uprightness is to be found in this."
>
> (13.18)

According to Confucius, uprightness was revealed when a father covered up his son's mistake or a filial son covered up his father's mistake. To bear witness to the misconduct of one's father or son regardless of the relationship was by no means uprightness. Thus, if loyalty is toward one's country and filial piety toward one's family, then a father or son's covering up for each other will imply violating the doctrine of loyalty. Mencius' standpoint on this issue quite clearly agrees with Confucius'. He puts forward a complex case involving a choice between loyalty and filial piety:

> Tao Ying asked, "When Shun was emperor and Gao Yao was the judge, if Gu Sou, Shun's father, killed a man, what was to be done?" Mencius said, "The only thing to do was to apprehend him." "In that case, would Shun not try to stop it?" "How could Shun stop it? Gao

Yao had his authority which he received from the law." "Then what would Shun have done?" "Shun would have looked upon casting aside the empire as no more than discarding a worn shoe. He would have secretly carried the old man on his back and fled to the edge of the sea and lived there happily, never giving a thought to the empire."[7]

(7A35)

Shun was in a dilemma as to whether he should allow his father to be executed or save him. As a son, he should have performed his filial duty and rescued his father. But as a ruler, he was required to be loyal to the country and avoid hindering enforcement of the law.[8] To Shun, this was a conflict between public and private interest, between loyalty and filial piety. In Mencius' opinion, Shun would take filial piety and forsake loyalty. He would have privately taken his father away and retired.

The above incident demonstrates clearly that filial piety is more important than loyalty in Pre-Qin Confucian thought. If filial piety and loyalty are in conflict and a choice has to be made, filial piety is always the first priority.[9]

The emergence of autocratic monarchy and the *Classic of Filial Piety*

With the establishment of a unified China by the Qin dynasty (221–206 BCE), the political arena was swept by drastic changes in its structure – the establishment of an autocratic monarchical system with centralized control. For the next two thousand years, Chinese politics and society were subject to variations of this system but with little change to its basic characteristics. Its uniqueness was such that the kingdom belonged to the royal family exclusively, and that only the ruling class could enjoy absolute power and superior status. This was the concept of a "familial state" 家天下, a political tradition of Chinese history that lasted until the end of the Qing dynasty.[10] It also leads to changes in the monarch–official relationship. Consequently, the concept of filial piety, which sometimes conflicts with political loyalty, was molded according to the development of the political structure and changes in the monarch–official relationship.

A unified China and a consolidated monarchical system gave rise to the situation of a monarch who became increasingly powerful at the expense of his subordinates. He became an indispensable element in the new system, while his officials became his servants. Exposed to this new political environment, the intelligentsia expounded new definitions of these relationships. One example was Dong Zhongshu's 董仲舒 (180–115 BCE) concept of the "three cardinal bonds." Based on his philosophy of heaven and man, Dong integrated the relationships between the monarch and official, father and son, and husband and wife into the concepts of heaven and earth, Yang and Yin. Proposing his theory of superior Yang and inferior Yin, Dong said:

The relationships between monarch and minister, father and son, and husband and wife, are all derived from the principle of Yin and Yang. The monarch is Yang, the minister is Yin; the father is Yang, the son is Yin; the husband is Yang, the wife is Yin . . . The three cardinal bonds of the Kingly Way may be sought in Heaven.[11]

Here, the three human relationships – those of monarch and minister, father and son, and husband and wife – are being singled out as the "three cardinal bonds." By linking minister to monarch, son to father, and wife to husband, Dong Zhongshu made the minister, son, and wife respectively the secondary appendages of monarch, father, and husband. In doing so, he gave these relationships metaphysical support by saying that they are all derived from the principles of Yin and Yang, Heaven and Earth. Dong said, "The subordinate serves the principal as the earth serves the heaven, it is called 'great loyalty'."[12]

According to Dong, loyalty should be practiced wholeheartedly and single-mindedly. A loyal minister should maintain absolute loyalty even if his monarch was being dethroned, and should not serve more than one monarch. The moral code of "loyalty" was restricted to the individual relationship between monarch and officials, and since the monarch considered the kingdom his private property, officials owed loyalty only to the individual person of the monarch, and not to the state as a separate entity.[13]

However, the new monarch–official relationship and the newly acquired definition of loyalty had created a dilemma between "loyalty" and "filial piety." All along, under the patronage of the Confucian school, filial piety was given top priority as compared to loyalty. Nonetheless, under the new political system, the monarch was equivalent to heaven, which rendered loyalty on the part of the officials as rightful. In this case, how could someone who plays the dual roles of an official and a son simultaneously resolve his "role conflict"? In the three cardinal bonds, the ruler guides the subject, the father guides the son, and the husband guides the wife. As such, how did one resolve the "power conflict" between monarchical power and parental power? How did one make a choice between being a loyal official and a filial son when the two sets of requirements clashed? The *Classic of Filial Piety* 孝經 was written to promote filial piety and to coordinate filial piety and loyalty in case of conflict.

The *Classic of Filial Piety* is a Confucian work especially prepared for elucidating the concept of filial piety. Although ascribed to Confucius' disciple Zeng Zi, it is a small work of unknown date and authorship, most likely compiled during the early Han period, reflecting the great emphasis placed upon the cardinal virtue of filial piety by the Confucian school.[14] The book, which consists of eighteen chapters, was included as one of the Seven Classics in the Han dynasty and one of the Thirteen Classics in the Song dynasty.

In this short work, which takes the form of a dialogue between Zeng Zi and Confucius, the concept of filial piety was redefined to suit the newly established monarchical system. As Ch'u Chai and Winberg Chai pointed out, social and political obligations on the one hand, and Chinese tradition of the veneration of ancestors on the other, are brought together in a single and practical doctrine.[15] The emergence of the *Classic of Filial Piety* saw the politicization of Confucian ethic in Han China. At the very beginning of the book, the "Starting Point and Basic Principles" 開宗明義 chapter, it says:

> Filial piety is the root of all virtues, and from which all teaching comes . . . The body, the hair and skin are received from our parents, and we do not injure them. This is the beginning of filial piety. When we have established ourselves in the practice of the Way, so as to make our name famous in future generation and glorify our parents, this is the end of filial piety. Filial piety begins with the serving of our parents, continues with the serving of our ruler, and is completed with the establishment of our own character.[16]

The *Classic of Filial Piety* puts forward a key concept that filial piety is the root of all virtues; thus anyone who possesses the virtue of filial piety would thereby possess all the other virtues. This is aimed at elevating the position of filial piety and broadening its scope. Filial piety was originally a familial ethic but, as reflected in the above passage which brings out the beginning and the end of the ethic, begins with the serving of the parents, continues with the serving of the ruler, and is completed with the establishment of one's own character. Its scope has been extended to the political sphere. Thus, to serve one's monarch is also one way of fulfilling one's filial duty. And, more importantly, it is even one stage further than serving one's parents. What is the purpose of making such an arrangement and dividing the practice of filial piety into beginning and the end? The *Xiaojing zhu* 孝經 注 by Emperor Xuanzong 玄宗 (reigned 712–756) of the Tang dynasty may be able to give us an answer. In his commentary Emperor Xuanzong said:

> The practice of filial piety begins with serving one's parents and continues with serving one's monarch. When the virtues of loyalty and filial piety are manifested, then one can make his name famous and glorify his parents. That is why it is said filial piety ends with establishing one's character.[17]

Sima Guang's 司馬光 (1019–1086) interpretation of the above commentary is quite explicit. He said: "To show that filial piety does not confine only to serving one's parents."[18] Obviously, the *Classic of Filial Piety* intends to establish the concept that serving one's parents could not attain the fullness of filial duty. Serving one's parents is only the beginning; one has to serve one's monarch and bring glory to one's parents, and only then could there be completion of filial duty.

The political nature of the book can also be shown from its table of contents. Rather than expounding the meanings of the virtue, the eighteen chapters discuss the practice of filial piety by different social classes and the general guiding principles.[19] The *Classic of Filial Piety* brought serving the monarch into the sphere of filial piety, perhaps as a means to resolve the conflict between loyalty and filial piety, and consolidated monarchical rule. Thus, in the chapter on the filial piety of the "scholars," it reads:

> One serves one's mother in the same manner in which one serves one's father, and the love toward them is the same. One serves one's monarch in the same manner in which one serves one's father, and the reverence toward them is the same. Thus, to the mother one shows love and to the monarch one shows reverence, but to the father one shows both love and reverence. Therefore, to serve the monarch with filial piety is to show loyalty; to serve the senior with reverence is to show obedience. Not failing in loyalty and obedience in the service of one's superiors, one will be able to preserve one's emolument and position and to carry on one's family sacrifices. This is the filial piety of the scholars.[20]

As a government official, a person has dual identities, being both son and subject. The father is the highest authority in a family, whom a son has to obey; the monarch is the highest authority in a state a subject has to obey. When the *Classic of Filial Piety* says that the reverence toward one's father and one's monarch are the same, it is a sign of integrating filial piety with loyalty, parental power with monarchical power.[21]

The linking up of the familial ethic of filial piety with the political ethic of loyalty had a profound effect on the development of the monarch–minister relationship, which is no longer on an equal and reciprocal basis but on a unilateral and absolute basis. Serving one's parents and being loyal to one's ruler were regarded as two levels of filial piety. This undoubtedly broadened the scope of filial piety and at the same time elevated the importance of loyalty. Thereafter, filial piety has included the practice of filial piety and loyalty. This process of amalgamation of filial piety and loyalty is explained in the "Illustration of Perpetuating the Name" chapter of the book:

> The Master [Confucius] said: "The gentleman serves his parents with filial piety; thus his loyalty can be transferred to his sovereign. He serves his elder brother with brotherly deference; thus his respect can be transferred to his superiors. He orders his family well; thus his good order can be transferred to his public administration. Therefore, when one cultivates one's conduct within oneself, one's name will be perpetuated for future generations."[22]

The most important message in this passage is that of "transferring" (*yi* 移). The attempt to transfer filial piety to loyalty is significant for two reasons.

First, to apply the filial attitude to one's parents to one's ruler as well would remold not only the connotation of filial piety but the definition of loyalty as well. The ambiguity is shown in Emperor Xuanzong's annotation to the passage, which says "loyalty is to serve your ruler with filial piety."[23] Second, loyalty is regarded as a continuation of filial piety. Filial piety at home is the beginning and loyalty to one's ruler is the second stage in the completion of filial piety. As a minister, practicing loyalty would also mean practicing filial piety. In this respect, it implies that loyalty could be a substitute for filial piety. When there is a conflict between loyalty and filial piety, a minister fulfilling his loyal duty would be considered to be fulfilling his filial duty.

Emperor Chengzu and the *Biographical Accounts of Filial Piety*

The interpretation of the relationship of filial piety to loyalty in the *Classic of Filial Piety* laid the foundation for later periods and gave inspiration to imperial rulers. For example, in the *Guidelines for Ministers* 臣軌 by Wu Zetian 武則天 (624–705) of Tang, the Empress measured the two moral principles as follows:

> There is an old saying, "A loyal minister could only be found in the family of filial sons." If he is not a filial son, he could establish the great loyalty . . . However, in order to honor one's parents, one should first honor one's monarch; in order to bring peace to one's family, one should first bring peace to the state. Therefore, loyal ministers of the past, without exception, would first consider their monarch and then their parents, their country and then their families. Why? The monarch is the root of the parents, without the monarch the parents would not survive; the state is the foundation of the families, without the state the families would not exist.[24]

The message behind this passage is that filial piety to parents depends on loyalty to the monarch and that the existence of families depends on the state. Two developments from pre-Qin onward merged: the "politicization of filial piety" as reflected in the *Classic of Filial Piety*, and the emergence of "personal loyalty" as marked by the "familial state". The monarch is considered to be more important than one's parents and the state is deemed more important than one's family. In other words, loyalty is more important than filial piety. And the interpretation of loyalty as a political moral ethic has changed through a shift from "public loyalty" to "personal loyalty."[25]

The *Biographical Accounts of Filial Piety* (*Xiaoshun shishi* 孝順事實) by Emperor Chengzu 成祖 of the Ming dynasty is another text that merits special attention for an understanding of the politicization of filial peity. Emperor Chengzu (1360–1424), the third emperor of the Ming dynasty and the fourth son of founding emperor Taizu, came to power by overthrowing his nephew in a usurpation that resulted in a three-year civil war. After

Emperor Chengzu gained ascendancy, he made an effort to consolidate his power and legitimize his accession. Among other priorities, he tried to establish his image as that of a Confucian sage king and to promote the virtue of loyalty to the sovereign. The *Biographical Accounts of Filial Piety*, in ten chapters, was compiled for this purpose.

The book consists of 207 filial examples. As well as compiling these stories, Emperor Chengzu wrote commentaries for each of them and a poem to sum up the pertinent points. The Imperial Edict 聖諭 at the beginning of the book, also commonly known as the Six Edicts, reflects the principles of the compilation: be filial to your parents 孝順父母; respect your seniors and superiors 尊敬長上; live in harmony with your fellow villagers 和睦鄉里; teach your children and grandchildren 教訓子孫; follow the normal functions and behave oneself 各安生理; do not commit any kind of outrage 毋作非為.[26] The Imperial Edict spells out the emperor's exhortation to the people and the social rules for avoiding acts in defiance of the law and public opinion. With the Imperial Edict as the introduction, the political motivation behind the compilation of biographical accounts of filial piety is quite obvious. As reflected in his preface, several reasons lay behind the compilation of this work:

> Filial piety is the root of all conduct and the origin of myriad good deeds. Its greatness is able to move heaven and earth, spirits and gods. Its subtleness is able to cultivate brutality and violence, pacify birds and animals, and inspire plants and trees. All these are natural phenomena of the heavenly principle and human life, not the outcome of affected manners. However, records of ancient emperors and ministers, as well as the commoners, who were extolled for their filial piety at that time and handed down to the later generations, are often scattered in different works and difficult to search for. I have been looking for distinguished filial cases in historical and biographical works, and collected the stories of 207, in ten *juan*, entitled *Xiaoshun shishi*. I have also attached my remarks to each biography, followed by a poem, so that readers would be able to understand the Way of filial piety. Spontaneously, parental love wells up in one's heart and everyone fulfills one's duty as a son happily. Hence, human relations will be distinct and customs will be beautified.[27]

The compilation of filial accounts is an attempt to promote the Confucian ethic of filial piety with the ultimate goal of contributing to the education of the common people. His aim also pertained to another realm. The emperor claimed to be a transmitter of the learning of the sages and, as a result, secured his reputation as a sage ruler. He also strengthened the political interpretation of placing loyalty above filial piety.

A glimpse of Emperor Chengzu's remarks on filial piety will give us some understanding of the nature of the book:

The filial piety of the sages is originated from love and respect and freed from affectation. That it can make the teaching of morality universal to the whole world and later generations, is due to the utmost result of parental filial piety.[28]

Filial piety is a natural outcome of the Heavenly principle, and common to all human hearts.[29]

As a son, it is not difficult to support your parents but difficult to please your parents. Supporting your parents but not pleasing them, cannot be regarded as serving your parents well.[30]

Filial piety is the perfection of the human Way and the root of myriad fortunes. If a son can observe the rites of supporting and mourning in serving his parents, things of the myriad fortunes will response naturally.[31]

When filial piety reaches perfection, it can move heaven and earth, spirits and gods, and transform thief and traitors.[32]

On numerous occasions Emperor Chengzu mentions that the act of filial piety can move heaven and earth, and communicate with spirits and gods.[33] When one's filial piety reaches perfection, one is endowed with divine enlightenment. One's virtuous influence illuminates the four seas and penetrates far and wide. The passages stress the influence and rewarding effect of filial piety.

The *Biographical Accounts of Filial Piety* also reinforce the dogma of "transferring filial piety to loyalty," a resolution to the possible conflict between filial piety and loyalty suggested by the *Classic of Filial Piety*. In a story about the filial devotion of Chen Xiaoyi 陳孝意 of the Sui dynasty, Emperor Chengzu made use of the subject under discussion to put forward his own views: "Filial piety begins with the serving of our parents, continues with the serving of our ruler. The loyalty for serving one's ruler is the same as the filial piety for serving one's parents . . . How can loyalty and filial piety be two different Ways?"[34] Since loyalty and filial piety are the same, transferring one to the other is considered to be a natural progression. Emperor Chengzu's views on this matter are basically a continuation of the *Classic of Filial Piety*. Two examples are:

Filial piety in the past did not refer only to serving your parents when alive and mourning after death. The important thing is to make a name for your parents. Serving when alive and mourning after death are certainly filial acts. However, if a son can study and establish himself, transfer filial piety to loyalty and win great renown, so that people can trace his virtue to his parents and say, "how lucky to have a son like this," this is called making a name for your parents and the greatness of filial piety.[35]

There are five human relationships, the sovereign and parents are the most important. Those who are filial to their parents will also be loyal to their ruler. Serving his parents with filial piety, thus his loyalty can be transferred to his sovereign.[36]

Emperor Chengzu is more explicit when he suggests the idea of "transferring filial piety to loyalty" 移孝為忠,[37] a further development from the *Classic of Filial Piety*. However, from the Han down to the Ming dynasty, the suggestion that the two virtues can be transferred confined itself only to transferring filial piety to loyalty, not vice versa.

Conclusion

The Ming emperors were notorious for their despotic rule, with imperial power rising to unprecedented heights.[38] An obvious example was the order of Emperor Taizu, founder of the Ming dynasty, that "scholars not willing to serve me will be put to death."[39] There are many examples in the history of the Ming dynasty of requests by government officials for early retirement in order to take care of their aged parents not being granted on the grounds that serving one's monarch is more important than serving one's parents. The compilation of the *Biographical Accounts of Filial Piety* is an example of strengthening the concept of loyalty by imperial rule at the expense of filial piety. The promotion of imperial filial piety reveals a continuation of the politicization of the concept of filial piety that had its origins in the Han dynasty.

The eminent Ming Neo-Confucian scholar Qiu Jun 丘濬 (1421–1495) wrote a play entitled *A Record of Loyalty and Filial Piety and the Completion of Five Human Relationships* 伍倫全備忠孝記. The play, as the title suggests, is intended to emphasize the importance of the five human relationships between monarch and minister, father and son, older and younger brothers, husband and wife, individual and friend. Consisting of twenty-nine acts, the story deals with the life and families of two half-brothers, Wu Lunquan 伍倫全 and Wu Lunbei 伍倫備 (their names are symbolic, both meaning completeness of five human relations). It shows how the two brothers, their wives, mother, and friends observed these five human relationships and were rewarded with prosperity. Aiming to imbue moralistic ideas and proper conduct, the author paid special attention to the concepts of filial piety and loyalty and stressed that the monarch and the state were of prime importance. The ending poem of the play may be cited here to conclude the position of filial piety in the imperial Ming dynasty:

Through the ages,
Loyalty is of the first importance;
Among the unalterable principles of heaven and earth,
Filial piety should come first.

One should transfer his care for the family to govern the country,
All along, the *Kun* [Yin] has to submit to the *Qian* [Yang].[40]

Notes

1 Xiao Xinyi 蕭欣義, "Shangdai xiaodao sixiang shishi" 商代孝道思想試釋, *Huaxue Yuekan* 華學月刊, 99, 1980, 30–42; Zheng Zhihui 鄭志慧, *Rujia xiaodao sixiang yanjiu – Qin Han zhiji ji qianqi* 儒家孝道思想研究－秦漢之際及其前期, Taipei: Furen University MA thesis, 1973, pp. 7–25.
2 Translation of the *Analects* in this chapter is based on D. C. Lau, *Confucius: The Analects*, Harmondsworth: Penguin Books, 1979, sometimes with alterations.
3 See *Mengzi zhushu jiejing* 孟子註疏解經,1887 edition, 7A24a.
4 Sun Jiazhou 孫家洲 "Xian Qin rujia yu fajia zhongxiao lunli sixiang shuping" 先秦儒家與法家忠孝倫理思想述評, *Guizhou shehui kexue* 貴州社會科學, 2, 1987, 44–9.
5 *Analects* 1.2.
6 Ibid.
7 Translation is modified from D. C. Lau, *Mencius*, Harmondsworth: Penguin, 1983.
8 Although "zhong" as a moral value in the pre-Qin period is often understood as "doing one's best" in one's duty, when it is used in political context it also refers to one's attitude toward to one's country. In some cases, "忠于社稷" is mentioned in pre-Qin writings.
9 For a more detailed discussion on the topic, see Lee Cheuk Yin, "The Dichotomy of Loyalty and in Confucianism: Historical Development and Modern Significance," in Silke Krieger and Rolf Trauzettel (eds), *Confucianism and the Modernization of China*, Mainz: V. Hase and Koehler Verlag, 1991, pp. 96–115.
10 For a detailed study of the establishment of the monarchical system in Chinese history, see Xing Yitian 邢義田, "Zhongguo huangdi zhidu de jianli yu fazhan" 中國皇帝制度的建立與發展, in *QinHan shi lungao* 秦漢史論稿, Taipei: Dongdai, 1987, pp. 43–84.
11 Dong Zhongshu, *Chunqiu fanlu* 春秋繁露, *Sibu beiyao* edition, *juan* 12, pp. 6a–b.
12 Ibid., *juan* 10, p. 8b.
13 Liu Jiyao 劉紀曜, "Gong yu si – Zhong de lunli neihan" 公與私－忠的倫理內涵, in Liu Dai (ed.), *Zhongguo wenhua xinlun: Tiandao yu rendao* 中國文化新論－天道與人道, Taipei: Lianjing, 1982, pp. 171–207.
14 For a detailed discussion on the compilation and history of the *Xiao jing*, see Ho Soo Guang, *Xiao jing de yanjiu* 孝經的研究, Singapore: Singapore Society of Asian Studies, 1984, Chapters 2 and 3.
15 Ch'u Chai and Winberg Chai, *The Humanist Way in Ancient China*, New York: Bantam, 1965, pp. 326–34. Translation of the *Xiao jing* in this chapter is based on their work, sometimes with alterations, included in Lynn Nelson and Patrick Peebles (eds), *Classics of Eastern Thought*, New York: Harcourt Brace, 1991.
16 *The Classic of Filial Piety* 孝經 (hereafter *Xiao jing*); see *Xiaojing Zhijie* 孝經直解, Ming Chongzhen period edition, *juan* 1, pp. 1b–2a.
17 Tang Xuanzong annotated, Sima Guang 司馬光 interpreted, *Xiaojing zhujie* 孝經註解, *Tongzhitang jingjie* 通志堂經解 edition, 1680, p. 2a.
18 Ibid.
19 The eighteen chapters are Starting Point and Basic Principles 開宗明義章; The Son of Heaven 天子章; The Princes 諸侯章; The High Officials 卿大夫章; The Scholars 士章; The Common People 庶人章; The Trinity 三才章; Government by Filial Piety 孝治章; Government of the Sage 聖治章; The Practice of Filial Piety 紀孝行章; The Five Punishments 五刑章; Illustration of the Right Way

廣要道章; Illustration of the Highest Virtue 廣至德章; Illustration of Perpetuating the Name 廣揚名章; The Duty of Admonition 諫諍章; Evocation and Response 感應章; Serving the Sovereign 事君章; Mourning for Parents 喪親章.

20　*Xiao jing, juan* 4, pp. 4b–5a; *Classics of Eastern Thought*, p. 94 with moderations.

21　For a discussion of the integration of parental power with monarchical power by the *Classic of Filial Piety*, see Feng Youlan 馮友蘭, *Zhongguo zhexue shi xinbian* 中國哲學史新編, Beijing: Renmin Publishing House, 1964, pp. 58–60. On the political significance of the *Classic of Filial Piety*, see Shen Shanhong 沈善洪 and Wang Fengxian 王鳳賢, *Zhongguo lunli xueshuo shi* 中國倫理學說史, Hangzhou: Zhejiang renmin Publishing House, 1985, vol. 1, pp. 377–82.

22　*Xiao jing, juan* 14, pp. 15b–16a; *Classics of Eastern Thought*, p. 98.

23　*Xiaojing zhujie*, p. 16b.

24　Wu Zetian, *Chen Gui* 臣軌, Dongfang Xuehui facsimile reprint of Japanese 1669 edition, 1924, *juan* 1, p. 5a.

25　On the concepts of "public loyalty" and "personal loyalty," see Liu Jiyao, "Gong yu si," pp. 171–207.

26　See *Xiaoshun shishi* 孝順事實, Ming Liu Yizhi reprint edition, inner front page.

27　Ibid., preface, pp. 2a–b.

28　*Xiaoshun shishi, juan* 1, p. 3b.

29　Ibid., *juan* 1, p. 7a.

30　Ibid., *juan* 1, pp. 12b–13a.

31　Ibid., *juan* 1, p. 21a.

32　Ibid., *juan* 1, p. 25a.

33　See, for examples, *Xiaoshun shishi, juan* 3, pp. 4a–b, 18b; *juan* 5, p. 3b; *juan* 7, pp. 16a–b.

34　Ibid., *juan* 5, pp. 21a–b.

35　Ibid., *juan* 6, pp. 4b–5a.

36　Ibid., *juan* 7, pp. 24a.

37　Ibid., *juan* 6, p. 9b.

38　On despotism in China, see Qian Mu 錢穆, *Guoshi dagang* 國史大綱, Shanghai, 1948, pp. 474–504; F. W. Mote, "The Growth of Chinese Despotism," *Oriens Extremus*, 8, 1961, 1–41.

39　For details, see Chiu Ling-yeong, "Lun Ming Taizu zhengquan xia zhi zhishi fenzi" 論明太祖政權下之知識份子, in *Mingshi lunji* 明史論集, Hong Kong: Society of Historical Research, 1975, pp. 1–13.

40　Qiu Jun, *Wulun quanbei zhongxiao ji* 五倫全備忠孝記, Ming Shidetang edition, *juan* 4, p. 39b.

9 Does *xiao* come before *ren*?

Alan K. L. Chan

The concept of *xiao*, commonly rendered "filial piety" or "filiality," occupies a privileged position in Chinese thought. It is not limited to the Confucian tradition, although as an ethical concept it develops largely in a Confucian framework. Specifically, the meaning of *xiao* is related closely to that of the cardinal Confucian virtue *ren* 仁, "benevolence" or "humanity." Often, *xiao* is understood as a concrete expression of *ren*. This suggests that *ren* is more basic, forming a deep moral presence that pervades and informs the fundamental nature of human beings. From this perspective, *ren* takes on universal ethical significance and moves beyond the confines of "benevolence" understood as a particular virtue, whereas *xiao* gains meaning from *ren* and can be said to be a function of it.

This view has been attributed to Zhu Xi 朱熹 (1130–1200), but it gives an incomplete picture of Zhu's assessment of the relationship between *xiao* and *ren*. Prior to Zhu Xi, the subject had already attracted considerable controversy. In the *Lunyu* (*Analects*), the disciple Youzi seems to suggest that *xiao* is the "root" (*ben* 本) of *ren*. During the Han dynasty (206 BCE to 220 CE), the relationship between *xiao* and *ren* forms the focus of an important debate. Although few details are available, according to the *Hou Hanshu* (History of the Later Han Dynasty) the debate centered on the relative priority of *xiao* and *ren*, whether one "comes before" (*xian* 先) the other. This indicates that the relationship between *xiao* and *ren* posed not only a philosophical challenge but also a hermeneutical problem. Presumably, the classics did not give a clear-cut answer, which gave rise to the "*ren–xiao* debate" during the Han and later compelled Zhu Xi to define clearly the relationship between the two in the Song period.

The changing relationship between *xiao* and *ren* brings into view a complex and dynamic process in the development of Chinese philosophy. Meaning takes shape and flourishes in specific linguistic and cultural contexts; philosophical concepts cannot be assumed to have "fixed" meanings independent of the matrix in which they stand and interact with one another. This I take to be uncontroversial. As a philosophical concept, *xiao* gains meaning from its relationships with other concepts, and its meaning changes when these relationships achieve new balances and configurations. It is generally recognized that *ren* increasingly came to be interpreted as an ideal humanity as the Confucian tradition developed.[1] As *ren* dominates the Confucian philosophical landscape, it demands adjustment to the meaning of *xiao* and other related concepts. This necessitates a fresh interpretation of *xiao* as it appears in the Confucian classics.

The philosophical and hermeneutical strategies that come into play in this realignment of meaning merit close attention. By the Han period, *xiao* and *ren* have already achieved a central place in the value system and a high degree of hermeneutical stability, which resists arbitrary interpretation and, still less, disregard. The primacy of *ren* may be emphasized, but the resultant inflation of meaning would not be acceptable if it entailed a depreciation of *xiao*. It is not my intention to offer a detailed survey of the "evolving" relationship between *xiao* and *ren*; my concern has to do more with what may be called the management of intellectual complexities in Chinese philosophy. In what follows, I begin with a discussion of the *Lunyu*, to show how it may generate conflicting accounts of the relationship between *xiao* and *ren*. This establishes a context in which the *ren–xiao* debate may be placed. The debate hinges on the sense in which one concept can be said to "come before" another. This raises the question not only of which comes first but more fundamentally of the ways in which concepts are secured and interpreted in certain relational frameworks. Thus, at a meta-interpretive level, I propose to explore several philosophical markers – especially "before" (*xian*) and "after" (*hou* 後), "roots" (*ben*) and "branches" (*mo* 末), and "inner" (*nei* 內) and "outer" (*wai* 外) – that serve to define the relationship between different concepts. They are widely used in Chinese philosophical writings; often, it is assumed that they are but different ways of representing the same relationship. This will be scrutinized, in the context of the relationship between *xiao* and *ren*. The suggestion here is that they serve as "structural" elements that guide reflection in approaching complex philosophical problems. Finally, on this basis I consider Zhu Xi's resolution of the *ren–xiao* debate.

Xiao in the *Lunyu*

The pre-Confucian view of *xiao* has been examined by Keith Knapp and Donald Holzman and need not be repeated here.[2] Suffice it to say that there is a strong religious dimension to the early usages of *xiao*. A deepening moral understanding gradually came to the fore and by the time of Confucius (551–479 BCE) *xiao* was fully registered in the ethical domain and formed a key thread in the Chinese cultural fabric. In the *Lunyu*, *xiao* assumes the primary meaning of "filial piety" in the sense of a moral duty to serve one's parents, which extends beyond their death to include proper mourning. Ancestors are not neglected, but on the whole *xiao* is directed primarily to one's parents (or parents-in-law, as several studies in this volume demonstrate). This forms a starting point for later interpretations of *xiao*.

Modern scholars generally agree that the *Lunyu* is a composite work. A diachronic analysis may show that the usage of *xiao* in the different books or chapters fits into a certain developmental pattern.[3] Nevertheless, for traditional commentators the text forms an integral and coherent whole, which guides their interpretation. If *xiao* seems to be used in different senses in the *Lunyu*, it is the task of the interpreter to make clear the context in which Confucius' remarks about *xiao* are made, show how they are connected with one another, and discern their "deeper," underlying meaning. On the whole, the *Lunyu* seems to present a consistent account of *xiao*, although it is not entirely clear how *xiao* is related to *ren*.

There is little disagreement that *xiao* is central to the ethical life. For example, Confucius remarks:

> A young man should be *xiao* at home, treat his elders properly when outside . . . extend his love to the multitude and draw close to those who are *ren*. If having devoted himself to these practices he had any strength left, he should, then, study the [classical] literature and the arts.[4]

A second common point of departure is that, for Confucius, *xiao* involves far more than merely providing for one's parents: "Nowadays, *xiao* is taken to mean that one is able to provide for one's parents. Yet even dogs and horses receive as much care. Without reverence, what is the difference?" (*Lunyu* 2.7; cf. 2.8).

The deeper meaning of *xiao* is here traced to "reverence" (*jing* 敬), which underpins the ideal ethical relationship between parents and children, especially between father and son. *Jing* is not an act that one performs among other acts; instead, it suggests an attitude of seriousness, respect, and devotion (*Lunyu* 1.5, 15.38). When serving one's parents – whether one is serving them food or "gently remonstrating" with them (4.18) – it is *jing* that distinguishes one's acts as being *xiao*. Of course one should always remember the age of one's parents (4.21), give them no other cause for concern than illness (2.6), or let them know where you are when you have to travel (4.19), but without *jing* these would not amount to acts of *xiao*.

Reverence is associated with *li* 禮 (rituals) – in modern Chinese, *li* and *jing* are still closely related. The *Lunyu* states, "When your parents are alive, serve them according to *li*; when they are dead, bury them and sacrifice to them according to *li*." In this sense, Confucius defines *xiao* as "not being contrary" to the requirement of the rites (2.5). Informed by *jing*, this goes beyond mere compliance with certain ritual forms, such as wearing the proper ritual garments during mourning. Perhaps the seriousness of ritual performance helps to instill a measure of reverence. To "instill *jing* in the common people," the *Lunyu* also relates, the ruler should "treat them with dignity" (2.20).

The question that arises is how reverence is related to love (*ai* 愛). In modern usage, *jing* is also associated with love. Is it the case that reverence in *xiao* stems from filial love? The rite of mourning is arguably one of the most important elements in the Confucian conception of *xiao*, and several passages in the *Lunyu* attest that the deep sorrow that one suffers at the passing of one's parents is what makes mourning an ethical act. For example, in response to a question about the "roots" of *li*, Confucius replies, "In mourning, it is better to err on the side of grief than on the side of formality" (3.4, D. C. Lau, trans.). Further, "The Master said, 'What can I find worthy of note in a man who is lacking . . . in reverence when performing the rites and in sorrow when in mourning?'" (3.26, Lau). Indeed, as Zengzi reports, Confucius once remarked that it is only in mourning that a person is likely to express his innermost feelings to the full (19.17; cf. 19.14 and *Mencius* 3A2). The sorrow that one experiences in mourning one's parents presumably stems from the love that one has for them.

Support for this view is found, interestingly, in the *Zhuangzi*, which recognizes the universality of filial love. "A child's love for his parents [*ai qin* 愛親] is destined: it cannot be dispelled from the heart . . . in the service of parents there is no higher degree of filial conduct [*xiao*] than to live contentedly wherever they may dwell."[5] Elsewhere, the *Zhuangzi* distinguishes *jing xiao* 敬孝 (filial acts conducted with reverence) from *ai xiao* 愛孝 (*xiao* with love), arguing that the former is "easier" than the latter.[6] If *xiao* can be traced ultimately to love, given that *ren* is also defined as love in the *Lunyu* (12.22) and in the light of other statements in the text that emphasize the primacy of *ren* (e.g. 3.3), there is thus a sense in which *ren* can be seen to be more "basic" than *xiao*.

Once this relationship is clarified, the meaning of *xiao* in other *Lunyu* passages falls into place. Thus, it can be argued that it is because of love that a son follows the *dao* of his father: "Observe what a man has in mind to do when his father is living, and then observe what he does when his father is dead. If, for three years, he makes no changes to his father's ways [*dao*], he can be said to be *xiao*" (1.11, Lau; cf. 4.20). When a son "covers up" for his father who has committed a crime, he acts out of love (13.18). Similarly, from this perspective the reason why Confucius considers "managing the expression on one's face" (Lau) – or "demeanor" (Waley), "showing the proper countenance" (Ames and Rosemont) – to be difficult in being *xiao* (2.8) is that one must always communicate love to one's parents, no matter how tired, busy, or stressed one may be.

This represents one approach to *xiao* and *ren* in the *Lunyu*. However, what the *Lunyu* has to say about filial piety may be interpreted in other ways, which would entail a different view of the relationship between *xiao* and *ren*. Perhaps it is the exacting demands of *li* that make maintaining a "proper countenance" difficult, for even expressions of love ought to be measured and appropriate to the situation, and to observe the rules of ritual propriety. The *dao* of the father from which a filial son would not deviate (1.11) may refer only to morally defensible ways, in which case love may not be the sole or most important factor in the shaping of *xiao*.[7] For Confucius, as Zengzi recalls, what is special about the *xiao* of Meng Zhuangzi, an officer of the state of Lu, is that "he left unchanged both his father's officials and his father's policies" (19.18, Lau). Without undermining the son's love for his father, it would appear that the virtue of the officials and the rightness of the policies also play a role in determining *xiao*. After all, Confucius did not advocate that a person must always wait for the instruction of his father and elder brothers before he acts (11.22), which introduces other considerations than reverence and love into an interpretation of filial piety.

When the disciple Zai Wo objected to the three-year mourning period, Confucius said that he was "not *ren*" (17.21): "a child leaves the arms of his father and mother only after he turned three . . . did he not have the three years' love from his father and mother?" Although love is cited as the reason for mourning, this would suggest that *xiao* is a necessary condition for *ren*. Moreover, as Confucius also asserts, "When the gentleman feels profound affection for his parents, the common people will be stirred to benevolence" (8.2, Lau). Thus, there is reason to believe that Youzi had got it right: "A gentleman [*junzi* 君子] devotes his efforts to cultivating the roots; once the roots are established, the *dao* will grow. *Xiao* and brotherly respect are indeed the roots of *ren*!" (1.2).

My point here is not to provide an exhaustive analysis or to argue for a particular reading of *xiao* and *ren* but to highlight that the *Lunyu* invites different interpretations. Filial love is no doubt important, but reverence may be derived from a number of sources, such as *li* and *yi* 義 (rightness). There is also the question of whether filial love is the same as or a subset of *ren*. Youzi's interpretation seems to find support from a number of early Chinese texts. For example, the *Guanzi* states, "*xiao* and brotherly respect are the progenitors of *ren*."[8] The *Zhuangzi*, too, seems to accept that *ren* is rooted in the love between father and son, although it also states that "perfect *ren* knows no filial love."[9] One of the recently discovered bamboo texts from Guodian (near Jingmen city in Hubei province), the *Yucong yi* 語叢一, defines "mourning" [*sang* 喪] as "the beginning [*duan* 端] of *ren*."[10] Another Guodian text, the *Tang Yu zhi dao* 唐虞之道, suggests that "those who love their kin [*ai qin*] but forget the worthy are *ren* but not *yi*."[11] The *Wuxing pian* 五行篇 places *ren* in a series after *qin* (kinship affection) and *ai* (love), and suggests that "loving one's father, and then loving the people is *ren*."[12]

The *ren–xiao* debate

The Confucian school evidently considered both *xiao* and *ren* to be extremely important; but it is difficult to pinpoint the relationship between the two. On the one hand, the *Daxue* (*Great Learning*) suggests that whereas *ren* rests with the ruler, *xiao* lies with the son, and that "*xiao* is that with which one serves his ruler."[13] The *Zhongyong* (*Doctrine of the Mean*), on the other hand, seems to locate *xiao* in *ren*: "*Ren* is what defines a person; of *ren*, affection for one's kin is the greatest."[14] The *Mencius*, like the *Zhongyong*, defines *ren* as *qin qin* 親親, "being affectionate toward one's kin" (6B3 and 7A15), and gives the impression that "filial sons and men of *ren*" refer to the same category of people (3A5).[15] However, the *Mencius* also defines serving one's parents as "the *shi* 實 of *ren*" (4A27). If one takes *shi* to mean "actuality," bearing in mind the contrast between "names" and "actuality" in Chinese philosophy, *xiao* would seem more important than *ren*.[16] For Zhu Xi, as we shall see, *shi* in this context should be taken to mean "seeds," which casts a different light on the *ren–xiao* relationship. Elsewhere, the *Mencius* distinguishes "being affectionate toward one's kin" (*qin qin*) from "extending *ren* to the people" (7A45). In the *Xiaojing* (*Classic of Filial Piety*), *xiao* is seen as the "roots" of all virtues, whereas *ren* does not seem to figure in the ethical equation at all.[17]

Taken out of context, these references do not tell us how the texts may have approached *xiao* and *ren*, but they reinforce the point that the *ren–xiao* relationship presented a problem to later Confucians. Of course, other early Confucians, notably Xunzi, also deliberated on these concepts; but the examples cited above should suffice to provide a background for the discussion that follows. During the Han dynasty, as the demand for a Confucian orthodoxy grew, the need to establish a clear relationship between *xiao* and *ren* also became more pressing. Increasingly, *xiao* came to be regarded as a prerequisite for entering government service; at the same time, no Confucian could overlook the value of *ren*. This set the stage for the *ren–xiao* debate in the Later Han.

The early dynastic histories contain numerous accounts of both exemplary and unorthodox filial behavior, but little has been preserved of the discourse on *xiao*. The *Hou Hanshu* reports an accusation that Kong Rong 孔融 (d. 208) had made a mockery of the Confucian doctrine of *xiao*: "Is there really any kinship affection that a father has for his son? Getting to the root of the matter, it is but the expression of desire. And what is so special about a son's relationship with his mother? It is like placing something temporarily in a jar. When it is taken out, the relationship is severed."[18] Later commentators generally discard this as a wrongful accusation, which led to the death of Kong Rong.[19]

The most extended discussion on the relationship between *xiao* and *ren* is found in the biography of Yan Du 延篤 (d. 167), who studied under the famous Confucian scholar Ma Rong 馬融 (79–166) and served as governor of the capital area during the reign of Han Huandi 桓帝 (reigned 146–168). Yan's argument has not been made available in English and deserves translation in full.

At the time, some people doubted the arguments for the relative priority of *ren* and *xiao*. Yan Du thus set out his view as follows: "Looking at the debate on the relationship between *ren* and *xiao*, one finds a plethora of views, each citing the classical texts as evidence and drawing support from historical events. It can be said to have been a thoroughly debated issue. Now, *ren* and *xiao* come from the same source and together command all human conducts. It is not as if they had a different weight that one could use to determine with certainty which one stands before the other. Nevertheless, if one were to distinguish the two generally and to identify their characteristics, one should say that whereas *xiao* lies in serving one's parents, *ren* is bestowed on all categories of things. Bestowed on things, *ren* brings relief to the world; in serving one's parents, one gathers virtue in oneself. As an individual effort, *xiao* is directed at a few, whereas in bringing relief to the world, *ren* benefits many. From this perspective, *ren* is indeed far-reaching. Nevertheless, things may start out inconspicuously and then become illustrious; affairs that were unrecognized may become celebrated in the end. Take as an example one's own body. The ears can hear, the eyes can see, the feet can take us to faraway places, the hands can serve to defend – although the effects are shown outside, they are all rooted [*ben* 本] in the heart. Consider something beyond oneself as another example. The growth of plants and trees begins with germs and shoots and ends with luxuriant, well spaced leaves and branches in full, magnificent display – although the branch tips [*mo* 末] are numerous and radiant, what make them so are the roots [*gen* 根]. Thus, a *ren*-person's possessing *xiao* may be likened to the four limbs' having the heart and abdomen, or the leaves and branches' having roots and trunk. The Sage knows this and therefore says [in the *Xiaojing*], "*Xiao*, indeed, is the constant thread of heaven, the righteous principle of earth, and the guide to man's conduct". [The *Lunyu* also states,] "A *junzi* devotes his efforts to cultivating the roots; once the roots are established, the *dao* will grow. *Xiao* and brotherly respect are indeed the roots of *ren!*" However, *xiao* and *ren* are so great that it is difficult [for a person] to be complete in both; the nature of things tends to favor one side over the other. Thus, what is manifested [*xiao* or *ren*] is different and it is rare that both are equally represented. If we had to assess their relative merit, then like the luxuriant and well spaced leaves and branches *ren* should be regarded as great [*da* 大], whereas *xiao* as the heart of a body or the roots and trunk of a tree comes first [*xian* 先]. This can be deemed to be beyond dispute. Now, some consider the claim that *xiao* comes first and *ren* comes after to be against Confucius' assessment of Yan Hui [known especially for his *ren* and as superior to the other disciples] and Zengzi [known especially for his *xiao*]. It should be pointed out that *ren* and *xiao* are born of the same substance [*zhi* 質]. For those who embody them fully, they can be referred to interchangeably as either [*xiao* or *ren*]. This is the case of [the sage-king] Shun and Yan Hui. But if the two were not equally embodied, then distinctions can be made. This is the case of Gong Liu [known for his benevolent government; see *Shijing*, ode 250 "Gong Liu"

公劉, *Shiji*, 4.11a and *Mencius* 1B5] and Zengzi. Now, Zengzi and Min Ziqian attain the height of virtue with their filial piety and brotherly respect, whereas Guan Zhong accomplishes the work of *ren* by [assisting Duke Huan of Qi] bringing together the various feudal lords nine times [see *Lunyu* 14.16]. In discussing virtue, it is impossible not to rank Yan Hui and Zengzi first; in terms of merit, none can surpass that of Guan Zhong. From this perspective, they are each accorded a proper place on account of their achievement.[20]

Terms and metaphors of relations

Perhaps because of the emphasis on "harmony" in Chinese philosophy, especially since the Han period, fitting various concepts into place and clarifying their relationship – as opposed to, say, rejecting one concept in favor of another – represents an important strategy in resolving philosophical disputes. Yan Du's resolution of the *ren–xiao* debate rests on the analogy of "roots" and "branches," which secures *xiao* and *ren* in an inseparable but distinguishable relationship. However, concepts can be accommodated in a variety of ways and attempts at imposing a certain order on competing concepts have a long history, which brings out a "structural" dimension to the development of Chinese philosophy. In other words, once the focus was shifted to appropriating concepts into a structured edifice, a number of relational terms and metaphors emerged as key to philosophic discourse. These are structural components in the sense that they serve to hold different concepts together and as the tradition developed would come to influence the process of philosophical hermeneutics itself.

Of particular interest are terms that indicate relative importance and/or priority between any two concepts or sets of phenomena. In the *Lunyu*, for example, the distinction between "great/big" (*da*) and "small" (*xiao* 小) is used in this way: "Zigong said, 'The *dao* of King Wen and King Wu has not fallen . . . Those who are worthy understand its greater [aspects], whereas unworthy individuals understand its smaller [aspects]" (19.22; cf. 1.12, 11.26, 13.17, 15.27, 15.34, 19.11). In D. C. Lau's translation, "greater" and "smaller" are rendered suitably as "what is of major significance" and "what is of minor significance," respectively.

In Confucian philosophy, what is "difficult" (*nan* 難) often also carries the connotation of what is important. Thus, to suggest that "managing the expression on one's face" is difficult in being filial is also to say that it is more important than, say, running errands for one's parents or serving them food (*Lunyu* 2.8). "High"/"above" (*shang* 上) and "low"/"below" (*xia* 下) can also help to clarify certain relationships. For example, the *Lunyu* (6.21) asserts that "only to those who are above [*shang*] the middle can one talk about what is *shang*" (Lau, "about the best"; Ames and Rosemont, "higher things"). Similarly, *xian* (what is prior to or comes before something else) and *hou* (what is posterior or comes after) are terms that place different concepts into a hierarchical framework. For example, as the *Lunyu* explains, a *junzi* "*xian* puts his words into action and afterwards [*hou*] allows his words to follow" (2.13). In certain contexts, a combination of relational terms and metaphors may be used. For example, the *Lunyu* contrasts what is "far" (*yuan* 遠) with what is "small" (19.4). Replying to a question about *ren*, Confucius also says, "The *ren* person *xian* pursues what is *nan* [difficult] and afterwards [*hou*] concerns himself with the result" (6.22).

Useful as these terms are in indicating generally the relationship between any two items on the Confucian agenda, they may not be sufficiently precise to dispel possible ambiguities. What is "big" may be inappropriate or impractical. What is "far" may suggest missing the mark. What is "difficult" need not always be more important in a comparative context: for example, it is certainly difficult to be a ruler, but it does not follow that the way of a minister or subject is therefore easy or less important (*Lunyu* 13.15). The *Mencius* also warns, "The *dao* is near and yet one looks for it afar; the thing to be done is easy and yet one looks for [a solution] in the difficult. If everyone would love their parents and treat their elders properly, the world would be at peace" (4A11).

Shang is generally the preferred term over *xia*, although a truly cultured or educated person is "not ashamed to learn from those who are below [*xia*] him" (*Lunyu* 5.15). The *junzi* "gets through to what is up above [*shang da* 上達]," whereas the *xiaoren* 小人 (mean or petty person) "gets through to what is down below [*xia da* 下達]" (14.23); nevertheless, Confucius also says, "In learning, I pursue that which is below [*xia xue* 下學] and get through to what is up above [*shang da*]" (14.35). These last two sayings have been interpreted in various ways – e.g. *xia xue* may mean what is commonplace – but they show that *shang* and *xia* do not always yield an unequivocal relational picture. If the latter (14.35) implies that one starts first from "below," perhaps in the sense that one should begin by acquiring elementary learning, then the *xian–hou* formula would also face difficulty in describing the relationship between *xia xue* and *shang da*, because what "comes first" is usually regarded as what is more important. This is addressed further below in the discussion.

Part of the difficulty is that these terms do not always specify whether the two items in a particular relationship are mutually exclusive, overlapping, or related to each other in some other way. Consider, for example, the seemingly straightforward distinction made by Zixia between "great virtue" (*da de* 大德) and "small virtue" (*xiao de* 小德) in the *Lunyu* (19.11). Does the latter form a subset of the former, do they overlap, or do they refer to two classes of ethical conduct? D. C. Lau translates *da de* and *xiao de* as "major matters" and "minor matters," respectively. Yang Bojun distinguishes "important moral integrity" (*zhongda jiecao* 重大節操) from "small details in style" (*zuofeng shang de xiaojie* 作風上的小節). Zhu Xi in this instance defines *de* as *jie* 節 (literally, a joint on a bamboo), which seems close to Lau's rendition, and comments, "This suggests that if a person could first [*xian*] establish what is great [in terms of his own self-cultivation], then although the small details [*xiaojie*] may not agree perfectly with principle, they are harmless." However, perhaps Zhu Xi senses that if the two are related, the neglect of *xiao de* cannot but have an impact on attaining *da de*; he also cites a comment to the effect that this saying is not free from shortcomings and that students should read it with care.[21]

Compared with some other terms of relations, *xian* and *hou* are able to provide a clearer picture of the relationship between *xiao* (filial piety) and *ren*. Both *xiao* and *ren* are generally understood to be "far" and "difficult," despite Confucius' well known saying, "Is *ren* really far away? No sooner do I desire it than it is here" (*Lunyu* 7.30, Lau). Both are major landmarks on the ethical map, which rules out a "great–small" relationship. In Yan Du's account, *ren* is said to be "far" and "great," without implying that *xiao* is therefore "small"; instead, what it shows is that the author was aware of the imprecision of these terms and sought to clarify the perceived relationship with other markers of relations. Although both *xiao* and *ren* are great and difficult, they can be distinguished in terms of their relative priority.

Whether any two concepts are independent or overlapping, *xian* and *hou* seem able to indicate their relative priority and/or importance. For example, the *Lunyu* considers the rites to "come after" (3.8), and commentators by and large agree that *ren* and *yi* are the implied prior conditions that must be established before the rites can "truly" flourish. Elsewhere, the *Lunyu* distinguishes those who "*xian* advanced in the rites and music" before they received an official appointment from those who "advanced after" they had received an appointment (11.1). Disagreement in interpretation notwithstanding, Confucius explicitly states that he sides with the former group. The *Mencius* generally seems to prefer confronting one concept or course of action against another in order to force a moral choice, but in dealing with *ren* and *xiao* it can hardly favor one over the other and comes close to situating the two in a *xian–hou* relationship: "As for a *ren* person, there is no one that he does not love, but he takes attending to his kin and those who are worthy to be the most pressing task."[22]

Even *xian* and *hou* are not unambiguous, however. When Zilu asked Confucius, "If the Lord of Wei left the administration of his state to you, what would you put first [*xian*]?" (*Lunyu* 13.3, Lau), there is little question that *xian* is considered more important.[23] However, when Zigong asked Confucius, "If you had to give up one of these three [food, arms, and trust], which one would you give up first?" (12.7), *xian* refers to the least important. After all, Confucius advises that those who are "*hou*-born," i.e. the young, should be "feared" or not underestimated (9.23).

Roots (*ben*) and branches (*mo*)

If *xian* and *hou* by themselves cannot always clearly explain the relationship between *xiao* (filial piety) and *ren*, *ben* and *mo* come to the rescue. What is interesting about Yan Du's resolution of the *ren–xiao* debate is that it assigns priority to *xiao* without implying that it is more important than *ren*. This is accomplished by the introduction of the *ben–mo* relationship, or more precisely a "value-neutral" version of the *ben–mo* relationship.

Although Confucius seems to prefer to speak of the substance or basic stuff (*zhi*) of a person or thing, the idea of *ben* – literally, the base of a tree – figures in the *Lunyu*.[24] As mentioned, Confucius was asked about the *ben* of *li*, and Youzi believes that *xiao* is the *ben* of *ren*. In addition, the *Lunyu* reports the following interesting exchange:

> Ziyou said, "The disciples and younger followers of Zixia can certainly cope with sweeping and cleaning, with responding to calls and replying to questions put to them . . . but these are only details [*mo*]. On what is basic [*ben*] they are ignorant. What is one to do with them?"
>
> When Zixia heard this, he said, "Oh! How mistaken Yan You [Ziyou] is! In the way of the gentleman, what is to be taught first [*xian*] and what is to be put last [*hou*] as being less urgent? The former is as clearly distinguishable from the latter as grasses are from trees. It is futile to try to give such a false picture of the way of the gentleman. It is, perhaps, the sage alone who, having started something, will always see it through to the end."
>
> (19.12, Lau)

Zixia's argument seems to be this. The way of Confucian learning begins with what appear to be easy and simple tasks and ends with the *dao* of the *junzi*. The way in which the two are related is analogous to the relationship between roots and branches. Elementary learning comes first in the sense that it is a necessary condition for the *dao* of the *junzi*. Perhaps it is the discipline involved or perhaps Zixia was thinking of such basic skills as reading and writing, but the point remains that the "higher" learning of the gentleman is not possible without basic training. Obviously, as a necessary but not sufficient condition, the roots may not develop; as the *Lunyu* puts it, "There are certainly young plants that do not blossom, and blossoms that do not bear fruit!" (9.22).

Ziyou's criticism shows that he considered elementary learning and the learning of the *junzi* to be disjointed. From Zixia's perspective, the assertion that his disciples are fine with "details" (*mo*) but lacking in fundamentals (*ben*) shows that Ziyou did not understand the relationship between roots and branches. Nevertheless, it seems odd to suggest that "sweeping and cleaning" constitute the roots of Confucian self-cultivation. I return to this point below.

In the *Mencius*, the idea that morality has "one root" is well known (3A5). How this relates to the *ren–xiao* debate will be considered in connection with Zhu Xi's interpretation. The analogy of roots and branches finds an influential patron in the "text" of the *Daxue*, attributed to Confucius:

Things have their roots [*ben*] and branches [*mo*]; affairs have their ends and beginnings. Know what comes before [*xian*] and what comes after [*hou*], then one is near the *dao* . . . From the Son of Heaven to the common people, all must take self-cultivation as *ben*. It is false to suppose that the branches can be well governed if the roots are in disorder.[25]

This seems close to Zixia's argument presented above. The *ben–mo* distinction signifies an ordering relation that explains the sense in which one thing can be said to be prior to another.

Applied to the *ren–xiao* debate, Yan Du thus comes to the conclusion that both arise from the same source, although as *ben*, *xiao* can be said to come before *ren*. In a *ben–mo* relationship, *xiao* is prior not necessarily in the sense that it is "higher" or "greater" than *ren* but only because it is necessary for *ren*. One could argue that what comes before is more important, but there is also a sense in which what comes after can be seen to be more important. Kicking or heading the ball in the direction of goal is necessary for a soccer player to score a goal, but it can be argued that scoring is more important. Building a first-class infrastructure is a prerequisite for economic success, but arguably it is the quality of life that economic success brings that really matters. In this same sense, "sweeping and cleaning" can be regarded as *ben* and *xian*, without undermining the importance of the way of the *junzi*. The *ben–mo* analogy is useful precisely because it allows a measure of hermeneutical flexibility in describing the relationship between two equally important concepts. It is not designed to measure relative importance, which involves other considerations (e.g. important for what and to whom); as the *Mencius* points out, "If you bring the tips [*mo*] to the same level without measuring the difference in the bases [*ben*], you can make a piece of wood an inch long reach a greater height than a tall building" (6B1, Lau).

Inner (*nei*) and outer (*wai*)

Up to this point, the argument has been that in Confucian philosophy the interpretation of *xiao* is not an isolated event but takes place in a relational framework, especially in the light of its relationship with *ren*. Again, given that both *xiao* and *ren* rank high on the Confucian ethical scale, familiar terms of relations such as great and small, and difficult and easy, cannot bring out fully their perceived relationship. In this context, the *xian–hou* relation became a focal point of discussion in the *ren–xiao* debate during the Han. Although it is clearer than other metaphors of relations in some respect, the *xian–hou* order remains ambiguous and may give the impression that what comes after is less important. This explains the introduction of the *ben–mo* relation into the *ren–xiao* debate. *Xiao* and *ren* are equally important, although conceptual priority can be assigned to *xiao* because the absence of *xiao* will entail the absence of *ren*.

The construal of a "value-neutral" *ben–mo* relation may be useful, but like the *xian–hou* relation, *ben–mo* often implies relative importance as well. For example, when Mencius advised King Xuan of Qi to "return to the *ben*" of government (1A7), it is unlikely that he was maintaining that what was classified as *mo* in government was just as important. This does not invalidate Yan Du's argument, but the "value-added" sense of the relationship between roots and branches renders the conceptual terrain more challenging.

Further, the *Daxue* introduces another theme, which seems to privilege a value-added interpretation of the *ben–mo* relation: "Virtue is the *ben*, and wealth is the *mo*. If the ruler took the *ben* as external and the *mo* as internal, he would be fighting with the people for wealth and governing the country like a robber" (Chapter 10). In this instance, not only is *ben* the higher term, it is also "internal." Is it the case, then, that the *ben–mo* relation can be subsumed under the more complex relationship between the "inner" (*nei*) and the "outer" (*wai*)? *Ben* (main or base trunk) is usually understood in the sense of *gen* (roots), which are hidden from view, and may thus be taken as analogous to what is internal. The *Mencius*, for example, specifically uses *gen* rather than *ben* in describing the "nature" (*xing*) of the *junzi*: "That which a gentleman follows as his nature, that is to say, benevolence, rightness, the rites and wisdom, is rooted in his heart [*gen yu xin* 根於心], and manifests itself in his face, giving it a sleek appearance. It also shows in his back and extends to his limbs, rendering their message intelligible without words" (7A21, Lau).

The *nei–wai* relation does not figure in a philosophically significant way in the *Lunyu*; the emphasis on self-examination (e.g. 2.9, 4.17) or self-criticism (e.g. 5.27) is not concerned directly with binary relationships. The *nei–wai* relation does figure prominently in the *Mencius*, sometimes with the implication that what is classified as "inner" is more important than what is considered "outer."[26] For example, in response to the assertion that "when one has something within, it necessarily shows itself without," Mencius seems to be saying that the "inner" intentions of Confucius are beyond "the understanding of the multitude."[27] Apparently linking the idea of *ben* to that of the "inner," the *Mencius* also states, "If a thing has no *ben*, it is like the rain water that collects after a downpour . . . It may fill all the gutters, but we can stand and wait for it to dry up. Thus a gentleman is ashamed of an exaggerated reputation" (4B19, Lau). This anticipates a serious concern that emerged during the Later Han and the Wei (220–265) and Jin (265–420) periods that followed: that a person selected for office or a member of a "great" family with a fine reputation had only the appearance of talent and/or virtue and lacked "substance."

Applying this to the relationship between *xiao* and *ren*, can it be said that whereas *ren* is internal, *xiao* is external? At first glance, the *nei–wai* distinction seems inapplicable to the relationship between *xiao* and *ren*. Characterized by reverence and love, *xiao* can also be seen as an "inner" phenomenon, and may be translated in this sense as "filiality" rather than "filial piety."

Ren is bestowed on things, as Yan Du points out, and as such it seems to have an external dimension as well. Nevertheless, one decisive consideration for later interpretations of *xiao* and *ren* may be Mencius' idea that morality has "one root" (3A5), which points to a weakness in Yan Du's resolution of the *ren–xiao* debate. *Xiao* may come before *ren*, but the two are said to have come from the same source. Are they endowed by "heaven," or do they arise from a deep, inner moral core, or both?

Zhu Xi on the relationship between *xiao* and *ren*

The relationship between *xiao* and *ren* requires further reflection. The *ren–xiao* debate evidently continued to attract attention during the Wei–Jin period, although much of the literature has been lost.[28] Wang Bi (226–249), for example, gives a succinct interpretation of Youzi's remark on the relationship between *xiao* and *ren*: "Love for one's kin that arises naturally [*ziran qin ai* 自然親愛] is what constitutes *xiao*; the extension of love to things is what constitutes *ren*."[29]

The *ben–mo* metaphor is critical to Wang Bi's reformulation of classical learning; it is by "honoring the roots and putting to rest the branches" (*chongben ximo* 崇本息末), as Wang explains in his *Laozi* commentary, that lasting order and peace may be attained.[30] But what exactly is the "root," the profoundly deep and nameless *ziran* that brings forth *xiao* and *ren*? This is not the place to discuss Wang Bi's "Learning of the Mysterious Dao" (*xuanxue* 玄學). For our purposes, the point to note is that, logically, what is considered *ben* need not have an "inner" origin. For example, one may consider learning and ritual instruction to be the roots of the Confucian *dao*, which usually implies that a person's inner nature requires rectification from without. However, as *ren* captured the Confucian imagination, increasingly *ben* came to be associated with *nei*, which put pressure on the kind of interpretation of the *ren–xiao* relationship that we find in Yan Du's essay. The intricate lines of relationship between *xiao* and *ren* demanded careful yet firm handling, which we find in the masterful work of Zhu Xi. Although it seems attractive to ground what is considered *ben* in an inner realm, it is my suggestion that Zhu Xi gives a different interpretation. To give an indication of Zhu Xi's approach, I will focus on his commentary on *Mencius* 3A5, *Lunyu* 1.2, and *Lunyu* 19.12.

In *Mencius* 3A5, Yizi, who is partial to Mohist philosophy, presents to Mencius what he takes to be a Confucian position: "Love has no distinctions; its application begins with one's kin." This may recall Mencius' own saying quoted above, "As for a *ren* person, there is no one that he does not love, but he takes attending to his kin and those who are worthy to be the most pressing task" (7A46). But Mencius criticizes Yizi's interpretation: "Does Yizi truly believe that a man loves his brother's son no more than his neighbor's child? . . . Moreover, when Heaven produces things, it gives them one *ben*, yet Yizi tries to give them two *ben*" (3A5, Lau, modified).

Zhu Xi begins his commentary on this exchange by saying that Yizi attempts to smuggle a Mohist idea into Confucian teaching. Love does have distinctions, because "the birth of each and every human being is necessarily rooted [*ben*] in one's parents and does not have two [roots]." Further, "this is the principle of *ziran*, like heaven had made it so. Thus, love among human beings is built on this, which is then extended to reach the rest of humanity." Nevertheless, the fact that Yizi at least knew the proper "*xian–hou* order" in the application of love – that it begins with one's kin – shows that the light that lies deep within his heart (*benxin* 本心) has not been extinguished, and this is what enables him to recognize the truth of Mencius' teaching.[31]

The *Zhuzi yulei* 朱子語類 (*Conversations of Master Zhu Arranged According to Topics*) reports a less sympathetic critique of Yizi. A disciple suggests that Yizi seems to know "what comes before and what comes after." In response, Zhu Xi is emphatic in pointing out that this is precisely where Yizi had gone wrong. What truly comes first is the *ben*, and there can only be one *ben* because we all come from our parents; in putting "love without distinctions" as the basis of kinship affection, Yizi attributes an additional source to filial love, which is like saying that "one tree trunk has two roots [systems]." The key to this exchange is thus not "the application of love begins with one's kin," which Yizi "made up on the spot" to make his view more palatable to Mencius; instead, Yizi's mistake lies fundamentally in saying that "love has no distinctions," which is akin to "taking the roots of that tree and forcibly attaching it to this tree."[32]

So, did Yizi get the *xian–hou* order right? The commentary on *Mencius* 3A5 indicates Zhu Xi's approach but does not resolve the problem of the relationship between *xiao* and *ren*. Granted that there can only be one root, what that root is remains a question. This is addressed in Zhu Xi's extended discussion of Youzi's remark in the *Lunyu* (1.2). Here, Zhu Xi begins by defining *xiao* as being good at serving one's parents (*shanshi fumu* 善事父母). What does Youzi mean by "cultivating the roots" (*wu ben* 務本) and by "*xiao* and *ti* [brotherly respect] being the *ben* of *ren* [*wei ren zhi ben* 為仁之本]"? As is well known, Zhu Xi takes the phrase "*wei ren*" to mean "practicing *ren*." Zhu Xi writes:

> "Cultivate" [*wu*] means concentrating one's effort; *ben* suggests the roots [*gen*]. *Ren* means the principle of love [*ai zhi li* 愛之理] and the virtue of the heart [*xin zhi de* 心之德]. "*Wei ren*" is like saying [in common parlance] practicing *ren* [*xing ren* 行仁] ... This means that the *junzi* in all things concentrates his efforts on [cultivating] the roots and trunk. When the roots and trunk are established, then their *dao* will grow naturally. What *xiao* and brotherly respect in the above passage refers to is the root of practicing *ren*. If students cultivate this, the *dao* of *ren* will develop from it. Master Cheng [Cheng Yi 程頤, 1033–1107] said,

". . . Virtue has roots; when the roots are established, then its *dao* develops and enlarges. When *xiao* and *ti* are practiced at home, then afterward *ren* and love can be extended to things. This is what is meant by 'he is affectionate toward his kin and then extends *ren* to the people' [*Mencius* 7A45]. Thus, in practicing *ren, xiao* and *ti* form the roots. In terms of human nature, then it is *ren* that forms the roots of *xiao* and *ti.*" Someone asked, "If *xiao* and *ti* are the roots of practicing *ren*, is it true that from *xiao* and *ti* one can attain *ren*?" Master Cheng replied, "It is not true. To say that practicing *ren* begins with *xiao* and *ti* means that *xiao* and *ti* are one issue of *ren*. To say that *xiao* and *ti* form the root of the practice of *ren* is acceptable, but to say that they are the root of *ren* is not acceptable. This is because *ren* is nature, whereas *xiao* and *ti* are functions."[33]

In the *Zhuzi yulei*, Lu Xiangshan 陸象山 (1139–1193) is quoted to have said that contrary to what Youzi has proposed, "*ren* is the root of *xiao* and *ti.*"[34] This would be a simple way of resolving the debate. But Youzi is not wrong, according to Zhu Xi: *xiao* does come first. This is why Mencius places filial affection before loving the people (7A45). This is also why the *Daxue* insists that things have their roots and branches and that it is crucial to understand what comes before and what comes after. Flowing directly from the heart, there is nothing in the world that is more fundamental than *xiao*; at this level, all the "four germs" and not only the practice of *ren* "are rooted in *xiao* and *ti* and appear only afterwards."[35] "It's like a tree that has roots, trunk, branches and leaves. Being affectionate toward one's kin is the roots, extending *ren* to the people is the trunk, loving things is the branches and leaves. This, then, is the meaning of *xiao* and *ti* being the root of practicing *ren.*"[36]

The assertion that *xiao* forms the root of *ren*-practice takes *ren* in the sense of love, which always begins with filial affection. Without this, there can be no goodness in the world. However, this still does not explain the source of filial love. The answer, according to Zhu Xi, can only be *ren* in a metaphysical sense. From this perspective, "*ren* is the root [*gen*], and love is the young shoots; and one cannot just call the young shoots the root."[37] Thus, Zhu Xi defines *ren* not as love but as the principle of love in his commentary to *Lunyu* 1.2. In this sense, *ren* is the root not only of *xiao* but also of all things. Neither great nor small, neither difficult nor easy, as a metaphysical principle *ren* cannot even be said to be "attainable."[38]

In the *Mencius*, as we have seen, *xiao* is described as the "*shi* 實 of *ren*" (4A27). To Zhu Xi, this brings out both senses of *ren* and the crucial place of *xiao*. In his commentary to this passage, Zhu Xi emphasizes the immediacy of *xiao* and connects it with Youzi's comment in the *Lunyu*. In the *Yulei*, Zhu Xi takes pains to explain that the word "*shi*" is used here not in the sense of "actuality" (as contrasted with "names") or "facts" (as contrasted with "principle") but in the sense of "seeds" (as contrasted with "blossoms" [*hua* 華]). As the first outflowing of *ren*, filial love may be likened to seeds, which makes possible the flowering of "extending benevolence to the people" and "loving all things."[39]

Commenting on *Lunyu* 19.12, Zhu Xi cites Cheng Yi extensively:

> Master Cheng said, "There is a certain order to the way the *junzi* teaches. He first passes on to his students what is small and near, and afterwards teaches them what is great and far . . . " He said also, "sweeping and cleaning and responding to calls and answering queries are already *xing er shang* 形而上 [above the realm of forms]. This is because principle does not admit of the distinction between great and small . . . " He also said, "The *dao* of the sage does not distinguish the subtle from the coarse. From sweeping and cleaning and responding to calls and answering queries to penetrating to the core of rightness and entering the realm of the spiritual, there is only one principle that cuts through them . . . " He also said, "All things have their roots and branches. One must not divide *ben* and *mo* into two separate things . . . " He also said, "From sweeping and cleaning . . . one can reach the affairs of the sage." In my view, the first quotation from Master Cheng gives the fullest account of the meaning of this passage. The remaining four are all concerned with clarifying that one principle underlies the distinctions between the subtle and coarse and between the roots and branches. Students should advance gradually in the prescribed order and must not despise the branches and seek only the roots . . . The point is not that the branches are the roots, but rather that in mastering the branches the roots are also there.

This sums up Zhu Xi's approach to *ben* and *mo* and also to the relationship between *xiao* and *ren*. In the *Yulei*, Zhu Xi admits that it had taken him a long time before he finally understood what Cheng Yi was trying to say. There are two difficulties. First, Zixia was clearly talking about a *xian–hou* order, whereas Cheng Yi seems to be emphasizing that there is no distinction between roots and branches.[40] Second, following Zixia's order, sweeping and cleaning would have to be recognized as the "root" of Confucian self-cultivation, the foundation of learning to become a sage. For Zhu Xi, "Cheng Yi's view is also the view of Zixia."[41] Cheng Yi is not denying the distinction between *ben* and *mo* and thus *xian* and *hou* in learning; he is simply saying that in the one we find also the other because they share the same principle. There is thus no reason to look down on seemingly trivial tasks, although it does not follow that one can become a sage merely by "sweeping and cleaning." Just as *xiao* at one level constitutes the root of *ren*, elementary learning comes before a greater understanding of the *dao*. Just as *ren* as nature is the root of *xiao*, "principle" is always one and transcends all "functions."

Conclusion

The word *"ren,"* as Zhu Xi intimates, is the most difficult to speak about.[42] Philosophically, *ren* as principle is all-encompassing. But from the perspective of the world of affairs and phenomena, *ren* is nothing but the extension of *xiao*. The *Yulei* in a number of places reports how Zhu Xi explains the relationship between *xiao* and *ren* by drawing a series of concentric circles: inside the innermost circle, write the word *"ren,"* as Zhu Xi tells one of his disciples, then write *"xiao* and *ti"* at the next outside circle, and *"ren min ai wu* 仁民愛物" at the next.[43]

In Zhu Xi's "Diagram of the Treatise on *Ren*," as is well known, *xiao* is placed at the very end of the diagram as a function of *ren*, which may give the impression that Zhu Xi was not interested in *xiao* at all.[44] However, taking into view Zhu Xi's complex approach to the *ren–xiao* relationship, this does not give the whole picture. In fact, Zhu Xi laments that "nowadays, people tend to underestimate *xiao* and *ti"* in their eagerness to rise above the mundane to reach the height of the sagely way.[45]

It would probably have been much easier if Zhu Xi had traced what is *ben* and what comes first to an inner realm. Why not trace both *xiao* and *ren* to the "heart" (*xin*), which comes before and is the root of everything else? In this case, both *xiao* and *ren* would be functions of *xin*. But he did not, for a reason. Discussing with his disciples Zixia's remarks, Zhu Xi explicitly rejects Xie Liangzuo's 謝良佐 (1050–1120) interpretation that what matters is not as much what one does as putting one's heart, as it were, in the right place.[46] The reason seems to be that Zhu Xi was alarmed by possible Buddhist and Daoist influence.[47] The concept of *xin*, of course, plays an important role in Zhu Xi's philosophy, but if one focuses only on the "inner," one may risk missing the *xian–hou* order on which Confucian learning depends: "If one only talks about the great root [*da ben*], this is the teaching of the Buddha and Laozi."[48]

Although the inner–outer distinction can serve to explain certain relations, it may create a sharp divide that gives rise to misunderstanding of the Confucian *dao*. Replying to a question from a disciple that the "investigation of things" (*ge wu* 格物) may lean too far in the direction of the external, Zhu Xi emphasizes that "if done in unison [*he* 合], then although it is a matter of governing the country and bringing peace to the world, it is also my own affair." This seems to echo the view of the *Zhongyong* that the height of virtue is the *dao* that "unites [*he*] the inner and the outer" (Chapter 25). Indeed, Zhu Xi is reported to have nodded with approval when the disciple concludes, "In this case, then one should not be talking about *nei* and *wai*, but rather about working in unison or not."[49] Nevertheless, the point is not to insist on the unity of the inner and the outer; instead, when extended to the full, the investigation of things would naturally reveal the oneness of the universe.[50] This refocuses attention on "principle," which as a metaphysical reality cannot be said to be either inner or outer but encompasses both.

Confucius and Mencius were concerned with making clear the ethical significance of filial piety. As the Confucian tradition developed, making sense of *xiao* in relation to other key ethical concepts became a major intellectual concern. The application of *xiao* to politics, law, and other spheres of life gives rise to a host of complexities – as the studies by Anne Cheng, Patricia Ebrey, and others in this volume amply illustrate – that require careful management and render the task of the philosophers all the more challenging and valuable. Yan Du in the Later Han saw the need to provide a balanced account of the relationship between *xiao* and *ren*; but it was not until Zhu Xi that the issue found a lasting resolution in the Confucian world. In everyday life, according to Zhu Xi, *xiao* always comes before *ren* and is the root of *ren* understood as love. As one penetrates the reason why this is the case, however, one realizes that *ren* in a "higher" metaphysical sense is the very principle of love and of life itself and as such constitutes the source of *xiao*. Zhu Xi's approach to the *ren–xiao* relationship reflects a deep concern for the integrity of the entire philosophical architecture. Terms and metaphors of relations provide the structural support that links together a network of ideas. There are only a limited number of such terms, and philosophers cannot but work with them. It would be an overstatement to say that they determine the direction of thought, but it seems reasonable to suppose that they play a critical role in the development of Chinese philosophy.

Notes

1 See W. T. Chan, "The Evolution of the Confucian Concept *Jen*," *Philosophy East and West*, 4, no.4, 1955, 295–319.

2 K. Knapp, "The *Ru* Reinterpretation of *Xiao*," *Early China*, 20, 1995, 195–222; and D. Holzman, "The Place of Filial Piety in Ancient China," *Journal of the American Oriental Society*, 118, no. 2, 1998, 185–99.

3 See K. Knapp, "The *Ru* Reinterpretation of *Xiao*," p. 205, n. 37. The composite nature of the *Lunyu* has been given extensive treatment by E. B. Brooks and A. T. Brooks, *The Original Analects*, New York: Columbia University Press, 1998.

4 *Lunyu* 1.6. Yang Bojun 楊伯峻, *Lunyu yizhu* 論語譯注, Beijing: Zhonghua shuju, 1982. Translation from the *Lunyu* is generally based on D. C. Lau, *Confucius: The Analects*, Harmondsworth: Penguin Books, 1979, with modifications where appropriate. In some cases, I differ from Lau's translation. Compare A. Waley, *The Analects of Confucius*, New York: Vintage Books, 1938; and R. T. Ames and H. Rosemont Jr, *The Analects of Confucius: A Philosophical Translation*, New York: Ballantine Books, 1998.

5 *Zhuangzi*, Chapter 4; translated in A. C. Graham, *Chuang-tzu: The Seven Inner Chapters*, London: George Allen and Unwin, 1981, p. 70.

6 *Zhuangzi*, Chapter 14; cf. B. Watson, *The Complete Works of Chuang Tzu*, New York: Columbia University Press, 1968, p. 155: "To be filial out of respect is easy; to be filial out of love is hard."

7 Yang Bojun, for example, holds this view; see his *Lunyu yizhu*, 1.11.

8 *Guanzi*, Chapter 26, "Jie" (Admonitions); cf. W. A. Rickett (trans.) *Guanzi*, Princeton, NJ: Princeton University Press, 1985, vol. 1, p. 380.

9 *Zhuangzi*, Chapter 14; B. Watson, *The Complete Works of Chuang Tzu*, p. 155.
10 Slip 98; in *Guodian Chumu Zhujian* 郭店楚墓竹簡, Beijing: Wenwu chubanshe, 1998, p. 198. For an introduction to the Guodian texts, see W. Boltz, "The Fourth-century BC Guodiann Manuscripts from Chuu and the Composition of the *Laotzyy*," *Journal of the American Oriental Society*, 119, no. 4, 1999, 590–608.
11 *Guodian Chumu Zhujian*, p. 157.
12 Ibid., p. 150; cf. Pang Pu 龐樸, *Zhubo wuxing pian jiaozhu ji yanjiu* 竹帛五行篇校注及研究, Taipei: Wanjuanlou chubanshe, 2001, pp. 140, 153. The *Wuxing pian* is found in both the Guodian and Mawangdui manuscripts; see also the studies by Ikeda Tomohisa 池田知久 cited in his contribution to this volume.
13 *Daxue*, Chapters 3 and 9; see Zhu Xi, *Daxue zhangju* 大學章句, pp. 3b and 7a; as translated in W. T. Chan, *A Source Book in Chinese Philosophy*, Princeton, NJ: Princeton University Press, 1963, p. 91. All references to Zhu Xi's commentaries to the Four Books are from the *Sishu jizhu* 四書集注, Sibubeiyao edition, Taipei: Zhonghua shuju, 1973.
14 *Zhongyong*, Chapter 20; Zhu Xi, *Zhongyong zhangju* 中庸章句, p. 12a; cf. W. T. Chan, *Source Book*, p. 104.
15 Yang Bojun, *Mengzi yizhu* 孟子譯注, Hong Kong: Zhonghua shuju, 1984; cf. D. C. Lau (trans.), *Mencius*, Hong Kong: Chinese University Press, 1984, pp. 111, 247, 269.
16 This is, for example, how W. T. Chan has understood it; see *Source Book*, p. 76.
17 Huang Deshi 黃得時, *Xiaojing jinzhu jinyi* 孝經今注今譯, Taipei: Taiwan Shangwu yinshuguan, 1986, Chapter 1.
18 *Hou Hanshu* 後漢書, *juan* 70, Beijing: Zhonghua shuju, 1982, p. 2278.
19 According to Yu Yingshi 余英時, Kong Rong was challenging the view that *xiao* could be understood merely in biological terms. See Yu, "Mingjiao weiji yu Wei Jin shifeng de yanbian" 名教危機與魏晉士風的演變, in his *Zhongguo zhishi jiecengshi lun, gudai pian* 中國知識階層史論, 古代篇, Taipei: Lianjing, 1984, p. 341.
20 *Hou Hanshu*, *juan* 64, pp. 2104–5.
21 Zhu Xi, *Lunyu jizhu* 論語集注, *juan* 10, p. 2b. See also *Mencius* 6A14 and 6A15 on the distinction between the "greater aspects" (*da ti* 大體) and "smaller aspects" (*xiao ti* 小體) of a person.
22 *Mencius* 7A46, following Zhu Xi's reading, in *Mengzi jizhu* 孟子集注, *juan* 7, p. 14a. D. C. Lau, *Mencius*, p. 285, and W. A. C. H. Dobson, *Mencius*, Toronto: University of Toronto Press, 1974, p. 146, give a different interpretation. Lau's translation reads: "A benevolent man loves everyone, but he devotes himself to the close association with good and wise men."
23 Cf. *Lunyu* 15.10: "A craftsman who wishes to practice his craft well must first sharpen his tools"; see also 12.21, 19.10.
24 The *Shuowen* lexicon by the Han scholar Xu Shen 許慎 (*fl.* 100 CE) defines *ben* as "the lower part of a tree" (*mu xia yue ben* 木下曰本); see Duan Yucai 段玉裁 (1735–1815), *Shuowen jiezi zhu* 說文解字注, Shanghai: Shanghai guji chubanshe, 1988, p. 248.
25 *Daxue zhangju*, pp. 1b–2a.
26 Two recent essays that address this theme in the *Mencius* are K. C. Chong, "Mengzi and Gaozi on *Nei* and *Wai*," in A. K. L. Chan (ed.), *Mencius: Contexts and Interpretations*, Honolulu: University of Hawaii Press, 2002, pp. 103–25; and J. Heng, "Understanding Words and Knowing Men," in *ibid.*, pp. 151–68.
27 *Mencius* 6B6, Lau, trans.; cf. Robert Eno, "Casuistry and Character in Mencius," in A. K. L. Chan (ed.), *Mencius: Contexts and Interpretations*, pp. 189–215.
28 The famous Cao Zhi 曹植 (192–232), for example, is known to have written a "Treatise on Benevolence and Filial Piety" (*Ren xiao lun* 仁孝論). The text no

longer survives, except for several sentences preserved in the Song encyclopedic work, the *Taiping yulan* 太平御覽 (*juan* 419, p. 5b); see Yan Kejun 嚴可均 (1762–1843), *Quan Shanggu Sandai Qin Han Sanguo Liuchao wen* 全上古三代秦漢三國六朝文, Beijing: Zhonghua shuju, 1995, p. 1150. Like Yan Du, Cao Zhi also holds that "*xiao* applies to what is near, whereas *ren* reaches far" (孝者施近, 仁者及遠). According to the *Jinshu* (*History of the Jin Dynasty*), Xun Yi 荀顗 (d. 274) and Wang Jun 王駿 debated on the relative priority of *ren* and *xiao*. Given that Xun Yi is known for his filial piety, perhaps he would emphasize its priority over *ren*; see *Jinshu*, Beijing: Zhonghua shuju, 1982, *juan* 39, p. 1150, biography of Xun Yi. During the Wei–Jin period, the *ren–xiao* question increasingly came under the debate on the relative priority of loyalty (*zhong* 忠) and filial piety. The potential conflict between the two cannot be dismissed; the *Sanguozhi* (*Records of the Three Kingdoms*), for example, relates that Cao Pi (187–226), when he was crown prince, raised the following question to his guests at a banquet: "Suppose your ruler and your father were both suffering from a terminal illness and you have one pill that could save one of them. Would you save your ruler or your father?" The guests debated at length, we are told, and were divided in their answer. Cao Pi then asked Ping Yuan 邴原, who did not participate in the discussion. Ping Yuan firmly replied, "Father!" See *Sanguozhi*, Beijing: Zhonghua shuju, 1982, *juan* 11, pp. 353–4. An attempt to reconcile loyalty with filial piety is found in the *Sanguozhi*, *juan* 22, p. 638, n. 1: "The man of *ren* loves his fellow men [cf. *Lunyu* 12.22]. When [this love is] applied to the ruler, it is called loyalty; when applied to one's kin, it is called filial piety. Loyalty and filial piety are derived from the same root." On this development, see Tang Changru 唐長孺, "Wei Jin Nanchao de junfu xianhou lun" 魏晉南朝的君父先後論, in his *Wei Jin Nan Bei chao shilun shiyi* 魏晉南北朝史論拾遺, Beijing: Zhonghua shuju, 1983, pp. 233–48.

29 Wang Bi, *Lunyu shiyi* 論語釋疑; in Lou Yulie 樓宇烈, *Wang Bi ji jiaoshi* 王弼集校釋, Beijing: Zhonghua shuju, 1980, p. 621.

30 The phrase is used in two senses, both directed primarily at the ruler: (a) to cultivate the fundamentals in self-cultivation and government so as to enable the people to grow and to nurture their "genuine" nature; and (b) to cultivate the roots in order to put an end to the false and deviant. See A. K. L. Chan, *Two Visions of the Way*, Albany: State University of New York Press, 1991, p. 77; Wang Xiaoyi 王曉毅, *Wang Bi pingzhuan* 王弼評傳, Nanjing: Nanjing daxue chubanshe, 1996, p. 265.

31 *Mengzi jizhu, juan* 3, p. 12b.

32 Li Jingde 黎靖德 (thirteenth century) (ed.), *Zhuzi yulei*, Beijing: Zhonghua shuju, 1986, pp. 1313–14.

33 *Lunyu jizhu, juan* 1, pp. 1b–2a.

34 *Yulei*, p. 458.

35 Ibid., p. 463.

36 Ibid., p. 472.

37 Ibid., p. 464.

38 Ibid., p. 475, referring to the question put to Cheng Yi whether one can attain *ren* from *xiao* and *ti*.

39 Ibid., pp. 1332–3; see also p. 463.

40 Ibid., p. 1208.

41 Ibid., p. 1210.

42 Ibid., p. 477.

43 Ibid., p. 462; see p. 473 for a variation of this diagram. See also W. T. Chan, "Analogies and Diagrams," in his *Chu Hsi: New Studies*, Honolulu: University of Hawaii Press, 1989, pp. 271–92.

44 *Yulei*, p. 2633; cf. Sato Hitoshi , "Chu Hsi's *Treatise on Jen,*" in W. T. Chan (ed.), *Chu Hsi and Neo-Confucianism*, Honolulu: University of Hawaii Press, 1986, pp. 212–27.
45 *Yulei*, p. 1333.
46 Ibid., p. 1209.
47 See ibid., pp. 2562–3 for Zhu's assessment of Xie's view of *ren*.
48 Ibid., p. 290.
49 Ibid., p. 288.
50 Ibid., p. 295.

10 Filial piety, commiseration, and the virtue of *ren*

Sin Yee Chan

In the *Analects*, filial piety and respect for one's elder brother have been described as the root of the virtue of *ren*: "It is rare for a man whose character is such that he is good as a son and obedient as a young man to have the inclination to transgress against his superiors . . . The gentleman devotes his efforts to the roots, for once the roots are established, the Way will grow therefrom. Being good as a son and obedient as a young man is, perhaps, the root of *ren*" (1:2). On the other hand, we find that Mencius refers to something else, namely commiseration, as the germination of the virtue of *ren*.[1] In the description of the four minds, commiseration is described as the germ of *ren* (*Mencius* 2A:6). In this chapter, I show how both commiseration and filial piety can be seen as essential to the development of the virtue of *ren*, as they pertain to the different aspects of *ren*. Commiseration is about a general concern for the well-being of people, and filial piety (as well as respect for the elderly brother) is about a special bonding with particular individuals. While the claim that commiseration and filial piety are both important for a person's moral development is not a novel claim, I hope to shed new light on it by showing how psychological theories can help to ground it.

A few clarifications are in order. First of all, my examination is based primarily on the texts of the *Analects* and *Mencius*. In other words, the examination is made in the context of philosophical Confucianism rather than imperial Confucianism.[2] And my primary textual references are made to the *Analects* and the *Mencius*, as the two are more detailed about interpersonal relationships, especially the familial relationships. Second, it is the aspect about benevolence that I emphasize when I discuss the concept of *ren*. *Ren* in the *Analects* and the *Mencius* can be seen as an ideal virtue that encompasses a variety of specific virtues such as courage, wisdom, and modesty, among others. As such it is closely connected to *li* (ritual) for its development and expression.[3] On the other hand, *ren* in the *Analects* and the *Mencius* sometimes is also described as a specific virtue of being benevolent or having affective concern for others.[4] "Fan Ch'ih asked about *ren*. Confucius said, 'Love your fellow men'" (*Analects* 12:22). Hence, arguably, benevolence in the sense of loving others can be seen as the quintessential component of the virtue of *ren* in the sense that all the other specific virtues, which are also the components of the ethical ideal virtue of *ren*, are seen as required for the sake of the achievement and the proper expression of one's love for others.[5]

Before we look at the psychological theories, we need to clarify the meaning of commiseration and filial piety. Let us first look at commiseration. There is no reference to commiseration in the *Analects*. In the *Mencius*, commiserative responses are described in a few instances. The most famous ones are the following.

> The King was sitting in the upper part of the hall and someone led an ox through the lower part. The King noticed this and said, "Where is the ox going?" "The blood of the ox is to be used for consecrating a new bell." "Spare it. I cannot bear [*buren*] to see it shrinking with fear, like an innocent man going to the place of execution."[6]
>
> (*Mencius* 1A:7)

> Mencius said, "Everybody who has a mind cannot bear others' [sufferings] (*buren ren*). The ancient kings have this mind of *buren ren*, hence they have policies of *buren ren* . . . My reason for saying that everyone has the mind of *buren ren* is this. Suppose a man were, all of a sudden, to see a young child on the verge of falling into a well. He would certainly feel fear and the mind of pain [*ceyin*]. This is not because he wanted to get in the good graces of the parents, nor because he wished to win the praise of his fellow villages or friends, nor yet because he disliked the cry of the child."
>
> (*Mencius* 2A:6)

We should note that Mencius uses two different terms in describing what I call the commiserative responses: the mind of *ceyin*, and the mind of *buren ren*. According to *Shuowen*, both characters *ce* and *yin* mean pain. The mind of *ceyin* can therefore be seen as referring to the feeling of pain. The mind of *buren ren* refers to the mind that cannot bear to see the suffering of others, and that contains a desire to do something to help to alleviate the pain. Putting these two minds together, we have something analogous to the English word "commiseration": when seeing others in pain, we feel the pain, and we have the desire to help others to get rid of the pain.

Commiseration can be seen as akin to sympathy or compassion, and as such it is important to distinguish it from both empathy and pity.[7] Empathy is marked by vicarious arousal. Basically, it is to share the same feelings of another person. When I empathize with the emotions of another person, I feel joyful if she is joyful, and sorrowful if she feels sorrow. Empathy is often achieved by imagining oneself in another's position, or even identifying with another. But sometimes empathy may occur in the form of affective contagion. That is, one is simply taken over by the affective state of another without a cognitive awareness of the situation or even a recognition of that affective state. For example, one feels joyful when one walks into a euphoric crowd.

As for commiseration or sympathy, philosophers such as Aristotle and Rousseau think that it requires identification with the object.[8] That is, one imagines oneself as being the other person, or at least imagines that one has similar degrees of vulnerability to misfortunes as the object. Hence, it is thought that if one has previously experienced the kind of misfortune that the object is undergoing, one may tend to experience a higher degree of commiseration. But this requirement seems to be too strong. Full identification in the sense of imagining oneself as another does not seem to be a necessary condition for one to have compassion. When I have compassion for the children who were sold by their parents to become child prostitutes, I may just be struck by their sense of helplessness, abandonment, loss, and desperation. Or when I feel compassion for the laboratory animals that underwent cruel and painful experimentations, I do not imagine that I were them, as I do not know what it feels to be animals like them.

Even the weaker sense of identification – that is, to imagine oneself as sharing similar degrees of vulnerability – need not be taking place in compassion. In explaining this weaker sense of identification, Nussbaum says: "the pain of another will be an object of my concern only if I acknowledge some sort of community between myself and the other, understanding what it might be for me to face such pain. Without that sense of commonness, both Aristotle and Rousseau claim, I will react with sublime indifference or mere intellectual curiosity, like an obtuse alien from another world."[9] She then concludes, "the judgment of similar possibilities is part of a construct that bridges the gap between prudential concern and altruism."[10]

It is unclear what it means to bridge the gap between prudential concern and altruism, and in what sense the community between oneself and the other is required for compassion. If understanding is construed as a form of community, so that the discernment of suffering in the other is seen as a form of community between oneself and the other, then compassion does require community. But this sense of community implies nothing about similar vulnerability. I can discern the suffering of a bat, without believing that I, who have significantly different physiological and psychological make-up, share vulnerability similar to that of a bat. More importantly, it is mistaken to think that altruistic compassion is related to prudential concern. Is it true that for me to feel compassion I must think that the suffering that the other undergoes could happen to me? I do not believe so. Compassion seems to be an other-oriented emotion that is instigated by the awareness of the suffering of others, instead of a self-oriented emotion based on one's consideration of one's own vulnerability. In Buddhism, the Bodhisattvas are said to have compassion for the myriad creatures, even though they themselves have achieved enlightenment, and are no longer subject to vulnerability or suffering of any sort.

What are the core characteristics of commiseration if it does not involve identification with the object of commiseration? Perhaps we can see them through the comparison between commiseration and empathy. The two emotions differ in the following ways. First, commiseration or sympathy implies a divergence of the feelings between the agent and the object of commiseration or sympathy. Mencius' own example of seeing a child about to fall into a well nicely illustrates the feeling of commiseration. The innocent child is totally unaware of the danger that befalls her, so she feels neither pain nor fear. The commiserating bystander on the other hand feels shocked and cannot bear to see the forthcoming suffering. A sympathetic agent witnessing another person in agony need not feel the pain herself even though she will feel bad, or discomfort, or sorrowful for the person. Second, while empathy can relate to both positive and negative emotions (that is, both joy and pain), sympathy or commiseration is a response to negative emotions only. One can be empathetic with one's happy friend, but cannot be sympathetic towards a happy friend, unless one detects pain beneath the surface of happiness. Third, commiseration presumes a clear distinction between the self and others. Hence it can come about only when a child has achieved a sense of self (we should note that Mencius' paradigm example of commiseration also features an adult responding to the potential suffering of a child). Empathy, on the other hand, can occur very early on, as it can take the form of affective contagion. Even three-day-old neonates are reported to mimic the crying of similarly aged neonates and respond to the cue of distress by experiencing the distress themselves.[11] Finally, commiseration is conceptually linked to the altruistic desire to alleviate the sufferings of others. Mencius talks about the desire to save the child who is about to fall into the well. As pointed out insightfully by D. C. Lau, this desire may not finally actualize into actions. Such motivation to help, however, may be absent in the case of empathy. Certain clinical psychological theories such as that of psychoanalysis even require the severance of empathy from an actional stance.[12]

Furthermore, commiseration is different from pity, in that the latter connotes condescension.[13] The rich pities the poor, the healthy pities the sick, the lucky pities the unfortunate. The pitying agent is seen to occupy a superior position. The superiority here does not necessarily refer to a social position. Instead, it refers to a more privileged position. Consequently, the pitying agent herself is aware of the superiority, though she need not exhibit or have a sense of superiority. A commiserating agent, on the other hand, need not be in a better position than the object of commiseration. A victim of an accident can sympathize with her fellow traveler, but not pity the latter. This discrepancy in status may explain why people sometimes resent being treated as objects of pity.

In summary, commiseration includes the discrepancy of feelings between the agent and the object, a response to the negative emotions of the object, an awareness of the distinction between the self and others, an altruistic motivation, and does not presume a superior status of the agent.

Let us now move on to look at filial piety. The filial duties described in the texts include the following: support one's parents (*Analects* 2:7), respect them (*Analects* 2:7), obey them (*Mencius* 4:18), please them (*Mencius* 4A:28), and not cause them worry (*Analects* 2:5), identify with them by taking up their values (*Analects* 4:20), treat them according to rituals (*Mencius* 3A:2), bury them and make sacrificial offerings to them according to rituals (*Mencius* 3A:2), bear descendents (*Mencius* 4A:26) so that the sacrificial offerings to them can be continued, behave properly so that one would not cause revenge to be inflicted upon one's parents (*Mencius* 7B:7), and remonstrate against them when they have deviated from the right path (*Analects* 4:18).

The most important constituent of filial piety, arguably, is affection or love. Although it is said in the text that "The greatest thing a dutiful son can do is to honor his parents, and the greatest thing he can do to honor his parents is to support them with the Empire" (*Mencius* 5A:7), we should also note that in characterizing the role model of filial piety, the sage Shun, it is his affection for his parents that is emphasized: nothing, not even the rank of emperor, can alleviate his sorrow for the lack of his parents' love. And great filial piety is described as including a life-long yearning for the parents' love (*Mencius* 5A:1). Furthermore, it is *qinqin*, or loving one's parents, that is described as *ren* (Mencius 6B:3, 7A:15), and deep mourning for one's parents is praised as filial (*Mencius* 3A:2) because it is the basic reason for the mourning rituals (*Analects* 17:21). The ability to love one's parents is also seen as instinctual, even though it is not among the four germs of human nature (Mencius 7A:15). Given the important role of human nature in *Mencius*, we can therefore infer the importance of affection as a constituent of filial piety.

We should note that affection for one's parents is not merely a transitory and whimsical feeling. Instead, it leads to strong altruistic concern for the physical, spiritual, and moral well-being of one's parents. Indeed, it constitutes such a devotion and commitment to one's parents that one is willing to risk one's moral integrity for the sake of one's parents: one may have to cover up for them when they have committed a crime (*Analects* 13:18), or steal them from prison if they have been jailed (*Mencius* 7A:35). Consequently, we can conclude that while filial piety has behavioral components, its essence is the special bond with and affection for one's parents.

In this way, both commiseration and filial piety can be understood as *affective altruistic concerns*. While commiseration is directed at anybody who is suffering or is expected to undergo some negative emotions, filial piety points to particularistic relationships in the sense that its objects are particular individuals who have special significance to the agent, and it has to be understood in the context of relationships that are cherished and seen as irreplaceable.

How are filial piety and commiseration as affective concern related to the development of the virtue of *ren*? Let us look at commiseration first. As explained above, commiseration includes the desire to relieve others' pain;

its association with altruistic behaviors is therefore obvious. The more pertinent question is what particular kind of virtue(s) can be seen as correlating to commiseration. For example, Nussbaum suggests that sympathy leads to the construction of an emotional analogue of Rawls's original position.[14] She reasons that the consideration of one's vulnerability to misfortunes makes one turn one's attention to the structure of society's allocation of goods and resources; one therefore desires the condition of the worst off people in society to be as good as it can be.

While the construction of the emotional analogue of the original position is not incoherent in the case of compassion, compassion alone is much too thin to generate something like the original position. Society may be in such an affluent and harmonious condition that even the worst off people are not in any sense suffering, they are just comparatively worse off than the other members of the society. But as said before, compassion is a response to suffering only; hence compassion will not be incited in this case. Alternatively, society may include a lot of people besides the worst off who are in miserable condition. In that alternative scenario, a compassionate person may choose to structure society in such a way that the average utility is maximized, rather than merely maximizing that utility of the worst off. In brief, whether one will choose something similar to Rawls's original position or not does not seem to depend very much on compassion.

Is compassion more related to *ren* than the emotional analogue of the original position then? Perhaps yes. As noted above, benevolence in the sense of loving others is the quintessential element of *ren* (*Analects* 12:22). Commiseration, in turn, can be seen as the germ of the virtue of benevolence because the expansion and development of commiseration results in benevolence. When we commiserate, we commiserate for people who are suffering, i.e. we only sympathize with people who are in pain and we have a desire to alleviate their pain. However, when a person is benevolent, she cares for everybody, not just those who suffer; and she desires to promote others' well-being, not just to alleviate their pain. Benevolence can be seen as the development of commiseration because the absence of pain is a component, indeed a very important one, of a person's well-being. By appreciating the importance of the removal of pain, we come to recognize the importance of protecting and promoting a person's well-being. Commiseration can therefore be seen as the germ of benevolence.

Darwall's observation about sympathy further supports this view about the relationship between commiseration and benevolence. According to Darwall, sympathy is an individual-regarding emotion in the sense that when one sympathizes, one does not just see the disvalue of or desire the removal of suffering, one has concern for the *person* for her own sake.[15] Hence, although it is the suffering that elicits the response of compassion, if Darwall is correct, then it is easy to see how one can transit easily from compassion to benevolence. Having concern for the other person, one will care about not just the suffering, but the other aspects of her well-being as well.

Filial piety can also be seen as the root of the virtue of *ren*, because benevolence or loving others does not only pertain to loving anybody, it also consists in loving some particular individuals in some special ways and developing bonding and close relationships with them. In Confucianism, relationship love is seen as having ethical priority over general benevolence (*Mencius* 7A:45). While this ability to love is described in the Mencius as innate, relationship loving can still be seen as requiring development. First of all, transient affection has to be developed to strong and reliable forces constituting commitment. Mencius shows how often one's innate love for one's parents becomes quickly replaced by one's love for one's wife, which in turn gives way to love for one's prince (*Mencius* 5A:1). Whimsical affection is shallow and fragile; it will not lead to life affirming relationships. While arguably affection must imply altruistic concern, the extent of one's willingness to make sacrifice for the sake of others can still be subject to further development. A child may be willing to share some of her favorite food with her parent, but it is hard to imagine that she will be willing to give it all up without being taught to do so. More basically, relationship love requires development because altruistic concern requires learning of skills to become effective. One needs to learn what constitutes the physical, material, and spiritual well-being of another, as well as how to go about promoting the well-being. Perhaps it is because of this kind of reasoning that the *Analects* emphasizes treating one's parents according to rituals, which can be understood as useful guides to how to behave in a beneficial manner (*Analects* 2A:5).

To sum up, if we understand the virtue of *ren* as essentially about loving, in the form of both general benevolence and relationship affection, then we can see how commiseration and filial piety as different forms of affective altruistic concern can help to develop the virtue of *ren*.

How does this Confucian insight of the relevance of commiseration and filial piety to moral development compare with contemporary psychological theories about moral development? While it is at odds with two prominent theories, it also coheres with other psychological theories about moral development.

The first theory that conflicts with the Confucian idea is Kohlberg's theory.[16] Kohlberg proposed a sequence of six developmental stages of moral judgment. Stage 1 is heteronomous morality, where the reason for doing the right thing is to avoid punishment. Stage 2 is marked by instrumental purpose and exchange. One follows rules when doing so serves one's interests. Right is understood as what is a fair exchange. Stage 3 is about living up to the expectations of the people close to oneself, showing concern for others and keeping mutual relationships such as trust and gratitude (golden rule). Stage 4 focuses on fulfilling duties and upholding laws; one also starts to take the point of view of the society (and conscience). Stage 5 is when one recognizes the distinction between the group-related values and the non-relative values and rights, like life and liberty. Stage 6 (later integrated with stage 5), the highest stage, is achieved when one follows self-chosen ethical principles that are universal principles of justice: the equality of human rights and respect for the dignity of human beings as individual persons. Kohlberg's theory upholds the importance of reasoning, especially in the form of universal principles, at the expense of affection. Affective altruistic concerns such as commiseration and filial piety are downplayed, as they are seen as exemplifying immature moral judgments of stage 3.

Another theory that conflicts with the Confucian idea is the psychoanalytic theory, as it denies the genuineness of altruistic concern. To understand this denial, we have to first understand how one's conscience is developed according to the psychoanalytic theory. According to the theory, a young boy desires erotic contacts with his mother and resents his father, who is seen as his rival. To relieve the anxiety that results from his fear of paternal revenge, he represses his resentment toward his father as well as any conscious desire for his mother. As part of this process, the boy identifies with his father; that is, adopts the values, beliefs, and behaviors of the father. Such identification results in the development in the boy of a superego, which consists in the two parts of the conscience and the ego ideal. When internalized moral standards or ideals are violated, the conscience punishes the individual with guilt feelings. These guilt feelings are the feelings of resentment formerly directed toward the same-sex parent that were turned inward as a result of identification. Guilt feelings dominate the workings of the superego. In Freud's view, guilt, envy, and self-destructive tendencies are the major forces underlying altruism and the sense of justice. Seemingly altruistic behaviors are often defense mechanisms used by the ego to deal with the superego. For example, by reaction formation (one form of defense mechanism), a person may act in an apparently altruistic manner to conceal and keep in check the greedy tendencies. In this way, the psychoanalytic theory denies the genuineness of both commiseration and filial piety, as it denies that one can really transcend one's own world and work for the sake of others.[17]

However, not every dominant psychological theory concurs with the downplaying of affects as Kohlberg's theory suggests, or the denial of the genuineness of altruistic motivations as psychoanalytic theory advocates. For example, Piaget, another important moral development psychologist, believes that affective development parallels the stages of cognitive development. The two follow parallel, complementary courses. Cognition is viewed as providing the structure for development; emotion supplies the fuel or energetic component. Indeed, one cannot occur without the other according to Piaget. In this theory, some intra-individual feelings are present from birth. Then between two and seven years of age, elementary interpersonal feelings and the beginnings of moral feelings, such as respect and obedience, emerge. It is then followed by the stage (seven to eleven years) where autonomous moral feelings will appear. Finally, between eleven and twelve years of age, idealistic goals and feelings for collective ideals emerge.[18]

With specific reference to commiseration, there are also supports for the link between sympathy and altruistic behavior.[19] Infants exhibit emotional responses to others' distress since very early age. Neonates of two and three days old cry to the sound of someone else's cry.[20] However, such response should be more appropriately seen as empathy and not compassion, for the latter requires the attainment of the concept of the self, and the ability to make the distinction between oneself and another. Yet it does not take long for infants to develop from empathy to sympathy. The following anecdote illustrates the sympathetic response of a twelve-month-old child:

> I know a child whose typical response to his own distress, beginning late in the first year, was to suck his thumb with one hand and pull his ear with the other . . . Something new happened at 12 months. On seeing a sad look on his father's face, he proceeded to look sad and suck his thumb, while pulling on his father's ear.[21]

The anecdote seems to suggest that this infant responds with both his own personal distress and sympathy to his father upon seeing his father's sad look. Hoffman claims that with their further cognitive development, infants later become aware of the distinctive needs of others as different from their own. Hence when they try to alleviate others' suffering, they will act in ways that can effectively address others' needs instead of only appealing to means that work in their own case. Instead of pulling on the father's ear, the infant may now give the father a kiss or touch his hand.

Compassion once developed is a powerful motive for altruistic behavior.[22] Empirical research shows that even pre-schoolers frequently justify their own helping behaviors with rationales suggesting that they acted so because of an awareness of another's need; for example, statements such as "he's hurt" or "she needs help."[23] Moreover, it is found that socializers' (parents, teachers, and others) use of disciplinary techniques that are likely to focus the child's attention on another's affective state or plight seem to correlate with degree of altruistic responding.[24] Indeed, such appeals have been found to be effective when power-assertive (for example, involving threats of disapproval), normative (referring to norms relating to altruism), or self-oriented (referring to egoistic reasons for assisting) appeals fail.[25] As noted by Hoffman, though very young children may only empathize but not help, with age, children's emotional reactions are more likely to involve sympathetic concern as they learn how to assist and that assisting can produce positive consequences.[26]

Sympathy remains a powerful altruistic motive for adults. Batson conducted an experiment in which the subjects were asked either to imagine how the other person who was in a difficult situation felt, or to be as objective as possible, just attending to the objective feature pertaining to the situation of the other person.[27] The study showed that subjects who attended to how the other person felt were more sympathetic than the other subjects. Moreover, they helped approximately the same amount no matter whether they could relieve their own distress (induced by discerning the distress of the other person) by helping or by other means. However, the subjects who were instructed to be objective helped less in situations in which they could relieve their distress by means other than helping. In real-life settings, more than half of the rescuers of Jews from Nazis during the Second World War who were interviewed reported empathy and sympathy as the primary motives for their actions.[28]

With regard to filial piety, as we have seen, the core element is the child's love for his or her parents. There is little doubt that bonding with one's parents, or the primary caretaker, is something instinctive and immensely significant. As early as six days, infants prefer mother's breast to that of another woman.[29] They start to react to strangers with apprehension at six months. By eight to nine months, bonding is evident, in that infants begin to show separation anxiety when they are separate from the primary care-takers.[30] And it can be argued that this bonding is an affective one similar to love, rather than merely about trust, security, and fulfillment of physical needs. Young children clearly express positive emotions such as joy and delight in the company of their caretakers, and they are more responsive and alert when interacting with their caretakers. Another reason can be seen in the children's identification with their parents, in the sense of adopting their values and morals, and trying to live up to their parents' wishes and expectations.[31] Certainly when children grow older and become more autonomous they may outgrow the identification and seek to develop their own individuality. But such changes do not preclude that the earlier identi-fication may have come about as a result of the children's affection and admiration for their parents. The changes only mean that the children have come to realize that bonding and affection can coexist with individuality and autonomy, and that they have found other ways to express their affec-tion for the parents.

What is important to note is that filial piety reinforces and strengthens the bonding between the child and his or her parents. Since the 1970s, develop-mental research began to change from a unidirectional to a bidirectional understanding of parent–child interaction.[32] And psychological research on filial piety in Chinese societies also confirms the idea that filial piety contrib-utes to the establishment of a cohesive and close family.[33]

There is ample evidence that severe neglect and failure to develop a successful attachment are associated with a broad range of cognitive, emotional, and social deficits, which may include a virtual disruption of development and a blunting of the capacity for social relationships.[34] More importantly, there is some evidence that future relationships and the capacity to love may be determined to some extent by the quality of this early attachment between infants and their primary caretakers.[35]

Before we conclude, I would like to mention one point about the psycho-logical theories concerning early bonding. While there is an immense amount of psychological studies on this topic, and the significance of early bonding is very much emphasized, few have related early bonding to moral development. One exception is the research of Hoffman, who links beginnings of sympathy, which is often seen as closely related to moral development, to the mother–child interaction. Unfortunately, this conclusion faces much criticism. The reason for the reluctance to connect early bonding to moral development, I suspect, is because morality is conceived as being about either general benevolence or principles of justice. Few seem to share the Confucian idea that particularistic relationships are an equally important aspect of morality as general altruism. But if justice and general altruism are cherished because they represent a transcendence of the narrow egoistic world, then there is no reason why particularistic relationships should not share the same regard, especially when the commitment to particularistic relationships is accompanied by a commitment to general altruism.

To conclude, what I have said so far does not establish the superiority of the Confucian insight over conflicting theories such as that of Kohlberg or psychoanalytic theory. But it is not my aim to establish such superiority anyway. The merit of a psychological theory has to be determined by its ability to accurately describe and explain the facts, and make predictions. Hence we cannot evaluate a psychological theory just from the armchair. That means that the task of evaluation cannot be accomplished by doing philosophy alone, though philosophy can still contribute to clarify the concepts, as well as draw out the implications. What is significant is that the Confucian notion of moral development does have psychological backing. As Owen Flanagan has noted, a minimum requirement of our moral theories is that they make demands on us in conformity with our psychologies. And the Confucian moral theory, at least with regard to commiseration and filial piety, seems to pass the test.

Notes

1 Throughout this chapter, I use the term "commiseration" interchangeably with "compassion" and "sympathy."
2 Donald Munro makes the distinction between philosophical Confucianism and Imperial Confucianism. The former refers to the system of ideas as expressed in the Confucian philosophical texts. The latter aims at promoting the authority of the ruler by emphasizing the virtue of loyalty and obedience to the ruler. Its main architect is Dong Zhongshu of the Han Dynasty. See, K. Lieberthal, S. F. Lin, and E. Young (eds), *Constructing China*, Ann Arbor: Center for Chinese Studies, The University of Michigan, 1997, pp. 26–7.
3 For this interpretation of *ren*, see, for example, W. T. Chan, *A Source Book in Chinese Philosophy*, Princeton, NJ: Princeton University Press, 1963; and B. Schwartz, *The World of Thought in Ancient China*, Cambridge, MA: Belknap Press of Harvard University Press, 1985.
4 K. L. Shun, "*Jen* and *Li* in the *Analects*," *Philosophy East and West*, 43, July 1993, 457–79.
5 For the interpretation of *ren* as essentially about social relationships and love for others, see Qian Mu, *Lun-yu-xin-jie,* Taibei: Lantai chubanshe, 2000, and Tang

jun-yi, *Zhongguo zhe xue yuan lun, yuan dao bian*, Hong Kong: Xinya yanjiusuo, 1975.

6 My translations are adapted with modifications from D. C. Lau (trans.), *Mencius*, New York: Penguin, 1970.

7 In this chapter, I am using commiseration as interchangeable with compassion and sympathy. I take commiseration as being within the family of emotions that include compassion and sympathy. Commiseration basically has the same meaning as compassion, whereas compassion and sympathy seem to share important core characteristics, and perhaps differ only in the degree of misfortune that is involved. Snow, for example, has argued that compassion is a response to the *serious* misfortune of another, whereas sympathy covers responses to a wider range of misfortunes, including minor ones. N. Snow, "Compassion," *American Philosophical Quarterly*, 28, no. 3, 1991, 197.

8 Ibid., and M. Nussbaum, "Compassion: The Basic Social Emotion," *Social Philosophy and Policy*, 13, 1996, 27–58.

9 Nussbaum, "Compassion," p. 35.

10 Ibid., p. 36.

11 M. Hoffman, "Empathy, Guilt, and Social Cognition" in W. F. Overton (ed.), *The Relationship Between Social and Cognitive Development*, Hillsdale, NJ: Lawrence Erlbaum Associates, 1983.

12 N. Sherman, "Empathy and Imagination," *Midwest Studies in Philosophy*, 22, 1998.

13 Nussbaum also alludes to this point. M. Nussbaum, "Compassion," p. 29.

14 On Rawls's concept of "the original position," see J. Rawls, *A Theory of Justice*, New York: Oxford University Press, 1973, Chapter 3.

15 S. Darwall, "Empathy, Sympathy, Care," *Philosophical Studies*, 89, 1998, 261–82, p. 275.

16 L. Kohlberg, *The Philosophy of Moral Development: Moral Stages and the Idea of Justice*, New York: Harper and Row, 1981.

17 S. Freud, *The Ego and Mechanisms of Defense*, London: Hogarth, 1937.

18 J. Piaget, *The Moral Judgment of the Child*, New York: Free Press, 1965.

19 See, for example, N. Eisenberg, *Altruistic Emotion, Cognition, and Behavior*, Hillsdale, NJ: Lawrence Erlbaum Associates, 1986.

20 M. L. Simmer, "Newborn's response to the cry of another infant," *Developmental Psychology 5*, 1971, 136–50.

21 M. Hoffman, "Empathy, Guilt, and Social Cognition."

22 This is not to claim that compassion is the only or necessary motive behind altruistic behaviors. Adherence to moral values or principles certainly can motivate altruistic actions as well.

23 N. Eisenberg *et al.*, "The Relations of Quantity and Mode of Prosocial Behavior to Moral Cognitions and Social Style," *Child Development*, 55, 1984, 1479–85; and N. Eisenberg-Berg and C. Neal, "Children's Moral Reasoning about Their Spontaneous Prosocial Behavior," *Child Development*, 51, 1980, 552–7.

24 D. Bar-Tal *et al.*, "The Relationship Between Israeli Children's Helping Behavior and Their Perception on Parents' Socialization Practices," *Journal of Social Psychology*, 111, 1980, 159–67; M. L. Hoffman, "Moral Development" in P. H. Mussen (ed.), *Carmichael's Manual of Child Development*, New York: Wiley, 1970.

25 D. G. Perry *et al.*, "Impact of Adults' Appeals for Sharing on the Development of Altruistic Dispositions in Children," *Journal of Experimental Child Psychology*, 32, 1981, 127–38; N. Eisenberg-Berg and E. Geisheker, "Content of Preachings and Power of the Model/Preacher: The Effect on Children's Generosity," *Developmental Psychology*, 15, 1979, 168–75; B. R. Burleson and D. A. Fennelly, "The Effects of Persuasive Appeal Form and Cognitive Complexity on Children's Sharing," *Child Study Journal*, 11, 1981, 75–90.

26 M. L. Hoffman, "Empathy, role-taking, guilt, and development of altruistic motives," in T. Lickona (ed.), *Moral Development and Behavior: Theory, Research and Social Issues*, New York: Holt, 1976.

27 M. Toi and C. D. Batson, "More Evidence that Empathy Is a Source of Altruistic Motivation," *Journal of Personality and Social Psychology*, 43, 1982, 281–92.

28 S. P. Oliner and P. M. Oliner, *The Altruistic Personality: Rescuers of Jews in Nazi Europe*, New York: Free Press, 1988.

29 J. MacFarlane, "Olfaction in the Development of Social Preferences in the Human Neo-nate," in R. Podrter and M. O'Connor, *Parent-infant Interaction, Ciba Foundation Symposium 33*, New York: Elsevier Exerpta Medica, 1975, pp. 103–13.

30 K. Minde and B. Robson, "Normal Child Development," in P. Steinhauer and Q. Rae-Grant (eds), *Psychological Problems of the Child in the Family*, New York: Basic Books, 1977, p. 15.

31 Ibid. Even though psychoanalytic theory can also explain a child's identification with a parent by reasons other than affection, it suggests that the identification is only with one's same sex parents. But there is no reason to think that children only identify with their same sex parent instead of with both parents.

32 For a review, see B. Martin, "Parent–Child Relations," in F. D. Horowitz (ed.), *Review of Child Development Research 4*, Chicago: University of Chicago Press, 1975.

33 K. H. Yeh, "The Beneficial and Harmful Effects of Filial Piety: An Integrative Analysis," in K. S. Yang *et al.* (eds), *Asian Social Psychology: Conceptual and Empirical Contributions*, Westport, CT: Greenwood, 2002.

34 W. Goldfarb, "Emotional and Intellectual Consequences of Psychologic Deprivation in Infancy: A Re-evaluation," in P. M. Hoch and J. Zubin (eds), *Psychopathology of Childhood*, New York: Grune and Stratton, pp. 105–19.

35 L. Matas *et al.*, "Continuity of Adaptation in the Second Year and the Relationship between Quality of Attachment and Later Competence," *Child Development*, 49, 1978, 547–56.

11 Filial piety as a virtue

Philip J. Ivanhoe

> Gentlemen work at the root of the matter.
> Once the root is well established, the Way will flourish.
> Filial piety and brotherly respect – are these not the root of perfect
> goodness!
>
> (*Analects* 1.2)

Introduction

Filial piety was an important virtue in early Confucianism and was recognized even by critics of the tradition, such as Zhuangzi, as an unavoidable part of human life.[1] Such a deep and abiding concern with filial piety is not unique to China alone. Many cultures throughout the world value filial behavior and record, retell, and advocate acts of filial devotion and sacrifice.[2] Such behavior is often explained, as Zhuangzi seems to have done, by appeals to human nature. At times, along with religious warrants, such appeals are offered not only as explanations for filial behavior but also as justifications for filial piety as a duty, obligation, or virtue.[3] However, Chinese culture is distinctive in the amount of attention paid to and the importance claimed for this particular virtue. In contrast, contemporary philosophers pay scant attention to filial piety. Among those who offer a defense of at least some form of filial obligation, the most interesting and persuasive views base filial piety on the model of friendship or a sense of gratitude for the various sacrifices that good parents make on behalf of their children.[4] I argue that such arguments offer an important source for a viable defense of filial piety but fall short because they fail to capture important features of the child–parent relationship. This in turn leads them to miss important and characteristic features of the virtue of filial piety.

In this chapter, I explore some of the central justifications for filial piety as a virtue that one can find in the early Confucian tradition. Specifically I describe, discuss, and evaluate several arguments that were offered in support of a general obligation to care for, protect, defer to, and revere one's parents while they are alive and to remember and sacrifice to them when they have died. I then argue that some of the explicit or implied justifications for such an obligation are not well founded and no longer offer compelling reasons for cultivating and valuing the virtue of filial piety. However, others do provide solid and persuasive justification for filial piety as a virtue and offer considerable support for at least some version of traditional belief and practice. Equally importantly, these arguments and the related descriptions of the nature of the child–parent relationship offer important contributions to the contemporary philosophical discussion of filial piety. In particular, they are useful for both correcting and augmenting contemporary accounts of filial piety as an expression of gratitude. In conclusion I argue that a proper understanding of these early Chinese beliefs about the relationship between children and parents also offers important insights into other, related aspects of traditional Chinese ethics.

Early Confucian conceptions of filial piety

Before we turn to the early Chinese views on filial piety that contribute to my contemporary account, it is important to clear away some traditional claims that are better left behind. The first claim that I explore and then leave behind is that filial piety is based on a special sense of gratitude that children should feel toward those who brought them into being. The thought is that parents are the source of the existence of the children they beget and that this fact somehow establishes an obligation on the part of the children to honor, defer to, and serve their parents. Similar ideas are widespread in contemporary culture, where it is not uncommon to find parents insisting that because their children "owe" their very existence to them, this establishes a debt that the children can *never* fully repay.[5] Related to this idea is the view that parents are entitled to nearly complete control over the lives of their children.

In the early Confucian tradition, we see various expressions of this kind of argument and the special nature of this appeal is used to justify some of the more distinctive characteristics of the tradition's conception of filial piety. For example, children were thought to be physical extensions of their parents and this was seen as establishing an overriding debt on the part of children. Such a view was also the basis of early Confucian taboos about physically harming or defacing one's body. Both of these ideas are seen in the opening chapter of the *Xiaojing* (*Classic of Filial Piety*): "One's body, hair, and skin are received from one's father and mother. Not to injure or harm these is the beginning of filial piety."[6]

As common as such appeals are in China and in other cultures, they provide no credible justification for filial piety. While it is true that a child "owes" its existence to its parents, this fact alone does not support any sort of obligation on the part of the child. It seems that at least part of the force of this kind of "genetic argument" derives from a conflation of two distinct senses of the word "owe." In the case of children, they "owe" their existence to their parents in the sense that certain of their parents' actions were the sufficient causes for their coming into being. However, this sense of "owing" is distinct from the sense in which one "owes" someone money as a result of borrowing it earlier. The analogy with borrowing or any sense of contractual obligation is clearly inappropriate in the case of child–parent relationships because the child did not exist when such a purported debt is claimed to have been incurred.

One might try to argue that children still owe their parents some kind of obligation as an expression of gratitude for being brought into existence. However, upon further consideration, such appeals prove unconvincing. In order for any action to be a legitimate source of gratitude, it must not only be in the actual interest of the recipient, but also be done out of an attitude of caring *for her*.[7] On these criteria, it should immediately be clear that many children owe their parents nothing for being brought into existence. On the one hand, one would first have to show that existence itself is a good. As I argue below, this is not at all evident. On the other hand, it should be clear that a good number of children are created as a result of their parents seeking each other's or their own sensual gratification. Other children are born because their parents believe that having children will improve their lives or marriage or because they have a religious duty to procreate. In such cases, the object of care is not the child itself.

In the case of the early Confucian tradition, having children clearly was thought to be a religious duty. Those who failed to have children failed not only their parents but also their entire clan lineage. Mencius singles out a failure to have children as the most unfilial of actions: "Mencius said, 'There are three unfilial things [that a child can do] and to leave behind no posterity is the greatest'."[8]

In this last case, as well as those sketched above, it is clear that the child's existence is not something that is sought for *her good*. It is not at all clear why a child should feel gratitude for being brought into existence in order for her parents to fulfill *their* felt obligation to continue the family line. And so, even if one grants that existence itself is a good thing, in many cases it is clear that it is not a good sought for the good of any child. There is an even more serious weakness in this kind of appeal, which makes it clear that begetting a child could never constitute doing good *for that child*. For prior to conception, there is no specific person about whose good one could be concerned.[9]

Mary Shelley's story *Frankenstein* is instructive both for illustrating why begetting is not enough and for pointing toward the true basis for a sense of filial gratitude. As we know, in this story, Victor Frankenstein brought the Creature into existence. However, as we have argued, that act in itself established no obligation on the part of the Creature toward Frankenstein. Given the nature of the Creature, it did not need or want many of the kinds of goods that human parents must provide for their children and for which their children should feel gratitude. The Creature did not need to be protected and provided for in the ways that human infants do – both during a pregnancy and for many years thereafter. Nevertheless, what it *did* need and crave was the kind of attention, instruction, nurturance, and guidance that is essential to good parenting. Most of all, it needed to be loved *for its own sake*. Frankenstein withheld his love and even his approval. Unlike a good parent he made these *conditional*: his approval and affection depended on the creature meeting certain prior expectations that were in fact expressions of Frankenstein's good, not the good of his creation.[10] At least some of the sympathy we feel for the Creature is founded on the perceived failure of Victor Frankenstein to love his creation. At the very least, we do not feel that the Creature owed Frankenstein gratitude simply for bringing him into existence. At least according to the Creature, existence was a torment and not a good.[11]

Mary Shelley's story also helps us to see the legitimate bases for feelings of gratitude, reverence, and love on the part of children toward their parents. While Frankenstein's Creature did not need to be provided for, or at least not as badly as human infants do, it would seem that one source of filial feelings should be the remarkable range of protection, nurturance, and material support that children receive from good parents. Such support normally begins soon after conception and is particularly direct and complete in the case of one's mother. For good mothers sustain, nurture, and protect their children in a comprehensive and intimate way. A father who supports and cares for his spouse and child during this period is also offering the kind of person-specific care that is a legitimate basis for filial gratitude.[12] The fact that the need for such goods is simply a matter of the kinds of creatures we are in no way detracts from their value. Indeed, quite the reverse is true, for by providing for one's children in these ways parents are expressing a distinctively human form of care. Early Confucians recognized that such care was one of the most powerful bases for filial piety.

> Oh father, you begot me!
> Oh mother, you nourished me!
> You supported and nurtured me,
> You raised me, and provided for me,
> You looked after me and sheltered me,
> In your comings and goings,
> You [always] bore me in your arms.
> The kindness I would repay,
> Is boundless as the Heavens![13]

Of course, the very first line of this verse supports the view that I have argued against above and which I do not accept as offering any legitimate justification for filial piety. However, the main point of this passage is to express the broad range of goods that parents provide for their children and the immense debt this appears to create. The following poem, by the poet Meng Jiao (751–814), expresses similar sentiments.

Thread, in the hands of a loving mother,
Becomes the coat to be worn by her wandering son.
As the time draws near for his departure, she stitches it tightly,
Fearing that he may be slow to return.
Who would claim that a tender blade of grass,
Could ever repay the warmth of three Springtimes?[14]

Another good that children receive from their parents, and one that we shall return to below, is education, very broadly construed. For early Confucians, the most important education that one receives from one's parents concerns issues of ethics, character, and culture – an introduction to what it is like to live as an aware and engaged human being within human society. Good parents teach their children directly, but perhaps more effectively through example, how to be good and decent people and can go a long way to instill in them a love for learning and an appreciation of the arts. On the traditional model, parents play a critical role in shaping their children into full human beings by introducing them into the humane social life described by Confucian rituals and norms. Without a proper introduction to the social nature of human life, the child at best would remain a "petty person," someone who is not capable of leading a full and satisfying life. This is a special contribution that for the most part only parents provide, and it establishes a particularly intimate relationship between children and parents. Parents play a remarkably important role in influencing and shaping the early development of their children. If they regularly care for their children for the children's own good, they contribute in profound and enduring ways to the future character, attitudes, sensibilities, and inclinations of these young people.[15]

The sustained attention and care that one receives from one's parents are unique in nature. These not only sustain one's life, they play a central role in the formation of one's character and the development of one's capabilities to live well as a human being. The love that good parents provide cannot be paid back through efforts like caring for them in their old age, because, among other things, there is an unavoidable asymmetry between these cases. No matter what one might do for aged parents, one is not helping to form them into the people they will become. At best one is doing something very different: helping them to face and pass through the dissolution of self that is an inevitable part of the human condition.

The only reasonable response to those who have provided one with good parental care throughout the most vulnerable years of one's life is a special form of gratitude, reverence, and love, one that recognizes and responds to the unique nature of the kindness received. I take it that one of the points of the verses cited above is to acknowledge that one cannot really repay one's parents for all that they have done. The only appropriate response is to keep in mind the nature of their love and, in the warmth of this light, to cultivate a reciprocal feeling for them.

Seeing that what is called for is a certain critically informed attitude or state of character shows why filial piety is best thought of as a virtue. It is not something that one can *command* another to have and hence it is not a duty, at least not in the strict or "perfect" sense of duty.[16] Nevertheless, it is something that one can insist people have an obligation to cultivate. Parents can hope that their children cultivate the virtue of filial piety but in a certain sense they cannot *demand* that they do so. For even if a child were to successfully generate some sense of filial obligation out of a sense of duty, this would fall short of the lively, spontaneous state of heart and mind that is the ideal for this virtue. This is what makes cases of genuinely ungrateful children so tragic. When good parents lament that their children appear to be "ungrateful" for all their sacrifices, what they often are expressing is a desire to be loved and cared for, not a desire to be paid in full for services rendered. This is particularly clear with regard to the desire on the part of elderly parents to play some active role in the lives of their adult children. Non-family members can provide for aging parents, but they cannot give them the love and sense of common familial purpose that only their children can provide. As Confucius said, "Those who are considered filial these days are those who are able to provide for their parents. However, even dogs and horses are able to find this kind of support. If there is no feeling of reverence, wherein lies the difference?"[17] One cannot think about any form of gratitude or reverence on the model of debts or duties without distorting something central to its value. In this regard, these attitudes differ fundamentally from the case of attitudes like respect. For if I have to demand or even repeatedly ask for gratitude or reverence from another, then they have failed to manifest the kind of attention and care that in important ways *constitute* being grateful or reverent. In a similar way, if I regularly have to *ask* you to show me that you love me, it means that you don't love me, at least not in a certain way.

If one grants something along the lines of what has been argued for above, then one will accept, as a number of contemporary philosophers do, that filial piety is an expression of gratitude. As such it could be considered as a token of a general attitude or virtue, something along the lines of what we call "being grateful." Filial piety would then be distinguished from other expressions of gratitude at best only in terms of its particular sphere of activity and the ways in which it is manifested within the course of a human life.[18] While such an understanding of filial piety does capture important aspects of its special value, it would be difficult to reconcile such an account with the importance that Confucian thinkers claim for filial piety. For, as seen in the epigram that opens this chapter, among other things Confucians claim that filial piety is the root of "perfect goodness" or *ren*.[19] In some way, it is supposed to be the basis of other virtues and paradigmatic for ethical behavior in general. In the following section, I expand on some aspects of our earlier discussion and extend these in order to defend versions of these more dramatic claims. In conclusion, I use this account of filial piety to show how it can help us to understand several other aspects of traditional Confucian ethics.

The first thing I would like to argue for is the claim that filial piety is in some clear way the source of other virtues and paradigmatic for ethical behavior in general. The case here is not all that difficult to make, for parental care is in fact the first experience most children have of someone else thinking of and working for their good.[20] From the third-person perspective, the care that good parents show to their children, attending to the good of their children for the children's own sake, is paradigmatic of an ethical point of view. Often such focused and sustained concern offers a vivid illustration of compassion or care.[21] Seen in this way, the gratitude, reverence, and love that one feels for the love of parents is not just a token of some general attitude of gratitude but also, in most cases, the source of and paradigm for our sense of what it is to respond to care.

Another distinctive feature of Chinese conceptions of filial piety highlights an additional characteristic of this virtue. In most descriptions of filial piety there is an explicit recognition of the helplessness of the child and the power of the parents. Filial piety is not just a general feeling of gratefulness for a kindness done for one's own sake. It is partially constituted by the sense that this kindness was done by someone who was dramatically more powerful than oneself and who sacrificed substantial goods of their own in order to care for one in these ways. This is important from an ethical point of view: acts of parental love express the priority of love and care over power and prerogative. One must keep in mind the vast difference in power that separates infants and young children from their parents in order to appreciate the special sense of *filial* gratitude. As we shall see below, this aspect of filial piety also helps us to understand related aspects of traditional Chinese ethical and political thought.

The final feature of traditional accounts of filial piety that I would like to draw attention to concerns the nature of the types of care that one receives. As noted above, parents not only protect, support, and nurture their children – both during pregnancy and after birth – they also play a critical and decisive role in the formation of the child's character, values, and sensibilities. Good parents prepare their children to go out and live good lives and one important way they do this is by providing a good example through living their own lives well. This is a role that very few people play in any child's life and good parents fulfill it in a distinctive way. Often what a child learns from her parents is a general attitude or sensibility rather than a specific fact or body of knowledge. For example, a child may not end up sharing her parents' particular intellectual interests but could still learn from them the "love of learning" that Confucius cherished and worked so hard to inculcate in others.

These last two features of filial piety show why it cannot be adequately described in terms of friendship, as a number of contemporary philosophers have tried to do.[22] Friendship characteristically exists between equals or at least between people similar in status, power, and abilities. In addition, the value of friendship derives much of its force from the shared activities in which friends engage. However, throughout infancy, we are not in any significant sense the equals of our parents, nor do we share in any common activity with them. We do not change our diapers *with* our parents; they change us. Friendship is closer to what two parents share, though even here it is wrong to allow the unique kinds of activities that a married couple share to be reduced to the general notion of the shared activities of friends.

While filial piety cannot be properly understood on the model of friendship, the notion of friendship does have much to contribute to our understanding of the child–parent relationship. As children age, they can and should become friends with their parents. As adults they can indeed share as equals in the common activities that often define friendship. This, however, does not erase their earlier history, which should and does inform even the nature of their later friendly activities and relationship.

Conclusion

I have described three distinctive aspects of early Chinese conceptions of filial piety in order to show why filial piety cannot be reduced to an expression of a general virtue of gratitude or friendship. Filial piety represents a distinct and important virtue in its own right. In conclusion I would like to show how each of the points I argued for above can help us to understand other important aspects of traditional Chinese ethics.

The first point I argued for is that filial piety can be seen as the source of other virtues and a paradigm for ethical behavior in general. Appreciating what this claim entails helps us to see what Confucian thinkers mean when they insist that filial piety is the "root" of the other virtues and has an especially close relationship to the virtue of compassion or care. It is interesting to note that even some thinkers who rejected the family-based view of Confucians accepted that the child–parent relationship serves an important role as the source of and paradigm for ethical behavior. For example, while the Mohist Yi Zhi argues for "impartial care" as his ethical ideal, he accepts that this ideal can only be reached by extending the feelings we naturally have for our parents. For Yi Zhi the ancient sage-kings cared for all their people equally but the quality of their care was that of someone "watching over an infant."[23]

The second point I made was that filial piety is not just a general feeling of gratitude for a kindness done for one's own sake. It is partially constituted by the sense that this kindness was done by someone who was dramatically more powerful than oneself and who sacrificed substantial goods of their own in order to care for one. This can help us to understand why Confucian thinkers regularly assert that filial piety is the proper paradigm for the subject–ruler relationship as well as the child–parent relationship. A good ruler clearly is more powerful than and willingly sacrifices substantial personal prerogatives and goods in order to provide for, nurture, and guide his people. Not only his care for others but also his ability to restrain himself are important for a full appreciation of the value of his actions.

My third and final point was that part of what makes filial piety a unique and important virtue is the intimate and sustained role that parents play in helping to shape and direct the character, sensibilities, and interests of their children. Among other things, I noted that this is something that one could never hope to "repay," for there is a fundamental dis-analogy between what parents do for their children and what even the most caring and supportive adult children can do for their parents. They may support their parents and comfort them in old age, but they will not play a sustained and critical role in helping to make their parents into the kind of people they will become. The only adequate way for children to respond to the special kindness that they have received is by living out of an attitude of loving care, appreciation, and reverence for their parents.

While the special role of parents is unique in this way it is not without close relatives. Excellent teachers of various kinds, especially those who provide the early lessons and models for children, often play this kind of role as well. This similarity helps us to understand why Confucians have tended to see teachers as second parents – referring to good teachers as *shifu* or *shimu* – and why teachers have been accorded the special sense of respect that they enjoy throughout East Asian societies. The only way to respond to the best kind of teacher is with an attitude of loving care, appreciation, and reverence. In other words, they too are appropriate recipients of filial piety.[24]

The right kind of teachers are most worthy of the special favor that is the heart of filial piety and this points toward additional insights regarding the nature and exercise of this virtue. First, as I have argued, filial gratitude is not grounded on the fact that a child is brought into existence. It is something one should feel toward those who have shown one a special and sustained form of kindness during a particularly critical period of one's life. The true basis of filial piety lies in the well intentioned benefits that others have bestowed upon us, people who not only played a critical role in our survival and material well-being but also helped to shape, prepare, and direct us in the task of living well. Given this, it should be clear that filial piety can and should be felt equally toward good adoptive parents and good biological parents. In either case, what matters is how people have behaved toward one another. The challenge for children is how they choose to respond.

The view of filial piety that I have argued for above may seem to raise insuperable difficulties for other aspects of traditional Chinese beliefs. In the traditional account, children seem to have an absolute obligation with regard to their parents, an obligation that trumps all other demands and moral concerns. This idea is at least raised in the famous passage in *Analects*

13.18 that describes how a son conceals the wrongdoing of his father and is even more dramatically stated in *Mencius* 7A35.[25] In the latter passage, Mencius argues that Emperor Shun would happily have abandoned his kingdom and stolen away in the middle of the night, carrying his father on his back, to live hidden by the side of the sea in order to prevent his father from having to face the consequences of having committed murder. I don't see any way to preserve this kind of absolute and overriding obligation in its traditional form. However, it would make perfect sense to argue that filial piety obliges us to stick with those we love, even when they do something terribly wrong. Such a view could retain a very strong commitment to stand by, support, and comfort parents, regardless of what they have done, but not require a filial son or daughter to transgress the demands of justice. According to the view that I have argued for, good sons or daughters would have to pursue such a balanced course of action if they are to remain true to the best that their parents have taught them.[26]

Finally, we might ask what becomes of filial piety for those children who suffer from being raised by despicable parents. The Confucian tradition again seems to require too much, insisting that such children simply grin and bear it, no matter how bad their parents happen to be. One of the clearest examples of this problem is found in the *Mencius*. In 5A2 Mencius discusses how Emperor Shun endured repeated attempts on his life by his father, stepmother, and half-brother yet continued to love, support, and take joy in them. In 4A28 we are told that in the end Shun's perseverance so moved his father that he abandoned his wicked ways and became a model parent. That makes for a fine story. However, does it describe a reasonable ideal or at least suggest one?[27]

The account of filial piety that I have presented could incorporate certain aspects of this traditional view but would abandon others. It should be clear that it would not endorse an absolute and overriding commitment on the part of any child to parents who utterly failed to provide those goods that I have endeavored to enumerate above. Parents who are consistently and uniformly bad do not perform the kinds of acts that are the true basis of filial piety and so their children are under no obligation to show them this special form of gratitude, reverence, and care. However, even the children of bad parents – and Shun's parents seem clearly to qualify as bad parents – may still elect to cultivate and show their parents at least some degree of filial piety.[28] One can still find the institution of parenting to be something worthy of respect, admiration, and reverence, even if one's own parents failed miserably to fulfill such an ideal. It seems clear that at least some good parents become good parents because they seek to realize an ideal they cherish but did not benefit from themselves. Having a sense of what it is like to feel filial gratitude can help one to be a better parent, even if one feels little or no such gratitude toward one's own parents. Expressing some degree of filial piety toward even bad parents can serve as an example and inspiration for others. Perhaps the value of such examples might warrant actually cultivating and expressing some level of filial piety even toward bad parents, though it would fall well short of the absolute devotion that Shun purportedly maintained. Finally, such a show of filial virtue might at least improve if not convert poor parents and move both parents and child closer to an important source of human meaning and value.

Notes

1 See *Zhuangzi,* Chapter 4, "In the Human World," where we are told "That children should love their parents is a matter of destiny." Thanks to Eric L. Hutton and T. C. Kline III for helpful comments and suggestions on earlier drafts of this chapter.

2 For a discussion of ideals of filial piety in the Western tradition, see J. Blustein, *Parents and Children: The Ethics of the Family*, New York: Oxford University Press, 1982. For representations of filial piety in Japanese drama, see M. J. Smethurst, *Dramatic Representations of Filial Piety: Five Noh in Translation*, Ithaca, NY: Cornell University Press, 1998.

3 Saint Thomas Aquinas is an excellent example of someone who develops a sophisticated defense of filial piety combining both Aristotelian accounts of human nature and biblical commands. For an excellent discussion of his views, see J. Blustein, *Parents and Children*, pp. 56–62. Chinese beliefs about ancestor worship and in particular the need to carry on sacrifices to ancestral spirits also provided important warrants for Chinese belief and practice. Such beliefs in fact contribute a great deal to the sense of "piety" in Chinese conceptions of filial piety.

4 There are a number of interesting contemporary defenses of filial piety. Christina Hoff Sommers argues for the importance of tradition and convention and attempts to combine this with claims about the rights of moral patients. See "Filial Morality," *Journal of Philosophy*, 83, 1986, 439–56. Jane English argues against the notion that children "owe" their parents anything and for a relationship of love or friendship between children and parents; see "What Do Grown Children Owe Their Parents?," in O. O'Neill and W. Ruddick (eds), *Having Children: Philosophical and Legal Reflections on Parenthood*, New York: Oxford University Press, 1979, pp. 351–6. For the friendship model of filial piety, see also N. Dixon, "The Friendship Model of Filial Obligations," *Journal of Applied Ethics*, 12, no. 1, 1995, 77–87. Nancy S. Jecker argues that children have an obligation to treat their parents with filial piety out of gratitude for the supererogatory acts and duty-meeting acts of benevolence parents did on behalf of their children; see "Are Filial Duties Unfounded?" *American Philosophical Quarterly*, 26, no. 1, 1989, 73–80. A good general introduction to filial piety is, M. Wicclair, "Caring for Frail Elderly Parents: Past Parental Sacrifices and the Obligations of Adult Children," *Social Theory and Practice*, 16, no. 2, 1990, 163–89. The most thorough and incisive monograph on this topic is J. Blustein, *Parents and Children*.

5 Nancy Jecker argues against the idea that parents are owed gratitude from their children merely for the act of begetting them, a view that she identifies as the "Law of Athens"; see "Are Filial Duties Unfounded?" Aristotle advocates a view similar to the one that Jecker rejects; see the discussion in J. Blustein, *Parents and Children*, pp. 31–46.

6 *Xiaojing*, Chapter 1. See also *Analects* 8.3. The filial obligation that one has to protect and nurture one's parents is so great that it even trumps this standing obligation to protect one's own body. This is seen in various stories about filial

children sacrificing themselves in order to preserve their parents. For example, there is the well known story, alluded to by Su Shi in one of his poems, of a filial child who cuts the flesh from his leg in order to make medicinal cakes to cure his ailing parents. The original source is a passage in the *Songshi*.

7   Nancy S. Jecker argues a similar line in holding that an obligation of gratitude is incurred only in cases where one not only benefits from the actions of another but also when what is done for one is done out of benevolence; see "Are Filial Duties Unfounded?"

8   *Mencius* 4A26. The other two were to aid and abet one's parents in wrongful actions and to fail to protect and provide for them in old age. In *Mencius* 4B30, Mencius describes a list of five unfilial actions. These all concern various ways that children can, through lack of effort or self control, bring disgrace to, fail to support, or endanger their parents.

9   Nancy S. Jecker is the first to make this kind of argument against begetting as establishing filial obligation; see "Are Filial Duties Unfounded?"

10 Frankenstein created the Creature in order to serve as a witness to his genius and his vaulting ambition to play the role of God. When the Creature did not live up to Frankenstein's expectations, he considered it a failure and turned away from it.

11 Commenting on a presentation by Bernard Williams at Stanford University, Philip Clark raised the fascinating idea that Frankenstein's Creature might offer a rare example of a being that regrets its own existence. This seems right to me. A Confucian might argue that in denying the Creature the love that every child should have, Frankenstein cut off the opportunity for it to become part of the human community and thereby set it on its course of destruction, death, pain, and anguish. On such an interpretation, the fact that the Creature itself could not die, or at least was very hard to kill, serves to emphasize the point that begetting is in no way a ground for gratitude.

12 The difference in the level and type of support that mothers and fathers can provide can be understood as the basis for a number of traditional beliefs and attitudes. While it has been notoriously undervalued in many traditional cultures, the love between mothers and their children often serves as the paradigm of filial love. There may be good reasons for the special sense of closeness and obligation that many children feel toward their mothers. Miranda Brown argues that in China, during the Han dynasty, mourning for mothers surpassed that accorded to fathers. See her "Men in Mourning: Ritual, Politics, and Human Nature in Eastern Han China, AD 25–220," PhD dissertation in history, University of California, Berkeley, 2002.

13 From the *Shijing*; cf. J. Legge, *The Chinese Classics*, Hong Kong: Hong Kong University Press, 1960, vol. 4, p. 352.

14 Meng Jiao's poem is entitled, "The Wandering Son."

15 It is most important to keep in mind that the goods that I have been describing as the basis of filial gratitude must be given out of love for and for the good of the child. They are expressions of love, not an investment given with an eye on future returns. This is where Victor Frankenstein made his greatest mistake. His science created the Creature, but his failure to love it turned his creation into a monster.

16 The distinction between "perfect" and "imperfect" duties goes back at least to Pufendorf. It played an important role in Hume's distinction between natural and artificial virtues and of course was made famous by Kant. While certain accounts of "imperfect duty" can capture part of what I describe as the virtue of filial piety, for reasons that I provide below, even such a conception of duty falls short of the ideal as I understand it. For an informative and revealing discussion of the history of the distinction between perfect and imperfect duties,

see J. B. Schneewind, "The Misfortunes of Virtue," reprinted in R. Crisp and M. Slote (eds), *Virtue Ethics*, New York: Oxford University Press, 1997, pp. 178–200.

17 *Analects* 2.7. This aspect of filial piety helps to explain at least part of the general attitude of respect and reverence that is shown to elderly people in traditional Chinese society.

18 I adopt the expression "sphere of activity" from Martha Nussbuam; see her "Non-relative Virtues: An Aristotelian Approach," in M. C. Nussbaum and A. Sen (eds), *The Quality of Life*, New York: Oxford University Press, 1993, pp. 242–69.

19 I translate *ren* as "perfect goodness" in the context of the *Analects*. In the later Confucian tradition, and as early as the *Mencius*, it came to be used in the more restricted sense of "compassion" or "care." The argument I make works equally well on either understanding of *ren*.

20 As should be clear from my arguments against the ethical significance of begetting for filial gratitude, my account applies equally well to adoptive and biological parents. Of course, good biological parents will also have provided for one prior to one's birth and so the two cases are not in every respect the same. This difference offers one way of supporting some sense of filial gratitude to one's biological parents, or at least one's mother, on the part of children given up for adoption at birth. Biological parents who have good reasons to believe that they cannot possibly care for their children as well as good adoptive parents and who make every effort to secure such care-givers for their children can also be seen as caring for their children for the child's own sake. This too offers a legitimate reason for a sense of gratitude to one's biological parents.

21 My views here have been influenced by the line of reasoning presented by Stephen Darwall concerning the nature of moral value. See his "Empathy, Sympathy, Care," *Philosophical Studies*, 89, 1998, 261–82.

22 For example, see the essays by Jane English and Nicholas Dixon cited in n. 4 above.

23 See *Mencius* 3A5. Yi Zhi begins this discussion by quoting from the "Announcement to the Prince of Kang" section of the *Shujing*.

24 The Qing dynasty Confucian Zhang Xuecheng sharply criticized Han Yü for failing to recognize precisely these features of the best kind of teacher. Zhang argues that there are "replaceable teachers" (those who transmit information) and "irreplaceable teachers" (those who teach the essence of the Way). The latter teach by way of their style and example as well as their mastery of the tradition and constitute a mind-to-mind tradition of moral intuition. For a brief description of Zhang's views, see D. S. Nivison, *The Life and Thought of Chang Hsüehch'eng (1738–1801)*, Stanford, CA: Stanford University Press, 1966, pp. 169–71.

25 For an interesting discussion of this particular issue, see G. Whitlock, "Concealing the Misconduct of One's Own Father: Confucius and Plato on a Question of Filial Piety," *Journal of Chinese Philosophy*, 21, 1994, 113–37.

26 Striking the balance that I am advocating is not always easy. It should though be clear that one cannot aid, abet, or actively conceal serious wrongdoing on the part of one's parents. This does not mean that one cannot seek to make amends on their behalf that might help them to avoid prosecution. It may even warrant legal exemptions to the duty to provide testimony in cases where the defendant is one's parent. The idea that true filial piety is to follow a moral way and not just to obey one's parents is clearly seen in the early Confucian tradition. For example, in the twenty-ninth chapter of the *Xunzi*, called "The Way of Sons," we are told that "great filial piety" requires one to "follow the Way and not one's lord, follow the proper norm and not one's father." Thanks to Eric Hutton for pointing this passage out to me.

27 Jack Kline has pointed out to me that one of the likely motivations behind the "grin and bear it" view was that the children of rulers and ministers were well situated to betray their kingdoms to neighboring states. Strongly advocating perpetual patience and an attitude of deference would have worked to prevent the children of politically powerful people from causing considerable mischief. A similar kind of argument from social conditions is offered by Dora Dien for both filial piety and *ti*, "respect for one's elder brother." See D. S. S. Dien, "Gender and Individuation: China and the West," *Psychoanalytic Review*, 7, 1992, 105–19 and "Chinese Authority-directed Orientation and Japanese Peer-group Orientation: Questioning the Notion of Collectivism," *Review of General Psychology*, 3, no. 4, 1999, 372–85. Of course, as they stand, these kinds of arguments no longer offer contemporary people good reasons for such an attitude or practice.

28 We don't know much about Shun's early childhood or the nature of his relationship to his parents during the formative period of his life. There may have been good treatment in the past that would serve to establish some reasonable grounds for filial gratitude. The stories of his persevering in the face of cruel treatment all concern his life as an adult.

12 Filial piety as respect for tradition

A. T. Nuyen

The notion of filial piety in Chinese philosophy has received a great deal of attention recently. To a large extent, this is due to the current interest in "family studies."[1] Within philosophy, there is a growing literature on duties and obligations in the context of family relationships, and some philosophers have turned to Chinese philosophy, Confucianism in particular, for insights.[2] With few exceptions, commentators have been largely critical of the idea of filial piety, so much so that one wonders if the idea still has any relevance to twenty-first-century morality. However, as usually is the case with most concepts and ideas in ancient Chinese philosophy, it is all a matter of interpretation. Given the admittedly common reading, critics of filial piety certainly have a case. But as Heiner Roetz has pointed out, the "words of the ancients are for the most part anything but clear, often timid, and always subject to interpretation."[3] Critics would no doubt argue that while this may be so with many concepts, the pronouncements on filial piety are clear enough, and clearly an indictment of that idea. Supposing the critics are right, the question is still whether there can be some understanding of the concept that, on the one hand, stays close to what the ancient Chinese thinkers had in mind and, on the other, has some relevance for contemporary morality. The aim of this chapter is to offer a reading of filial piety that meets this requirement. It is not as much an interpretation of "the words of the ancients" on filial piety as a suggestion concerning one possible way in which the notion might be understood and appropriated. More specifically, I suggest that we understand filial piety as respect for tradition, where tradition is understood in the Gadamerean sense.

The critics' case

The picture of the traditional Confucian family painted by many anthropologists on the basis of their empirical data is not an appealing one, not just to the modern mind that subscribes to equality and personal liberty, but to most of those caught up in that family structure. Numerous social and psychological problems have been attributed to the attempt by contemporary Asian families to maintain the Confucian family structure. The victims are said to be not just the children and the wives, but the fathers and the husbands as well. The indictment is so severe that one wonders how the Confucian family has survived for so long and why East Asia does not follow Communist China in denouncing it, along with Confucianism, for its terrible effects on the family, among other things. Indeed, one wonders why, despite the efforts of the Communist regime, traces of the Confucian family structure can still be found in many parts of China itself. What, then, is the case against the Confucian family? How much of it is also against Chinese philosophy?

For one commentator, the traditional Confucian family format reinforces the "hierarchical social structure" designed to entrench the authority of those in power, that of the husband and the father in the family context.[4] In particular, the effect on the child is appalling: "[it] was to reduce the child . . . to impotence – helpless, frustrated, furious, and floundering."[5] The enforcement of the father's authoritarian domination results in "fear, dependency, and hostility" within the family.[6] For another commentator, the "moral axiom . . . [of] filial piety" has resulted in "*a sense of guilt*" in family members who "cannot fulfill their moral responsibilities," and in "*the suppression of hostile feelings* toward parents."[7] These commentators have no doubt that the idea of filial piety is to blame. According to the first of the two authors quoted here, "Confucianism was based on authoritarianism, and filial piety was the principal instrument through which it was established and maintained."[8]

As for textual evidence, critics typically point to writings on the doctrine of the Three Bonds, on the assumption that the idea of filial piety is embedded in it. The first textual appearance of this doctrine is in the *Hanfeizi*, in the chapter called "Zhongxiao" ("Loyalty and Filial Piety"). The often-quoted passage is the following: "The minister serves the king, the son serves the father, and the wife serves the husband. If the three are followed, the world will be in peace; if the three are violated, the world will be in chaos."[9] The common interpretation of the doctrine of the Three Bonds is that it seeks to establish the authority of the king over his minister, of the father over his son, and of the husband over his wife. A strict application of the Three Bonds doctrine requires, among other things, the son to yield to the authority of the father. Other writings on filial piety have also been commonly cited. Even if we dismiss the notorious *Ershisi xiao* (*Twenty-four Examples of Filial Piety*) as non-canonical, there is enough in the canonical works to serve as grist for the critics' mill. In the *Analects,* filial piety is often referred to as a key virtue. A favorite of critics is *Analects* 1.11: "Confucius said, 'When a man's father is alive, look at the bent of his will. When his father is dead, look at his conduct. If for three years [of mourning] he does not change from the way of his father, he may be called filial'."[10] Other often-quoted passages include *Analects* 2.5 ("Meng I Tzu asked about filial piety. Confucius said: 'Never disobey'") and *Analects* 2.7 ("Confucius said, 'Filial piety nowadays means to be able to support one's parents. But we support even dogs and horses. If there is no feeling of reverence, wherein lies the difference?' "). From passages such as these, critics draw conclusions such as: "The most salient feature of filial piety is the subordination of the will and welfare of each individual to the will and welfare of his or her real classificatory parents"; and "Filial Piety is quintessentially described as the subordination of a son to his father."[11]

Filial piety has also been implicated in the authoritarianism of the social and political structure in ancient China. The obedience to one's sovereign, as stated in the Three Bonds doctrine, is seen as an extension of the obedience to one's father demanded by filial piety. Roetz cites one critic as saying that filial piety, *xiao*, "is the entrance door to *zhong*, loyalty to the ruler."[12] *Analects* 1.2 is often cited in support of this view: "Few of those who are filial sons and respectful brothers will show disrespect to superiors." In the *Xiaojing* (*Classic of Filial Piety*) itself, we read that because "the gentleman is filial when serving his parents, he can be loyal to his ruler."[13]

For many critics, filial piety and, for that matter, the Three Bonds doctrine are rooted in the Confucian notion of *li* (propriety). The respect, reverence, obedience, loyalty, etc. that must be shown by the son toward his father are aspects of *li*. *Analects* 2.5 is often cited in partial support of this claim. Thus, "Confucius said, 'When parents are alive, serve them according to the rules of propriety. When they die, bury them according to the rules of propriety and sacrifice to them according to the rules of propriety'." As one critic sees it, *li* was "a core concept for Confucius [and] was demanded of all."[14] This rather uncontroversial claim is followed by the claim that *li* "defined the correct, stylized behavior which was attached to social roles and forestalled the idiosyncrasies of individual expression."[15] It is by *li* that society is ordered "into a hierarchy of superior and subordinate roles."[16] The implication is that it is by *li* that the family is likewise ordered, with wives and children occupying subordinate roles. This is how *li* ultimately gives rise to authoritarianism and totalitarianism in the family and in the social and political order.

As if totalitarian and authoritarian family and social structures are not bad enough, critics point out that filial piety requires obedience from the children. There is of course nothing wrong with obedience in the case of very young children. However, the idea of filial piety applies to grown-up children, or to people who have reached the "age of reason." What is wrong, according to many critics, is that children must yield to their parents, particularly fathers, even if they know their parents are in the wrong, morally or otherwise. Purportedly quoting from the *Mencius* and elsewhere, Zhu Xi (1130–1200) made the following claims:

Li Tong said: "The fact that Shun could help Gusou [his criminal father] to achieve delight was simply because he fulfilled the way of serving the parents to the utmost, discharged the duties of a son, and shut his eyes to the wrongdoings of the parents."

Luo Zhongsu [Luo Congyan] once remarked to this, "It was simply because *there are no parents in the world who are not right.*"

When Liaoweng [Chen Guan] heard this, he found it excellent and said, "Only then the roles of father and son in the world were fixed. Whenever subordinates have murdered their rulers and sons have murdered their fathers, this has always started with their finding fault with them."[17]

In what follows, I ignore the claim that filial piety is responsible for adverse political, social, and psychological effects, focusing instead on the claim concerning the moral status of filial piety. If to be filial is to obey one's father, no matter what, then little can be said in reply to the critics. Naturally, the question is whether absolute obedience is the essential element of filial piety. Many commentators have pointed out that the "words of the ancients" allow for interpretations that move away from the idea of absolute obedience.

Reviewing the critics' case

To begin with, it is interesting to note that the Three Bonds doctrine was nowhere discussed by Confucius and major Confucians, such as Mencius. Dong Zhongshu discussed it in his writings but he was a minor philosopher who managed to play a large role in politicizing Confucianism. The *Hanfeizi* in which the Three Bonds doctrine made its first appearance is a text of the Legalist school. The doctrine came to be regarded as part of Confucianism only through the politicization of Confucianism during the Han dynasty and subsequently. As Wei-ming Tu sees it, "the Han ideologists, like the Legalists, were mainly concerned about the functional utility of the Three Bonds as mechanism of symbolic control for the primary purpose of social stability."[18] Indeed, "the politicized Confucian implementation of the Three Bonds is much more demanding than their legalist origin and nature may suggest."[19] Given this history, it is not unreasonable to suggest that the Three Bonds doctrine is not canonically Confucian. Those critics who cite the doctrine against filial piety have largely failed to make the distinction between Confucianism and what Tu calls "the politicized implementation" of it. The only thing that bears any resemblance to the Three Bonds doctrine in canonical Confucian writings is the notion of the Five Relationships found in the *Mencius.* But as Tu has pointed out, the "ethics of the Three Bonds as an integral part of [the] politicized Confucian mechanism of symbolic control is a far cry from the Mencian idea of the Five Relationships."[20]

The statement of the Five Relationships occurs at *Mencius* 3A4: "the sage *Shun . . .* appointed Hsieh to be the Minister of Instruction, to teach the relations of humanity: – how, between father and son, there should be affection; between sovereign and minister, righteousness; between husband and wife, attention to their separate functions; between old and young, a proper order; and between friends, fidelity."[21] It is interesting to note that righteousness governs only the relationship between the sovereign and the minister. The family relationships of father and son and husband and wife are governed respectively by affection, or love, and separateness, or distinction. Tu concludes that, for Mencius, "the proper relationship between [father and son] is mutual affection rather than one-way obedience."[22] At *Mencius* 4A28, it is said that the effect of "great filial piety" was that "all fathers and sons in the kingdom were established *in their respective duties*" (original emphasis). Zhu Xi, as we saw above, made a great deal of this passage, but it is clearly possible to read it as saying that it is not the case that only children have duties toward their fathers. For Mencius, fathers have certain duties toward their children, which include the duties of love and benevolence. To be served by one's children is the fruit of the benevolence one shows toward them. Thus, at *Mencius* 4A27, it is said that the "richest fruit of benevolence is . . . the service of one's parents." These passages lend support to Roetz's contention that "*ci*, kindness, [is] the counterpart of *xiao* on the side of the parents."[23] It is no wonder that critics typically ignore the *Mencius* when it comes to textual support for the reading of filial piety as something that demands absolute obedience, relying instead on later appropriations of it, such as Zhu Xi's.

More importantly, direct textual evidence is available to support the view that filial piety does not require absolute obedience, particularly when it comes to moral matters. In Chapter 15 of the *Xiaojing*, we find that the Master denies that "filiality consists in simply obeying a father." Indeed, the filial son must "reason" with his father and "must never fail to warn his father against [moral wrong]." It may be said that reasoning and warning are not sufficient. If the son is convinced that his father is wrong, he must not obey. The question is whether filial piety allows for going against the father. *Analects* 4.18 may be cited on behalf of the skeptics. However, Roetz points out that the verb *wei* in *Analects* 4.18 does not have a clear reference and the passage can be translated either as "If you see that [your parents] do not follow your will, then keep on being respectful, and do not resist [*wei*]," or as "If you see that they do not follow your will, then keep on being respectful, but do not abandon [*wei*] your purpose."[24] In the latter version, the son's "moral firmness . . . is . . . just as important as a tactful tone and a sympathetic understanding which reflect [his] subordinate position in the family and probably increase the chances of the moral engagement."[25]

In *Mencius* 6B3, it is said that while the parents' small faults may be tolerated, their big faults should be pointed out to them, out of our affection for them: "Where the parents' fault was great, not to have murmured on account of it would have increased the want of natural affection . . . [which] would have been unfilial." This is reinforced by Xunzi. Thus, in Book 29 on "The Way of the Son" (*Zidao*) in the *Xunzi*, section 29.2, we find that great filial piety requires getting a clear insight into the principle of when to follow and when not to follow the father's order, and applying this insight with courtesy, respect, and all the other virtues.[26]

Clearly, then, the words of the ancients are quite ambiguous. It is arguable that the ancient Chinese thinkers would happily endorse the adaptation of their teachings, within limits, to suit the prevailing social conditions. At any rate, the later Legalists adapted the idea of filial piety and made it into a key component of their idea of a hierarchical social structure. Any such adaptation must be defended on its own. While the earlier Confucians might not have endorsed the Legalists' adaptation, it is clearly not inconsistent with their flexible notion of filial piety. With this in mind, I shall defend the view that we can take the idea of filial piety as respect for tradition where tradition is understood in the Gadamerean sense.

The father as tradition

According to Hans-Georg Gadamer, understanding and interpretation are one and the same process.[27] To have an understanding of something, oneself included, is to have interpreted it. To interpret something, in turn, is to stand within a tradition and to bring to bear what one has already understood in it to the new situation. This includes a particular self-understanding. One's tradition provides one with one's own "horizon of understanding," or the perspective necessary for the task of interpretation. The object of understanding too comes to us with its own horizon determined by the tradition in which it is embedded. Understanding is the "fusion" of the two horizons. Just as no object is presented to understanding in its nudity, so to speak, no subject embarks on the task of interpretation, or understanding, as a tabula rasa. Tradition, for Gadamer, supplies the subject with the necessary preconditions of understanding, the "prejudices" as Gadamer calls them. Without tradition, understanding is not possible, not just because one lacks certain necessary cognitive preconditions, but also because one lacks self-understanding. Tradition nourishes and maintains the subject, and guides the subject in its task of understanding, as well as serves as the subject's source of cognitive authority. It is not a Wittgensteinian ladder to be kicked away once there is understanding, but something that accompanies every act of interpretation. The subject grows with and through tradition.

Alan Chan argues that the idea of tradition having "superiority in knowledge and insight," as Gadamer himself has put it, can be found in Chinese philosophy: "Confucian philosophy . . . seems to find in tradition a reservoir of insight and truth."[28] As Chan points out, Confucius thinks of himself as merely a transmitter of the wisdom embedded in a tradition going back to the Zhou dynasty and beyond, exemplified by the thoughts and deeds of sages such as King Wen, King Wu, and the Duke of Zhou. According to Confucius, the Zhou culture in turn was built on the achievements of previous dynasties: "The Master said, 'the Zhou is resplendent in culture, having before it the example of the two previous dynasties'" (*Analects* 3.14). Indeed, it may be said that for Confucius, to follow tradition is to follow the Dao. As in the case of Gadamer's hermeneutics, in which tradition nurtures and guides one who seeks knowledge and understanding, the Dao plays the role of nurturing and guiding the knowledge seeker. While the workings of the Dao are mysterious, their manifestations in the ways of tradition are not, and we can follow the Dao simply by following tradition. Given the role of tradition, knowledge cannot be had outside of tradition. Thus, Confucius declares: "I believe in and love the ancients" (*Analects* 7.1) and "I am not one who was born with knowledge; I love ancient [teaching] and earnestly seek it" (*Analects* 7.20). Also, as in the case of hermeneutics, personal development is a process that takes place within tradition. As Confucius admits, "in how to be a practicing gentleman, I can . . . claim no insight" (*Analects* 7.33).

Given that this is so, it is natural enough to take the idea of filial piety as a component part of the Chinese respect for tradition. This makes sense because the father is not an independent figure of authority. The father has his own father and the latter his and so on. Filial piety requires the son to defer not to the father pure and simple, but to the father who defers to his, and the latter in turn is someone who defers to his, and so on. Filial piety is intergenerational. It makes no sense to speak of it as something that stops with one's own father. Thus, the father is really a father figure representing a tradition. Just as the wisdom of the Zhou culture was formed, "having before it the example of the two previous dynasties" (and the latter, presumably, with the example of dynasties before them), the views of the father, to which the son is meant to defer, are not entirely his own, but views formed "having before him the example" of previous fathers. In the father, then, we have a "reservoir of insight and truth," to borrow Chan's words. Alternatively, a father who has learned from examples of all the fathers before him may be assumed to have "superiority in knowledge and insight," in Gadamer's words. In this way, the idea of filial piety as obedience to the father can be taken to refer to the necessity to stand within a tradition in the seeking of wisdom and knowledge. Disobedience, in turn, can be taken to refer to the disregard of tradition, or traditional knowledge.

As pointed out above, Gadamer thinks of tradition as something that nurtures, maintains and guides the individual, intellectually speaking. This makes it quite appropriate to equate the father with the father figure representing tradition. This is so because the father, together with the mother, in following their parents before them, nurture, maintain, and guide the child, literally so until a certain age, and are in the position to do so long after. Furthermore, Gadamer takes self-understanding as understanding one's own tradition, which in turn is the precondition for further understanding. In a similar way, to have filial piety is to have understanding of the tradition handed down by the fathers, and to have the appropriate fore-knowledge for the acquisition of knowledge and wisdom. One must first learn to be filial before one can learn anything, just as one must acquire a perspective by immersing oneself in one's tradition before one can embark on the task of interpretation and understanding. Some textual evidence can be found in support of this view. For instance, at *Analects* 1.2, we find: "Filial piety and brotherly respect are the root of humanity." This can be read as saying that to be a person with a certain level of understanding, a person with *ren*, one has to learn the way of the fathers, the way of tradition, or simply the *Way*. Elsewhere, we find that filial piety means much more than just to follow the instructions of one's immediate parents; it means to follow the tradition, the *Way*. Thus, in Chapter 29 (29.1) of the *Xunzi*, we find: "Inside the home to be filial . . . and outside the home to be courteous . . . constitute the minimal standard of human conduct. . . . To follow the dictates of the Way rather than those of one's lord and to follow the requirements of morality rather than the wishes of one's father constitute the highest standard of conduct." In the line of fathers stretching back to antiquity, one's own father could well be out of line. If this is the case then "great" filial piety requires that one does not follow the father; it requires instead that one follows justice as laid out in the tradition of the fathers of one's father, or the Dao. Juggling the words of the ancients, we can certainly take Confucius' saying at *Analects* 2.5 to the effect that filial piety means "Never disobey" to mean never to place oneself outside of the tradition of one's forefathers.

The advantage of reading filial piety as respect for tradition is that we can render consistent all the seemingly conflicting statements found in the literature. Thus, all those pronouncements that urge obedience can be read as referring to the hermeneutic necessity of staying within a tradition. They are quite consistent with all the seemingly more liberal sayings that allow for deviation from the rulings and judgments of the father, such as those canvassed above. The father in the latter is the father that is out of line with tradition. As respect for tradition, filial piety not just permits but requires one to reason or "remonstrate" with the father who is out of line. Of course, in the tradition of *ren* and *li*, one must do so with tact and propriety.

Appropriating the idea of filial piety along the lines suggested here takes away some of the sting in the critics' attack. However, a large dose of it remains, in that it can be said that the way of tradition is not infallible. Critics may go along with the suggestion here and still charge Chinese philosophy, or the idea of filial piety, with conservatism. As it turns out, the charge of conservatism has been raised against both Confucianism and Gadamer's hermeneutics. As Chan points out, in urging us to follow the wisdom of antiquity, Confucius "can be described as a 'conservative' thinker."[29] As for Gadamer, Georgia Warnke acknowledges that in saying that we "must accept the authority of the tradition because we cannot know enough to be certain of our criticism of it," Gadamer's thesis is "fundamentally conservative."[30] The problem is that we cannot rule out the possibility of the way of tradition, or the way of antiquity, being fundamentally unjust, or "systematically distorted," as Habermas, a critic of Gadamer, has put it. Fortunately, both Gadamer's hermeneutics and Confucianism can be defended against the charge of conservatism. Neither advocates a blind obedience to tradition. For both, to follow tradition is to contribute to the flourishing of tradition. Both leave room for a critical engagement with tradition.

In the case of Gadamer, the charge of conservatism came originally from the Critical Theorists Habermas and Apel, elaborated respectively in their *Zur Logik der Sozialwissenschaften* and *Hermeneutik und ideologiekritik*.[31] As they see it, the problem is that, without being able to stand outside and look back on tradition, hermeneutics will fail to reveal what might be wrong with tradition itself. Differently put, if hermeneutics is the placing of oneself in tradition then hermeneutical understanding will fail to detect any pathology that besets the tradition. To avoid this problem, Critical Theory advocates the creation of an independent standpoint, external to tradition, an *Archimedean* position, from which to examine ourselves and the world in which we live. Apel advocates something like the objective scientific viewpoint, and Habermas advocates a viewpoint reached via undistorted communicative means, or what he calls the "ideal speech situation." Both would hold the same objection to filial piety understood as respect for tradition. For both, "the root of humanity" lies not in tradition but outside it. Both would say that humanity requires being, in a sense, unfilial to tradition.

In his own defense, Gadamer has stressed the fact that hermeneutics is a dynamic process of dialogical discourse, the aim of which is to reach agreement on meaning and truth. As such, no viewpoint can remain unquestioned in hermeneutical understanding. In the section on the application of legal tradition in *Truth and Method*, Gadamer argues that the hermeneutical process does not leave tradition unaffected after application. The attribution of "superiority in knowledge and insight" to tradition should not be taken to mean that tradition is beyond question. One is here reminded of Otto Neurath's metaphor of repairing the boat while staying afloat in it. Gadamer's hermeneutics has to be interpreted in such a way that we "must accept the authority of the tradition" only insofar as it is tradition that keeps us afloat. This acceptance does not imply that tradition is beyond questioning. Indeed, it may turn out that tradition, like the leaking boat, has to be *extensively* repaired if we are to remain afloat in it. The application of tradition in interpretation is really a conversation with tradition. As such, hermeneutics contains resources adequate to the task of providing a critique of tradition and to change it. All that is needed is the power of imagination to bring to the foreground different possibilities; that is, possibilities different from that which would result from a strict application of tradition. Given these possibilities, tradition itself can be questioned. Gadamer himself thinks of the hermeneutical process as a to-and-fro movement resulting in a "reflective equilibrium," to borrow Rawls's words. It is precisely the relentless hermeneutical process that will prevent being locked into a systematic distortion.[32]

The same thing can be said about the "conservatism" in Confucianism. According to Alan Chan, Confucius is a "conservative" thinker only in the technical sense of wanting to preserve antiquity. Chan goes on to argue that the "conservative Confucian understanding of *li* does not entail a set of rigid rituals and rules of behaviour, which inhibit criticism and change." This is because "Confucius' devotion to antiquity . . . implies a sharply honed historical consciousness." [33] I take it that Chan means here the equivalent of Gadamer's "effective historical consciousness," which is not a passive consciousness of tradition, but an active application of it, an application that will not leave tradition itself unaffected. Chan points out that Confucius advocated tempering *li* with *ren*. We may add to this the emphasis, found particularly in the Neo-Confucians, on the virtue of *cheng* (sincerity) as a virtue that moderates all others, including *li*. So when Confucius says that filial piety is observance of *li*, he does not mean any strict application of *li*. It is instead the observance of *li* moderated by a sense of humanity (*ren*) and against the background of sincerity (*cheng*). The virtues of *ren* and *cheng*, not to mention practical considerations, could well require one to question what might be thought to be traditionally demanded by *li*, such as using linen for ceremonial caps, or bowing before ascending the hall. The filial person's respect for the way of the fathers does not take away the motivation, and does not leave him or her bereft of resources, to engage critically the traditional viewpoints.

How, exactly, can tradition be questioned? Here, Chan appears to take the Habermasian line that we must appeal to an ideal external point of view in our questioning of tradition. He then argues that the "ideal sage" supplies such an external viewpoint: "With a growing community of *junzi*, whose sight is set firmly in the direction of the ideal sage, the threat of 'conservatism' diminishes in that Confucian learning ensures a thoroughgoing interrogation and appropriation of tradition."[34] However, we have to ask whether the viewpoint of the ideal sage is within or without the tradition. To perform the Habermasian task of critique of ideology, it must be some ideal speech situation outside of tradition. This seems to undercut my suggestion that one must be filial to tradition in the sense of not going outside it. Gadamer would certainly resist the idea of appealing to the viewpoint of the ideal sage as something arrived at independently of tradition. He would ask how one arrives at the point of view of the ideal sage in the first place. How do the *junzi* know what would be prescribed and proscribed by the ideal sage if the latter speaks outside of the tradition? To remain within the Gadamerean framework, we have to say that our understanding of what is sagely ideal comes from within tradition itself. Only in this way can the *junzi*'s appeal to the sagely ideal be said to stay within tradition; that is, to stay filial to tradition. As it turns out, the ideal sage that Confucians spoke of is very much Confucian, not someone alien to the Chinese tradition. Of course, the effectiveness of an immanent critique may be doubted. However, the dynamic play of the numerous different virtues, including the overarching virtue of *cheng* (sincerity), and the Confucian requirement of eternal moral vigilance that Chan himself has drawn our attention to,[35] should be sufficient to ensure an effective immanent critique. Gadamer never tires of reminding us that hermeneutics is a to-and-fro movement. Given the richness of moral resources within Chinese philosophy, the to-and-fro movement is bound to keep stirring the tradition, reducing, if not eliminating, the danger of stagnant conservatism. Yet, while stirring the tradition, we remain filial to it.

If I am right in reading filial piety as respect for tradition, the idea is not some outmoded and disreputable teaching of Chinese philosophy. What happens at the social and political level is not a true reflection of the philosophical significance of the idea of filial piety. Indeed, understood in the way suggested here, the idea of filial piety can be used to correct the "traditional" Chinese family structure that has been the subject of social critics. If filial piety is responsible for the social and political ills noted by critics, how could it be part of a long Chinese tradition of harmonious existence? To question this family structure and to correct its defects is not to do away with filial piety. On the contrary, it is just to obey Confucius's command to the filial son never to disobey; that is, never to disobey the tradition of harmonious existence. To reason with, or deviate from, an authoritarian father, who is a source of disharmony in the family or the community, is not unfilial. On the contrary, it is to uphold the tradition of harmonious existence, *and* to do so in the name of the fathers.

Notes

1 See, for instance, W. H. Slote and G. A. de Vos (eds), *Confucianism and the Family*, Albany: State University of New York Press, 1998.
2 See, for instance, O. O'Neill and W. Ruddick (eds), *Having Children: Philosophical and Legal Reflections on Parenthood*, Oxford: Oxford University Press, 1979; D. Archard, "Filial Morality," *Pacific Philosophical Quarterly*, 77, 1996, 179–92; and D. Archard, *Children, Family and the State*, Aldershot: Ashgate, forthcoming.
3 H. Roetz, *Confucian Ethics of the Axial Age*, Albany: State University of New York Press, 1993, p. 58.
4 W. H. Slote, "Psychocultural Dynamics within the Confucian Family," in W. H. Slote and G. A. de Vos (eds), *Confucianism and the Family*, p. 39.
5 Ibid., p. 43.
6 Ibid., p. 46.
7 D. Yim, "Psychocultural Features of Ancestor Worship in Modern Korean Society," in W. H. Slote and G. A. de Vos (eds), *Confucianism and the Family*, p. 165, original emphasis.
8 W. H. Slote, "Psychocultural Dynamics," p. 46.
9 As translated in B. Watson, *Han Fei Tzu: Basic Writings*, New York: Columbia University Press, 1964.
10 Translation of the *Analects* is by W. T. Chan, *A Source Book of Chinese Philosophy*, Princeton, NJ Princeton University Press, 1963. Chan's Wade-Giles romanization is retained.
11 D. K. Jordan, "Filial Piety in Taiwanese Popular Thought," in W. H. Slote and G. A. de Vos (eds), *Confucianism and the Family*, pp. 268, 269.
12 H. Roetz, *Confucian Ethics*, pp. 54–5.
13 English translation is by M. L. Makra, *The Hsiao Ching*, New York: St John's University Press, 1961.

14 S. B. Young, "The Orthodox Chinese Confucian Social Paradigm versus Vietnamese Individualism," in W. H. Slote and G. A. de Vos (eds) *Confucianism and the Family*, p. 139.

15 Ibid.

16 Ibid., p. 138.

17 Cited in H. Roetz, *Confucian Ethics*, p. 57.

18 W. M. Tu, "Probing the 'Three Bonds' and 'Five Relationships' in Confucian Humanism," in W. H. Slote and G. A. de Vos (eds) *Confucianism and the Family*, p. 122.

19 Ibid., p. 123.

20 Ibid., p. 124.

21 Translation of *The Mencius* is by J. Legge, *The Chinese Classics*, Vol. 2, *The Works of Mencius*, Hong Kong: Hong Kong University Press, 1960. I retain Legge's punctuation and Wade-Giles romanization.

22 W. M. Tu, "Probing the 'Three Bonds'," p. 125.

23 H. Roetz, *Confucian Ethics*, p. 56.

24 Ibid., p. 59.

25 Ibid.

26 Translation of *The Xunzi* is by J. Knoblock, *Xunzi: A Translation and Study of the Complete Works*, Stanford, CA: Stanford University Press, 1994, vol. 3.

27 H.-G. Gadamer, *Truth and Method*, G. Barden and J. Cummings (trans. and ed.), New York: The Seabury Press, 1975.

28 H.-G. Gadamer, "Replik," in K. O. Apel (ed.), *Hermeneutik und Ideologiekritik*, Frankfurt: Suhrkamp Verlag, 1977, p. 73. A. K. L. Chan, "Confucian Ethics and the Critique of Ideology," *Asian Philosophy*, 10, 2000, 245–61, p. 245.

29 A. K. L. Chan, "Confucian Ethics," p. 246.

30 G. Warnke, *Gadamer*, Cambridge: Polity Press, 1987, p. 136.

31 J. Habermas, *Zur Logik der Sozialwissenschaften*, Frankfurt: Suhrkamp Verlag, 1970, and K. O. Apel, *Hermeneutik*.

32 For a detailed discussion, see my "Critique of Ideology: Hermeneutics or Critical Theory?," *Human Studies*, 17, 1995, 419–32.

33 A. K. L. Chan, "Confucian Ethics," p. 249.

34 Ibid., p. 257.

35 Ibid., p. 252.

13 Reflections on filiality, nature, and nurture

Lisa Raphals

In this chapter I reflect on filiality (*xiao* 孝) from two distinct directions. One applies what in Greek would be called a *Nomos–Phusis* perspective to filiality, namely to offer a gendered perspective on the differences between filiality for men and women. The other is to consider *xiao* as an emotion, rather than as a virtue. (This is a matter of emphasis; I am not suggesting that filiality is *not* a virtue!) I concentrate on the strict sense of the term, filial duty to parents, rather than husbands or other relatives. If we adopt a gendered perspective on filiality, there is a radical difference between filiality as it is defined for men and for women. Men's filiality is "genetically" defined by lineage throughout life, but women's filiality is expected to shift to the new environment of her husband's ancestral lineage at marriage. My second nature–nurture continuum concerns whether we are to regard filiality as an emotion, which is arguably "natural," at least in much traditional theory of the emotions, or as a virtue, which is a product of culture and upbringing.

Differences between male and female filiality

I begin by arguing that classical texts tend to treat filiality as an emotion that is part of the "natural" human endowment. (Needless to say, they also recognized that there were unfilial sons, and that virtues required cultivation.) This expectation of filiality is tenable for males, but problems arise when it is applied to females, because there is no biological bond to the husband's parents.

In other words, filiality is described as "natural" to males, in that men's filiality is genetically defined throughout life. Women's filiality is entirely a product of nurture, since there is no "natural" justification for the expectation that they will shift the emotion of filial love from its "natural" object, their (natal) parents, to a husband's ancestral lineage at marriage.

Because the tradition does not make a linguistic distinction between male and female filiality, this difference creates tensions in the textual tradition, expressed by the relative absence of early narratives about filial women. I also show how some Ming accounts of filial women were constructed from earlier narratives. The problem of gendered filiality provides a new perspective on the problem of whether the potential for self-cultivation is gendered, a question I have explored elsewhere.[1]

A virtue or an emotion? Biological versus cultural theories of emotion

Theories of the emotions provide a perspective to examine the basis for filiality as an emotion and for claims that it is "natural." Research on the cross-cultural study of emotion has challenged earlier biological and psychological theories of emotion as instinctive and primarily biologically determined.[2] Such theories associated the emotions with instinct and uncritically viewed them as biologically determined universals. Psychologists tended to adopt an essentialist view of emotion as some entity, something "there" to which the word "emotion" refers. While there is evidence that there are some universal emotions, the problem is complicated by a tendency within cross-cultural studies of emotion for Western ideas about emotion and Anglophone emotion concepts to be taken as conceptual universals.[3]

Recent approaches to the category of emotion within the social sciences, especially anthropology and sociology, have stressed the social construction of emotion, and have drawn attention to the nuanced and culturally specific character of some emotions. In these views emotion is culturally determined. Some are delimited in both time and space. Some emotions have limited lifetimes. Consider, for example, *accidie*, a kind of boredom and dejection at fulfilling one's religious duty, experienced by hermits and others. This has been described as an example of an emotion that became obsolete when the conditions that produced it ceased to be widespread.[4]

Since the seventeenth century, most philosophers have tended to construe emotion as simple, involuntary, affective and non-cognitive. Spinoza is an exception, as is Aristotle in the Classical world. Aristotle's discussion of emotions (*ta pathē*) is highly nuanced; for him, they are (affective) impulses that cause people to change their judgments, and are accompanied by pain (*lupē*) and pleasure (*hedonē*); they include anger (*orgē*), pity (*heleos*), and fear (*phobos*), their opposites, and emotions like them.[5] Aristotle's subvarieties of emotions are very subtle. Consider the correlates of anger: slight (*oligōria*), contempt (*kataphronēsis*), and insult (*hubris*). Its opposite is mildness (*praünsis*). Other emotions discussed include love and friendship (*philia*), hatred (*ekhthros*), fear (*phobos*) and its opposite, boldness or confidence (*tharsos*), shame (*aiskhunē*) and its opposite, benevolence (*kharis*) and its opposite, virtuous indignation (the opposite of pity) and envy. Filiality would fit well into this list, as a variety of love. It is in this broad context of the relation of local moral orders and languages to the experience of emotion that I want to consider *xiao* as a specifically Chinese emotion that is gendered in very different ways for men and for women.

A note on the controversy about *qing* 情

For purposes of my argument it is not necessary to resolve the controversy surrounding Graham's assertion that *qing* never means "passions" (even in *Xunzi*), but means "the facts" or "genuine," and responses to it by Chad Hansen, Irene Bloom, and others.[6] Whether we understand the phrase *qing yu* as "emotions and desires" or, following Graham, as "essential desires," it seems clear from both text and context that joy, anger, sadness, and the rest do refer to the "basic" emotions of love, hate, pleasure, anger, sorrow, and joy. References to these six states appear in a range of Warring States texts, including the *Zuo zhuan*, *Guo yu*, *Liji*, *Guanzi*, *Zhuangzi*, *Xunzi*, *Lüshi chunqiu*, and *Huang Di neijing*. Consider these three, from the *Zuo zhuan*, *Guanzi*, and *Xunzi*, respectively.

> People have love and hate, pleasure and anger, sorrow and joy. These are born from the six *qi*. Therefore be careful to choose your models from the fitting categories, in order to regulate the six intentions.[7]

> Love and hate, pleasure and anger, and sorrow and joy are the transformations of life.[8]

> Our nature's liking and disliking, pleasure and anger, sadness and joy, is called "the genuine in us" (*qing*).[9]

By contrast, the *Li ji* refers to seven feelings:

> What is meant by the genuine (*qing*) in man? Pleasure, anger, sadness, fear, love, hate, desire, these seven we are capable of *without having learned them*.[10]

The *Zuo zhuan* passage describes the six *qing* as byproducts of the six *qi*. Heaven and earth produce the six *qi*, which become the five flavors, extend outward as the five colors, and manifest as the five sounds. In the Admonitions (*Jie* 戒) chapter of the *Guanzi* they are "the transformations of life." Unnamed *qing* are a source of argument between Zhuangzi and Huizi.[11]

(Male) filiality as a natural emotion

In the light of research on the spatially and temporally local social construction of emotions, I want to offer the speculative suggestion that Confucius and his intellectual descendants valorized filiality, *xiao*, as a very culturally specific variant of love, and considered it a natural emotion. For men.

The understanding of filiality as a natural human emotion is strengthened, in the case of men, by its biological basis. From a biological perspective, the expectation of married women, that they transfer their "natural" solicitude toward their natal parents to their husbands' parents, is correspondingly unnatural. Girls who have not yet reached marriageable age, but who are expected to marry in future, represent a third group who, for the present, are permitted and expected to feel "biological" filiality, but on a temporary basis. The expectations of female filiality, both for girls and for married women, pit a set of arguably "natural" emotions against another set that are clearly culturally constructed. Now let us see how this problem plays out in the textual record, and consider the status of filiality as a natural emotion in Warring States texts.

A Warring States consensus

The antiquity and importance of family relations centered on filiality is undisputed, and there remained a remarkable consensus about the desirability of filial piety and its related virtues, as attested by the papers of Livia Kohn and others in this volume. We may note the antiquity of the vocabulary for family relationships, including words for filial piety, deference to elder brothers, and other role-specific virtues, well before the formulations of Confucius. A wide range of Warring States thinkers after him, including his critics, maintained this consensus. For example, even the *Mozi* chapter "Exaltation of the Virtuous" argues that rulers who fail to exalt the virtuous will be surrounded by men who neglect filiality toward their parents and the proper distinction of the sexes.[12] Han Fei devotes a chapter (51) to filiality on account of its usefulness to the state.

According to *Analects* 1.2, the roots of *ren* are filial piety and brotherly deference.[13] Nourishing these roots is crucially important to the *junzi*, because, once established, "dao will grow from them." Yu Jiyuan argues that for Confucius *xiao* is thus a *natural* emotion: "Filial love as natural sentiment is inborn and not culturally specific. What is required is to cherish and nurture it." He points out that, for Confucius, love must be rooted in family love because of its inherent intimacy between affection and ethical training. For Confucius, this intimacy is crucial for complying with *li*.[14] Mencius, too, describes filiality as natural. In a debate with the Mohist Yizu (3A5), he describes cases where sons failed to bury their parents, later found their bodies mutilated by animals, and broke out in sweat and could not bear to look. The sweat was not put on for others to see, but was an expression of their inmost hearts (*zhong xin* 中心). The question of the "naturalness" of the emotional dispositions connected with the cultivation of virtue is also central to the dispute between Mencius and Xunzi concerning human nature. That subject is beyond the scope of this chapter, but it is worth mentioning that Xunzi too defines emotions as inborn. He defines the *qing* (whether understood as "feelings" or as "essential nature") as liking, disliking, pleasure, anger, sadness, and joy.[15]

A Han example

A Han example of "natural" filiality shows that a filial son remains filial even to a depraved parent. The *Shiji* biography of Empress Lü relates how she murdered her rival Lady Qi in so brutal a fashion as to alienate the affections of her own son:

> The Empress Dowager cut off Lady Qi's hands and feet, put out her eyes, burned her ears out, [forced her to] drink a muteness-inducing drug, imprisoned her in a latrine, and named her the Human Pig. After some days had passed, she summoned Emperor Xiao Hui to view the Human Pig. When he had seen, asked, and finally learned it was Lady Qi, he burst into tears, and fell so ill that he could not get up for over a year. He sent a messenger to say to the Empress: *"This is not the deed of a human being! As I am the Empress' son, I will never be able to govern the empire."*[16]

Xiao Hui is so upset by the perception that his mother is "not human" that he attempts to decline the throne, but remains filial to her nonetheless. The *Hanshu* eulogy (he eventually ascends the throne as Hui Di) describes him as cultivated, *filial*, generous and kind, even though the Empress Dowager Lü "damaged and injured his perfect virtue."[17]

Of course there are also many references to unfilial sons, but ample evidence from the Warring States and Han attests to the view that human feelings, including filiality, were considered "natural," even in cases where the parent did not deserve this regard.

The problem with female *xiao*

There is a marked contrast in the treatment of male and female gendered *xiao* in these texts. The importance of implicitly male-gendered *xiao* in Warring States and Han texts, "Confucian" and otherwise, is unequivocal; we need only recollect the legends of such filial sons as Shun and Shen Sheng. Yet there is a curious dearth of filial daughters (and daughters-in-law). When filial daughters do make an appearance, they tend to be praised for something else, often intelligence or cleverness. The treatment of the earliest work on female virtues, the *Lienü zhuan*, neglects filiality to a striking degree. (I use this term to refer to the Han–Song *Lienü zhuan*, as distinct from later Ming editions.[18])

The silence of the Lienü zhuan

It is striking that filiality is of so little account in the earliest versions of the *Lienü zhuan*, which devotes two chapters to the "womanly" virtues of chastity and obedience, and three to what I have elsewhere somewhat maladroitly called the "intellectual virtues" of wisdom, benevolence, sagacity, and rhetorical skill. The fifth chapter of the *Lienü zhuan* contains examples of women who are "filial" to husbands, elder brothers, and family lineage, but rarely to their natal parents. The exceptions are stories of resolution of conflict between duty to a husband and duty to a father or brother.

The life stories of the *Lienü zhuan* are organized into six chapters based on virtues, but *xiao* is not one of them. It is full of stories of wives who advance the interests of their husbands (another form of filiality), but there is only one story in the *Lienü zhuan* that explicitly deals with filiality toward parents or parents-in-law, the story of the "Filial Wife," a Widow of Chen County in the chapter "Chaste and Obedient" (*zhen shun* 貞順).[19] "Filial Wife" was an honorific title awarded to a young widow of Chen who keeps her promise to her husband, cares for her mother-in-law, and defies her parents' wishes to remarry her. The prefect of Huaiyang, upon hearing of her virtuous conduct, recommends her to the emperor Xianwen, who awards her the title (*xiao fu* 孝婦) as well as forty catties of gold, and establishes her position to the end of her life.[20] (This is one of several cases in the *Lienü zhuan* where women receive special honorary titles, as distinct from rank and court titles by virtue of birth or marriage.[21])

Whether this relative disinterest arose from a lack of acceptable paragons or from the relative disinterest of the original *Lienü zhuan* compilers, filiality toward parents (in-law), as distinct from husbands, seems not to have been a priority in accounts of women's virtue in this period.

The intellectual virtues of filial girls

Despite the apparent disinterest in filiality, there are any number of filial girls in the *Lienü zhuan*. One saves the life of her half-brother (which is indirect filiality toward her father), who has been (probably justifiably) captured by her husband for violating a treaty, by threatening to kill both herself and their children, including the heir apparent (which would have been profoundly *unfilial* to her parents-in-law).[22] Another saves her father from a death sentence that resulted from his own fault by arguing that the sentence was unjust because the law valued the life of a tree above that of a person.[23] When her father is discovered asleep at his post, the daughter of a ferry officer attempts to take his punishment upon herself, argues on his behalf, and even does his job, violating propriety in the process. She wins a pardon for her father and marriage to the king.[24] All these girls are classified in the chapter titled "Skill in Argument" (*Bian tong* 辯通).

Perhaps the most important, and certainly the best documented, of them is Ti Ying 緹縈, the daughter of the Taicang of Qi. Her story is the last in the *Lienü zhuan* chapter, and also appears in the *Shiji*. Ti Ying saves the life of her father, the Han physician Chunyu Yi, a near contemporary of Sima Qian.[25] When he refused to treat certain illnesses, some of the families of the sick held grudges against him, and he was denounced to the throne in the fourth year of the reign of Emperor Xiao Wen (Chunyu had no sons). Ti Ying followed him to the capital and submitted a petition for his release.[26] The *Shiji* and *Lienü zhuan* give almost identical versions of her argument, which both secured the release of her father and persuaded Xiao Wen to modify the laws on mutilating punishments.

In the postscript to *Shiji* 105, Sima Qian states explicitly that "It was only because Ti Ying sent forward a document of petition that her father was able to live out his days in peace."[27] His reference to her by name, rather than as Chunyu Yi's daughter, underscores her agency in her father's fate. Sima Qian may have felt the contrast between her intervention and his own fate when he said: "My family was poor and our wealth was insufficient to commute the punishment. Of those nearest to me, no one sought to help and none of the officials near to the throne spoke a single word for me."[28]

The Xiaojing *and the* Nü Xiaojing

Like the *Lienü zhuan*, the *Xiaojing* also neglects filial women. It has no references to girls (*nü* 女) or women (*furen* 婦人), and mentions mothers (*mu* 母) only six times, and then in the context of mothers and fathers (*fumu* 父母).[29] The *Nü Xiaojing*, a Tang dynasty women's instruction manual, emphasizes distinctions between men and women, but also stresses the importance of women cultivating talent, both in household management and in their ability to admonish their husbands indirectly. The work was written by a woman for a woman. Ten of its eighteen chapter titles are identical to corresponding chapter titles in the *Xiaojing*. Thirteen chapters cite the explicit authority of Ban Zhao, but several take their quotations not from the *Nü jie* but from the *Lienü zhuan*.[30]

Several recount the stories of wives who remonstrate with their husbands. For example, Chapter 9, "Sage Intelligence" (*xian ming*), includes the story of Fan Ji, wife of King Zhuang of Chu, who successfully admonished her husband against hunting and music, and helped him select good men.[31] Chapter 15, "Remonstrance and Admonition," asks whether a woman who follows her husband's commands can become a sage. Ban Zhao cites the examples of Empress Jiang's admonitions to King Xuan of Zhou and Ban Jieyu's admonitions to Han Cheng Di.[32] Her overall argument is that, during the Three Dynasties, discerning kings all had sagely ministers (and their wives) to reprimand them, and that a man with such a wife never goes against the Way.[33] In Chapter 18, "Prosperity and Evil," Ban Zhao cites the legendary examples of the wives and consorts whose influence caused the rise and fall of the first dynasties (Tu Shan and Moxi for the Xia, You Shen and Danji for the Shang, and Tai Ren and Bao Si for the Zhou). Girls are enjoined to practice virtue, to eschew the vicious examples.[34]

Although the chapter titles of the *Nü Xiaojing* are identical to those of the *Xiaojing*, it more closely resembles the *Lienü zhuan*. It focuses on virtue(s) rather than on life-cycle roles, and emphasizes the importance of independent-mindedness in a wife, and of the intellectual and ethical virtues of women. Thus as late as the Tang we see an emphasis on the intellectual and ethical comparability of men and women, albeit given a new framework within the emphasis on filiality.

Female filiality in the Ming

In Ming dynasty editions of the *Lienü zhuan* the situation changes completely, and filiality is introduced as an important category in classifying the life stories of virtuous girls and women. Editions such as the *Gui fan* reflected changes in cultural vocabulary, with a growing stress on filiality, construed as loyalty (or chastity) to the family and the state, which replace earlier *Lienü zhuan* chapters on "Benevolent Wisdom" (*ren zhi* 仁智) and "Skill in Argument" (*Bian tong*).[35]

The *Gui fan* stories are classified not according to virtue, but according to life-cycle role: Daughters, Wives, and Mothers. These in turn are subclassified, according to a new list of virtues, prominently including filiality. The second book, Girls, contains thirty stories, eight from the (original) *Lienü zhuan*. Its first section, Filial Daughters (*Xiao nü* 孝女), contains fourteen stories, including the three "filial daughter" stories from the original *Lienü zhuan*, discussed above.[36] Wives (Book 3) contains a short section on Filial Wives (*Xiao fu* 孝婦), with six stories, including the "Filial Wife" from the original work.[37] Filiality, by its nature, is not applied to mothers (Book 4).[38] This transformation of the clever girls of the original *Lienü zhuan* into filial daughters is also accomplished by the illustrations that accompany each story.

Conclusion

In this chapter I have attempted to contextualize filiality as a Chinese culturally constructed emotion that is experienced very differently by women when compared with men. Applying the theory of the cultural construction of emotions to filiality in this way opens a Pandora's box. In conclusion, let me review some of what might be in that box. On the positive side, this approach may offer a convincing explanation of why filiality is treated so differently in texts about men and women. Given the political aspects of the reification of filiality in late imperial China, it may also explain why filiality for women was simply less important than filiality for men, until social changes in the Ming put it into a new perspective. Finally, this approach de-universalizes filiality. Is filiality, like *accidie*, an emotion whose time has come and gone, an artifact of a strongly hierarchical Confucianism that is obsolete? Or can (and should) it be reconceived in ways yet to be determined, and is it being done, as we speak here?

Notes

1 See L. A. Raphals, *Sharing the Light: Representations of Women and Virtue in Early China*, Albany: State University of New York Press, 1998; "Gendered Virtue Reconsidered: Notes from the Warring States and Han," in C. Y. Li (ed.), *The Sage and the Second Sex*, LaSalle: Open Court, 2000, pp. 223–47; "A Woman Who Understood the Rites," in B. W. Van Norden (ed.), *Essays on the Analects of Confucius*, New York: Oxford University Press, 2002, pp. 275–302; "Arguments by Women in Early Chinese Sources," *Nan Nü*, 3.2, 2001, 157–95; and "Gender and Virtue in Greece and China," *Journal of Chinese Philosophy*, 29, no. 3, 2002, 415–36.

2 J. Boucher, "Culture and Emotion," in J. Marsella *et al.* (eds), *Perspectives on Cross-cultural Psychology*, London: Academic Press, 1979, pp. 159–78; R. Harré (ed.), *The Social Construction of Emotions*, Oxford: Blackwell, 1986; P. Heelas, "Emotion Talk across Cultures," in ibid., pp. 234–66; A. Hochschild, "Emotion Work, Feeling Rules, and Social Structure," *American Journal of Sociology*, 85, 1979, 551–75; H. Leventhal, "Towards a Comprehensive Theory of Emotion," *Advances in Experimental Social Psychology*, 13, 1980, 139–207; M. Rosaldo, "Toward an Anthropology of Self and Feeling," in R. Shweder and R. A. LeVine (eds), *Culture Theory: Essays on Mind, Self, and Emotion*, Cambridge: Cambridge University Press, 1984; E. Schieffelin, *The Sorrow of the Lonely and the Burning of the Dancers*, New York: St Martins Press, 1976. For a recent review of some of these issues see R. Mallon and S. Stich, "The Odd Couple: The Compatibility of Social Construction and Evolutionary Psychology," *Philosophy of Science*, 67, March 2000, 133–54.

3 C. A. Lutz, "Emotion, Thought and Estrangement: Emotion as a Cultural Category," *Cultural Anthropology*, 1, 1986, 297–309; and C. A. Lutz and L. Abu-Lughod (eds), *Language and the Politics of Emotion*, Cambridge: Cambridge University Press, 1990.

4 R. Harré and R. Finlay-Jones, "Emotion Talk across Times," in R. Harré (ed.), *The Social Construction of Emotions*, Oxford: Basil Blackwell, 1986, 220–33, p. 221.

5 Aristotle, *Rhetoric* 1378a20ff, W. D. Ross (ed.), *Ars Rhetorica*, Oxford: Clarendon Press, 1959. He considers understanding of the emotions necessary to convince an audience of a speaker's good will.

6 A. C. Graham, "The Mencian Theory of Human Nature," *Studies in Chinese Philosophy and Philosophical Literature*, Singapore: Institute of East Asian Philosophies, 1986, p. 59, and response by Chad Hansen, "Qing 情 in Pre-Buddhist Thought," in J. Marks and R. T. Ames (eds), *Emotions in Asian Thought: A Dialogue in Comparative Philosophy*, Albany: State University of New York Press, 1995.

7 民(有)好惡喜怒哀樂・生于(六)氣・是故審則宜類・以制(六)志. *Zuo zhuan*, Duke Zhao 25.3. Yang Bojun 楊伯峻 (ed.), *Chunqiu zu zhuan zhu* 春秋左傳注, Gaoxiong: Fuwen tushu chubanshe, 1991, p. 1458.

8 *Guanzi* 10, *juan* 26, p. 2a, *Sibu beiyao* edition. 好惡喜怒哀樂, 生之變也.

9 性之好惡善怒哀樂謂之情. *Xunzi* 83/22/3, *Xunzi yinde* 荀子引得, Shanghai: Guji chubanshe, 1986, trans. A. C. Graham, "Mencian Theory of Human Nature," p. 65.

10 謂人情・喜・怒・哀・懼・愛・惡・欲・(七)者弗(學)而能・*Li ji*, Chapter 9, *Li ji zhushu* 禮記注疏, *juan* 5/20A/15, Ruan Yuan (ed.), *Shisan jing zhushu* 十三經注疏, 8 vols, Taibei: Yiwen jushu, 1980, trans. A. C. Graham, "The Mencian Theory of Human Nature," p. 64 (emphasis added).

11 *Zhuangzi*, Chapter 5, pp. 217–21, Guo Qingfan 郭慶藩 (ed.), *Zhuangzi jishi* 莊子集釋, Beijing: Zhonghua shuju, 1961, trans. A. C. Graham, "The Mencian Theory of Human Nature," pp. 61–2.

12 *Mozi yinde* 墨子引得, Shanghai: Guji chubanshe, 1982, 10/9/29.
13 *Lunyu yinde* 論語引得, *Mengzi yinde* 孟子引得, Shanghai: Guji chubanshe, 1986.
14 J. Y. Yu, "Virtue: Confucius and Aristotle," *Philosophy East and West*, 48, no. 2, 1998, 323–58.
15 See n. 7. Elsewhere he states that our natures (*xing*) flow from heaven, and their basic stuff is *qing*; and further that desires (*yu*) are reactions to *qing* (85/22/63).
16 *Shiji* 史記, Beijing: Zhonghua shuju, 1959, *juan* 9, p. 397 (emphasis added).
17 *Hanshu* 漢書, Beijing: Zhonghua shuju, 1962, *juan* 2, p. 92, H. Dubs (trans.), *History of the Former Han Dynasty*, Baltimore: Waverly Press, 1958, vol. 1, pp. 186–7.
18 L. A. Raphals, *Sharing the Light*, Chapter 5.
19 Liang Duan 梁端 (*c.* 1793–1825) (ed.), *Lienü zhuan jiaozhu* 列女傳校注 (abbreviated LNZ), Taibei: Zhonghua shuju, 1983, *juan* 4, story 15.
20 LNZ 4:10a (*juan* 4, p. 10a); 4.15 (*juan* 4, story 15).
21 Similar cases include the "Mother-teacher" of Lu, who is granted the title *mu shi* 母師 by Duke Mu of Lu after the Grand Master of Lu recommends her (LNZ 1:12a in LNZ 1.12). The "Honorable Lady" wife of Bao Su of Song receives the title *nü zong* 女宗 when the Duke of Song hears of her virtuous conduct; he also recognizes her village (LNZ 2:5b in LNZ 2.7).
22 Ji, the Wife of Duke Mu of Qin (LNZ 2.4), discussed in Raphals 1998.
23 The Daughter of Shanghuai of Qi (LNZ 6.4).
24 The Girl Ferry Officer of Zhao (LNZ 6.7).
25 He was from Linzi 臨菑, and born in Qi in 216 BCE. His name as it appears in the biography (*cangong*) is derived from his title, *cang zhang*, Chief of the Granary. He practiced medicine more or less between 175 and 150 BCE.
26 *Shiji, juan* 105, pp. 2794–5. A summary of the same events also appears in LNZ 6:13b–14a.
27 *Shiji, juan* 105, p. 2817.
28 *Hanshu, juan* 62, p. 2730.
29 *Xiaojing* 孝經, *Shisanjing zhushu*. Sinica Scripta, http://www.sinica.edu.tw
30 Zheng Shi 鄭氏, *Nü xiao jing* (NXJ) 女孝經, in Zhang Zhengxie (ed.) *Nü'er shu ji* 女兒書輯, *Tingyutang congke* 聽雨堂叢刻, Jiaozhou: Ting yu tang, 1901. The *Nü Xiaojing* lends some support to traditions that attribute the *Lienü zhuan*, in part, to Ban Zhao. A certain Madame Zheng 鄭氏 wrote the *Nü Xiaojing* as an aid to her niece, who had married a prince. For discussion see T. Martin-Liao, "Traditional Handbooks of Women's Education," in A. Gerstlacher *et al.*, *Women and Literature in China*, Bochum: Brockmeyer, 1985, pp. 173–4. Chapters 1, 7, 8, 9, 10, 11, 12, 14, and 15 share chapter titles with *Xiaojing* chapters of the same number. These and chapters 16, 17, and 18 all cite the authority of Ban Zhao 班昭. Ban Zhao, *Nü jie* (NJ) 女戒, *Hou Hanshu* 後漢書, Beijing: Zhonghua shuju, 1965, *juan* 84, pp. 2786–92.
31 NXJ 9:5a–6b, LNZ 2.5.
32 LNZ 2.1 and 8.15.
33 Ji of Wei's remonstrance to Duke Huan of Qi (against licentious music) and Jiang of Qi's to Chong Er (that he regain his kingdom in Jin). NXJ 15:10a–b. These stories appear at LNZ 3.2 and 3.3, respectively.
34 NXJ 18:12a–b.
35 For detailed discussion see L. A. Raphals, *Sharing the Light*, Chapter 5.
36 The daughter of Shanghuai of Qi (LNZ 6.4), also in Lu Kun 呂坤 (1536–1618), *Gui fan* (GF) 閨範, Xin'an (Huizhou): She Yongning, 1618, facsimile edition in Harvard-Yenching library, 2.1.1; the girl ferry officer of Zhao (LNZ 6.7, GF 2.1.2) and Ti Ying (LNZ 6.15, GF 2.1.3). Girls or daughters are otherwise classed as: daring (*lie* 烈), chaste (*zhen* 貞), incorruptible (*lian* 廉), sage and intelligent (*xian ming* 賢明), and literary (*shi nü* 詩女).

37 Its more populous sections are: (3.4) Wives who die for chastity (*si jie* 死節), thirteen stories, one from the *Lienü zhuan*; (3.5) Wives who protect chastity (*shou jie* 守節), ten stories, two in the *Lienü zhuan*; (3.8) Intelligent and penetrating (*ming da* 明達), ten stories, four in the *Lienü zhuan*; (3.1) Husband and Wife (*fu fu* 夫婦), nine stories, none in the *Lienü zhuan*; and (3.6) Sage wives (*xian fu* 賢婦), eight stories, seven in the *Lienü zhuan*. Only three sections have fewer stories than Filial Wives: these are (3.2) All virtues (*jian de* 兼德), (3.7) Protectors of the Rites (*shou li* 守禮), and (3.9) Learned (*wen xue* 文學), with five stories in each section.

38 They are described as: teachers of rites (*li* 禮), upright (*zheng* 正), benevolent (*ren* 仁), just (*gong* 公), unavaricious (*lian* 廉), stern (*yan* 嚴), knowing (*zhi* 智), tender stepmothers (*ci ji mu* 慈繼母), and tender foster-mothers (*ci ru mu* 慈乳母).

14 Filial daughters-in-law
Questioning Confucian filiality

Sor-hoon Tan

The passages about the sage-king Shun's filiality in the *Mencius* sometimes remind me of the melodramatic stereotype of the filial daughter-in-law in the Hong Kong soap operas of the 1960s and 1970s.[1] The heroine was usually beautiful and always virtuous. Her lot in life was a series of misfortunes and injustices, which she faced with tear-wrenching courage. Throughout her trials and tribulations, she remained the ever-faithful wife to her husband, loving mother to her children, caring sister-in-law to her husband's siblings, and filial to her parents-in-law. Her filiality never wavered even when, as often happened, she was confronted with a shrewish, abusive, or downright vicious mother-in-law.

The filial daughter-in-law of popular Chinese culture has the tougher task but less reward. Being filial to one's natural parents seems easier than being filial to people who are usually strangers until one marries into the family, and moreover who are likely to be rivals for one's husband's affection and resources. While Shun was rewarded with an empire for being filial, no filial daughter-in-law had such luck, not even in a myth.

Male exclusivity of pre-Qin Confucianism

While the filial son is a central figure in Confucianism from the very beginning, the filial daughter-in-law was conspicuously absent in the early Confucian texts. This is not surprising given that these texts seldom discuss women. The rare passages that mention women are all too easily given sexist readings. For example, some scholars read *Analects* 17.25 to mean that girls are difficult to educate. The *Analects* has a couple of passages about Confucius teaching his son, but no mention of any education for his daughter and niece. The only favor he had done them, which was considered worthy of comment, was finding them good husbands (*Analects* 5.1, 5.2, 11.6).

The *Mencius* and the *Xunzi* are hardly any more informative about ethics for women generally, let alone the daughter-in-law specifically. Two *Mencius* passages (5B5 and 7A22) implicitly acknowledge the woman's role as daughter-in-law, but the focus is on the ethics of the son, not the daughter-in-law. These passages imply that a daughter-in-law's filiality is an extension of her husband's filiality, grounded in the wife's responsibilities as a helpmate. While other Warring States texts contain an implicit argument for female virtue – though the paradigm of exemplary womanhood was that of the wise mother or wife, not the daughter-in-law – pre-Qin Confucianism was basically a school of thought and practice limited to a small male minority.

Filial daughters-in-law in the Han dynasty

This male exclusivity is a historical contingency, and could not be maintained once Han Confucians made their bid to establish Confucianism as a state orthodoxy that not only justified political unification under the Han dynasty, but also aimed at social and moral unification of the empire. The influence of women on society and even state politics was already a subject that attracted some attention in early texts like the *Odes* and the *Spring and Autumn Annals*, which were considered canonical works during the Han. Scholars like Han Ying 韓嬰 (*c.* 200–120 BCE), an older contemporary of Dong Zhongshu 董仲舒, already paid significant attention to the importance of women's virtues from a Confucian perspective in the *Hanshi waizhuan* 韓詩外傳.[2] The Han Confucians' comprehensive goals of sociopolitical and moral unification could hardly ignore half the population. The prominent woman scholar of Eastern Han, Ban Zhao 班昭 (*c.* 48 to *c.* 117 CE), argued in the second chapter of her *Admonitions for Women* (*Nüjie* 女誡) that educating girls was as important as educating boys in regulating the husband–wife relation, which was central to the Confucian ritual order.[3] The *Book of Rites* (*Liji* 禮記) also mentions education for women to prepare them for their roles as wives and daughters-in-law.[4]

This chapter examines the extension of Confucian filial ethics to daughters-in-law between the Warring States and Han periods, even though the honorific of "*xiao* 孝" was seldom conferred on women until later. Although family and social structures today, even in societies long influenced by Confucianism, are significantly different from those in Han China, so that hardly any of the specific filial requirements of a daughter-in-law of that time remain relevant, this extension of Confucian filial ethics to the daughter-in-law illuminates certain important characteristics of Confucian filiality and related aspects of Confucianism still relevant to contemporary moral reflection. Given that little research has been done on the literature of filial daughters-in-law, I begin with a survey of the key texts that bear on this discussion.

In the *Biographies of Women* (*Lienü zhuan* 列女傳) – comprising 125 life stories of women compiled by Han Confucian scholar Liu Xiang 劉向 (79–8 BCE), as positive and negative examples of how women influenced social order at all levels for the moral edification of the Han Emperor Cheng 成帝 – a few stories mention the woman's role as daughter-in-law in passing. There is, however, only one story of a filial daughter-in-law, "The Filial Wife, A Widow of Chen County (陳寡孝婦)," under the "Chaste and

Obedient (*zhenshun* 貞順)" section.[5] That this story is from the Han period probably indicates that Liu Xiang had not found any story of filial daughters-in-law in earlier texts and oral tradition.

Another work, the *Shuo Yuan* 說苑, also believed to have been assembled by Liu Xiang, includes a story of a filial daughter-in-law from the Eastern Ocean district who was falsely accused of killing her mother-in-law. The official, Yu Gong 于公, who insisted on the daughter-in-law's innocence against the presiding official, was praised for never failing to dispense justice in the cases he adjudicated, and therefore his descendents would prosper. His son, Yu Dingguo 于定國, became prime minister in 51 BCE, during the reign of emperor Xuan 宣帝. This story also occurs at the beginning of the biography of Yu Dingguo in the *History of the Former Han (Hanshu* 漢書).[6] The filial daughter-in-law, though a crucial part of the story, is not the focus.

Filial daughters-in-law came to occupy a more important position in Confucian ethics between the former and the later Han dynasties. The *History of the Later Han (Hou hanshu* 後漢書) includes a section of seventeen biographies of women, in which there was one about a filial daughter-in-law, Jiang Shi's wife 姜詩妻. In addition, the biographies of Master Yue Yang's wife 樂羊子妻 and Wu Xusheng's wife 吳許升妻 mention filiality toward the mother-in-law as one of the virtues of each woman.[7] This focus on the filial daughter-in-law in the narratives is significantly reinforced by the inclusion of the entire text of the *Admonitions for Women* in Ban Zhao's biography.[8]

Ban Zhao's *Admonitions*, the earliest extant instructional text for women, applies Confucian thought and practice to the life of married women. Quoting from the *Analects* as well as works that had gained the status of Confucian Classics by Han dynasty – the *Odes*, the *Book of Changes*, and the *Book of Rites* – Ban Zhao counseled her audience to obey their mothers-in-law without questioning, regardless of her personal opinion, so that she is "like an echo and a shadow." This could be seen as a "survival skill" to help daughters-in-law to navigate the minefield of family *realpolitik* in aristocratic Han families like Ban Zhao's.[9] But that is more Daoist, or even Legalist, than Confucian. Confucian filiality is not merely a means; it is a constitutive virtue of the exemplary person and the sage. Given the syncretistic climate of the Han dynasty, it would not be surprising to have non-Confucian elements in texts that also proclaim a Confucian lineage. However, beyond advocating manipulation to gain one's way when faced with the harsh realities that often awaited daughters-in-law of those times, Ban Zhao's *Admonitions* shows genuine concern about educating women in Confucian virtues.

Ban Zhao's *Admonitions* depicts a married woman's life as revolving around her husband. "To win the love of one man is the crown of a woman's life; to lose the love of one man is her eternal disgrace." A married woman's status and power in her family depended on her husband's love and esteem. Although the husband may be the central figure in her life, he was not the final arbiter of her fate. Of the five unfilial behaviors Mencius acknowledged, one was the neglect of one's parents through partiality toward one's wife (*Mencius* 4B30). According to the *Book of Rites*, if a man "very much approves of his wife, but his parents do not like her, he should divorce her. If he does not approve of his wife, and his parents say, 'she serves us well,' he should behave to her in all respects as his wife."[10] Disobeying her parents-in-law was one of the seven grounds for divorcing a woman, while having mourned her parents-in-law for three years was one of the three circumstances protecting a woman from being divorced.[11]

While Ban Zhao deals only with obedience as the main constituent of daughters-in-law's filiality, the *Biographies of Women* recognizes a less subservient role, describing daughters-in-law who were "conscientious in caring for their mothers-in-law [*yang gu shen qin* 養姑甚勤]."[12] The widow of Chen, the exemplary filial daughter-in-law, even took over the role of the breadwinner in supporting her mother-in-law.[13] According to Mencius, "Though caring for his parents is not the reason for marrying, there are times when a man takes a wife for the sake of his parents."[14] For the most part, societies influenced by Confucianism have accepted caring for parents-in-law as a daughter-in-law's responsibility. Just how much obedience is required is a more controversial issue.

We must not underplay the oppression of women resulting from the very unequal power relations inherent in the social structure of Han or later times. Neither do we need to exalt unacceptable actualities into normative goals. In today's context, the lesson we learn from a Confucian ethics of the daughter-in-law is different from that of Ban Zhao's day. Women today, even in societies heavily influenced by Confucianism, are no longer as dependent on their husbands. But for those who choose to marry, the relationship between husband and wife deserves serious reflection and conscientious effort. Ban Zhao's teaching about a daughter-in-law's filiality illuminates how no relationship exists in a vacuum any more than individual selves exist in isolation. The relationship between husband and wife is embedded in a network of interlocking social relations of varying complexity. The *Book of Rites* also links the daughter-in-law's obedience with harmony within the home.[15] To make the most of one relationship, one needs to work on the surrounding interdependent relationships. Even within a social structure with gender equality, Ban Zhao's teachings about the filial daughter-in-law could still illuminate the connection between the ethics of filiality and a more general relational ethics by highlighting the interlocking nature of the network of relationships constituting a person's life and selfhood.

From filial sons and daughters to filial daughters-in-law

The daughter-in-law's role comes about by a woman's marriage and the relationship is formed through her husband. Her filiality is part of her responsibilities toward her husband. This is already implicit in the *Mencius*.

Ensuring that one's wife would be filial toward his parents is part of the filiality of a son. The daughter-in-law's filiality could be a substitute for the son's filiality.

In Liu Xiang's *Biographies of Women*, the widow of Chen refused remarriage and continued to care for her mother-in-law after her husband's death because of a promise to her husband on the eve of his departure for military duties that she would care for his mother in his absence. She justified her refusal to remarry on the grounds that breaking her promise would betray her husband's trust (*xin* 信), and that her unfilial behavior would highlight her husband's failure as a son. The filial daughter-in-law's obedience, Ban Zhao emphasized, also contributes to the husband's filiality, as she thereby avoids causing friction between her husband and his parents.[16]

The attempt to promote a Confucian ethos at all levels of society and in all areas of life, as well as the increasing emphasis on gender difference, not surprisingly led to some – albeit still very little – attention to daughters' filiality during the Han period, even though it was not considered a subject worthy of serious philosophical discussion. Among Liu Xiang's biographies is a famous one of Ti Ying 緹縈, who saved her father in 176 BCE from cruel corporal punishment by petitioning the Han Emperor Wen 文帝 (also known for his filiality) to punish her in her father's place.[17] However, Ti Ying was praised specifically, not for her filiality, but for her skill in argument (*biantong* 辯通). It is only in the seventeen Biographies of Women of the *Hou Hanshu* that we find two biographies (of Cao E 曹娥 and Shu Xianxiong 叔先雄) that focus on the daughter's filiality.[18]

A daughter-in-law's filiality is also part of her filiality as a daughter. From pre-Qin to the Ming and Qing dynasties, the marriage rituals included parents instructing their daughters "to be respectful, circumspect and obedient" in their new homes.[19] In disobeying her parents-in-law, like disobeying her husband, a woman would have disobeyed her own parents. Ban Zhao began her *Admonitions* with expressions of gratitude to her parents, followed with an admission that, after her marriage, "she feared constantly that she might disgrace her parents." She worried that her daughters, by their "failure in good manners in other families will humiliate both their ancestors and clan."[20] This parallels Confucian views that the son's filiality includes "honoring his parents" and "bringing honor and glory to his ancestors" by his behavior outside the family.[21] The *Book of Rites* considers marriage the basis of the ritual order, and its purpose is to "unite the merits of two surnames."[22] The filiality of a daughter-in-law is part of her filiality as a daughter because failing as a daughter-in-law would harm her own parents by undermining the alliance forged through the marriage, as well as advertising her parents' failure in educating her.

Although the daughter-in-law's filiality could be seen as an extension of the son's and the daughter's filiality, it differs from them in certain aspects. The requirement of obedience from daughters-in-law is more stringent than what is required of sons. The *Analects* emphasizes obedience in filiality, but allows for remonstration when parents err. "In serving your father and mother, remonstrate with them gently. On seeing that they do not heed your suggestions, remain respectful and do not act contrary. Although concerned, voice no resentment."[23] Ban Zhao, in contrast, advises, "Whenever the mother-in-law says, 'Do that,' even if what she says is wrong, still the daughter-in-law submits unfailingly to the command."[24]

That Ban Zhao did not advocate remonstration might be attributed to the fact that erring parents-in-law were even less likely to listen to a daughter-in-law than their son (or daughter), and rather than improving matters, remonstration might cause further problems, sometimes with dire consequences. If this renders the filial ethics of the daughter-in-law more stifling of conscientious expression than the filial requirements of the son or daughter, we may balance it with the observation that Ban Zhao did not expect a daughter-in-law to maintain "the way" of her mother-in-law after the latter's death, whereas a filial son, according to Confucius, would "refrain from reforming the ways of his late father" for three years (*Analects* 1.11, 4.20).

Given that roles differ according to one's position in the family or society, and gender differences were firmly established as part of the social as well as moral (even cosmological) framework of Han Confucianism, it is only to be expected that Han Confucian ethics would require different filial acts from daughters-in-law compared with sons or daughters. Yet there is an important similarity in the fundamentals despite differences in details. Differences in the acts required of the filial son/daughter and the filial daughter-in-law notwithstanding, both sets of requirements could be accommodated within a Confucian filial ethics embodied in a ritual order.

The capacity for filiality

Confucian requirements of filiality from daughters-in-law assume that such acts are within the capacity of any daughter-in-law. Is the daughter-in-law's capacity for filiality toward her parents-in-law similar to the son's filiality toward his parents? Is this capacity inborn or acquired? According to Mencius, "There are no young children who do not know loving their parents" (*Mencius* 7A15). Citing this passage, Cheng Chung-ying claims that "filial piety and fraternal duty are feelings of human instinct."[25] If the "human instinct" of filiality is dependent on the existence of biological relationship, then it is irrelevant in the case of the daughter-in-law.

Although "biological bondage provides an opportunity for personal realization,"[26] we are not hard-wired to be filial. An instinct for filial love, even assuming one is born with such, could be lost in the process of growing up. Hence Yu Ji-yuan, while believing that "filial love as natural sentiment is inborn and not culturally specific," nevertheless emphasizes that "what is required is to cherish and nurture it."[27] Filiality is an important part of Confucian self-cultivation. There would have been no need to discuss filiality as much as the early Confucian texts did if it were such a "natural" virtue that no effort would be required to be filial.

The biological fact that our parents give us life might not be the cause of their having a special place in our affection, and certainly does not necessitate a filial ethics. What D. C. Lau translates as "young children" for brevity and fluency in the *Mencius* may be more literally rendered as "children held in the arms 孩提之童."[28] It could be the process of nurturing a child during its helpless years that forms the most powerful ties. We could read *Analects* 17.21 to mean that three years' mourning for parents is something one *feels* compelled to do because of the "three years of loving care" one has received from one's parents – hence Confucius' criticism of Zaiwo being comfortable with a shorter mourning period as "unfeeling [*buren* 不仁]" (*Analects* 17.21). However, there are difficulties with this reading. According to the *Book of Rites*, wives of rulers and great officers do not nurse their own children. Those employed to nurse the baby, though involved in the care of the helpless infant – and literature of all periods often portrays them as receivers of great affection from the child – nevertheless have no claims on the latter in terms of mourning rituals, but were instead awarded materially after the three years' service.[29]

Based on contemporary psychological studies, I am more inclined to give weight to nurture over nature in seeking the source of filial capacity. However, as far as textual evidence goes, both find support within the Confucian tradition. Confucian teaching on filiality is normative endorsement of feelings of attachment that develop in the nurturing relationship that exists usually, but not always, between biological parents and child. While capacity, whatever its source, is a precondition, it does not constitute filiality. Filiality is realized in action; more specifically, it is embodied in ritual action. The Confucian ritual order is not a simple expression of biological instincts or nurtured feelings. The distinction between what is and what should be is often blurred in early Chinese texts. The normative dimension is implicit in Mencius' emphasis on spontaneous concern for those closely related to oneself by blood in his use of the concept of "*qin qin* 親親." With his emphasis on "artifice," Xunzi considered *qin qin* "treating relatives in a manner befitting their relation," which is part of "the graduated scale of humane conduct."[30]

Confucian ritual order is a normative system that values some instincts and feelings above others. The ritual texts show how biological relationship, nurtured feelings, and normative reasoning interact to produce a complex system of behavioral requirements aimed at cultivating Confucian character, of which filiality is an important quality, and creating a harmonious Confucian community. At constant risk of reification, this system is nevertheless capable of change over time through the dynamic play of the tension among its various determinants.

The ritual system of mourning, designed to distinguish symbolically, through dress and period of mourning, the varying degrees of kinship, is a good example of normative distinction that cuts across both biological relations and feelings of affection arising from daily interaction.[31] One's father and mother are equally close in biological terms, and the *Book of Rites* acknowledges that "the love is the same for both," but "heavier" mourning (of unhemmed sackcloth for three years) is worn only for the father to signify his higher position and the greater importance of the patrilineal relation.[32] Although there is no biological relationship, the ruler is mourned like one's own father. Adopted sons wear the same mourning as biological sons. Whether or not the people involved live in the same household also makes a difference in the mourning dress prescribed for relatives by marriage, indicating that, compared with biological ties, at least equal if not greater weight is sometimes given to affection and mutual obligations arising from daily interactions in non-biological relations governed by rituals.

While the biological relationship with one's mother cannot change, the mourning the child wears varies, depending on circumstances such as whether the father is still alive, or whether the mother has been divorced. An unmarried daughter wears the same mourning for her parents as a son; but once married, a woman wears the heaviest mourning (unhemmed sackcloth for three years) only for her husband, and lighter mourning (sackcloth with even edges for only one year) for both her own parents and her parents-in-law, although elsewhere in the *Liji*, having mourned her parents-in-law for three years is said to provide protection against divorce.

Stepmothers are mourned in the same manner as one's biological mothers. The "Biography of Gongsun Hong 公孫弘" in the *Hanshu* mentions that this Han prime minister, a favorite of the Han Emperor Wu 武帝, wore three years' mourning dress for his stepmother.[33] It is the stepmother's relationship to the father that determines the mourning dress the stepson wears. According to the *Book of Ceremonial Rituals* (*Yi Li* 儀禮), besides one's step-mother, one's *cimu* 慈母 – James Legge translates this as "indulgent mother" – should also be mourned like one's own mother.[34] While a stepmother is one's father's wife, the *cimu* is a concubine who has been commanded by the father to take care of a child whose mother had died in its infancy. In the "Questions of Master Zeng" chapter of the *Book of Rites*, Confucius is quoted as denying that mourning one's *cimu* like one's own mother is "ancient ritual" and attributing it to a practice first introduced by Duke Zhao of Lu 魯昭公 (reigned 541–516 BCE), against the advice of his own officials, out of his affection for his own *cimu*.[35] Clearly, neither biological relationship nor nurtured affections alone determine the ritual obligations of mourning dress.

Extension of filial love

The so-called "instinct" for filial love is more nurtured than inborn. The child's love is for the one who nurtures her, regardless of whether they are biologically related. Although such affection might make it easier, or "natural" in a loose sense, for one to be filial toward one's parents, it cannot be a necessary condition for filiality, as otherwise it would be impossible for daughters-in-law to be filial unless their parents-in-laws had given them "three years of loving care" when they were babies. As Chenyang Li has pointed out, the justification for Confucian filiality is not only purely backward-looking, but also looks toward the future creation of self and community.[36] If filial love is limited by biological ties or affection arising from past nurturing relationships, filiality will not be a suitable basis for the broader virtue of *ren*, by which we "love others," including those who neither cared for our young selves nor are biologically related to us.

Mencius gives us some idea of how the transition from filiality to *ren* is effected. "Treat the aged of your own family in a manner befitting their venerable age and extend this treatment to the aged of other families" (*Mencius* 1A6). The *Book of Rites* requires that daughters-in-law "serve parents-in-law like serving parents."[37] There is some ambiguity whether that means "as she serves her own parents" or "as her husband serves his parents." However, both readings require analogizing in-law relationship and parent–child relationship. In explaining the Han Chinese terms for parents-in-law, *jiugu* 舅姑 (*jiu* also refers to the mother's brother and *gu* also refers to the father's sister), the *Baihu tong* 白虎通 suggests that one's parents-in-law are those who, though not one's parents, are "as close as" one's parents.[38]

One might respond that love cannot be commanded: if one loves one's parents because of the care they have given us and the times we shared with them, there is no way we could ever treat others, whose past interactions with us are quite different, in the same way. However, some kind of "love" might be amenable to the control of thought. The usual distinctions between feeling, thought, and action are often unclear in early Chinese works; but I think it significant that the character "*xin* 心" refers to both "heart" and "mind." Filial love and the authoritatively humane (*ren*) person's love for others are constituted by action, embodied in rituals, enlightened by the wisdom of recognizing how our past relationships make us who we are today, and who we will be tomorrow will depend on what we make of our relationships today.[39]

The "extension" of filial love – if that is what it is – will be neither simple nor easy. Otherwise Ban Zhao, who indicated no worry about her daughters' behavior as daughters, would not have to worry about their not knowing how to be daughters-in-law.[40] Where some indulgence might be expected from parents because of their affection for a daughter, parents-in-law are more likely to be critical to begin with. A woman upon marriage could not simply behave toward her parents-in-law as she was wont to do as a daughter of the house, even if she could bring herself to feel toward them what she felt toward her own parents.

Ban Zhao's recommended approach to disagreements and conflicts that she acknowledged as common in in-laws relationship, "obedience which sacrifices personal opinion," is unacceptable to us today. But it should make us wary of self-assertive confrontation as a knee-jerk reaction, and prompt us to reflect more carefully upon the difficult problem of how one could maintain harmony without becoming a doormat or a shrew. The lesson is relevant beyond the daughter-in-law role: finding the middle path between submissiveness and domination is important to human relationships in general.

The daughter-in-law's filial ethics is an important link in understanding the transition from filiality to *ren*. It shows us both the practical difficulty and the conceptual complexity of Mencius' idea of "extension." People we encounter probably resemble parents-in-law more than parents: their interests are often different from our own, and they are likely to use any power they have over us to our detriment, especially if we go against them. It is naive to expect strangers to bear any good will toward us; one cannot even assume that in one's own family, if some of the news headlines are anything to go by. If Confucianism still has any relevance today, we must understand the Confucian ideal as advocating that we be "broadly generous with the people and to help the multitude" (*Analects* 6.30), despite the preponderance of indifference or ill will rather than good. Taking the filial requirements of the daughter-in-law seriously will help us to understand better the difficulty of the Confucian ideal as well as how much we need to reinterpret it to avoid obsolescence. The extension of filial love involves a cognitive analogizing of different relationships and a practical striving to realize the analogy that must overcome many odds and often go against one's initial feelings.

The binding power of rites

The possibility of extending filial love to love for those with no family ties to oneself is critical to Confucian ethics. Failure would mean a pernicious familism that justifies the charge that Confucian emphasis on the family precludes concern for the wider community.[41] One could cite textual evidence showing that Confucianism insists that personal cultivation is inseparable from the ordering of family relations and ethical interactions within the wider community (the most oft-quoted being the beginning passage of the *Great Learning*), but this is insufficient without a persuasive account of *how* this process works.

Confucius taught his favorite student Yan Hui that *ren* is achieved by "returning to the rites" (*Analects* 12.1). Another student of Confucius comforted a fellow student that, when people "are respectful and impeccable in their conduct, are deferential to others and observe the rites, everyone in the world is their brother" (*Analects* 12.5; *Liji* 9.1/59/29). This chapter cannot give a complete account of how rites bring about the extension of filiality to *ren*, from love for parents to love for those outside the family, nor is there space for a detailed study of the ritual constitution of the daughter-in-law's filial ethics, as evident in the Han texts. But I would take this opportunity to suggest that a more serious study of such material would help us to understand how Confucian rites could create a harmonious community of cultivated persons in orderly families.

In the Han texts, the daughter-in-law's filiality is circumscribed and constituted by ritual acts – just as the filial son should serve his parents "according to the observances of ritual propriety" when they are alive and, when they are dead, "bury and sacrifice to them according to the observances of ritual propriety" (*Analects* 2.5). The *Analects* is explicit about harmony being the most valuable function of rituals (*Analects* 1.12). The *Xunzi* elaborates on how this process works: rituals ensure that "desires and goods sustain each other over the course of time" by "apportioning things, nurturing desires and satisfying wants."[42] Confucian ritual order institutes clear division of labor in social endeavors and distribution of privileges and rewards. In doing so, it attempts to match expectation and action in any social relationship. When a woman first arrives in her husband's home, everything is new and strange. Learning her way around her new relatives by trial and error would not only be inefficient, but might cause serious misunderstandings and lasting resentment. The ritual prescriptions of how a daughter-in-law should behave facilitate that induction. Furthermore, they minimize conflicts arising from competing interests and desires by ranking the appropriate priorities within the household.

Han ritual texts elaborate on the daily acts a daughter-in-law must perform to serve her parents-in-law from dawn to dusk. The "pattern of the family [*neize* 內則]" chapter in the *Book of Rites* begins with a description of how the son should wash up and dress as soon as he wakes in the morning in preparation for a visit to his parents. This is followed by a closely paralleled description of how his wife should prepare herself for the visit. Once appropriately dressed, husband and wife "should go to their parents and parents-in-law . . . with bated breath and gentle voice, they should ask if their clothes are [too] warm or [too] cold, whether they are ill or pained, or uncomfortable in any part; and if they be so, they [the son and daughter-in-law] should proceed reverently to stroke or scratch the place."[43]

Although many of the ritual acts were required of both sons and daughters-in-law, given that men were expected to work outside the family, while women were expected to be concerned only with what lay within the family, it was the daughters-in-law who took care of every detail of the old folks' comfort and well-being: helping and supporting their parents-in-law in leaving or entering, bringing in the basin for the parents-in-law to wash in the morning, preparing their bath, fetching and carrying respectfully and with "an expression of pleasure to make their parents-in-law feel at ease," encouraging them to eat and ensuring that they get the choicest food at meal times, and so on. In the presence of her parents-in-law, a daughter-in-law's every move, every expression, every detail of her dress, must be respectful and circumspect.

These detailed prescriptions might seem at best obsolete, at worse oppress-ive, to us today. But like Book 10 of the *Analects*, which describes in seemingly banal details Confucius' every expression, manner, movement, and dress on various occasions, these descriptions of ritual acts of caring for her parents-in-law give us a glimpse of the surface of an entire way of life. Though ritual "begins from outside," the visible details of behavior, the ritual requirements, would be oppressive if these acts elicit no more than external conformity. If so, the ritual process would have failed. To achieve the aims of personal cultivation and social harmony, rituals must become a deeply personal experience, embodying the ways people relate to one another, their appropriate feelings and attitudes.

Rituals are not merely utilitarian tools for reducing the chances of friction in social interaction. To fulfill their role within Confucian ethics, rituals must transform the people and their relationships. The *Xunzi* asserts that "rituals nurture," not in the sense of purely physical sustenance, but in the sense of ethical refinement achieved through physical means. Specifically, Xunzi suggests that rituals nurture the emotions.[44] Instead of simply going through the motion, all the while chafing at the imposition, a successful ritual performance must fully engage one's heart, mind, and body. Getting all the minute tangible details as well as the expression (which is often emphasized) right will eventually engender the emotions that harmonize the relationship. It is only when external form and inner content are mingled in action that ritual becomes the central process that could produce a sage.[45] Hypocrisy is of course possible, but difficult to sustain over the long run. To appreciate how ritual acts transform a person and her relations, one must avoid over-intellectualizing, and realize that exalting respect for elders, com-passion for others, and so on will bear little fruit if one does not take specific, and sometimes very mundane, action. It is not just the thought, but thoughtful action, that counts.

A Confucian daughter-in-law's filiality is embodied in ritual acts per-formed respectfully, caringly, with feelings that constitute humanity (*ren*). This does not mean that we should revive specific prescriptions in the tra-ditional ritual texts. Any top-down prescriptive approach to a revival of rituals will only lead to oppression. But there are more rituals in our lives than we are usually aware of; rituals need not involve elaborate ceremonies or formal acts, they could be inconspicuous habits. Their ritual function lies in their communicative and stabilizing potential. Reflecting on the ritual con-stitution of filiality should prompt us to ponder the little habitual acts that sustain relationships of any permanence in our lives. What do they express? Do they nurture the right kind of feelings? In which direction are they driving the relationship? However outmoded the figure of the Han Con-fucian daughter-in-law may seem in this day and age, a closer scrutiny reveals some important lessons about Confucian ethics of filiality, and its impli-cations beyond immediate family relations in a Confucian understanding of how to build communities through ritual acts.

Notes

1 For Shun's filiality and his parents' atrocious treatment of him, see D. C. Lau, *Mencius*, Hong Kong: Chinese University of Hong Kong Press, 1984, 4A28, 5A1, 5A2, 5A4, and 7A35.

2 Xu Fuguan 徐復觀, *Intellectual History of the Former and Later Han* 兩漢思想史, Taipei: Student Book Co., 1979, vol. 3, pp. 42–5.

3 N. L. Swann, *Pan Chao: Foremost Woman Scholar of China*, New York: The Century Co., 1932, pp. 84–5.

4 D. C. Lau and F. C. Chen (eds), *A Concordance to the Li Ji*, Hong Kong: Commercial Press, 1992, 12.52/79/19; 12.54/79/29–30; 45.7/168/8–9.

5 Liu Xiang, *Biographies of Women* 列女傳, *Sibucongkan*, Shanghai: Commercial Press, 1936, p. 59.

6 D. C. Lau and F. C. Chen (eds), *A Concordance to the Shuo Yuan*, Hong Kong: Commercial Press, 1992, 5.23/36/24–5.23/37/7; Ban Gu 班固, *History of the Former Han* 漢書, Beijing: Zhonghua, 1997, p. 3041.

7 Fan Ye 范曄 (398–455), *History of Later Han* 後漢書, Beijing: Zhonghua, 1997, pp. 2783, 2793, 2795.

8 Ibid., pp. 2786–91.

9 S. Wawrytko, "Prudery and Pruprience: Historical Roots of the Confucian Conundrum Concerning Women, Sexuality and Power," in C. Y. Li (ed.), *The Sage and the Second Sex*, La Salle: Open Court, 2000, pp. 163–98; Y. S. Chen, "The Historical Template of Pan Chao's *Nü-chieh*," *T'oung Pao*, 82, 1996, 230–57; X. H. Lee, *The Virtues of Yin: Studies on Chinese Women*, Broadway: Wild Peony, 1994, p. 4.

10 *Liji* 12.12/74/24.

11 D. C. Lau and F. C. Chen (eds), *A Concordance to the Da Dai Li Ji*, Hong Kong: Commercial Press, 1992, 13.2/78/5; D. C. Lau and F. C. Chen (eds), *A Concordance to the Kong Zi Jia Yu*, Hong Kong: Commercial Press, 1992, 26.1/50/6. Three years' mourning for parents-in-law is more than what is required in the *Liji* 15.28/88/30.

12 Liu Xiang, *Biographies of Women*, pp. 28, 30; Fan Ye, *History of Later Han*, pp. 2783, 2793. The *Book of Rites* covered both aspects in the chapters on "the Pattern of the Family [*neize* 內則]" and "the Meaning of the Marriage Ceremony [*hunyi* 昏義]."

13 Liu Xiang, *Biographies of Women*, p. 59.

14 D. C. Lau, *Mencius*, 5B5.

15 *Book of Rites* 45.6/168/6.

16 N. L. Swann, *Pan Chao*, p. 88.

17 Liu Xiang, *Biographies of Women*, pp. 88–9.

18 Fan Ye, *History of Later Han*, pp. 2794, 2799.

19 D. C. Lau, *Mencius*, 3B2; D. C. Lau and F. C. Chen (eds), *A Concordance to the Yi Li*, Hong Kong: Commercial Press, 1994, 2/10/16–18. *Shuo Yuan* 19.12/163/8; Ban Gu, *Comprehensive Discourses of the White Tiger Hall* 白虎通, Tjan Tjoe Som (trans.), Leiden: E. J. Brill, 1952, p. 248.

20 N. L. Swann, *Pan Chao*, p. 82.

21 D. C. Lau, *Mencius*, 5A4; *Liji* 4.4/29/22–4.4/30/9; D. C. Lau and F. C. Chen (eds), *A Concordance to the Erya and Xiaojing*, Hong Kong: Commercial Press, 1992, 2/1/10 to 5/1/30.

22 *Liji* 28.2/135/22 and 45.1/167/16. See also *Da dai Liji* 1.3/6/9.

23 *Analects* 4.18, in R. T. Ames and H. Rosemont Jr (trans.) *The Analects of Confucius: A Philosophical Translation*, New York: Ballantine, 1998. The *Mencius*, *Xunzi*, and *Xiaojing* all advocate opposing parents when they are morally wrong. D. C. Lau, *Mencius*, 4B30; *Xiaojing* 15/4/3–7; *Xunzi* 29.1/141/19, in D. C. Lau

and F. C. Chen (eds), *A Concordance to the Xunzi*, Hong Kong: Commercial Press, 1996.
24 N. L. Swann, *Pan Chao*, p. 88.
25 C. Y. Cheng Chung-ying, "On Confucian Filial Piety and Its Modernization: Duties, Rights and Moral Conduct," *Chinese Studies in Philosophy*, 20, 1989, p. 60.
26 W. M. Tu, "Probing the 'Three Bonds' and 'Five Relationships' in Confucian Humanism," in W. H. Slote and G. A. de Vos (eds), *Confucianism and the Family*, Albany: State University of New York Press, 1998, p. 128.
27 J. Y. Yu, "Virtue: Confucius and Aristotle," *Philosophy East and West*, 48, 1998, p. 332.
28 Cheng Chung-ying translates this passage as "an infant once held in the arms will love his parents," C. Y. Cheng, "Confucian Filial Piety," p. 60.
29 *Liji* 12.50/79/14.
30 *Xunzi* 27/127/26, in J. Knoblock (trans.), *Xunzi*, Stanford, CA: Stanford University Press, 1994, vol. 3, p. 211.
31 "Mourning Ritual," in *Yi Li*; "Record of Smaller Matters in the Dress of Mourning," "Record of Greater Matters in the Dress of Mourning," and "Four Principles underlying the Dress of Mourning," in the *Liji*. There are inconsistencies both within each text and between them. But I shall not discuss all of them in detail, as they do not affect the point being made here.
32 *Liji* 50.5/174/31.
33 Ban Gu, *History of the Former Han*, p. 2619.
34 J. Legge, *The Li Ki (I–X)*, Oxford: Oxford University Press, 1885, vol. 27, p. 473; *Yi Li* 11/64/7.
35 *Liji* 7.18/53/13. Sun Xidan 孫希旦 comments that *cimu* 慈母 in this case refers to the practice, mentioned in the "Patterns of the Family" chapter of the *Liji*, of involving various concubines of good characters in the raising of the heir to a ruler or feudal lord, one of whom would be the "indulgent mother," whether or not the biological mother is alive. In such a case, the rule of "mourning *cimu* like one's own mother" did not apply. Sun also quoted Zhengxuan 鄭玄 that this story could not be true of Duke Zhao, whose biological mother died when he was thirty years old, according to the *Zuo Zhuan* 左傳: Sun Xidan (ed.), *Book of Rites with Collected Annotations* 禮記集解, Beijing: Zhonghua, 1998, p. 527. For Duke Zhao's mother's death in the eleventh year of his reign (531 BCE), see Yang Bojun 楊伯峻 (ed.), *Annotated Zuo Commentaries on the Spring and Autumn Annals* 春秋左傳说, Beijing: Zhonghua, 1990, p. 1321.
36 C. Y. Li, "Shifting Perspectives: Filial Morality Revisited," *Philosophy East and West*, 47, 1997, 211–32.
37 *Liji* 12.3/73/13.
38 Ban Gu, *Comprehensive Discourses*, p. 564.
39 For a more detailed account of filial piety as a requirement of both self-realization and *ren*, as a Confucian alternative way of understanding the role of filial piety in morality, see C. Y. Li, "Shifting perspectives."
40 N. L. Swann, *Pan Chao*, p. 82.
41 For examples of such criticisms, see B. Russell, *The Problem of China*, London: Allen & Unwin, 1922, p. 40; Liang Shuming 梁漱溟, *Complete Works*, Shandong: People's Press, 1989, vol. 3, p. 30; Lin Yu-tang, *My Country and My People*, New York: Halcyon House, 1938, p. 180. For a recent argument that the Confucian tradition presents a mixed picture and is not devoid of counter tendencies, see S. H. Tan, "Between Family and State: Relational Tensions in Confucian Ethics," in K. L. Chan (ed.), *Mencius: Contexts and Interpretations*, Honolulu: University of Hawaii Press, 2002, pp. 169–88.
42 *Xunzi* 19/90/4–5, J. Knoblock, p. 55.

43 *Liji* 12.3, J. Legge, *Li Ki*, p. 450.
44 *Xunzi* 19/90/15, J. Knoblock, p. 56.
45 *Xunzi* 19/92/21–19/93/3, J. Knoblock, p. 62. In this connection, we must note that sincerity (*cheng* 誠) is also a highly valued Confucian virtue, though further elaboration would digress too much.

Index